Rethinking Statehood in Palestine

Rethinking Statehood in Palestine

Rethinking Statehood in Palestine

Self-Determination and Decolonization Beyond Partition

———

Edited by

Leila H. Farsakh

UNIVERSITY OF CALIFORNIA PRESS

University of California Press
Oakland, California

Suggested citation: Farsakh, L. *Rethinking Statehood in Palestine:
Self-Determination and Decolonization Beyond Partition*. Oakland: University
of California Press, 2021. DOI: https://doi.org/10.1525/luminos.113

Library of Congress Cataloging-in-Publication Data

Farsakh, Leila, editor, contributor.
Title: Rethinking statehood in Palestine : self-determination and
    decolonization beyond partition / [edited by] Leila Farsakh.
    Other titles: New directions in Palestinian studies; 4.
Description: Oakland, California : University of California Press, [2021] |
    Series: New directions in Palestinian studies; 4 | Includes
    bibliographical references and index.
Identifiers: LCCN 2021012044 (print) | LCCN 2021012045 (ebook) |
    ISBN 9780520385627 (paperback) | ISBN 9780520385634 (ebook)
Subjects: LCSH: Self-determination, National—Palestine. |
    Arab-Israeli conflict.
Classification: LCC KZ4282. R48 2021 (print) | LCC KZ4282 (ebook) |
    DDC 341.26095694/2—dc23
LC record available at https://lccn.loc.gov/2021012044
LC ebook record available at https://lccn.loc.gov/2021012045

25   24   23   22   21
10   9   8   7   6   5   4   3   2   1

CONTENTS

LIST OF ILLUSTRATIONS

MAPS

FIGURES

ACKNOWLEDGMENTS

The genesis of this book was a research program on alternative models for state-formation in Palestine. It was launched by the Center for Development Studies at Birzeit University in 2013, under the directorship of Dr. Samia Al-Botmeh. The aim of this research was to explore Palestinian understandings of statehood, democracy, and citizenship in view of the regional upheavals ushered in by the Arab uprisings and the failure of the Oslo peace process to bring about a viable two-state solution to the Israeli-Palestinian conflict. A grant from the Soros Foundation financed this project, enabling the Center for Development Studies to commission six papers and conduct a survey on Palestinians' attitudes toward the one-state solution that included the views of Palestinians in Gaza and the West Bank as well as those living in Israel. The findings of this research were presented at a conference held at Birzeit University in 2015.

I was involved in this project from its inception. Upon its completion, it became clear to me that its findings should be accessible to everyone, as they expressed the voices of a new generation of scholars who are central to the definition of Palestinian political liberation in the twenty-first century. Like every book, though, this one has undergone various transformations, especially as some contributors dropped out and I persevered to have others join. I deeply regret that Samia Al-Botmeh could not remain my coeditor as we had originally planned. Her commitment and work at Birzeit University left little room for anything else, especially after she became dean of the Faculty of Business and Economics. Linda Tabar, who was central to the inception of this project and to the Soros grant, also could not remain in it, as her important research and teaching took all her time. I remain deeply indebted to Samia and Linda for their intellect, their precious friendship, the solidarity we developed over the years, and for their incredible generosity towards me in some of the hardest times I endured as we were trying to get this project off the ground.

I also wish to thank the contributors who persevered with me and those who came on board to bring this book to fruition. Adam Hanieh and Mazen Masri are among the former. Tareq Baconi, Hania Assali, Maha Nassar, Hanan Toukan, and Nadim Khoury are among the latter. They all made it possible not only to transcend the academic and physical fragmentation that Oslo created but also to institute gender balance in this academic conversation on Palestine. The fact that two honorary Palestinians, as I like to call Susan Akram and Ilan Pappe, joined this project, ensured that we transcended a myopic nationalist understanding of political engagement, while honouring these two scholars' dedication to the Palestinian cause.

Moving the book from conception, compilation, and completion to the actual process of publication took more time and nerves than I thought possible. For that, I want to thank a number of people who helped me along the way. They include Andre Zaaman for reminding me that this intellectual project is important for any viable political work, Gil Anidjar for his insight and for inviting me to speak about its early findings at Columbia University, and Sherene Seikaly for her encouragement and growing friendship. I am deeply indebted to Kinga Karlowska, my excellent research assistant, and Kate Rouhana for her editing of various parts of this work; Nancy and Hubert Murray for offering me the space to write in peace during the Covid-19 pandemic; Heike Schotten for her encouragement and advice with various versions of the introduction; Susan Jacoby for her fine-tooth editorial combing of that same introduction; and Sahar Bazzaz for her reading and support in more than one way. I also would like to thank Beshara Doumani for his interest in the book and eagerness to have it published in the New Directions in Palestinian Studies (NDPS) series. I am both honoured by and appreciative of this fitting home. A special thanks goes also to the editorial board of NDPS, whose assiduous readings and invaluable comments helped me situate this book within the larger ongoing debate on the meaning of liberation and self-determination in the twenty-first century, as well as to the book's two anonymous reviewers for their suggestions and enthusiastic endorsement.

Last but not least, I am most grateful to Franz, my partner of more than twenty-five years, for his patience and unwavering belief in me, and to my daughters, Selma and Frida, for their understanding and love. I look forward to sharing their joy as they traverse their own paths and carve out their own unique places in this world.

Self-determination, statehood, and partition are dominant political concepts that shaped the formation of the modern global order following World War I. The resistance of the Palestine question to any attempt at resolution guided by the logics of these concepts has generated a veritable industry of academic publications—buttressed by and even bigger industry of documentation, reports, initiatives, resolutions, and summits—on how to secure a two-state solution. Most of this scholarship, regardless of the political position of the authors, uncritically dwells within the confines of this nationalist conceptual architecture, thus reproducing the very epistemological climate that made possible the ongoing dispossession, displacement, and statelessness of the Palestinians. It is ironic, but hardly surprising, that the "peace process" launched by the 1993 Oslo Accords, based on the partition logic of "land for peace," greatly accelerated the tempo of Israeli colonization of Palestine.

The spectacular contrast over the past three decades between state-centric discourses in the public sphere and settler-colonial practices on the ground has pushed a new generation of scholars to consider intellectual exit strategies from the identity/territory/sovereignty matrix and to experiment with alternative paradigms. *Rethinking Statehood in Palestine: Self-Determination and Decolonization beyond Partition* is an outstanding collection of essays, mostly by leading Palestinian scholars of this new generation, that forensically explain the operations of partition logic on the ground and point to different paths to decolonial futures.

Statehood was never the sole mission of decolonization movements globally, and there is a rich tradition of thinking beyond the telos of the state among anti-colonial intellectuals. The Palestinians are no exception. Indeed, an outpouring of scholarship, activist initiatives, literary writing, and cultural projects have shifted the focus from the state to the nation. The concept of nation is more capacious engine for political struggle, as it privileges people over territory and recognizes the critical importance of the everyday lived experience.

This outpouring was especially noticeable in the period following the 1982 Israeli invasion of Lebanon, which sought to destroy the institutional infrastructure of the Palestine Liberation Organization and to make irreversible the colonization of the territories occupied in the 1967 war. Nevertheless, the hold of partition logic remains especially strong in the Palestinian case for a variety of historical reasons, not the least of which are the modalities of international interventions.

Rethinking Statehood encapsulates the mission of the New Directions in Palestinian Studies book series in that most of the authors draw on their intimate familiarity with the Palestinian condition to provide fresh perspectives, from the inside out, so to speak, on larger theoretical and global concerns. The editor, Leila Farsakh, assembled scholars from a variety of disciplines—political economy, law, international relations, history, and cultural studies—all of whom deliver crisp, concise, informative, and robustly insightful essays honed by years of research in their respective fields as well as by activist work. This makes the book an important inspiration for scholars, a go-to resource for teachers, and a stimulating read for anyone interested in understanding the deeper structures of the Palestine question and its relationship to central debates about, among other things: colonialism and self-determination, the political economy of state formation, legal constructions of nation and state, settler-colonialism and citizenship, international law, and the promise and limits of cultural decolonization practices informed by the politics of indigeneity.

Rethinking Statehood directly engages with the dominant debates on the question of Palestine and pushes against their limits. Deeply informed, theoretically engaged, and accessible, this anthology is designed as a long-term resource for all those interested in understanding the Palestinian struggle for a just and equitable future.

Beshara Doumani
Series Editor

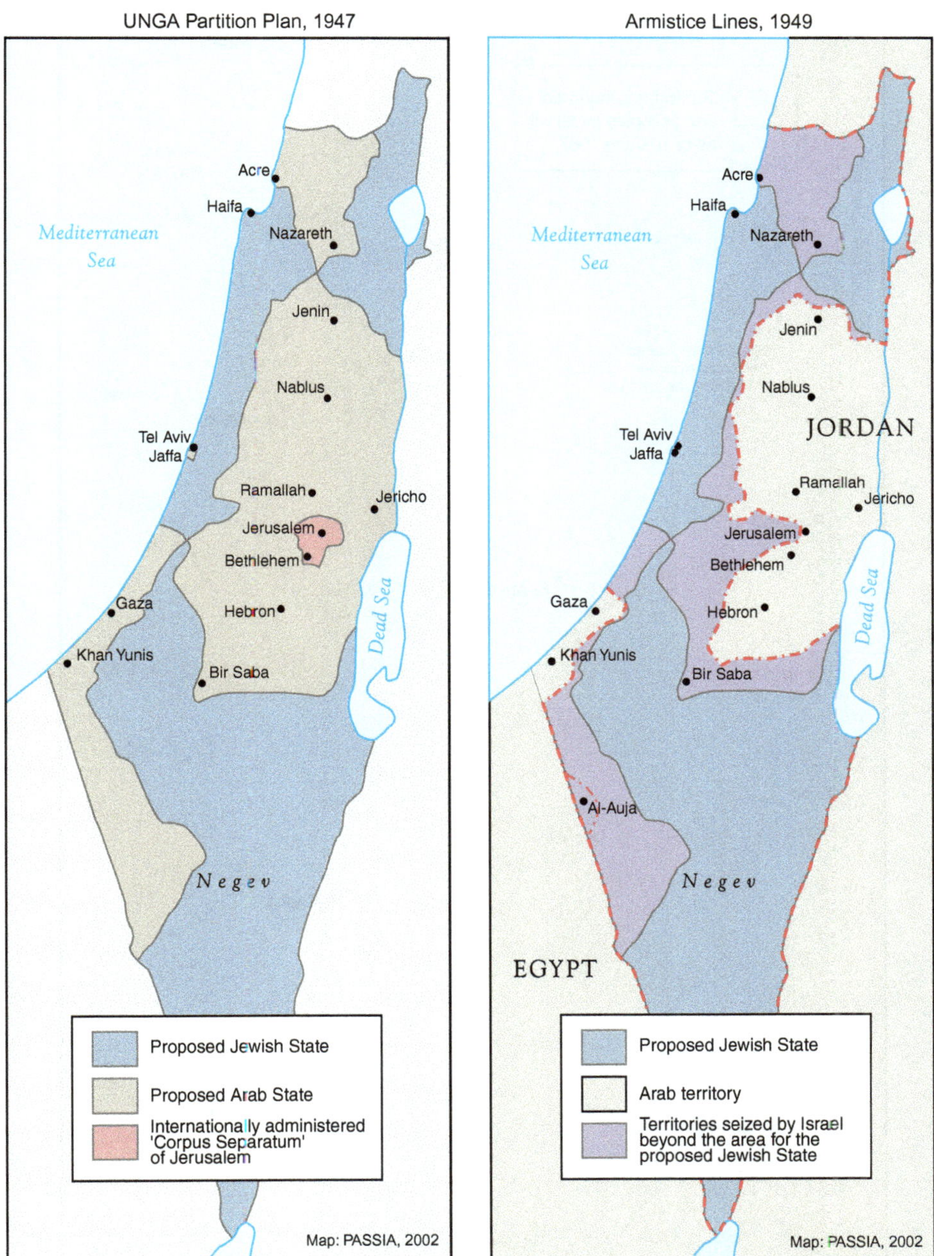

MAP 1. Palestine under the 1947 UN Partition Plan, and with the 1949 armistice lines. Source: Palestinian Academic Society for the Study of International Affairs.

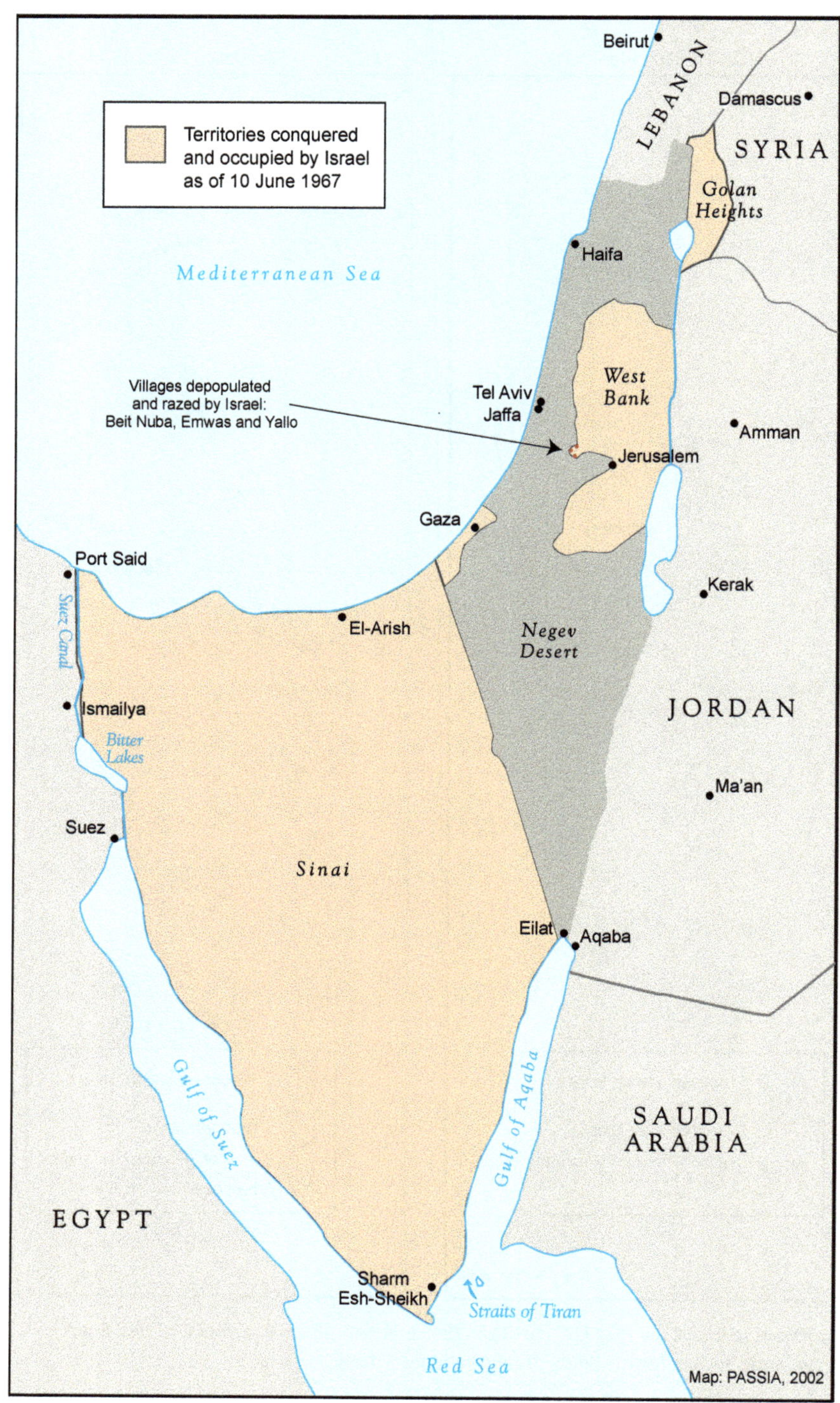

MAP 2. Israel, the West Bank, and the Gaza Strip, July 1967. Source: Palestinian Academic Society for the Study of International Affairs.

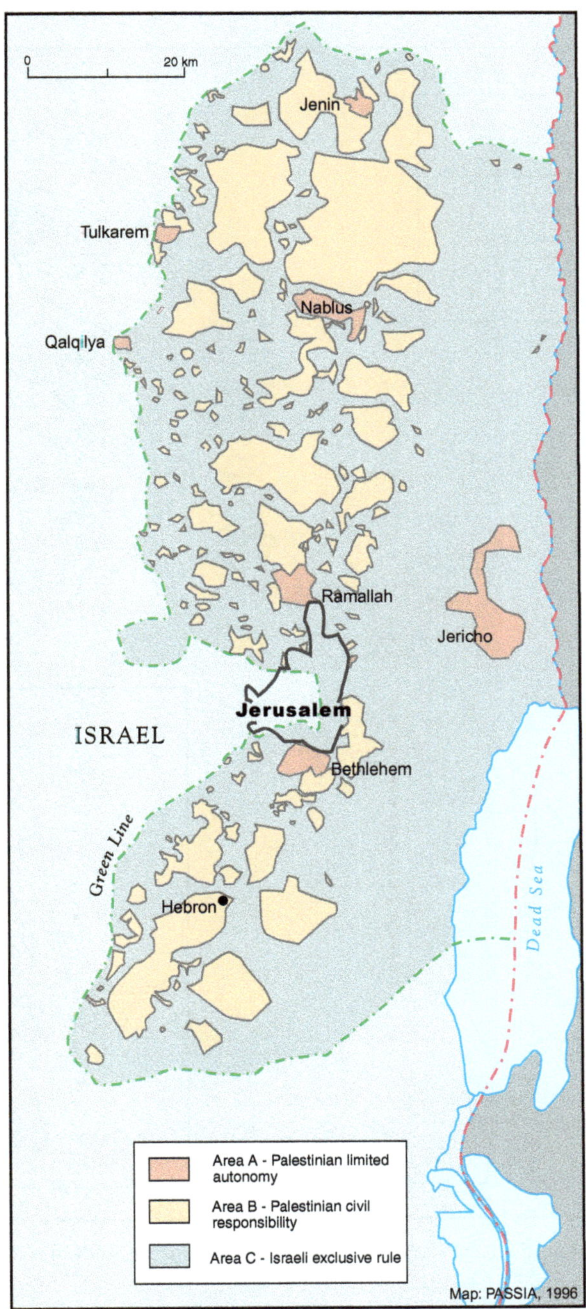

MAP 3. Division of the West Bank according to the Interim Agreement on the West Bank and Gaza Strip (Oslo II), September 1995. Source: Palestinian Academic Society for the Study of International Affairs.

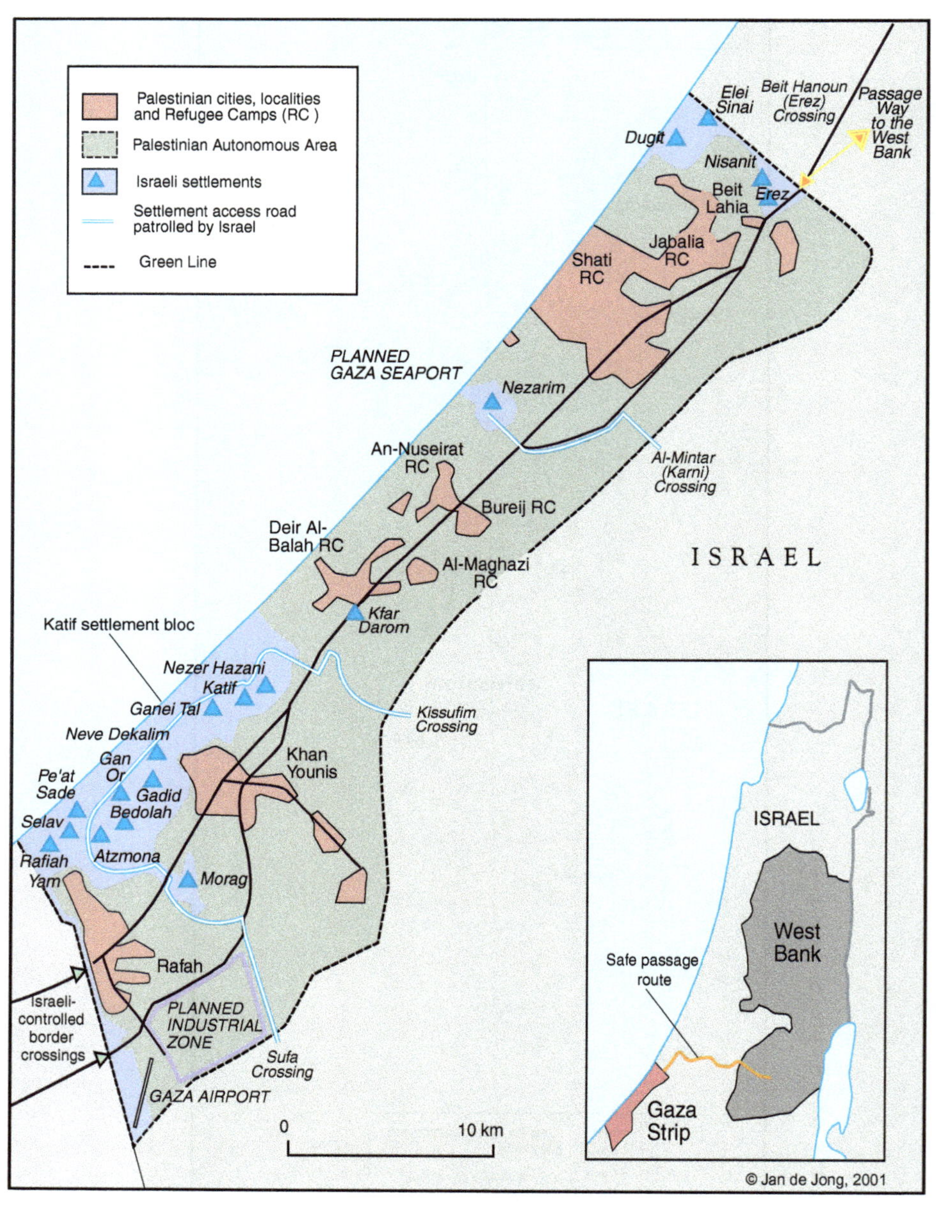

MAP 4. Gaza Strip, 2000. Source: Palestinian Academic Society for the Study of International Affairs.

Introduction

*The Struggle for Self-Determination and the Palestinian
Quest for Statehood*

Leila Farsakh

The quest for an independent Palestinian state has been at the core of the Palestinian national struggle for a very long time. It has been central both to the assertion of the Palestinian right to self-determination and to challenging Zionist attempts to erase the Palestine question.[1] In 1971, the Palestine Liberation Organization (PLO) declared the creation of a democratic state in Palestine inclusive of Christians, Jews, and Muslims to be its goal and the only just solution to the Israeli-Palestinian conflict. In 1988, it went further by issuing the Declaration of Independence and having its chairman, Yasser Arafat, officially recognize Israel. This paved the way to the Oslo peace process in 1993 and implied that the Palestinian state was to be confined to the West Bank and Gaza Strip. By 2019, the state of Palestine was officially recognized by 137 states and admitted into the United Nations as a nonmember state. It remains, though, under occupation and is far from being independent or sovereign.

The aim of this book is to rethink the Palestinian state project and the challenges facing any alternative to it. It sheds new light on the ways in which the past three decades of peace process have transformed the meaning of Palestinian statehood and, with it, the solution to the Israeli-Palestinian conflict. As many have argued, the Oslo peace process reformulated, rather than ended, Zionist colonization, thereby undermining the possibility of a viable Palestinian state.[2] Israel's continuous war and siege of Gaza, the presence of over 650,000 Israeli Jewish settlers in the West Bank (including East Jerusalem), the 708-kilometer Separation Wall and the institutionalization of over ninety-nine Israeli checkpoints have destroyed the two-state solution, long considered the only option for ending the Israeli-Palestinian conflict. Despite the Trump administration's 2020 peace plan, which put the final nail in the coffin of that solution, the Palestinian Authority, Hamas, and the international community remain committed to Palestinian national independence.[3] The Arab Peace Initiative and the 2003 internationally sponsored Quartet Road Map to Peace consider the creation of such a Palestinian state not only a right but also the only means to end the Israeli-Palestinian conflict.[4]

Rethinking Statehood delves into the ways Palestinians are redefining the relationships among self-determination, decolonization, and political liberation today, given the territorial impossibility of a Palestinian state. The contributors, mostly young Palestinian scholars, move away from the conflict resolution approach that has dominated the peace discourse and the political science literature on Palestine. They provide instead a critical political perspective that situates the Palestinian state project within its regional context, rather than confining it to the limits of a narrow nationalist paradigm. At the same time, they go beyond the ongoing debate over the inevitability of a one-state solution or its political danger, by focusing on the political challenges Palestinians need to address in articulating an alternative to the present impasse.[5] These include analyzing the extent to which Palestinian political rights, both collective and individual, can be protected outside the international consensus on partition as the paradigm for resolving the Palestinian-Israeli conflict.

In this regard, *Rethinking Statehood* engages with an emerging trend in Palestine studies that advocates for breaking out of national frames to understand the Palestine question.[6] Its main contribution lies in examining the opportunities and costs of moving away from the pursuit of territorial sovereignty as a means to achieve political liberation. As this introduction argues, the quest for a Palestinian state was not in vain, but its historical role has come to an end. It is thus necessary to reexamine this role and explore how the failure of national independence enables us to rearticulate the relationship between self-determination and decolonization away from the telos of the nation-state. Such a rearticulation requires transcending the partition paradigm that has dominated all international attempts to resolve the Israeli-Palestinian conflict. It entails defining the elements of a political alternative that is democratic, viable, and economically feasible. It also must address the question of Zionism and explain how the political rights of Jewish Israelis can be reconciled with Palestinian rights in any attempt to decolonize the ongoing settler-colonial reality.

SELF-DETERMINATION AND STATEHOOD

At the heart of the Palestinian struggle is a yearning to return home and for freedom—freedom from settler-colonialism, as much as from oppression and exile.[7] Ever since they were expelled from their land during the 1948 war and the creation of the State of Israel, Palestinians have sought to fulfill their right of return, which is enshrined in UN Resolution 194, issued on December 4, 1948. The establishment of the PLO by the Arab League in 1964 reaffirmed this right, as its charter called for the liberation of Palestine from Zionist imperialism. The PLO charter did not specify statehood as part of its mission, though, since it envisaged Palestine as part of a larger Arab collectivity. It was only in the aftermath of the 1967 Six Days War and the international consensus on UN Security Council (UNSC) Resolution 242 as a framework for peace in the Middle East that the Palestinian national movement made the project of an independent state the vehicle for decolonizing Palestine from Zionism and affirming the Palestinian right to self-determination.

In this regard, the Palestinian national movement was not much different from most anticolonial liberation movements of the twentieth century. Self-determination, a concept internationalized with Lenin's defense of people's right to national independence and reframed by Wilson's Fourteen Points in 1918, laid the foundation of a twentieth-century world order composed of nation-states.[8] By 1960, it became "the juridical component of international non-domination," as Adom Getachew put it.[9] Yet, as she and others have shown, self-determination was a concept used by imperial powers to reorganize their spheres of control, as much as it was claimed by every national liberation movement demanding freedom from colonialism. Imperial powers viewed it a principle that colonized people could exercise once they prove fit to do so, thus tying it to imperial racial and political considerations. Anticolonialists, on the other hand, defined self-determination as an inalienable *right* to achieve freedom from external domination.[10]

UN Resolution 1514, adopted in 1960 by the UN General Assembly (UNGA), affirmed the status of self-determination as a human right, one that is necessary in order to fulfill all other rights. It also declared colonialism a crime and specified that "all people have an inalienable right to complete freedom, the exercise of their sovereignty and the integrity of their national territory."[11] It thus inadvertently made self-determination synonymous with national territorial sovereignty, that is, statehood.[12] While many were aware of the inherent contradiction of the nation-state as protector as well as violator of human rights, an international consensus had formed around the necessity of independent statehood as a first, if not sufficient, step towards political liberation. This is because the nation-state was conceived as the internationally recognized sovereign entity that ensures citizens their political rights, including their right to security and protection from external domination.

For many anticolonialists, though, the creation of an independent state was not the only, or optimal, means to guarantee people's freedom and their national sovereignty. They considered the right to self-determination as a people's right to define their political future and choose their political *form*, or system, of government for managing their affairs. It did not need to be territorially bound, since sovereignty is enshrined in the people, or the nation, not in the state per se. Instead it can be fulfilled through various political configurations, such as transforming empires into representative federations, or confederations, of equal citizens. As Wilder and Getachew have shown, anticolonial proponents of the right to self-determination envisaged its implementation as part of a larger project of remaking the world beyond the Westphalian order of sovereign states, one that required transforming political and economic structures, both domestically and internationally, in ways that would guarantee the freedom and equality of all people.[13] They were cognizant of what revolutionaries from Toussaint Louverture to Fanon have warned against, namely that national independence does not guarantee liberation, for it can create new forms of domination that deny citizens their political and economic rights.

The Palestinian struggle for self-determination carried within it this ambiguity concerning the relationship between national liberation and statehood. As Edward Said put in 1978, the PLO never resolved "the question of whether it is really a national independence or a national liberation movement."[14] Since the arrival of Fatah at the head of the PLO in 1968, the Palestinian national discourse has tied return with liberation and conscripted the notion of self-determination to the right to establish an independent Palestinian state. In 1971, the eighth Palestinian National Council (PNC) convention adopted a unanimous resolution specifying that "the armed struggle of the Palestinian people is not a racial or religious struggle directed against the Jews. This is why the future state that will be set up in Palestine liberated from Zionist imperialism will be a democratic Palestinian state. All who wish to will be able to live in peace there with the same rights and the same duties."[15] What came to be known as the Palestinian version of a one-state solution was presented as the means to protect Palestinian political rights by affirming the right to an independent, decolonized nation-state. It asserted Palestinian political existence in the face of international denial, as best exemplified with UNSC Resolution 242. This resolution, adopted on November 22, 1967, acknowledged the right of each state in the region to "live in secure and recognised boundaries." It did not, though, mention the Palestinians nor any of their UN-protected rights, such as those detailed in UN Resolutions 181 and 194. It simply referred to them as refugees in need of a humanitarian solution, not a national group with a right to self-determination.[16]

From its inception, the Palestinian state project was a project of national self-affirmation as well as of political actualization. Its aim was to assert Palestinian "peoplehood," which Zionism sought to eradicate, as much as to articulate a just political future inclusive of all those who live on the land. While many doubted the sincerity of its inclusive vision, which Israel outrightly rejected, Palestinian nationalists were clear about opposing Zionism as a racial colonial project of domination rather than rejecting Jews for their identity. The PLO's diplomatic and legal efforts in this regard came to fruition in 1974 with UNGA Resolution 3236, which affirmed the legitimacy of Palestinian anticolonial struggle and right to "national independence and sovereignty." In UNGA Resolutions 3236 and 3237, the international community—as represented by the UN—also recognized the PLO as the sole legitimate representative of the Palestinian people and invited it to participate in the works of the General Assembly like any nonmember state, such as the Vatican.[17] The PLO, meanwhile, acted as a state in exile, with its various political

institutions, electoral structures, and economic services, representing and providing for Palestinians in the diaspora as well as for those under Israeli occupation.[18]

Linking self-determination with statehood, in other words, gave the Palestinian revolution a concrete political meaning in an international system that recognized the legitimacy of decolonization struggles in the post-WWII era and bestowed on states the primary responsibility of representing and protecting the human and political rights of citizens. What remained contested within the Palestinian national movement was the content and shape of this state, as much as the extent to which its creation would be the means to, or the end of, decolonization.

By 1974, the PLO gave up on the idea of remaking the regional and international order of nation-states and defeating imperialism. It accepted instead the confines of realpolitik and the international consensus on UN Resolution 242, which it officially recognized in 1988. In 1974, the twelfth PNC adopted the Ten Points transitional program, which became known as the pragmatic, or step-by-step, route to decolonization. It specified that "the PLO will employ all means . . . . for the liberation of Palestinian land and *setting up a patriotic*, independent fighting *national authority* in every part of the Palestine territory that will be liberated . . . . The PLO will consider any step toward liberation which is accomplished as a stage in the pursuit of its strategy for the establishment of a democratic Palestinian state."[19] Although many contested the possibility of a Palestinian state without fully dismantling Zionism, the majority accepted the view that national independence was a first step towards national liberation. This view gained further strength after Israel's war against the PLO in Lebanon in 1982 and the failure of the Arab states to come to the rescue of the Palestinians. The PLO's Declaration of Independence in 1988, announced in the wake of the First Intifada, which erupted in the Gaza Strip and the West Bank in December 1987, represented the official Palestinian acceptance that national self-determination could only be fulfilled on part of historic Palestine, and that it is attainable by negotiating with, rather than defeating, Israel.[20]

The Palestinian state project thus became the price for the Palestinian historic compromise with Israel. Herein too lies its historical importance. It was the only way for the Palestinians to advocate for themselves at any peace negotiations bounded by the parameters of the international consensus on partition as the solution to the Arab-Israeli conflict as set out in UN Resolution 181, and more specifically by UNSC Resolution 242. A Palestinian state on only 22 percent of Palestine was considered better than no state, because it promised political independence. It offered recognition and a historical compromise with an enemy, even if it could not bring about full liberation. It allowed a means for the return of the refugees, even if it could not restore justice to the Palestinians for the Nakba. Above all, it promised citizenship rights to Palestinians denied of these rights, whether in the diaspora or under Israeli occupation. In other words, the Palestinian state project affirmed the Palestinian "right to have rights" to quote Arendt.[21]

PALESTINIAN STATEHOOD AND THE OSLO
PEACE PROCESS

The Oslo peace process in 1993 provided an opportunity for the Palestinian national movement to reap the fruits of Palestinian resistance by territorializing the dream of a Palestinian state, at least from the point of view of the PLO leadership. With the signing of the Declaration of Principles in 1993 and Interim Agreement on the West Bank and Gaza Strip in 1995, the PLO acquiesced to a conflict resolution approach intrinsically tied to the concept of territorial partition as a paradigm for achieving a minimum of Palestinian rights. It accepted Israel's insistence that the starting point of the conflict was the 1967 war—not the 1948 war. Although fully aware that the Oslo peace process did not end the occupation or specify as its end goal the creation of a Palestinian state, the Palestinian leadership remained committed to proving that Palestinian statehood was both necessary and achievable. It was bolstered by international community support in this regard, especially as expressed by the Arab Peace Initiative in 2002 and the Quartet Road Map to Peace in 2003.

Starting with Arafat's return to Gaza in 1994 and role as the head of a democratically elected Palestinian National Authority (PNA) in January 1996, the Palestinian official narrative shifted from decolonization to state-building. The PNA focused on behaving as a state in order to be recognized as one, embarking on a wide variety of activities that ranged from setting up a new police force and various ministries and ritualizing presidential salutes and national anthems while receiving foreign ambassadors, to devising national development strategies and filing petitions against Israel's separation barrier to the International Court of Justice (ICJ) in 2005. Such performances of statehood sought to abstract the reality of occupation, not so much in order to deny it but rather to refuse to be constrained by it. They were not simply acts of "make believe," even if they appeared at times delusional. They were rather attempts to affirm Palestinian agency and legitimate national existence despite Israel's continuous obstructions, a legitimacy recognized by the international community, which admitted the State of Palestine into the UN in 2012, as well as into the UNESCO, International Criminal Court, and other international fora.

The PNA's belief that national independence was attainable through state-building in the present, rather than by revolutionary armed struggle resistance as in the past, was best exemplified by the Fayyad technocratic government in 2007. This government, which was set up in the aftermath of the international boycott of Hamas's electoral victory in 2006 and the Fatah-Hamas debacle in June 2007, defined its mission as providing "the final push to statehood."[22] It worked on proving Palestinian institutional readiness for independent statehood by laying the foundation of a modern state, as advised by PNA's new international sponsors, the World Bank and International Monetary Fund. It confined the meaning of self-determination to the establishment of a neoliberal state, as defined by Washington's conception of good governance. State-building thus became about law and order, not about national unity or democratic representation. Its mission was to foster "institution-building" and fiscal transparency in order to ensure the development of a vibrant private sector. It was sustained by the creation of large bureaucracy who produced, as much as depended on, the institutional edifice of this neoliberal state.[23] State-building implied that the PNA was performing "a kind of statehood not based on sovereignty but on management of financial resources and credible claims to management of an uncertain future."[24]

More assiduously, this state-building effort proved to be a site of governance and control. It became an effort by which the PNA shaped power relations over space and people, rather than a strategy that could effectively halt Israeli settlement construction, end the siege on Gaza, or bring liberation. This was visible at the macro level, in the creation of a repressive police force and prison system in the West Bank and Gaza Strip and in the failure to create independent and transparent judiciary. It also was clear in the way state-building efforts reshaped access to resources and power at the micro level, whether in developing the housing and land markets, encouraging public-private partnerships, or setting up the infrastructure for a modern electricity grid and road system. As a new generation of scholars have demonstrated, the development of modern electricity grids, new housing projects, or even "national environmental policies" does not only highlight the PNA's attempt to affirm a certain sovereign modernity.[25] Such projects also reflect the kind of polity the PNA is seeking to create, one that promotes a transactional, individualized relation between the central authority and the Palestinian population, rather than encourages collective representations and accountability. This state-building apparatus inevitably produced a political entity that was increasingly authoritarian, serving mostly an emerging private sector tied to the PNA and international capital. The PNA became unable, or unwilling, to undo the settler-colonial reality, given how embedded it was with safeguarding Israeli security through the Oslo peace agreement and its state-building efforts.

With the signing of the Oslo peace accords, the historical role of the Palestinian state project for the Palestinian cause was thus bound to come to an end. This was confirmed with the failure of the final status negotiations, after the Camp David Summit in 2000, to bring about Palestinian territorial independence, despite all the compromises that the Palestinian Authority was willing to make towards Israel.[26] The pursuit of a state had been essential for achieving Israeli and international recognition of the Palestinians as a collective, or national, political entity. However, Israel's recognition of the PLO had proved to be a means to fragment the Palestinian people and undermine their right to self-determination. Attempts to counter this fragmentation remained ineffective because the Palestinian leadership, the international community, and the regional powers all remained committed to partition as the only way to achieve Palestinian independence. The PNA's insistence that the problem is not partition in itself, but in the lack of implementation of UN resolutions did not carry much sway since the international community proved unwilling to exert pressure on Israel to retreat fully from the West Bank and Gaza or even to adhere to the terms of the Oslo agreements.

Indeed, it is impossible to explain the persistence of the Palestinian state project, as much as its failure, without considering the international investment in it.[27] The Quartet on the Middle East (UN, European Union, United States, Russia) has been the major advisor and funder of the Palestinian state project, dispersing over twenty-seven billion dollars to the Palestinian territories since 1994, making the Palestinian Occupied Territories one of the world's largest recipients of aid per capita.[28] Although the international community has been frustrated with Israel's continuous construction of settlements and its violation of Palestinian human rights, its approach has been to reform, rather than reject, the principle of partition. It focused its energy on improving the PNA's institutional capability to prove Palestinian readiness for political independence, giving special attention to enhancing the PNA's monopoly over the use of violence in the West Bank and Gaza. The international community thus restricted the meaning of statehood to the power of an internationally recognized authority to impose law and order over a specific population. It did not tie it to fostering democratic accountability or ensuring Palestinian unity, let alone adhering to international law or forcing Israel to withdraw from Palestinian land.[29] It ignored the importance of territorial contiguity for the physical viability of any state by prioritizing Israel's security concerns in delineating the extent of Palestinian territorial and demographic jurisdiction.

In acquiescing to the prioritization of Israeli security demands, the international community and the PNA thus contributed to transforming the Palestinian state project from a vehicle for national independence to a regionally and internationally sponsored endeavor to dissolve the Palestine question. Juridically, the Palestinian state project under Oslo confined the Palestinian nation to the West Bank and Gaza Strip. It thus compromised the unity of the Palestinian people and the political rights of those Palestinians not included in the new territorial nation-state, that is, the Palestinian citizens of Israel and refugees, who are at the crux of the Palestinian question. It also undermined the national Palestinian political system with the creation of new territorially confined political bodies, namely the PNA and the Palestinian Legislative Council. These political entities de facto superseded the Palestinian Liberation Organization and its Palestinian National Council, the bodies that had historically represented Palestinians both inside and outside the West Bank and Gaza Strip.[30] The Palestinian national collective, or "we," was thus compromised, especially as no new encompassing entity was created to represent and reunite all Palestinians as the PLO had before 1993.

The territorialization of the Palestinian dream of national self-determination has thus been emptied of any emancipatory potential. Rather than undo the unequal power relations imposed by Israel and the international order, the project of statehood introduced instead new structures of domination that perpetuate, rather than dismantle, the settler-colonial reality Palestinians are forced to endure. The Palestinians living in the West Bank and Gaza are effectively living in a one-state condition, with Israel as the only sovereign a reality that has been increasingly described as apartheid.[31] The entrenchment of the PNA's authoritarian regime and its refusal to revive the PLO or hold elections have compromised Palestinian citizenship rights.[32] Meanwhile, the PNA's obsession with statehood risks reducing the Palestinian struggle to a humanitarian problem once again; Palestinians leaders are now more focused on finding means to combat Covid-19 and prevent poverty levels from rising further in the Gaza Strip while keeping a captive economy afloat through international aid. They are not focused on ensuring an inclusive national debate on how to protect Palestinian rights in the face of continuous Israeli colonial onslaught, as seen in the latest war on Gaza in 2021.

RETHINKING DECOLONIZATION, TRANSCENDING PARTITION

If the past fifty years of Palestinian struggle prove that the quest for a Palestinian state was necessary to affirm a people's collective political existence, they also indicate that the pursuit of statehood can compromise national rights, especially when such a state is confined to an international neoliberal understanding of political sovereignty. The experience of the past fifty years makes it clear that national independence cannot be achieved through partition or in a context of ongoing Zionist colonization. As Dubonov and Robson have most recently argued, partition plans are intrinsic to imperial strategies to divide and conquer.[33] They have been proposed to "resolve" ethnic or national conflicts by steering ethnic or national groups into divided spaces. However, they have not succeeded in bringing about enduring peace, let alone reconciliation between conflicting parties, whether it is between Hamas and Fatah, Israel and the Palestinians, India and Pakistan, or the UK and Northern Ireland, among other examples.

The crisis that the Oslo peace process created for the Palestinian national cause has led to a renewed call for a return to the original tenets of the Palestinian political struggle, namely its commitment to liberation from settler-colonialism. The question that took hold of Palestinian activists and academics became how to think of "liberation beyond the not yet fully realised and yet already mutilated project of the nation-state."[34] This did not mean that the "national as a horizon of liberation" has lost its importance, as Salih and Richeter-Devroe put it, but rather that it has become a more contested space, since people in the Occupied Territories and in the diaspora questioned the PNA's attempted monopoly at defining the contour and content of this nation. A new discourse started to emerge, focused on articulating the elements of a new political strategy able to unite the Palestinian body politic and protect Palestinians rights. Such a strategy unequivocally rejects partition as a solution and relies on settler-colonialism as an analytical paradigm

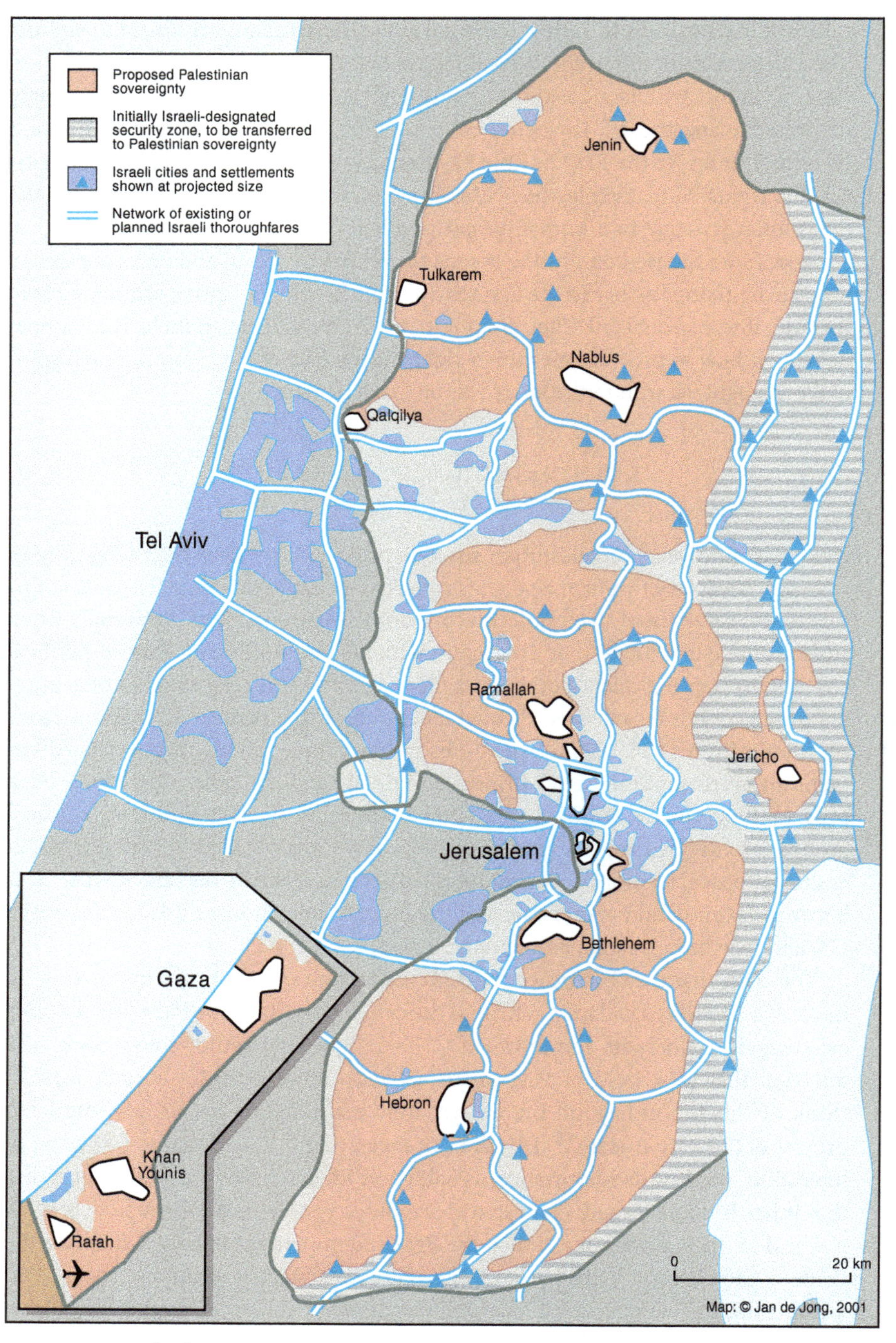

MAP 5. Scope of Palestinian sovereignty proposed at the Camp David Summit, 2000. Source: Palestinian Academic Society for the Study of International Affairs.

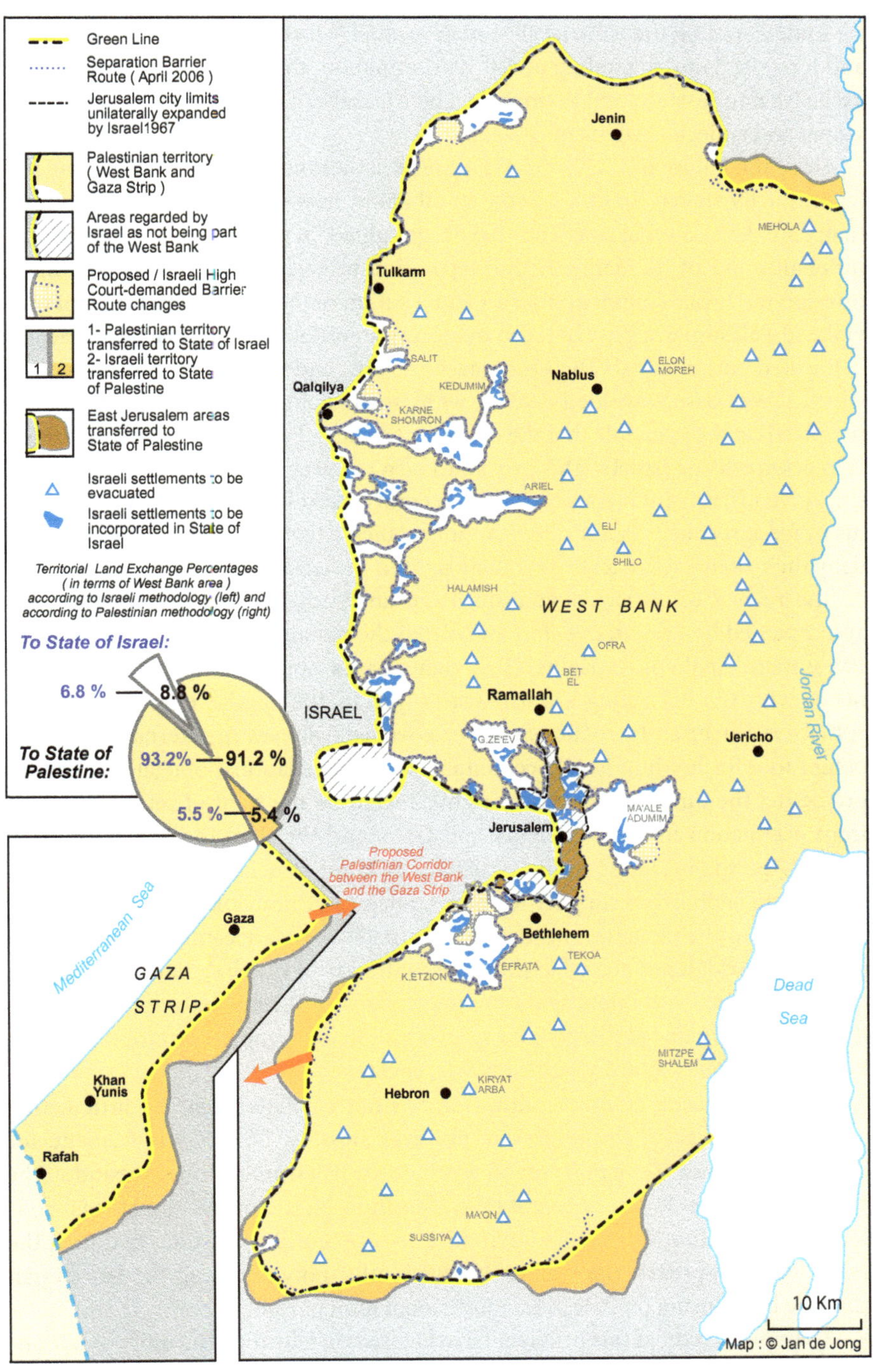

MAP 6. The Separation Wall and boundaries of the Palestinian state according to the Olmert Peace Plan, 2008. Source: Palestinian Academic Society for the Study of International Affairs.

for understanding the Israeli-Palestinian conflict.[35] It seeks to transcend an ethnic and territorial understanding of self-determination, that is, the framework of the exclusive nation-state, and to propose a political alternative that protects the individual and collective rights of citizens.

Since the failure of the Camp David negotiation in 2000, Palestinian academics and activists have become more vocal about how Israel reformulated, rather than ended, its colonial rule. They have highlighted, in particular, how Oslo's institutionalization of the demographic separation between Israelis and Palestinians through territorial fragmentation and annexation of Palestinian land has not only violated Palestinian rights but also made any solution based on partition racially delineated and unequal. The Oslo peace process, and the partition paradigm on which it was based, avoided dealing with Israel's colonial foundation, for it was premised on the principle that the only way to affirm Palestine's political existence is to acknowledge Israel's. This proved to be a real trap for the Palestinian leadership, given Israel's insistence on being recognized as a Jewish state in any final status peace agreement. Palestinians cannot acquiesce to such a demand, for it would deny their political existence and their right to the land.

The revival of settler-colonialism as an analytical framework has also been accompanied by a discursive shift away from the pursuit of statehood and towards Palestinians' inalienable rights. This rights-based approach has gained prominence with the ICJ ruling against Israel's wall in 2005 and the rise of the Boycott, Divestment and Sanctions (BDS) movement. It sees in international law a potent tool for holding Israel accountable to its international obligations and for protecting the unity of Palestinian rights, including the right of return, freedom from occupation in the West Bank and Gaza, and the right to equal citizenship for the Palestinians living inside Israel. The BDS movement has been particularly effective in mobilizing support for new strategies of nonviolent resistance as an alternative to the violence of the Second Intifada, which became demonized in a post-9/11 world. It has helped to show the continuity of Israeli settler-colonial policies that violate Palestinian rights and to generate a growing international solidarity with Palestinians at the grassroots level and in different policy circles (such as local governments, unions, and churches, et cetera).

The rights-based discourse, however, has not been sufficient for articulating a political alternative to the present political impasse. The BDS movement, for example, does not take a position on whether the Palestinians should abandon the pursuit of a state. It also does not take a position on the international legal consensus on partition or offer an alternative to it. According to some critiques, the rights-based approach risks, albeit inadvertently, individualizing the Palestinian struggle by focusing on Palestinian individual human rights.[36]

Attempts to redress this problem have focused on affirming the unity or nationhood of Palestinian people, albeit by proposing two different approaches. The first rejects the very idea of a Palestinian state as a political aspiration. Led mainly by anthropologists and historians, this approach calls for transcending nationalist frames, given that such frames prioritize the creation of a state over the Palestinian people.[37] It considers the state a site of inherent violence and thus bound to be oppressive, especially in the absence of a free and active civil society. It emphasizes that sovereignty lies with the people, not with the state, and highlights that globalization has undermined the importance of territorial sovereignty. Politically, this approach affirms the political agency of the Palestinians everywhere, not just in the Occupied Territories. It embraces the fragmented and exilic Palestinian experience rather than negates it, as the state project tried to do.

This anti-statist approach has gained traction in the diaspora promoted among Palestinians living in Western societies. While this discourse may sound reminiscent of the PLO's original prioritization of return over statehood, its main focus is on redefining the relationship between identity and place beyond the territory of the nation or the boundaries of the state. In this regard, the anti-statist critique of the Palestinian state project provides a resounding rejection of the PNA attempt to monopolize who the Palestinian collective, or "we," is. It gives space to counternarratives created through Palestinian grassroot initiatives to reclaim the public sphere by challenging hegemonic power structures. Yet this anti-statist critique does not solve the political and humanitarian problems of those living with no legal protection or citizen rights in Lebanon or Syria, for example. It also overlooks the fact that vibrant autonomous public spheres usually exist only in democratic societies where residents have the legal and political tools to challenge state violence and where state power is both limited and circumscribed by law. This anti-statist critique remains pertinent, though, insofar as it highlights the importance of taming state power by emphasizing the creation of representative counterpowers and the protection of spaces for public engagement. It is helpful in pointing out the importance of defining the kind of political community, or polity, that the struggle for self-determination seeks to create in order to ensure that it does not compromise its people's rights.

The second approach for reaffirming Palestinian national rights does not bypass the state. It rather considers the one-state solution the only means to decolonize Palestine.[38] Most of the critical writings by political scientists, legal scholars, and activists over the past twenty years have revolved around defining the political shape, and ethical value, of such a state. There is no consensus, however, on whether such a state should be a liberal democratic state or a binational one. Defenders of the former remain fundamentally attached to the importance of Palestinian territorial sovereignty over the whole of Palestine. They are committed to the principle of individual political equality between all the inhabitants of the land while emphasizing the indigenous sovereignty of the Palestinian people. According to Abunimeh (2014), Israeli Jews living in Palestine have legitimate individual political rights as equal citizens, but not a collective, or national, right to self-determination: this is largely because whenever they have had such a right, it has come at the expense of the Palestinians. Abunimeh and others reject binationalism as an option since, in their view, it entails an endorsement, however oblique, of Zionism and thus of colonialism.[39] The 2018 Israeli nationality law, which bestowed the right to self-determination in the whole area Israel controls only to the Jews, is a case in point. According to Omar Barghouti, a democratic state in all of Palestine offers the only ethical solution to the Israeli-Palestinian conflict, for it dismantles Zionism while allowing Israelis to remain in the land and live in the new polity as equal citizens. Its erodes the native/settler dichotomy by proposing the "de-dichotomisation" or "hybridisation" of individual identities.[40]

The binationalists, on the other hand, are concerned with the ethical problems involved in denying different ethnic groups their histories and collective political identities. Like the advocates of the democratic secular state, binationalists reject the ethno-exclusionary character of Zionism. They also agree on the impossibility of partition, given the growth of settlements and the multilayered, unequal interdependence between the colonizer and colonized that Israel produced over the past seventy years.[41] Binationalists, however, accept the enduring nature of Palestinian and Israeli national identities and recognize the political potency of national markers (language, religion, traditions, et cetera). They acknowledge that both Israelis and Palestinians have collective, not just individual, rights, including a right to self-determination. Their central argument is that this right does not need to be territorially conscripted and cannot be fulfilled through partition or in a nation-state. Instead, it can be protected only in a civic state, one that is not ethnically based but is established through a democratic, inclusive process of constitutional self-creation. The underpinning assumption here is that the state is a juridical order that is accountable to its citizens and responsible for protecting their equality. Such an understanding of the state echoes Hannah Arendt's argument that "our political life rests on the assumption that we can produce equality through organisation." As she put it, "we are not born equal; we become equal members of a group on the strength of our decision to guarantee ourselves mutual equal rights."[42]

Binationalists thus consider that the only way forward is for Palestinians and Israelis to come together to create a new organization, or polity, that guarantees their equal collective and individual rights. Only then will it be possible to overcome the political inequalities that both nationalism and colonialism foster. The question then becomes how it could be possible to engage in such a process of decolonization, given the unequal power realities on the ground. Some scholars, including authors in this volume, call for adopting a new framework of analysis, one that focuses on indigeneity or indigenous people's rights as a way to decolonize Israel from within. They are supported by legal scholars using international law to challenge Israel from outside its borders. As discussed by Susan Akram in chapter 8, such a legal strategy emphasizes a civic, rather than an ethnic, definition of nationality, and perceives the state as a juridical order responsible for protecting the equal rights of its citizens. Others emphasize that decolonization is not an event but a *process* that involves decolonizing Israeli-Palestinian *relationships*, rather than simply the land. According to Bashir and Busbridge, it requires placing Arab-Jewish relations at the center of the decolonization process, allowing "for the narration of Palestinian and Jewish experience in the Middle East alongside each other," rather than at the expense of each other.[43] Such an approach engages, rather than avoids, the enemy, in order to unravel the intertwined history of the settler and the native. It works through history rather than negates it, both at the local and regional level. It is a process that also seeks to tackle questions concerned with historical reconciliation, national trauma, and transitional justice.[44]

Engaging in such a decolonization process is not easy, especially given the privileges and international immunities that Israelis continue to enjoy today. For most Palestinians, especially for those living under Israel's continuous assault on the Gaza Strip, the West Bank, and East Jerusalem, as much as for those living in refugee camps in the diaspora, it is unrealistic, if not defeatist, to engage a conversation about the rights of Israelis in a future democratic state. It is, however, going to be necessary to identify who could lead such a conversation and how to create a representative platform that articulates the shape of a decolonized polity that would end Palestinian dispossession and provide equality for all. According to Edward Said, it falls on the Palestinians, as unfair as this might sound, since "no people, for bad or for good, is so freighted with multiple, and yet unreachable or indigestible significance as the Palestinians . . . . Their relationship to Zionism, and ultimately to political and spiritual Judaism, gives them a formidable burden as interlocutors of the Jews."[45]

Decolonizing Palestine would require articulating the components of a new political framework that acknowledges the violence and injustices of the past and the present while prioritizing citizenship rights over territorial sovereignty. It cannot be divorced from the larger struggle within the Arab region, where citizens are defying their oppressive governments, reminding them of their responsibility towards their citizens: to represent rather than oppress them, to honor rather than crush their diversity, and to acknowledge that the acceptance of differences forms the basis of any democratic polity that ensures equality for all.

RETHINKING STATEHOOD

Rethinking Statehood exposes how Palestinian scholars are redefining the political meaning of decolonization given the end of the historical role the Palestinian state project played for the Palestinian cause. The first part of the book highlights the importance of resituating the Palestinian struggle for liberation within both its regional and its settler-colonial contexts to understand the costs to the Palestinians of remaining confined to the partition paradigm as a means to achieve political independence. The second part exposes the legal and political possibilities in imagining an alternative to partition that protects Palestinian rights. It analyzes how the relationship between the nation and the state is being rearticulated to protect both the individual and collective rights of all those living in Israel/Palestine. It also discusses how international law continues to be a powerful instrument to defend Palestinian nationhood. Together, the chapters included here advance a new epistemology of the Israeli-Palestinian conflict, one that sees the Palestinian struggle not solely through the prism of the nation-state or as confined only to Palestinians, but rather enables us to construct a new critical way of thinking about political liberation that allows people to live in equality and dignity, irrespective of their ethnicity.

In chapter 1, Adam Hanieh provides a political economy critique of the Palestinian state project. Hanieh argues that the Palestinian obsession with statehood cannot be understood by remaining confined within a nationalist framework of analysis and without unpacking the political economy of state, and class, formation. He sheds lights on the PNA's institutional role as a facilitator of capital accumulation and highlights the role of regional capital originating in the Arab Gulf states in the development of a Palestinian capitalist class that sustains the Palestinian state project and depends on it. This class, or elite, is supported by a regional and international capitalist system that is key to understanding the obduracy of the status quo, despite it failing the Palestinian people.

Chapter 2 looks more closely at the Gaza Strip as a microcosm of the limitations of the Palestinian state project and the crisis it created, rather than resolved, for the Palestinian national struggle. Tareq Baconi argues that one of the unexpected effects of the Oslo Accords was the split of the Palestinian national movement into two projects: one that adopted the diplomatic route to achieve Palestinian independence, as represented by Fatah and the PNA; the other committed to armed struggle for liberation, albeit in an Islamist guise, as represented by Hamas. Although divisions within the Palestinian movement are not new, the persistence of this political infighting for over fifteen years despite many reconciliation attempts leads to the conclusion that the Palestinian state project is sustained by an elite more interested in power than in national liberation.[46] Baconi argues that the Gaza Strip has become the lynchpin for determining the future of the Palestinian national movement; its present humanitarian crisis demonstrates the costs of remaining committed to the tenets of Palestinian national liberation and seeking to assert political independence in a context of ongoing colonization.

Chapter 3 provides a micro-picture of how the Palestinian state project disempowered different Palestinian constituencies, denying their political rights and dream of liberation. Hania Assali focuses on East Jerusalem to show how Jerusalem's position as the capital of a future Palestinian state has been undermined by the failure of the PNA to counter Israel's decision to sever the Holy City from the rest of the West Bank. She provides a review of Israel's legal, demographic, and territorial assaults on Palestinians living in East Jerusalem and the ways in which they resist it, as exemplified by the "prayer intifada" in the summer of 2017 and again during Ramadan in April and May 2021.

Hanan Toukan in chapter 4 touches on the symbolic and aesthetic dimension of the Palestinian state project as represented by the construction of the Palestinian Museum. National museums have typically been markers of national independence. They can thus provide a discursive means to affirm the existence of a people whose history has been denied by the colonizer. The construction of the Palestinian Museum in Birzeit in 2016, however, elicited criticism for being a selective and an elitist endeavor that siphoned money away from more urgent needs. Toukan unpacks the political economy of the Palestinian Museum, arguing that its construction cannot be understood without situating it in a larger regional attempt to shape the discourse around art, identity, and modernity outside the confines of the Western world. Her analysis complements Hanieh's argument in chapter 1 by emphasizing the role of the museum's investors, mostly based in the Gulf and closely tied to the PNA, in seeking to shape the meaning of independence and resistance against Israel's physical, cultural, and economic domination. She shows that the Palestine Museum's political value lies in its temporal orientation, namely its focus on the present. Unlike the Darwish or Arafat museums, which are dedicated to the past and display the contours of the national narrative of dispossession and historical struggle, the Palestinian Museum leaves an open space for engaging the present and rethinking the future. Its architecture reveals an engagement with the continuing reality of dispossession and an attempt to disrupt hegemonic understandings of statehood, peoplehood, space, and time. Whether the Palestinian Museum will succeed in this mission is still to be seen, but so far it shows both the scope and limits of Palestinian agency in a context of ongoing colonization.

Chapter 5 provides a glimpse of the political opportunities that can emerge from resituating the Palestinian cause away from the paradigm of statehood and within a rights discourse instead. Yousef Munayyer in this chapter argues that a political strategy focused on defending Palestinian rights, rather than statehood, is more successful in generating international support today, particularly in the United States. He shows that US support for Palestinians' rights has grown since 2000, highlighting the paradoxical opportunities offered by the Trump era for activists emphasizing Palestinian demands for equality and dignity. Their activism draws on the intersectionality of political struggles, making connection between Trump's and Netanyahu's racist policies to build new international networks of solidarity for the Palestinian people.

Munayyar's analysis provides a segue to the second part of the book, which explores the legal and political dimensions that must be revisited in order to construct a viable political alternative to the current colonial reality. Nadim Khoury in chapter 6 examines the question of transitional justice and the way the Palestinian state project avoided it. He argues that the term has been raised by Palestinian critiques of Oslo to stress the impossibility of peace without providing justice for the full range of Palestinian rights, including the right of return, recognition of the Nakba, and an end to the ongoing Israeli violence. The Oslo peace agreements sought to settle the Israeli-Palestinian conflict by sidetracking the question of historical reconciliation. As Khoury demonstrates, the concept of transitional justice could spark new conversations about moving forward but it is also a deeply contested concept since there remain fierce disagreements over whose historical injustices need to be addressed, with what mechanisms, and toward what ends.

Chapter 7 examines how the first Zionist and Palestinian alternatives to partition sought to protect the individual and collective rights of Palestinians and Jews in a single polity. In this chapter, Leila Farsakh examines how early protagonists of a one-state solution conceptualized the notion of the nation and how separate it could be from the state. She also assesses Palestinian and Zionist attempts to incorporate the "other" in their conception of a one-state solution and points to the economic and political challenges that continue to haunt any binational or democratic alternative to partition today.

Chapter 8 focuses on how international law protects Palestinian rights, not only the right of return but also the right to a Palestinian nationality. Susan Akram in this chapter argues that Palestinian nationality is a legally protected concept, despite the Balfour Declaration, the creation of the state of Israel in 1948, and the establishment of the Palestinian Authority in 1995. She unpacks the international legal definition of nationality, which emphasizes the direct relation between a people and a land, rather than the ethnic criteria or a sense of an "imagined community" that sociological use of the term implies. She thereby challenges Israel's denial and elimination of Palestinian nationality in 1948, as well as its creation of a Jewish nationality that is open to all Jews in the world. Akram maintains that Israel's notion of Jewish nationality is not legitimate from an international legal perspective because Israel based it on a religious and extra-territorial definition of the nation. Her analysis suggests that while the concept of Israeli nationality, which presently does not exist and which would bestow equal citizenship rights on both Jews and non-Jews born and living in Israel, would be a legally binding category, Israel's latest nationality law is not.[47]

The legal persistence of the concept of the Palestinian nation has significant ramifications for any post-Oslo political configuration. Mazen Masri in chapter 9 looks more closely at various constitutional frameworks for a single state in historic Palestine. He provides a comparative lens to assess which of the various models of federalism, binationalism, and/or liberal democracy can best protect Palestinian and Israeli individual citizenship rights without compromising their collective or national rights. These rights include not only the freedom to speak one's own language, levy taxes, and elect representatives, but also to acknowledge historical grievances, establish mechanisms for reparation and reconciliation, and decolonize economic and social relations.

Chapters 10 and 11 meanwhile zoom in on Palestinian citizens in Israel, core constituents of the Palestinian people, to consider how they are rethinking the relationship between the nation and the state in envisaging a political future. Maha Nassar in chapter 10 examines the historical origins and ongoing challenges that Palestinian citizens of Israel confront in trying to both defend their individual and collective rights within Israel and remain part of the Palestinian national movement. She focuses on the evolving positions of Palestinian citizens of Israel in the one-state or two-states debate, exposing the tension they experience between asserting their intrinsic link to the Palestinian national struggle and finding a solution to the Israeli-Palestinian conflict that is politically feasible. Ilan Pappe complements this discussion in chapter 11, where he makes a case for the notion of indigenous sovereignty. He argues that Palestinians citizens of Israel are at the forefront of reclaiming indigeneity as a way to assert the sovereignty of the Palestinian people. Indigenous sovereignty helps resituate the Palestinian struggle within a decolonization paradigm and offers new forms of resistance that challenge the nation-state as a solution.

The conclusion wraps up the book by highlighting some of the line of inquiries that emerge from its chapters and the areas of new research needed to expand our understanding of the meaning and locus of political liberation moving forward.

NOTES

1. Edward Said, *The Question of Palestine* (New York: Vintage Books, 1979).

2. Sari Makdisi, *Palestine Inside Out: An Everyday Occupation* (New York: W.W. Norton & Company, 2007); Hani Faris, *The Failure of the Two-State Solution: The Prospects of One State in the Israel-Palestine Conflict* (London: I.B. Tauris, 2013); Mehran Kamrava, *The Impossibility of Palestine: History, Geography and the Road Ahead* (New Haven, CT: Yale University Press, 2017); Economic and Social Commission for Western Asia, *Israeli Practices towards the Palestinian People and the Question of Apartheid* (New York: United Nations, 2017).

3. Michael Crowley and David M. Halbfinger, "Trump Releases Mideast Peace Plan That Strongly Favors Israel," *The New York Times*, January 28, 2020.

4. The Quartet was established in 2002 and includes the United States, European Union, UN, and Russia. Its aim has been to support Oslo peace process and advice the PNA.

5. Ali Abunimeh, *One Country: A Bold Proposal to End the Israeli-Palestinian Impasse* (New York: Metropolitan Books, 2006); Ali Abunimeh, *The Battle for Justice in Palestine* (Chicago: Haymarket Press, 2014); Virginia Tilley, *The One-State Solution: A Breakthrough for Peace in the Israeli-Palestinian Deadlock* (University of Michigan Press, 2005). Benny Morris, *One State, Two States: Resolving the Israel/Palestine Conflict* (New Haven, CT: Yale University Press, 2010); Hussein Ibish, *What's Wrong with the One-State Agenda? Why Ending the Occupation and Peace with Israel is Still the Palestinian National Goal* (Washington DC: American Task Force on Palestine, 2009); Gershon Shafir, *A Half Century of Occupation: Israel, Palestine and the World's Most Intractable Conflict* (Oakland: University of California Press, 2017); Mark LeVine and Mathias Mossberg, *One Land, Two States: Israel and Palestine as Parallel States* (Berkeley: California University Press, 2014).

6. Beshara Doumani, "Palestine Versus the Palestinians? The Iron Laws and Ironies of a People Denied," *Journal of Palestine Studies* 36, no. 4 (Summer 2007): 49–64; Ruba Salih and Sophie

Richter-Devroe, "Palestine beyond National Frames: Emerging Politics, Cultures and Claims," *South Atlantic Quarterly* 117, no. 1 (2018): 1–20.

7. Said, *The Question of Palestine*; Fayez Sayigh, *Zionist Colonialism in Palestine* (Beirut: PLO Research Center, 1965).

8. Joseph Massad, "Against Self-Determination," *Humanity Journal* 9, no. 2 (2018).

9. Adom Getachew, *Worldmaking after Empire: The Rise and Fall of Self-Determination* (Princeton, NJ: Princeton University Press, 2019), 74.

10. Getachew, *Worldmaking after Empire*; Gary Wilder, *Freedom Time: Negritude, Decolonization and the Future of the World* (Durham, NC: Duke University Press, 2015).

11 See the text of UN Resolution 1514, at http://undocs.org/A/Res/1514(XV).

12. As Wilder put it, "a procedural understanding of self-determination as a people's free choice about its future political status, about a specific framework for self-government, was conflated with a limited understanding of self-determination as state sovereignty for a national group." Wilder, *Freedom Time*, 88–89.

13. Getachew, *Worldmaking after Empire*, chapter 3; Wilder, *Freedom Time*, chapter 4.

14. Said, *The Palestine Question*, 134.

15. Quoted in Alain Gresh, *The PLO: The Struggle Within* (London: Zed Books, 1988), 48.

16. See the text of UNSC Resolution 242 at https://www.securitycouncilreport.org/atf/cf/%7B65 BFCF9B-6D27-4E9C-8CD3-CF6E4FF96FF9%7D/IP%20S%20RES%20242.pdf.

17. The Arab League recognized the PLO as the sole and legitimate representative of the Palestinian people in a meeting of the Rabat Arab League in June 1974, thus delegitimizing claims by any Arab state to represent the Palestinians. For more details, see Noura Erakat, *Justice for Some: Law and the Question of Palestine* (Stanford, CA: Stanford University Press, 2019).

18. Yazid Sayigh, *Armed Struggle and the Search for State: The Palestinian National Movement 1949-1993*, (Oxford: Oxford University Press, 1997). In 1976, the municipal elections that Israel held in the West Bank and Gaza Strip brought to power mayors who were supportive of the PLO.

19. Italics added. See political program adopted at the twelfth session of the Palestinian National Council, in Cairo, June 1974, available at www/pnic.gov/ps/Arabic/semester12.html; my translation.

20. Rashid Khalidi, *The Iron Cage: The Story of the Palestinian Struggle for Statehood* (Cambridge: Beacon Press, 2007); Gresh, "The PLO and the Naksa."

21. Leila Farsakh, "The 'Right to Have Rights': Partition and Palestinian Self-Determination," *Journal of Palestine Studies* 47, no. 1 (Fall 2017): 56–68.

22. See PNA, "Palestinian Reform and Development Plan," 2008–10, available at https://www.un .org/unispal/document/auto-insert-208834/; and PNA, "National Development Plan 2011–2013: Establishing the State, Building our Future," available at http://www.mot.gov.ps/wp-content/uploads /Portals/_Rainbow/Documents/Establishing%20the%20State%20Building%20our%20Future_%20 NDP%202011-13.pdf.

23. The PNA became the largest single employer. Since 2000 it employed 31–48 percent of the total employed labor force in the Gaza Strip and over 15 percent in the West Bank. Central Bureau of Statistics, *Statistical Yearbook*, Ramallah, various years, available at http://pcbs.gov.ps/PCBS-Metadata -en-v4.3/index.php/catalog/Employment-Unemployment, accessed May 2021.

24. Sophia Stamatopoulou-Robbins, "An Uncertain Climate in Risky Times: How Occupation Became Like the Rain in Post-Oslo Palestine," *International Journal of Middle East Studies* 50, no. 2 (2018): 383–404, 400.

25. See for example Stamatopoulou-Robbins, "An Uncertain Climate in Risky Times,"; Omar Jabary Salamanca, "Hooked on Electricity: The Charged Political Economy of Electrification in Palestine," paper presented at the first New Direction in Palestine Studies Workshop, Brown University, March 2014; Kareem Rabie, "Housing and the Future of Palestine," paper presented at the New Direction in Palestine Studies Workshop, Brown University, March 2019; and Kareem Rabie, *Palestine Is

Throwing a Party and the Whole World is Invited: Capital and State in the West Bank (Durham, NC: Duke University Press, 2021)

26. For a comprehensive review of the negotiations and their failure, see Shafir, *A Half Century of Occupation*, George Mitchel and Alon Sachar, *A Path to Peace: A Brief History of Israeli-Palestinian Negotiations and a Way Forward in the Middle East* (New York: Simon and Schuster, 2016); Khaled Elgindy, *Blind Spot: The US and the Palestinians from Balfour to Trump* (Washington DC: Brookings Institute, 2019).

27. Michael Keating and Anne Le More, *Aid, Diplomacy and Facts on the Ground: The Case of Palestine* (London: Chatham House, 2005); Toufic Haddad, *Palestine Ltd: Neoliberalism and Nationalism in the Occupied Territories* (London: I.B. Tauris, 2016); Linda Tabar, "Disrupting Development, Reclaiming Solidarity: The Anti-Politics of Humanitarianism," *Journal of Palestine* Studies 45, no. 4 (Summer 2016): 16–31; Alaa Tartir and Timothy Seidel, *Palestine and Rule of Power: Local Dissent vs. International Governance* (Cham: Palgrave Macmillan, 2019).

28. Leila Farsakh, "Undermining Democracy in Palestine: The Politics of International Aid since Oslo," *Journal of Palestine Studies* 45, no. 4 (Summer 2016).

29. Farsakh, "Undermining Democracy in Palestine"; Tabar, "Disrupting Development."

30. Jamil Hilal, *Where Now for Palestine? The Demise of the Two-State Solution*, (London: Zed Books, 2006); Jamil Hilal, "Rethinking Palestine: Settler-Colonialism, Neo-liberalism and Individualism in the West Bank and Gaza Strip," *Contemporary Arab Affairs* 8, no. 3 (July–September 2015).

31. Ariella Azoulay and Adi Ophir, *The One-State Condition: Occupation and Democracy in Israel/Palestine* (Stanford, CA: Stanford University Press, 2012); Leila Farsakh, ed., "Commemorating the Naksa, Evoking the Nakba," special issue, *Electronic Journal of Middle Eastern Studies* 8 (Spring 2008); Omar Barghouti, *Boycott, Divestment, Sanctions: The Global Struggle for Palestinian Rights* (Chicago: Haymarket Press, 2011); Virginia Tilley, "After Oslo, a Paradigm Shift? Redefining Sovereignty, Responsibility and Self-determination," *Conflict, Security and Development* 15, no. 5 (2015): 425–53; Economic and Social Commission for Western Asia, *Israeli Practices*.

32. See for example the latest annual report of the Jerusalem Legal and Aid Center, http://www.jlac.ps/userfiles/file/Annual_Reports/AnRep2018.pdf; Human Rights Watch Report, *Two Authorities, One Way, Zero Dissent: Arbitrary Arrest and Tortures Under the Palestinian Authority and Hamas*, https://www.hrw.org/report/2018/10/23/two-authorities-one-way-zero-dissent/arbitrary-arrest-and-torture-under.

33. Arie Dubonov and Laura Robson, *Partition: A Transnational History of Twentieth-Century Separatism* (Stanford, CA: Stanford University Press, 2019).

34. Salih and Richter-Devroe, "Palestine beyond National Frames," 8.

35. See among others, Lorenzo Veracini, "The Other Shift: Settler Colonialism, Israel and the Occupation," *Journal of Palestine Studies* 42, no. 2 (2013): 26–42; Omar Salamanca, Mazna Qato, and Kareem Rabie, "The Past Is Present: Settler Colonialism in Palestine," *Settler Colonial Studies* 2, no. 1 (2012): 1–8; Francesco Amoruso, Ilan Pappe, and Sophie Richter-Devroe, "Introduction: Knowledge, Power, and the 'Settler Colonial Turn' in Palestine Studies," *Interventions: The International Journal of Postcolonial Studies* 21, no. 4 (2019): 451–63.

36. Hazem Jamjoum, "Reclaiming the Political Dimension of the Palestinian Narrative," *Al-Shabaka: The Palestinian Policy Network*, September 12, 2018, https://al-shabaka.org/circles/reclaiming-the-political-narrative-in-palestinian-politics/.

37. Amoruso, Pappe, and Richter-Devroe, "Introduction"; Rana Barakat, "Writing/Righting Palestine Studies: Settler Colonialism, Indigenous Sovereignty and Resisting the Ghost(s) of History," *Settler Colonial Studies* 8, no. 3 (2018): 349–63; Salih and Richter-Devroe, "Palestine beyond National Frames."

38. Abumineh, *Battle for Justice in Palestine*; Bashir Bashir, "The Strengths and Weaknesses of Integrative Solutions for the Israeli-Palestinian Conflict," *Middle East Journal* 70, no. 4 (2016): 560–78;

Faris, *Failure of the Two-State Solution*; Leila Farsakh, "The One-State Solution and the Israeli-Palestinian Conflict: Palestinian Challenges and Prospects," *Middle East Journal* 65, no. 1 (2011): 55–71.

39. Abunimeh, *The Battle for Justice in Palestine*; Omar Barghouti, "The Secular Democratic State Is the Only Possible and Ideal Solution," *Journal of Palestine Studies* 76 (2008): 8–25 [Arabic].

40. Omar Barghouti, "The Secular Democratic State."

41. Nadim Rouhana, *Israel and its Palestinian Citizens: Ethnic Privileges in the Jewish State* (Cambridge: Cambridge University Press, 2017); Asaʻed Ghanem, "The Bi-National State Solution," *Israel Studies* 14, no. 2 (Summer 2009): 120–33; Farsakh, "The One-State Solution;" Bashir, "The Strengths and Weaknesses of Integrative Solutions."

42. Hannah Arendt, *The Origins of Totalitarianism* (New York: Harcourt, Brace and Jovanovich, 1968 [1951]), 301.

43. Bashir Bashir and Rachel Busbridge, "The Politics of Decolonization and Bi-Nationalism in Israel/Palestine," *Political Studies* 67, no. 2 (2019): 388–405.

44. Bashir Bashir and Amos Goldberg, *The Holocaust and the Nakba* (New York: Columbia University Press, 2019).

45. Said, *The Question of Palestine*, 122.

46. The periods of infighting were: between 1983 and 1986, during the camp wars in Lebanon and the split of Fatah, and between 1996 and 1999, during the PNA/Fatah assault on Hamas, which did not lead to a severance between the two political parties.

47. Israel offers Israeli *citizenship* to both Jews and non-Jews. Israel defines *nationality* on the basis of the religious affiliation of its citizens, for example, Jewish nationality, Christian nationality, Muslim nationality, or Druze nationality. For an excellent analysis and a genealogy of Israel's legal separation of citizenship from nationality as a way to protect the notion of a Jewish, versus Israeli, nationality, see Shira Robinson, *Citizen Strangers: Palestinians and the Birth of Israel's Liberal Settler State* (Stanford, CA: Stanford University Press, 2013).

BIBLIOGRAPHY

Abunimeh, Ali. *The Battle for Justice in Palestine*. Chicago: Haymarket Press, 2014.

———. *One Country: A Bold Proposal to End the Israeli-Palestinian Impasse*. New York: Metropolitan Books, 2006.

Amoruso, Francesco, Ilan Pappe, and Sophie Richter-Devroe. "Introduction: Knowledge, Power, and the 'Settler Colonial Turn' in Palestine Studies." *Interventions: The International Journal of Postcolonial Studies* 21, no. 4 (2019): 451–63.

Arendt, Hannah. *The Origins of Totalitarianism*. New York: Harcourt, Brace and Jovanovich, 1968 [1951].

Azoulay, Ariella, and Adi Ophir. *The One-State Condition: Occupation and Democracy in Israel/Palestine*. Stanford, CA: Stanford University Press, 2012.

Barakat, Rana. "Writing/Righting Palestine Studies: Settler Colonialism, Indigenous Sovereignty and Resisting the Ghost(s) of History." *Settler Colonial Studies* 8, no. 3 (2018): 349–63.

Barghouti, Omar. *Boycott, Divestment, Sanctions: The Global Struggle for Palestinian Rights*. Chicago: Haymarket Press, 2011.

———. "The Secular Democratic State Is the Only Possible and Ideal Solution." *Journal of Palestine Studies* 76 (2008): 8–25. [Arabic.]

Bashir, Bashir. "The Strengths and Weaknesses of Integrative Solutions for the Israeli-Palestinian Conflict." *The Middle East Journal* 70, no. 4 (2016): 560–78.

Bashir, Bashir, and Rachel Busbridge. "The Politics of Decolonization and Bi-Nationalism in Israel/Palestine." *Political Studies* 67, no. 2 (2019): 388–405.

Bashir, Bashir, and Amos Goldberg. *The Holocaust and the Nakba: A New Grammar of Trauma and History*. New York: Columbia University Press, 2019.

Busbridge, Rachel. "Israel-Palestine and the Settler Colonial 'Turn': From Interpretation to Decolonization." *Theory, Culture and Society* 35, no. 1 (2018): 91–115.

Doumani, Beshara. "Palestine Versus the Palestinians? The Iron Laws and Ironies of a People Denied." *Journal of Palestine Studies* 36, no. 4 (2007): 49–64.

Dubonov, Arie, and Laura Robson. *Partition: A Transnational History of Twentieth-Century Separatism*. Stanford, CA: Stanford University Press, 2019.

Economic and Social Commission for Western Asia. *Israeli Practices towards the Palestinian People and the Question of Apartheid*. New York: United Nations, 2017.

Elgindy, Khaled. *Blind Spot: The US and the Palestinians from Balfour to Trump*. Washington, DC: Brookings Institute, 2019.

Erakat, Noura. *Justice for Some: Law and the Question of Palestine*. Stanford, CA: Stanford University Press, 2019.

Faris, Hani. *The Failure of the Two-State Solution: The Prospects of One State in the Israel-Palestine Conflict*. London: I.B. Tauris, 2013.

Farsakh, Leila, ed. *Commemorating the Naksa, Evoking the Nakba*. Special issue, *Electronic Journal of Middle Eastern Studies* 8 (2008).

———. "The One-State Solution and the Israeli-Palestinian Conflict: Palestinian Challenges and Prospects." *Middle East Journal* 64, no.1 (2011): 20–45.

———. "The Right to Have Rights: Partition and Palestinian Self-Determination." *Journal of Palestine Studies* 47, no. 1 (2017): 56–68.

———. "Undermining Democracy in Palestine: The Politics of International Aid since Oslo." *Journal of Palestine Studies* 45, no. 4 (2016): 48–63.

Getachew, Adom. *Worldmaking after Empire: The Rise and Fall of Self-Determination*. Princeton, NJ: Princeton University Press, 2019.

Ghanem, Asa'ed. "The Bi-National State Solution." *Israel Studies* 14, no. 2 (2009): 120–33.

Gresh, Alain. *The PLO: The Struggle Within*. London: Zed Books, 1988.

———. "The PLO and the Naksa: The Search for a Palestinian State." *Electronic Journal of Middle Eastern Studies* 8 (Spring 2008): 81–93.

Haddad, Toufic. *Palestine Ltd: Neoliberalism and Nationalism in the Occupied Territories*. London: I.B. Tauris, 2016.

Hilal, Jamil. "Rethinking Palestine: Settler-Colonialism, Neo-liberalism and Individualism in the West Bank and Gaza Strip." *Contemporary Arab Affairs* 8, no. 3 (2015): 351–62.

———, ed. *Where Now for Palestine? The Demise of the Two-State Solution*. London: Zed Books, 2006.

Ibish, Hussein. *What's Wrong with the One-State Agenda? Why Ending the Occupation and Peace with Israel Is Still the Palestinian National Goal*. Washington DC: American Task Force on Palestine, 2009.

Jamal, Amal. *Arab Minority Nationalism in Israel: The Politics of Indigeneity*. London: Routledge Press, 2011.

Kamrava, Mehran. *The Impossibility of Palestine: History, Geography and the Road Ahead*. New Haven, CT: Yale University Press, 2017.

Keating, Michael, and Anne Le More, eds. *Aid, Diplomacy and Facts on the Ground: The Case of Palestine*. London: Chatham House, 2005.

Khalidi, Rashid. *The Iron Cage: The Story of the Palestinian Struggle for Statehood*. Cambridge, MA: Beacon Press, 2007.

LeVine, Mark, and Mathias Mossberg. *One Land, Two States: Israel and Palestine as Parallel States*. Berkeley: California University Press, 2014.

Makdisi, Sari. *Palestine Inside Out: An Everyday Occupation*. New York: W. W. Norton & Company, 2007.

Massad, Joseph. "Against Self-Determination." *Humanity Journal* 9, no. 2 (2018): 161–91.

Mitchel, George, and Alon Sachar. *A Path to Peace: A Brief History of Israeli-Palestinian Negotiations and a Way Forward in the Middle East*. New York: Simon and Schuster, 2016.

Morris, Benny. *One State, Two States: Resolving the Israel/Palestine Conflict*. New Haven, CT: Yale University Press, 2010.

Nassar, Maha. *Brothers Apart: Palestinian Citizens of Israel and the Arab World*. Stanford, CA: Stanford University Press, 2017.

Pace, Michelle, and Sen Somdeep. *The Palestinian Authority in the West Bank: The Theatrics of Woeful Statecraft*. New York: Routledge, 2019.

Pappe, Ilan. *The Forgotten Palestinians: A History of the Palestinians in Israel*. New Haven, CT: Yale University Press, 2011.

———, ed. *Israel and South Africa: The Many Faces of Apartheid*. London: Zed Books, 2015.

Rabie, Kareem. "Housing and the Future of Palestine." Paper presented at the New Direction in Palestine Studies Workshop, Brown University, March 2019.

Robinson, Shira. *Citizen Strangers: Palestinians and the Birth of Israel's Liberal Settler State*. Stanford, CA: Stanford University Press, 2013.

Rouhana, Nadim. "Decolonization as Reconciliation: Rethinking the National Conflict Paradigm in the Israeli-Palestinian Conflict." *Journal of Ethnic and Racial Studies* 41, no. 4 (2018): 643–62.

———, ed. *Israel and its Palestinian Citizens: Ethnic Privileges in the Jewish State*. Cambridge: Cambridge University Press, 2017.

Said, Edward. *The Question of Palestine*. New York: Vintage Books, 1979.

Salamanca, Omar Jabary. "Hooked on Electricity: The Charged Political Economy of Electrification in Palestine." Paper presented at the New Direction in Palestine Studies Workshop, Brown University, March 2014.

Salamanca, Omar, Mazna Qato, and Kareem Rabie. "The Past Is Present: Settler Colonialism in Palestine." *Settler Colonial Studies* 2, no. 1 (2012): 1–8.

Salih, Ruba, and Sophie Richter-Devroe. "Palestine beyond National Frames: Emerging Politics, Cultures and Claims." *South Atlantic Quarterly* 117, no. 1 (2018): 1–20.

Sayigh, Fayez. *Zionist Colonialism in Palestine*. Beirut: PLO Research Center, 1965.

Sayigh, Yazid. *Armed Struggle and the Search for State: The Palestinian National Movement 1949–1993*. Cambridge: Cambridge University Press, 1997.

Shafir, Gershon. *A Half Century of Occupation: Israel, Palestine and the World's Most Intractable Conflict*. Oakland: University of California Press, 2017.

Stamatopoulou-Robbins, Sophia. "An Uncertain Climate in Risky Times: How Occupation Became Like the Rain in Post-Oslo Palestine." *International Journal of Middle East Studies* 50, no. 3 (2018): 383–404.

Tabar, Linda. "Disrupting Development, Reclaiming Solidarity: The Anti-Politics of Humanitarianism." *Journal of Palestine Studies* 45, no. 4 (2016): 16–31.

Tartir, Alaa, and Timothy Seidel. *Palestine and Rule of Power: Local Dissent vs. International Governance.* Cham: Palgrave Macmillan, 2019.

Tilley, Virginia. "After Oslo, a Paradigm Shift? Redefining Sovereignty, Responsibility and Self-determination." *Conflict, Security and Development* 15, no. 5 (2015): 4252–53.

———. *The One-State Solution: A Breakthrough for Peace in the Israeli-Palestinian Deadlock.* Ann Arbor: University of Michigan Press, 2005.

Veracini, Lorenzo. "The Other Shift: Settler Colonialism, Israel and the Occupation." *Journal of Palestine Studies* 42, no. 2 (Winter 2013): 26–42.

Wilder, Gary. *Freedom Time: Negritude, Decolonization and the Future of the Work.* Durham, NC: Duke University Press, 2015.

PART ONE

Partition and the Cost of Statehood

1

The Political Economy of State Formation in Palestine

Adam Hanieh

The question of state formation in Palestine has attracted a great deal of attention from scholars and activists alike since the establishment of the Palestinian National Authority (PNA) in 1994. Much of this debate has focused upon questions about three matters: (1) the relationship between peace and "state-formation", (2) the priorities and nature of Palestinian Authority institution-building, and (3) the linkages between donor funding and the emerging features of Palestinian government. Given the nature of the Oslo Accords and subsequent negotiations between Israel and the Palestine Liberation Organization (PLO), the discourse surrounding these debates has tended to be based almost exclusively on some version of a "two-state" solution—typically with greater attention given to the West Bank as the spatial center of PNA institution-building.

The aim of this chapter is to present a critique of this state-formation literature, focusing in particular on the analytical silence it shows concerning the wider political economy of the Middle East region as a whole. I argue that much of the debate around Palestinian state formation tends to a methodological perspective that views Palestinian society in the Occupied Palestinian Territories (OPT)—and in the West Bank specifically—as a self-contained social formation in which state-civil society relations are implicitly assumed to exist as separate and distinct from the wider region. In this sense, state-formation literature is typically characterized by a form of methodological nationalism, in which the territorial borders of the national state—or the Palestinian state-in-formation—are considered as the exclusive vantage point from which to understand the various modalities of state-building.[1] This is not to deny that much of the literature considers the impact of various trade and financial relationships between a future Palestinian state and neighboring countries. The point, however, is that these relationships are considered as *external* to Palestinian social formation as such. It is the contention of this chapter that it is necessary to consider the ways in which the developmental tendencies of the regional scale already exist *internal* to Palestinian social formation. Without considering the ways that these regional processes have been internalized into the nature of Palestinian state and class formation under the PNA, it is not possible to accurately assess the likelihood of any state-building trajectories over the coming period (including both one- and two-state options).

The chapter is divided into two main parts. The first begins with a survey of the general state-building literature as expressed in the policies of international agencies and government donors. This literature has identified three supposed characteristics of "successful" states—authority, legitimacy, and capacity—and aims to develop these features through technical support and financial aid. The section then concretizes these formulations in the Palestinian context, looking at both the dominant approach towards state-building in Palestine and the criticisms that have been raised against this within the literature. The final part of this section presents a reexamination of the state-formation debate (both generally and in Palestine) based upon a critique of the way that much of this literature conceives of the state itself at a theoretical level. In counterposition to the neo-Weberian understanding of the state that dominates most state-formation discussions, this section puts forward an alternative conception of the state based upon an understanding of the prevailing social and power relations that exist under capitalism.

The second part of the chapter aims to build upon this alternative conception of the state to assess how the regional context has determined the character of state formation in Palestine. In this vein, I present an overview of Palestine in the regional context, and the ways in which global relations of power have shaped the nature of the state-building project in Palestine. I also look at the implications of these regional trajectories for the nature of Palestinian class and state formation, arguing that the particular social base of the PNA has come to rest upon a business class that is largely drawn from a layer of Palestinian diaspora capital—one that has been fully integrated into the modalities of state formation under the PNA. The concluding section examines what this particular class-state structure means for the possible future trajectories of Palestinian self-determination.

THE STATE FORMATION DEBATE

Authority, Legitimacy, Capacity

The explosion of the state-building literature through the 1990s and 2000s was closely related to two important developments in the global political economy at the time. The first of these was the emergence of the neoliberal economic paradigm as the virtually unchallenged policy model. This framework promoted market liberalization and deregulation, and the opening up of economies to cross-border trade and finance. Closely connected to the breakup of the Soviet Union and the emergence of newly independent states across Europe and Central Asia—the so-called "transition economies"—this new era of neoliberal globalization raised a series of questions about how best to move from centrally planned, bureaucratic economies to market-based systems of accumulation. At the same time in the South, a range of conflicts and wars across numerous countries—notably Somalia, Iraq, Afghanistan, the Democratic Republic of Congo, and Sudan—placed the issue of rebuilding apparently dysfunctional state systems firmly on the map of international institutions and development practitioners.

These trajectories of neoliberalism and conflict were to shape the content of the emerging state-building debate, which crystallized around two key theoretical propositions. The first of these was the linkage between "democratization" (or "democracy-promotion") and neoliberal models of development. The creation of liberal democracies and market-based economies were said to be mutually reinforcing processes that offered the best guarantors for stability. In Europe, newly established institutions such as the European Bank for Reconstruction and Development (EBRD) consciously twinned the rebuilding of former Eastern bloc states with free-market principles, providing loans and grants to promote the privatization of infrastructure and industry. Elsewhere, notably in the Middle East, the US government was to launch a policy framework based on what George W. Bush described in 2004 as "free elections and free markets."[2] The initial testing-ground for this policy was post-2003 Iraq, where the US government stated they sought to see a narrow form of liberal democracy that could provide legitimacy for free-market economic measures. Accompanying this policy turn, a host of quasi-governmental institutions such as the US National Endowment for Democracy (NED), the National Democratic Institute (NDI), the International Republican Institute (IRI), the Center for International Private Enterprise (CIPE), and the Solidarity Center were to employ the same basic argument linking "free markets" and "a vibrant civil society" with the new state-building emphasis.

The second key theoretical proposition of the state-building literature was the explicit argument that effective state building was causally related to more peaceful states. This "liberal peace" perspective claimed that "conflicts could be defused by encouraging the liberalization of the political and economic structures of post-conflict societies."[3] If a state were governed along liberal democratic lines, it would be less likely to go to war because of the inherent reluctance of the population to engage in military conflict. "Democracies," as one perceptive critic of the liberal peace paradigm noted, "do not go to war with one another."[4] Through the 1990s and 2000s, this perspective was supplemented with further arguments—both theoretical and empirical—that intra-state violence was also less likely to occur within liberal democracies.[5] Francis Fukuyama, for example, was to link state weakness to a long list of internal crises, claiming that "weak or failing states commit human rights abuses, provoke humanitarian disasters, drive massive waves of immigration, and attack their neighbors."[6] Likewise, the World Bank would explain the rationale behind its State and Peace Building Fund as one in which building states and building peace are considered as complementary processes.[7]

Nonetheless, beyond the emphasis on neoliberal economic models and the claims around peace, the question of state-building raises a range of related theoretical and practical issues. What is meant by state building in practice? How is the state conceived of theoretically, and what particular institutional features characterize a successful state? What is the most appropriate temporal sequencing for the process of building state institutions? What actors should drive this process? Although there exists a wide variety of specific approaches to these questions, the starting point for the vast majority of relevant literature is an ideal-type definition of the state drawn from neo-Weberian sociology.[8] According to this perspective, a state is defined through its "monopoly of the legitimate use of physical force within a given territory."[9] Flowing from this definition, there are three supposed features of all states that are typically highlighted across the literature:

1. Authority, defined as "the ability of the state to project its political power over all its territory, to reach all citizens regardless of their location, to maintain law and order and protect citizens from predation and violence. It is the ability of the laws and rules of the state to trump all other laws and rules."
2. Capacity, or "the ability of the state to deliver or procure goods and services, design and implement policies, build infrastructure, collect revenue, dispense justice, and maintain a conducive environment for the private sector."
3. Legitimacy, or "whether citizens feel the government has the right to govern—and whether they trust the government."[10]

Each of these three features is postulated to be interrelated to the others and self-reinforcing. Successful states are able to enforce authority over their populations within a defined territory, and this helps to sustain their legitimacy. But authority stems not only from the use (or threat) of violence, but also from the generalized belief of the subject population in the legitimacy of the state's right to act as the supreme monopoly of force. In turn, this legitimacy arises from the state's capacity to ensure that needs such as security, stability, and provision of basic services are met.

Successful states are therefore characterized by the right balance of this interconnected triumvirate—authority, legitimacy, and capacity. When this balance does not exist, a state is said to be in crisis. As the United States Agency for International Development (USAID) was to put it in the mid-2000s, such states are defined by a "central government [that] does not exert significant control over its own territory or is unable or unwilling to assure the provision of vital services to significant parts of its territory where legitimacy of the government is weak or non-existent, and where violent conflict is a reality or a great risk."[11] By assessing states' relative degrees of authority, legitimacy, and capacity, academic and development research attempted to correlate gaps in one or more of these attributes with what were described as weak, fragile, fragmented, or stressed states.

Throughout these debates, the case of Palestine and the Palestinian National Authority has provided a prominent laboratory for these theoretical claims. Large levels of donor funding have gone towards building the institutions of the Palestinian National Authority since its establishment in 1994. In many ways, as numerous government and donor reports have noted, the PNA's institutional capacity has consistently been viewed as an international exemplar in relation to state-building.[12] Moreover, given the ongoing reality of Israel's occupation, Palestine also remains a key focus of the debates around "peace-building" and state formation. In this respect, it is instructive to turn to how these state-formation debates have unfolded in the Palestinian context.

State-Building in Palestine

The debates around state formation in Palestine are closely linked to an assessment of the negotiations process between Israel and the PLO that began in the early 1990s with the Oslo Accords. Drawing upon the "liberal peace" theory, the creation of a functioning Palestinian state was portrayed as means of fostering a successful peace process—typically understood through the lens of guaranteeing Israel's security. A particularly significant role in this was played by the World Bank, which issued its influential six-volume study, *Developing the Occupied Territories: An Investment in Peace*, in early 1993, laying out "a path to reforming, reorganizing and stabilizing the OPT's economic and social balance . . . and preparing its economic integration into the broader set of regional neoliberal interests."[13] According to one critic, the logic essentially came down to the argument that "building a democratic Palestinian state would buttress the peace process."[14] The European Union was a prime advocate of this approach, arguing in its 1999 Berlin Declaration that it was "convinced that the creation of a democratic, viable and peaceful sovereign Palestinian state . . . would be the best guarantee of Israel's security."[15]

Based on this perspective, and drawing heavily from the wider theoretical literature outlined above, donor support to the PNA since the mid-1990s has focused on building the institutional elements of the PNA's capacity and authority. Following the end of the Second Intifada in the early 2000s, the death of Yasser Arafat in 2004, and the split between the West Bank and Gaza Strip in 2006—leading the PNA to become largely territorialized in the West Bank—this orientation was codified in the November 2007 *Palestinian Reform and Development Plan for 2008–2010* (PRDP). Written with the assistance of the World Bank and other IMF advisors, the PRDP became the guiding framework for Palestinian development policy, particularly in the West Bank areas where the PNA was well established. In many ways, the PRDP explicitly confirmed the neoliberal orientation of state-building highlighted above. It committed the PNA to undertaking a series of fiscal reforms aimed at reducing public expenditure on public sector wages and employment, as well as supporting private sector-led development of key sectors such as housing, infrastructure, and industry. The overall goal was to reach a "diversified and thriving free market economy led by a pioneering private sector that is in harmony with the Arab world, [and] is open to regional and global markets."[16] External donor funding to the PNA was linked to its implementation, and these flows were to be controlled through a dedicated bank account managed by the World Bank.

The other aspect of PNA state formation that was heavily promoted as part of the PRDP and other donor assistance was security. Connected explicitly to the notions of state "authority" and "peace through state-building," security expenditure was to become a major focus of foreign support. Essential to this was the reconstitution and unification of PNA security forces through the open financial and logistical support of Western military and intelligence agencies. The PNA security budget was allocated the largest portion of all funding in the PRDP (257 million dollars), with money going to the training of new police and intelligence forces as well as the construction of new prisons. A US Army officer, Lieutenant General Keith Dayton—fresh from his position as head of the search for alleged "weapons of mass destruction" in Iraq, following the 2003 US-led invasion—served as the key point person for the training of Palestinian police from 2005 to 2010. Headquartered in Tel Aviv and supported by British, Canadian, and Turkish personnel, Dayton's mission involved running two training compounds in Jordan and the West Bank for Palestinian security forces.[17]

In this manner, PNA state formation was largely conceived through a technocratic lens, with a focus on building the (neoliberal-oriented) capacity of state institutions, and developing the "monopoly of violence" within the territories administered by the PNA (understood, as noted, through the perspective of ensuring Israeli security). These themes—encapsulating the authority and capacity features of the state-building theory—were strongly supported by US and EU policymakers, institutions such as the Quartet, the World Bank and the International Monetary Fund (IMF), as well as nongovernmental donor organizations.

Despite the uniformity in international support for this model of state-building, a number of important studies have raised significant critiques regarding donor approaches to state-building in Palestine.[18] One early influential critique of the dominant approach to state formation in Palestine has been offered by Mushtaq Khan. Echoing a shift in the focus of state-building discourse towards the question of legitimacy, Khan has highlighted the problematic nature of donor support for the PNA's technocratic capacities—in which emphasis is placed on the effectiveness and viability of state functions rather than popular endorsement of PNA rule.[19] Identifying a two-way relationship between what he describes as state functions and state legitimacy, Khan notes three possible feedback routes through which these two variables could potentially impact one another. First, state legitimacy is partially dependent upon the provision of functions by the state. In the case of the PNA, this has been the traditional focus of donor assistance, which has consequently emphasized the building of the technical and bureaucratic capacities of the state-in-formation. Secondly, however, Khan notes that the *choice* of what functions are provided is inherently a political one—if certain functions are prioritized over others, and these do not correspond with the "distribution of political values, organizations and aspirations in a country," then the legitimacy of the state is likely to be undermined.[20] In the case of Palestine, Khan argues that this process of prioritization has largely been determined by external powers and has traditionally focused upon the provision of security guarantees to the occupying power and a developmental model that reflects the concerns of foreign interests. Finally, a third possible feedback route is the impact that declining legitimacy has on the viability of the state itself. If a state lacks legitimacy, according to Khan, then it becomes more and more difficult for it to provide the requisite services. What may ensue is a vicious cycle, in which declining legitimacy fuels declining ability to provide functions, leading to further declines in legitimacy.[21]

Similarly, other scholars have focused on the contradiction between attempting to build "normal" state institutions in the context of an ongoing—and deepening—Israeli occupation.[22] As the International Crisis Group noted in 2002, for many Palestinians, "the idea of modernising the PNA and instruments of governance—while under military occupation is either impossible or meaningless."[23] Precisely because the PNA was established with the prioritization of Israeli security in mind, and with its sovereignty and extent of authority contingent on fulfilling this task, it "might be more accurately characterised as an extension of the Israeli security apparatus."[24] As Mandy Turner put it in her analysis of Hamas' electoral victory in 2006, "we are, at present, witnessing the problems inherent in a peace process which created an institution, the PA, whose primary task was to deliver security to a powerful neighbour who retained control over PA borders and economy. This task . . . is in contradiction to promoting the development of a sovereign and democratic Palestinian state—a process that is dependent upon a resolution of the conflict and the end of Israeli occupation."[25]

In this context, flows of aid to the PNA take on a particularly pernicious role, as they are "mostly geared toward enhancing, if not engineering, the legitimacy of the PNA in the West Bank within the straightjacket imposed by the Oslo peace process and in accordance with the exigencies of the Israeli occupation."[26] Because "the real obstacles to the economic development of the territories were not weak institutions but instead the intensifying occupation-related elements which donors were refusing to deal with," donor activity served to depoliticize the occupation itself.[27] In this sense, Israeli settler-colonialism comes to be seen as a question of administrative regulations that may potentially constrain Palestinian development (or indeed, assist it), rather than as a form of power that necessarily penetrates all aspects of Palestinian society.[28] The technocratic approach towards state-building thus involves an elision of power relations, which leads to the incorporation of Israeli colonialism into the process of development itself.[29] In short, the pacification of the Palestinian population, rather than any genuine concern with Palestinian self-determination or conditions of life in the OPT, becomes the primary goal and result of Western (and Israeli) policy.[30]

All of these critiques make important contributions to unpacking the supposed neutrality of the dominant approach to Palestinian state-building and revealing the relations of power that continue to structure development options in the area. Yet while this literature stresses the ongoing reality of Israeli occupation and its relationship to the politics of the PNA, it is a contention of this chapter that the problem with the dominant literature is a broader one, which lies in its theoretical conception of the state. Specifically, the neo-Weberian understanding of the state is itself flawed, in that it constructs an ideal-type of the state that is premised on an artificial separation between "state" and "society" (or "politics" and "economics") and thus abstract the power relations—particularly those of class—that necessarily typify all capitalist societies, from its analysis of the state and state-building.

Rethinking State Theory: Alternatives to Neo-Weberianism and Neoliberal Approaches

Hugo Radice has noted the relationship between much of the general state-formation literature and the "developmental state" approach that was popularized in the 1980s and 1990s during the so-called East Asian miracle.[31] The latter explains the impressive growth rates of countries such as South Korea, Taiwan, and Japan on the basis of the supposed autonomy of their states, which was said to enable a balance of contending social interests and well-coordinated government-led policies prioritizing growth and domestic industrial development. In this sense, both sets of literature share a neo-Weberian conception of the state, rooted in liberal ideology that thinks of the state as "as a public realm separate from the private realm of civil society."[32] The core assumption is a conception of the state as an autonomous body that stands above social relations, with its primary function the facilitation of markets and the rule of law.

Against these neo-Weberian perspectives, Radice and numerous other critics have argued that the state, as an institution, is never and cannot be neutral—rather, it should be understood as a "form of appearance" of the social relations that constitute society. The state is an institutional form of these social relations, one which acts to maintain the existing class structure, mediate the conflicts that inevitably appear between and within classes, and allow these relations to reproduce themselves.[33] The apparent neutrality of the state and its separation from society is thus ideological—acting to conceal the relations of power that underlie all capitalist social formations.[34] Although the state may really appear to us in this neutral form, we need to penetrate below this appearance to grasp the state as a social relation, which, in the words of the philosopher Bertell Ollman, constitutes a "set of institutional forms through which a ruling class relates to the rest of society."[35] The state is not an independent, distinct sphere, severed from the social structure that generates its character, rather "state and society are interdependent and interpenetrate in a multitude of different ways."[36]

Seen in this manner, the separation between politics (embodied in the state) and a supposedly independent civil society (encompassing the market) is illusory—even as a normative goal. Academic approaches that present the ideal of liberal democracy as the desired policy end—supposedly guaranteeing the same rights and responsibilities for all "civil society actors" regardless of wealth, social status, or accident of birth—act to obscure the reality of social power that is foundational to the ways that markets work. These approaches abstract the real, substantive differences of power among individuals due to their socioeconomic role, that is, their class position, instead positing individuals as equal citizens with the same rights and responsibilities vis-à-vis the state. Within these neo-Weberian conceptions, markets are also neutralized, seen as instruments of "resource allocation rather than exploitation."[37] As a result, much of both the developmental and state-formation literature wields concepts such as "governance," "civil society," and "participation" in a principally obfuscatory manner—"deflect[ing] the citizen from class identification in favour of a contractual relationship with the state," while simultaneously, "the representative-politics component of the relationship has been largely reduced to a circulation of political elites through a banal and etiolated electoral form of democracy."[38] By treating the state as a disconnected and neutral "thing" rather than as a relation formed alongside the development of social structures, the dominant state-building literature treats the institutional forms of society as determinant rather than determined.[39]

The implications of this perspective for understanding state-formation in Palestine are two-fold. First, it allows us to penetrate the ideological form contained within the standard themes of authority, capacity, and legitimacy that dominate Palestinian (and the wider) state-building literature. While these features may indeed be necessary functions that all states perform, they are nonetheless functions of *capitalist* states (about this, the normative, market-oriented prescriptions of state-building literature are unequivocal). To pose these categories as if they can be understood in the abstract—or through undifferentiated aggregates such as "the people" or "the national interest"—only serves to conceal the ever-present relations of power. Instead, we should ask questions like: Authority—in whose hands? Capacity—to do what, and in whose interest? Legitimacy—in whose eyes? If the state is not, in fact, a neutral, distinct sphere then these questions are necessarily presupposed; to posit them in their abstract, general form only serves to disappear power itself.

Secondly, approaching the state through the social relations that produce its particular forms means that it is necessary to map these relations of power in their entirety. In the case of Palestine, this is clearly inseparable from the settler-colonial character of the Israeli state, as the critical literature surveyed above affirms. To treat Palestinian state-building as a technical exercise of authority, capacity, and legitimacy that can be achieved in partnership—or at least within and alongside—an ongoing colonial occupation acts again to disappear power relations. But the critical literature, in this respect, does not go far enough. It is the contention of this chapter that it is necessary to view Palestinian social relations in their regional context—to understand the way that class formation under the Palestinian National Authority is deeply interpenetrated with the regional political economy. This can tell us a great deal about the state-building project as it currently is framed, as well as the obstacles to alternative models of state formation.

SITUATING PALESTINE IN THE REGIONAL CONTEXT

Central to any understanding of the Middle East is an appreciation of the region's insertion within the global economy and its role in shaping the architecture of international power relations. In this respect, there are two interlinked dynamics that have shaped the region's development since the early twentieth century. The first of these is the fundamental place of hydrocarbons—oil and gas—in powering global capitalism. Oil and gas came to underpin the shifts in global production chains in the post–World War II era, constituting a strategic commodity that fueled industrial, transportation, and military networks, and formed the feedstock of petrochemical products such as synthetic rubbers, plastics, and fertilizers.[40] Through the postwar period, the Middle East—notably the oil-rich region of the Gulf Arab states—became the core global supply source for the extraction and export of relatively cheap and accessible hydrocarbons. Simultaneously, the sale of these hydrocarbons facilitated the flow of large amounts of capital, which came to be known as petrodollars, into the Gulf. The redirection of these petrodollar surpluses into US and European financial markets was a vital feature of the way that the architecture of global finance developed through the 1960s and 1970s, helping to underpin the reserve status of the US dollar as well as the emergence of debt and other financial markets through these decades.[41] In the context of these two interrelated dynamics of oil and finance, foreign domination of the region constituted a key strategic element to the balance of rivalries between different global powers; this was particularly significant with the shift from a largely European-centered colonial system to an international state system structured around US hegemony in the postwar period.

These global issues intersected with local, regional dynamics—most notably the various anticolonial and nationalist movements that emerged through the 1950s and 1960s in countries such as Egypt, Yemen, Algeria, Syria, and Iraq. As new governments came to power in these states, they attempted to pursue statist forms of development that prioritized domestic control of industry, the provision of social services backed by food and fuel subsidies, the expansion of higher education, and the guarantee of employment to university graduates within growing public sectors. These policies led to an improvement in living conditions for much of the region's population, but they were also characterized by repressive forms of rule aimed at curtailing any independent political action.[42] In response to these developments, Western governments—led by the United States—sought to roll back the growing independence movements in the region. At the political level, this was pursued through the consolidation of alliances with three main regional allies: Saudi Arabia, Iran, and Israel. Financial and military aid to these three countries helped to strengthen their positions within regional hierarchies, and, in return, these states moved to confront and undermine the nationalist or left-wing movements that were growing in influence across the Middle East.

Israel played a particularly significant role in this process. Because it had emerged as a settler-colonial state founded upon the expulsion of around three-quarters of the original Palestinian population, Israel depended upon foreign support for its ongoing viability and the maintenance of its ethno-religious character as a self-defined Jewish state.[43] In this sense, it was a much more reliable partner of foreign powers than Arab regimes that faced ever-present pressure from their own citizen populations. Following the 1967 war, in which the Israeli military dealt a devastating blow to Arab nationalist regimes in Syria and Egypt—and expanded its occupation of Arab land to the West Bank, Gaza Strip, (Egyptian) Sinai Peninsula, and (Syrian) Golan Heights—the United States became the country's key patron, supplying it annually with billions of dollars' worth of military hardware and financial support. Indeed, one former US intelligence officer has been quoted as claiming that the US-Israel military relationship was worth "five CIAs" and that upkeep of an armed force equivalent to Israel's in the Middle East would cost US taxpayers 125 billion dollars.[44]

In the wake of these military defeats—soon followed by the global economic recession of the early 1970s, and the subsequent erosion of Arab nationalist regimes—the door was opened for the reconfiguration of the regional political economy. Through the latter part of the 1970s and 1980s, virtually all Arab governments began laying the ground for a range of structural adjustment packages that embodied the basic precepts of neoliberal reform. Most notably, this involved the dismantling of collective and state property rights in land, the beginnings of privatization and cut-backs to the state sector, and opening up to foreign trade and financial flows. Although the pace of these changes varied considerably across the region, by the early 1990s most Arab states had made significant steps along this new path.[45]

The changes during this period coincided with—and were closely connected to—the rise to prominence of the state- and peace-building literature surveyed above. The cases of Iraq and Palestine were the two central foci of this policy shift in the Middle East. In Iraq, the themes of democracy promotion, regime change, and state-building adumbrated the devastating decade-long sanctions regime imposed on the country in the 1990s and the US/British-led invasion of 2003, which led to the overthrow of Saddam Hussein and the establishment of a new US-led Coalition Provisional Authority. Simultaneously, the Palestinian Authority was formed in 1994 as part of the Oslo peace process discussed above. These political developments were accompanied by a rearticulation of both US and EU policy towards the region itself. In the case of US policy, hegemony over the Middle East continued to center upon alliances with Israel, the Gulf states, and client regimes such as Egypt and Jordan (the strategic link with Iran was broken with the 1979 revolution). There was a change, however, in how these alliances were conceived. Most importantly, through the 1990s and 2000s, US policy shifted towards the explicit aim of developing closer political and economic ties between these three pillars of support within the region. Articulated under the concept of "the New Middle East," the policy sought to tie these different zones together within a single economic zone. To do so required the dropping of Arab boycotts towards Israel and the development of joint investments and other economic projects. "Normalization" of Israel's ties with Arab states thus became a central focus of US policy in the region.[46]

In this respect, the Oslo negotiations were an important feature of integrating Israel into the region. Most significantly, Oslo would provide a Palestinian "green light" for Arab normalization with Israel. For Israel, this process would also enable a shift in its own economic orientation. Following an economic crisis in 1985 the Israeli economy had moved towards high-value added exports connected to development of information technology, pharmaceuticals, and military industries. Growth in these sectors was enabled by US financial support—indeed, for many decades Israel had been the recipient of US aid without the conditions that were tied to loans made to Arab states. Moreover, since the signing of a US free trade agreement with Israel in 1985, the United States had run a significant trade deficit with Israel. In this context, the attempt to normalize Israel's relations with other Arab states would further facilitate the internationalization of Israeli capital itself—allowing foreign investors to invest in the country without fear of Arab boycotts and marking the expansion of Israeli companies through core stock markets in the United States and European Union.[47]

Between 1994 and 1998, a series of intergovernmental summits known as the Middle East and North Africa (MENA) Economic Summits codified this trend towards normalization. The first of these, held in Morocco in 1994, saw concrete steps towards the lifting of regional economic boycotts and the establishment of a Middle East-wide chamber of commerce. Then-US Secretary of State Warren Christopher was to note that "the Middle East is open for business . . . the conference could be the beginning of a beautiful friendship."[48] Subsequent MENA summits in Cairo and Amman explicitly tied normalization with the deepening of neoliberal reform processes, including—as the Cairo conference final resolution noted—"privatisation, structural reform, and removing trade barriers" which were said to provide "for a more business-friendly economic climate throughout the region."[49]

One important indication of these regional shifts was the establishment of qualified industrial zones (QIZ) in Jordan and Egypt. QIZ provided duty-free access to US markets for Jordanian and Egyptian exporters, provided that a certain percentage of inputs were from Israel (8 percent in the case of Jordan, 11.7 percent in the case of Egypt). Launched in 1997, these QIZ perhaps best symbolized the new era of normalization between Arab capital and Israel. In 2004, Egypt also launched its first QIZ in an agreement with Israel and the United States. Six more QIZs were approved in subsequent years, and from 2005 to 2008 exports from these zones grew at an annual average rate of 58 percent, ten times that of total exports from Egypt to the United States.[50] Since their establishment, they have come to dominate bilateral trade between the United States and Jordan and Egypt respectively. In 2007, the US government was reporting that exports from the thirteen QIZs established in Jordan accounted for a massive 70 percent of total Jordanian exports to the United States.[51] In 2008, close to one-third of Egypt's total exports to the United States came from QIZs.[52] By 2013, this figure had risen to nearly 50 percent.[53]

Despite the eruption of the Second Intifada in 2000, the orientation towards normalization, neoliberal reform, and the strengthening of US influence in the region continued to deepen. In mid-2003, George W. Bush announced the US aim to establish a Middle East Free Trade Area (MEFTA) by 2013, which was envisioned as encompassing the region from North Africa to the Gulf. The means to achieving this free trade area were a range of bilateral economic agreements between the United States and individual Arab states, eventually joined together within a single zone. Importantly, these free trade agreements contained clauses that committed these states to lift any boycotts on Israel. Pointedly, they were also connected within US government discourse with the "democratization" discourse described earlier. Robert Zoellick, for example, who acted as US trade representative in the early 2000s, was to note that the goal of this regional trading bloc was "to assist nations that are ready to embrace economic liberty and the rule of law, integrate into the global trading system, and bring their economies into the modern era."[54] Although MEFTA ultimately proved unable to reach its goal of establishing a regional free trade area, it did lead to four new free trade agreements with countries in the Middle East: Bahrain, Jordan, Morocco, and Oman. Prior to MEFTA, the only bilateral free trade agreement the United States held in the region was with Israel, completed in 1985.[55]

In parallel to these US trade agreements through the 1990s and 2000s, the European Union also sought to deepen its influence in the region. In this case, the focus was on countries surrounding the Mediterranean, reflecting the longstanding economic ties between Europe and North Africa in particular. The European Union's moves in this direction, like those of the United States, have promoted liberalization of economies and normalization with Israel. These goals were initially expressed in the Euro-Mediterranean Partnership (EMP), also called the Barcelona Process, which was established in 1995 with representatives from Algeria, Cyprus, Egypt, Jordan, Israel, Lebanon, Malta, Morocco, the PNA, Syria, Tunisia, and Turkey. The Barcelona Process aimed at creating "open economies by the opening-up of markets . . . [and] the elimination of trade barriers."[56] This would include a focus on "fiscal, administrative and legal reforms as well as deregulation of public services . . . in order to raise the level of foreign direct investment in the southern Mediterranean economies."[57] Following the establishment of the EMP, the European Union moved to sign a range of individual treaties, known as association agreements, with Mediterranean countries.[58] These association agreements required EMP countries to liberalize trade and domestic markets in order to receive access to financial aid and European export markets.

In the wake of these internationally driven restructuring processes—accompanied by the increased engagement of international financial institutions in the development of Arab government economic policy—was a pronounced deepening of neoliberal reform processes throughout the 2000s. By 2009, the Middle East as a whole was acclaimed by the World Bank as the region with the second greatest jump in liberalization measures of any in the world—seventeen out of nineteen countries recorded advances in this regard. This was most clearly marked in Egypt where the so-called "government of businessmen" of the mid-2000s won plaudits from the World Bank and other international institutions; but, more generally, Arab governments moved decisively in this period towards adopting policies such as privatization, labor market deregulation, and opening up to trade and financial flows. Importantly, however, this extension of neoliberalism did not only involve shifts in national economic policy. Accompanying these trends, large Arab conglomerates—most notably those based in the Gulf region—utilized market liberalization to expand their own regional activities. This internationalization of largely Gulf-based capital—facilitated by the rapid rise in oil prices (and hence surplus capital) from 2000 to 2008—meant that class structures within individual Arab states became increasingly imbricated with ownership structures involving Gulf investors.[59] This is partially indicated by figures on foreign direct investment (FDI) flows originating in the Gulf, notably to the Mashreq subregion: indeed, from 2003 to 2010, Gulf investments made up 75 percent of total FDI inflows for Lebanon, 69 percent for Jordan, 61 percent for Syria, 59 percent for Egypt, and 46 percent for Iraq.[60] These capital flows were especially marked in the real estate, financial, telecommunications, and retail sectors—but also involved the extension of Gulf-based ownership of logistics, manufacturing, and industrial assets.

This particular feature of the regional political economy has critical implications for understanding Palestinian state formation as it is currently conceived. From 2003 to 2008, more than two-thirds of total global FDI projects announced in PNA-controlled areas originated in the Gulf region.[61] These figures are a tiny proportion of total Gulf-origin FDI in the wider region (less than 1 percent), but for the Palestinian economy they are substantial. Moreover, they do not capture other important Gulf capital flows to the PNA—including budgetary support, development loans, and portfolio investment in the Palestinian stock market.

It is necessary, however, to conceptualize the internationalization of Gulf capital in a wider sense than simply FDI flows. Most significantly, internationalization has occurred through the "return" to Palestine of diaspora Palestinian groups who are headquartered or largely based in neighboring countries (particularly Jordan and the Gulf). Two prominent examples are the Al Masri and Khoury family groups, both of whom locate their origins in pre-1948 Palestine. The initial capital accumulation of these groups was closely connected to state formation in the Gulf states, through the establishment of companies involved in the laying of pipelines, engineering and construction, and the provision of services to the Gulf's oil and gas industries. Since that time, the original companies founded by these family groups have expanded across the Middle East, but a key zone of their accumulation remains located in the Gulf. Following the signing of the Oslo Accords and the establishment of the PNA in the 1990s, this diaspora capital became integral to the development of the new Palestinian economy in the West Bank and Gaza Strip. This took place through direct investments and the establishment of subsidiaries in the OPT, as well as through the formation of an important network of holding companies that linked this diaspora class to state capital (ultimately funded through foreign aid to the PNA) and local elites.

The outcome of these cross-border ownership ties linking the diaspora and the local Palestinian market has been an economy largely dominated by Palestinian capital groups based in the Gulf, as well as Gulf investors. In banking and finance, for example, such groups directly control fifteen out of the seventeen banks in operation in PNA-controlled areas.[62] These include the three most important banks (the Bank of Palestine, the Arab Bank, and Cairo Amman Bank), which between them operate nearly half of all bank branches in the Palestinian territories. In telecommunications, two companies—Paltel and Wataniya Mobile—completely monopolize Palestinian cellular, fixed landlines, and Internet service provision in the West Bank. The first is controlled through a holding company that is dominated by the Masri family and a range of other diaspora investors (mostly from the Gulf), while the second is a subsidiary of a Qatari telecom company. Similar patterns of ownership and control over key Palestinian economic sectors can be seen in real estate, manufacturing and transport, retail, and energy.[63]

These characteristics of Palestinian class structure help to illuminate the neoliberal form of state-building under the PNA. As noted earlier, in line with the wider regional trends, the PNA has pursued a clear neoliberal project over the past decade that has been codified in the PRDP and subsequent national development plans. This trajectory is not simply a reflection of policies driven by international financial institutions, but has actually helped constitute the PNA as a principal conduit of wealth transfer to the large, internationalized conglomerates that dominate the Palestinian economy. Affirming the perspective on state theory outlined above, the PNA appears as an institutional form (or social relation) expressing the dominance and interests of these (largely diasporic) capital groups.

Moreover, this configuration of class and state helps to clarify the social forces that underlie the PNA's incorporation into the structures of the Israeli occupation. Closely tied to the major regional powers in the Arab world, the social class embodied by these large conglomerates remains reliant upon power structures in the Gulf and the regional order constructed over recent decades. Moreover, in Palestine itself, its reproduction as a class is contingent upon the particular form of state-building materialized through the PNA—including the neoliberal policy trajectory and the economic policies that have unfolded through the Oslo process. Palestinian state and class structures are thus intimately linked, with each side of the equation shaping the characteristics of the other.

CONCLUSION: IMPLICATIONS FOR ALTERNATIVE MODELS OF STATE FORMATION

Before returning to the question of Palestinian state-building in light of these dynamics, it is necessary to briefly discuss how the regional framework has changed following the 2011 Arab uprisings. In their initial phases, the uprisings represented an important moment of popular hope across the region, embodying a rejection of neoliberal authoritarianism and aspirations for a long sought-after transformation in socioeconomic and political rights. In many ways, these uprisings represented the most significant upsurge of popular mobilization since the postwar Arab nationalist struggles; the striking manner in which their political and social forms generalized rapidly across all states in the Middle East indicated a profound challenge to the regional order of the past five decades.

Since this initial phase, Western powers and their regional allies have moved decisively in an attempt to reconstitute state structures and the local bases of support on which their hegemony depends. Despite ongoing struggles, established elites have largely been able to win back political power. Military- and state-supported repression was a critical element in this return to the status quo—seen, for example, in the assassinations of Tunisian opposition leaders Chokri Belaid and Mohammed Brahmi in 2013, and the May 2013 military coup in Egypt. Simultaneously, the devastating repression of the Assad regime in Syria and the ongoing disintegration of the Iraqi state helped to spur the growth of sectarian and Islamic fundamentalist movements across the region, further disrupting the social and political goals initially embodied in the uprisings.

Given the social justice aspirations of the uprisings, it is particularly significant that there has been little change in the near-universal hegemony of the neoliberal development model post-2011. The Deauville Partnership, an initiative launched at the May 2011 G8 Summit in France and led by the major international financial institutions, which promised up to forty billion US dollars in loans and other assistance towards Arab countries "in transition," was premised upon a neoliberal orientation in all its essential elements.[64] Since that time, both the World Bank and IMF have deepened their engagement in the region, rolling out new loan agreements and assistance that are in essential continuity with past programs—emphasizing private-sector driven growth, fiscal austerity (particularly subsidy and pension reform), and the liberalization of financial and labor markets.[65] International actors, notably the EBRD, have also entered the region for the first time—making explicit the argument that state-building necessarily involves the twinning of liberal democracy and neoliberal economic policy. Indeed, the current socioeconomic and political crises are frequently portrayed by IFIs as an opportunity to extend the policy trajectories of past regimes. As the European Investment Bank noted not long after the overthrow of Ben Ali and Mubarak, "moments of political change can also represent an opportunity to reinforce or improve already existing institutional frameworks."[66]

The Gulf states have played a central role in shaping the new political arrangements that emerged in the post-2011 period. This has involved financial and political support to new governments, political movements, and armed groups. The battle to assert regional hegemony has been marked by the surfacing of severe rivalries within the Gulf itself (e.g., between Saudi Arabia and the UAE on one side, and Qatar on the other), which has frequently led to different Gulf states sponsoring opposing forces in neighboring Arab states. Economically the Gulf also remained dominant in the years after the uprisings, with an ever-widening gap emerging between it and the rest of the region from 2011 to 2014. This differentiation of power and wealth can be attributed to both the ways in which different zones of the Middle East have been inserted into the world market as well as the enduring crises of the region. With the relatively stable emergence of the Gulf states from the global crisis of 2008 and the high oil prices that continued from 2010 to mid-2014, Gulf states were able to accumulate vast quantities of surplus capital. Even following the collapse in oil prices in 2014, the Gulf Cooperation Council states have continued to play a dominant political and economic role in the Arab world.[67] At the same time, the rest of the region has been faced with the ongoing weakness of major trading partners—particularly the European Union—and the political and social crises of states such as Egypt, Libya, Yemen, Iraq, and Syria. The ensuing regional differentiation is a critical characteristic of the contemporary moment.

Throughout these developments, Israel's integration into the Arab world continues to be an important focus of long-term Western policy—despite the popular Arab antipathy towards this goal. In particular, from 2015 onwards, the increasingly close relationship between Israel, Saudi Arabia, and the UAE has become apparent in joint military exercises, commercial and economic ties—most conspicuously in the security, surveillance, and high tech sectors—as well as open visits of high-ranking political figures. Israel also emerged as one of the earliest endorsers of the Saudi-UAE actions against Qatar in mid-2017, echoing its growing convergence with Saudi Arabia and the UAE on many of the key political questions in the region. These developments also set the stage for the Abraham Accords, signed in August 2020, which officially recognized the normalization of economic relations between Israel and the United Arab Emirates and Bahrain.

All of these features of the contemporary moment affirm that the characteristics of class and state formation in Palestine will continue to be shaped by developments at the regional scale. Given this fact, what does the analysis of this chapter say about the possibilities for models of state formation that could encompass the aspirations of Palestinian self-determination? Most significantly, what conditions are necessary for an alternative path that breaks from the current situation under the PNA, and moves towards including the totality of the Palestinian people—not least those that live outside the borders of the West Bank and Gaza Strip?

The first aspect to emphasize in this regard is one of the core premises of this chapter: the importance of not approaching the question of state formation in the abstract—that is, as simply a technocratic question of arranging institutional forms to best meet a checklist of preconceived functions such as authority, legitimacy, and capacity. The character of the state needs to be seen as reflective of social and other power structures that are delineated across various spatial scales. The state is not a neutral apparatus that sits above these structures, but rather a social relation that enables ruling groups to maintain their dominant position vis-à-vis those who are dominated. In this sense, it is imperative to consider, on the one hand, the social forces that underlie existing state arrangements, and, on the other hand, those that may enable alternative models of state-building to emerge. Without assessing these social forces, analyses of state formation that focus simply on a normative "recipe" of institution-building or establish moral criteria for how those states should function tend to abstract the concrete relations of power and thus—inadvertently or not—reinforce those very relations.

In the Palestinian case, this paper has surveyed the critical literature of state-building, which correctly highlights the ongoing reality of Israeli occupation and the importance of incorporating the impact of this settler-colonial context into an understanding of the PNA state-building project. It has also, however, argued for the need to situate this project within the wider context of the regional political economy. This includes an appreciation of the ways in which the state system arose in the Middle East, fully located within the global economy, and the more recent changes in regional accumulation patterns that have occurred under the aegis of US power. The significant realignment of the regional political economy through the 1990s and early 2000s was driven by a variety of intersecting factors: military conflict and state-building (with Iraq as the principle illustration of this); the widespread adoption of neoliberal policies by all states in the region; the impetus towards deepening regional trade and financial linkages embodied in the various projects promoted by the United States, European Union, and international financial institutions; and the increasing intermeshing of capital ownership across the regional space, typified most sharply in the internationalization of Gulf-based capital. All of these emerging features of the regional political economy were profoundly connected with the normalization of Arab relations with the Israeli state. And in this respect, the formation of the PNA and the extension of its state-building project across the West Bank was a central feature of the period.

The internationalization of regional capital—particularly that originating in the Gulf Arab states—is essential to understanding the nature of class formation under the Palestinian National Authority. The class that has emerged as a result of these processes is interiorized within the structures of the PNA state-in-formation, and simultaneously constituted at the regional scale through its ongoing accumulation activities in the Gulf and other neighboring countries. In this sense, Palestinian capital reproduces itself across different spatial scales that cannot be confined to the national "borders"—however ill-defined—that exist within the OPT. Breaking with nationalist methodological perspectives that treat social relations as neatly circumscribed within these borders is thus imperative to a full appreciation of state/class relations in the Palestinian context.

This internationalizing class is a particularly important frame through which to view the Palestinian state-building project as it is currently conceived. It constitutes the primary social base of the PNA within Palestinian society, shaping the character of its policy-making and institution-building at the domestic level. It does so in full interaction with international state-building actors and the structures of the Israeli occupation and thus—in terms of assessing the various social forces at play within the state-building project—needs to be viewed as both a key element of the obduracy of the status quo, as well as a fundamental obstacle to any alternative paths of state formation.

Given this arrangement of social forces, any alternative model of state formation—notably that embodied in a single-state solution—is necessarily premised on a fundamental challenge to the position of current Palestinian elites, particularly those whose accumulation is predicated upon the state/class relations analyzed in this chapter. Any just and progressive alternative model of state formation is thus unlikely to be an elite-driven project, but will take place in opposition to these elites and involve the dismantling and rejection of existing political economy structures in Palestine. It necessitates, in other words, not simply a political change, but must also involve tackling economic inequity and the dominance of the neoliberal paradigm. Moreover, because an alternative path in Palestine needs to occur in tandem with regional change, any full assessment of the prospects of Palestinian state formation is not solely a question of internal Palestinian (or indeed, Israeli) dynamics.

NOTES

1. Andreas Wimmer and Nina Glick-Schiller, "Methodological Nationalism and Beyond: Nation-State Building, Migration and the Social Sciences," *Global Networks* 2, no. 4 (2002): 301–34.

2. White House Office of the Press Secretary, "President Bush Discusses Importance of Democracy in Middle East: Remarks by the President on Winston Churchill and the War on Terror, Library of Congress, February 4, 2004," https://georgewbush-whitehouse.archives.gov/news/releases/2004/02/20040204-4.html.

3. Toufic Haddad, *Palestine Ltd.: Neoliberalism and Nationalism in the Occupied Territory* (London: I.B. Tauris, 2016), 25.

4. Mandy Turner, "Building Democracy in Palestine: Liberal Peace Theory and the Election of Hamas," *Democratization* 13, no. 5 (2006): 740.

5. Turner, "Building Democracy," 742.

6. Francis Fukuyama, *State Building: Governance and World Order in the Twenty-First Century* (London: Profile, 2005), 125.

7. World Bank, *The State and Peace-Building Fund*, https://www.worldbank.org/en/programs/state-and-peace-building-fund/overview, accessed May 2021.

8. See Haddad, *Palestine Ltd.*, for a comprehensive survey.

9. Max Weber, *Economy and Society. An Outline of Interpretive Sociology* (Berkeley: University of California Press, 1978), 54–55.

10. World Bank, *Strengthening Governance: Tackling Corruption. The World Bank Group's Updated Strategy and Implementation Plan* (Washington, DC: World Bank, 2012), 9–10.

11. United States Agency for International Development, "Fragile States Strategy," 2005, http://www.usaid.gov/policy/2005_fragile_states_strategy.pdf, 1.

12. Ad-Hoc Liaison Committee, "Meeting of the Ad Hoc Liaison Committee New York, Chair's Summary," September 18, 2011, United Nations Information System on the Question of Palestine, http://unispal.un.org/UNISPAL.NSF/0/25BBF4BD29E3590485257911004DE045#sthash.MQHI6cgs.vP7aIvLy.dpuf; World Bank, *The Underpinnings of the Future Palestinian State: Sustainable Growth and Institutions* (Washington, DC: World Bank, 2010).

13. Haddad, *Palestine Ltd*, 63.

14. Turner, "Building Democracy in Palestine," 740.

15. European Council, "Presidency Conclusions: Berlin European Council," March 24 and 25, 1999, United Nations Information System on the Question of Palestine, http://unispal.un.org/UNISPAL.NSF/0/F6ED2F19B37DACCA85256F95007A259F.

16. Palestinian National Authority, *Building a Palestinian State: Towards Peace and Prosperity* (Paris: PNA, 2007), 18.

17. Keith Dayton, "Speech to the Washington Institute's 2009 Soref Symposium," Washington Institute for Near East Policy, May 7, 2009, www.washingtoninstitute.org/html/pdf/DaytonKeynote.pdf.

18. Numan Kanafani and Samia Al-Botmeh, "The Political Economy of Food Aid to Palestine," *The Economics of Peace and Security Journal* 3, no. 2 (2008): 39–48; Iyad Riyahi and Nahed Samara, *Just Ahead of the Crisis: Policies Designed to Plunge the West Bank into Debt* (Birzeit: Centre for Development Studies, Birzeit University, 2014); Firas Jaber and Imad Sayrafi, *Lending and Development Policies in the Occupied Palestinian Territory* (Birzeit: Centre for Development Studies, Birzeit University, 2014); Samia Al-Botmeh, "Implications of the Kerry Framework: The Jordan Valley," *Journal of Palestine Studies* 43, no. 3 (2014): 49–51; Mandy Turner, "Peacebuilding as Counterinsurgency in the Occupied Palestinian Territory," *Review of International Studies* 41, no. 1 (2015): 73–98; Mandy Turner and Omar Shweiki, *Decolonizing Palestinian Political Economy: De-development and Beyond* (New York: Palgrave-McMillan, 2015); Haddad, *Palestine Ltd.*; Leila Farsakh, "Palestinian Economic Development: Paradigm Shifts since the First Intifada," *Journal of Palestine Studies* 45, no. 2 (2016): 55–71; Leila Farsakh, "Undermining Democracy in Palestine: The Politics of International Aid since Oslo," *Journal of Palestine Studies* 45, no. 4 (2016): 48–63.

19. Mushtaq Khan, "Palestinian State Formation since the Signing of the Oslo Accords," 2009, available at http://eprints.soas.ac.uk/9964/1/Palestinian_State_Formation_since_Oslo_Internet.pdf, 6.

20. Khan, "Palestinian State Formation," 9.

21. Khan, "Palestinian State Formation," 11.

22. Sara Roy, *Failing Peace: Gaza and the Palestinian-Israeli Conflict* (London: Pluto Press, 2007); Turner, "Building Democracy in Palestine"; Leila Farsakh, *Palestinian Labor Migration to Israel: Labor, Land and Occupation* (London: Routledge, 2005).

23. International Crisis Group, "The Meanings of Palestinian Reform," *Middle East Briefing*, November 12, 2002, 2.

24. Oliver Richmond, "Jekyll or Hyde: What Is Statebuilding Creating? Evidence from the 'Field,'" *Cambridge Review of International Affairs* 27, no. 1 (2014): 7.

25. Turner, "Building Democracy in Palestine," 740.

26. Farsakh, "Undermining Democracy in Palestine," 56.

27. Sahar Taghdisi-Rad, *The Political Economy of Aid in Palestine: Relief from Conflict or Development Delayed?* (London: Routledge, 2010), 10–11.

28. Adam Hanieh, "Development as Struggle: Confronting the Reality of Power in Palestine," *Journal of Palestine Studies* 45, no. 4 (2016): 32–47.

29. Turner and Shweiki, *Decolonizing Palestinian Political Economy*; Raja Khalidi and Sobhi Samour, "Neoliberalism as Liberation: The Statehood Program and the Remaking of the Palestinian National Movement," *Journal of Palestine Studies* 40, no. 2 (2011): 6–25.

30. Turner, "Peacebuilding as Counterinsurgency;" Khalidi and Samour, "Neoliberalism as Liberation"; Center for Development Studies, *Critical Readings of Development under Colonialism: Towards a Political Economy for Liberation in the Occupied Palestinian Territories* (Birzeit: Birzeit University, 2015).

31. Hugo Radice, "The Developmental State under Global Neoliberalism," *Third World Quarterly* 29, no. 6 (2008): 1,153–74.

32. Radice, "The Developmental State," 1157.

33. Neil Davidson, "The Necessity of Multiple Nation-States for Capital," *Rethinking Marxism: A Journal of Economics, Culture and Society* 24, no. 1 (2012): 24–46.

34. Raju J. Das, "State Theories: A Critical Analysis," *Science and Society* 60, no. 1 (1996): 43.

35. Bertell Ollman, *Dance of the Dialectic: Steps in Marx's Method* (Urbana: University of Illinois Press, 2003), 202.

36. Fred Block, *Revisiting State Theory: Essays in Politics and Post-Industrialism* (Philadelphia: Temple University Press, 1987), 21.

37. Radice, "The Developmental State," 1,163.

38. Radice, "The Developmental State," 1,157–58.

39. Greg Albo, "Contesting the 'New Capitalism,'" in *Varieties of Capitalism, Varieties of Approaches*, edited by David Coates, 63–82 (New York: Palgrave Macmillan, 2005), 74.

40. Simon Bromley, *American Hegemony and World Oil: The Industry, the State System and the World Economy* (Cambridge: Polity Press, 1991); Timothy Mitchell, *Carbon Democracy: Political Power in the Age of Oil* (London: Verso, 2011); Adam Hanieh, *Capitalism and Class in the Gulf Arab States* (New York: Palgrave-MacMillan, 2011).

41. Hanieh, *Capitalism and Class*; Adam Hanieh, *Money, Markets and Monarchies: The Gulf Cooperation Council and the Political Economy of the Contemporary Middle East* (Cambridge: Cambridge University Press, 2018)

42. Gilbert Achcar, *The People Want: A Radical Exploration of the Arab Uprising* (London: Saqi Books, 2013).

43. Ilan Pappe, *The Ethnic Cleansing of Palestine* (London: Oneworld Publications, 2006); Tikva Honig-Parnass, *The False Prophets of Peace: Liberal Zionism and the Struggle for Palestine* (Chicago: Haymarket Books, 2011).

44. Haddad, *Palestine Ltd.*, 43.

45. Adam Hanieh, *Lineages of Revolt: Issues of Contemporary Capitalism in the Middle East* (Chicago: Haymarket Press, 2013).

46. Hanieh, *Lineages of Revolt*, chapter 2.

47. Hanieh, *Lineages of Revolt*, 34.

48. Warren Christopher, quoted in Waleed Hazbun, *Beaches, Ruins, Resorts: The Politics of Tourism in the Arab World* (Minneapolis: University of Minnesota Press, 2008), 116.

49. US Embassy of Israel, "Text of Cairo Conference Declaration," November 14, 1996, www.usembassy-israel.org.il/publish/press/summit/es111115.html.

50. Barbara Kotschwar and Jeffrey J. Schott, *Reengaging Egypt: Options for US-Egypt Economic Relations* (Washington, DC: Peterson Institute for International Economics, 2010), 20.

51. Office of the US Trade Representative, "Trade Policy Agenda, Section III," 2007, https://ustr.gov/sites/default/files/uploads/reports/2007/asset_upload_file677_10626.pdf, 5.

52. Kotschwar and Schott, *Reengaging Egypt*, 20.

53. "Speech of Ann Paterson (U.S. Dept. of State) at Egypt-Israel QIZ Lunch in NYC," January 15, 2014, http://www.scribd.com/doc/201534696/Speech-of-Ann-Paterson-U-S-Dept-of-State-at-Egypt-Israel-QIZ-Lunch-in-NYC-Jan-15-2014, 7.

54. Robert Zoellick, "Global Trade and the Middle East: Reawakening a Vibrant Past," speech at the World Economic Forum, Amman, Jordan, June 23, 2003.

55. Rebecca M. Nelson, Mary Jane Bolle, and Shayerah Ilias, *U.S. Trade and Investment in the Middle East and North Africa: Overview and Issues for Congress* (Washington, DC: Congressional Research Service, 2012), 17.

56. European Commission, *The Barcelona Declaration, Five Years On 1995–2000* (Luxembourg: European Communities, 2000), http://www.emwis.org/overview/fol101997/fol221357/barcelona-5yrs_en.pdf/download/1/barcelona-5yrs_en.pdf, 17.

57. European Commission, *The Barcelona Declaration*, 17.

58. Association agreements with Israel, Jordan, Morocco, Tunisia, the Palestinian Authority, and Turkey were signed between 1995 and 1997; an association agreement with Egypt was signed in 2004.

59. Hanieh, *Money, Markets and Monarchies*.

60. World Bank, *Over the Horizon: A New Levant* (Washington, DC: World Bank Group, 2014), http://beta.cmimarseille.org/sites/default/files/Over%20The%20Horizon%20A%20New%20Levant_0.pdf, xix.

61. ANIMA, "Foreign Direct Investment Towards the Med Countries in 2008: Facing the Crisis," *Anima Investment Network Study*, no. 3, April 20, 2009, https://anima.coop/en/foreign-direct-investment-in-the-med-countries-in-2008-facing-the-crisis/, 155.

62. Analysis by author based on stock exchange data and bank lists from the Palestine Monetary Authority.

63. Adam Hanieh, "The Internationalisation of Gulf Capital and Palestinian Class Formation," *Capital and Class* 35, no. 1 (2011): 81–106. See Hanieh, *Lineages of Revolt* and Hanieh, *Money, Markets and Monarchies* for further detail on these ownership structures.

64. Sebastian Moffett, Nathalie Boschat, and William Horobin, "G-8 Pledges $40 Billion for 'Arab Spring,'" *Wall Street Journal*, May 28, 2011, http://online.wsj.com/news/articles/SB10001424052702304520804576348792147454956.

65. Adam Hanieh, "Shifting Priorities or Business as Usual? Continuity and Change in the Post-2011 IMF and World Bank Engagement with Tunisia, Morocco and Egypt," *British Journal of Middle Eastern Studies* 42, no. 1 (2015): 119–34.

66. European Investment Bank, *FEMIP Study on PPP Legal and Financial Frameworks in the Mediterranean Partner Countries*, (Luxembourg: European Investment Bank, 2011): 12.

67. Hanieh, *Money, Markets and Monarchies*.

BIBLIOGRAPHY

Achcar, Gilbert. *The People Want.* London: Saqi Books, 2013.

Ad-Hoc Liaison Committee, "Meeting of the Ad Hoc Liaison Committee New York, 18 September 2011 Chair's Summary," United Nations Information System on the Question of Palestine, http://unispal.un.org/UNISPAL.NSF/0/25BBF4BD29E35904852579110004D E045#sthash.MQHI6cgs.vP7aIvLy.dpuf.

Akhtar, Shayerah Ilias, Mary Jane Bolle, and Rebecca M. Nelson. "U.S. Trade and Investment in the Middle East and North Africa: Overview and Issues for Congress." Congressional Research Service, 7–5700, R42153, March 4, 2012, https://fas.org/sgp/crs/misc/R42153 .pdf.

Albo, Greg. "Contesting the 'New Capitalism.'" In *Varieties of Capitalism, Varieties of Approaches*, edited by D. Coates, 63–82. New York: Palgrave Macmillan, 2005.

Al-Botmeh, Samia. "Implications of the Kerry Framework: The Jordan Valley." *Journal of Palestine Studies* 43, no. 3 (Spring 2014): 49–51.

ANIMA. "Foreign Direct Investment towards the Med Countries in 2008: Facing the Crisis." *Anima Investment Network Study*, no. 3 (April 2009).

Block, Fred. *Revisiting State Theory: Essays in Politics and Post-Industrialism.* Philadelphia: Temple University Press, 1987.

Bromley, Simon. *American Hegemony and World Oil: The Industry, the State System and the World Economy.* Cambridge: Polity Press, 1991.

Center for Development Studies. *Critical Readings of Development under Colonialism: Towards a Political Economy for Liberation in the Occupied Palestinian Territories.* Birzeit: Birzeit University, 2015.

Das, Raju J. "State Theories: A Critical Analysis." *Science and Society* 60, no. 1 (1996): 27–57.

Davidson, Neil. "The Necessity of Multiple Nation-States for Capital." *Rethinking Marxism: A Journal of Economics, Culture and Society* 24, no. 1 (2012): 26–46.

European Commission. *The Barcelona Declaration, Five Years On, 1995–2000,* http://www .emwis.org/overview/fol101997/fol221357/barcelona-5yrs_en.pdf/download/1/barcelona -5yrs_en.pdf.

European Council. "Presidency Conclusions: Berlin European Council," 24 and 25 March 1999, United Nations Information System on the Question of Palestine, http://unispal .un.org/UNISPAL.NSF/0/F6ED2F19B37DACCA85256F95007A259F.

European Investment Bank. *FEMIP Study on PPP Legal and Financial Frameworks in the Mediterranean Partner Countries.* volume 1, May, 2011, https://www.eib.org/attachments /med/ppp-study-volume-1.pdf.

Farsakh, Leila. "Palestinian Economic Development: Paradigm Shifts since the First Intifada." *Journal of Palestine Studies* 45, no. 2 (2016): 55–71.

———. *Palestinian Labour Migration to Israel: Labour, Land and Occupation* (London: Routledge, 2005

———. "Undermining Democracy in Palestine: The Politics of International Aid since Oslo." *Journal of Palestine Studies* 45, no. 4 (2016): 48–63.

Fukuyama, Francis. *State Building: Governance and World Order in the Twenty-First Century.* London: Profile, 2005.

Haddad, Toufic. *Palestine Ltd.: Neoliberalism and Nationalism in the Occupied Territory*. London: I.B. Tauris, 2016.

Hanieh, Adam. *Capitalism and Class in the Gulf Arab States*. New York: Palgrave-MacMillan, 2011.

———. "Development as Struggle: Confronting the Reality of Power in Palestine." *Journal of Palestine Studies* 45, no. 4 (2016): 32–47.

———. "The Internationalisation of Gulf Capital and Palestinian Class Formation." *Capital and Class* 35, no. 1 (2011): 81–106.

———. *Lineages of Revolt: Issues of Contemporary Capitalism in the Middle East*. Chicago: Haymarket Press, 2013.

———. *Money, Markets and Monarchies: The Gulf Cooperation Council and the Political Economy of the Contemporary Middle East*. Cambridge: Cambridge University Press, 2018.

———. "Shifting Priorities or Business as Usual? Continuity and Change in the Post-2011 IMF and World Bank Engagement with Tunisia, Morocco and Egypt." *British Journal of Middle Eastern Studies* 42, no. 1 (2015): 119–34.

Hazbun, Waleed. *Beaches, Ruins, Resorts: The Politics of Tourism in the Arab World*. Minneapolis: University of Minnesota Press, 2008.

Honig-Parnass, Tikva. *The False Prophets of Peace: Liberal Zionism and the Struggle for Palestine*. Chicago: Haymarket Books, 2011.

International Crisis Group. "The Meanings of Palestinian Reform." *Middle East Briefing*, November 12, 2002.

Jaber, Firas, and Imad Sayrafi. *Lending and Development Policies in the Occupied Palestinian Territory*. Centre for Development Studies: Birzeit: Birzeit University, 2014.

Kanafani, Numan, and Samia Al-Botmeh. "The Political Economy of Food Aid to Palestine." *The Economics of Peace and Security Journal* 3, no. 2 (2008): 39–48.

Khalidi, Raja, and Sobhi Samour. "Neoliberalism as Liberation: The Statehood Program and the Remaking of the Palestinian National Movement." *Journal of Palestine Studies* 40, no. 2 (2011): 6–25.

Khan, Mushtaq. "Palestinian State Formation since the Signing of the Oslo Accords," 2009, available at http://eprints.soas.ac.uk/9964/1/Palestinian_State_Formation_since_Oslo _Internet.pdf.

Kotschwar, Barbara, and Jeffrey J. Schott, *Reengaging Egypt: Options for US-Egypt Economic Relations*. Washington, DC: Peterson Institute for International Economics, 2010.

Ministry of Planning and Administrative Development, State of Palestine. *National Development Plan, 2014–2016*. February 23, 2014.

Mitchell, Timothy. *Carbon Democracy: Political Power in the Age of Oil*. London: Verso, 2011.

Office of the US Trade Representative. "Trade Policy Agenda, Section III." 2007. https://ustr .gov/sites/default/files/uploads/reports/2007/asset_upload_file677_10626.pdf.

Ollman, Bertell. *Dance of the Dialectic: Steps in Marx's Method*. Urbana: University of Illinois Press, 2003.

Organisation for Economic Co-operation and Development. "Concepts and Dilemmas of State Building in Fragile Situations: From Fragility to Resilience." 2008, http://www .oecd.org/development/incaf/41100930.pdf.

———. "The State's Legitimacy in Fragile Situations: Unpacking Legitimacy," 2010, http://www.oecd.org/dac/incaf/44794487.pdf.

Palestinian National Authority. "Building a Palestinian State: Towards Peace and Prosperity," December 2007, https://unispal.un.org/pdfs/PRDPFinal.pdf.

Pappe, Ilan. *The Ethnic Cleansing of Palestine*. London: Oneworld Publications, 2006.

Pfeifer, Karen. "How Tunisia, Morocco, Jordan, and Even Egypt Became IMF Success Stories." *Middle East Report*, no. 210 (Fall 1999): 23–27.

Radice, Hugo. "The Developmental State under Global Neoliberalism." *Third World Quarterly* 29, no. 6 (2008): 1,153—74.

Richmond, Oliver. "Jekyll or Hyde: What Is Statebuilding Creating? Evidence from the 'Field.'" *Cambridge Review of International Affairs* 27, no. 1 (2014): 1–20.

Riyahi, Iyad, and Nahed Samara. *Just Ahead of the Crisis: Policies Designed to Plunge the West Bank into Debt*. Birzeit: Centre for Development Studies, Birzeit University, 2014.

Roy, Sara. *Failing Peace: Gaza and the Palestinian-Israeli Conflict*. London: Pluto Press, 2007.

Taghdisi-Rad, Sahar. *The Political Economy of Aid in Palestine: Relief from Conflict or Development Delayed?* London: Routledge, 2010.

Turner, Mandy. "Building Democracy in Palestine: Liberal Peace Theory and the Election of Hamas." *Democratization* 13, no. 5 (December 2006): 739–55.

———. "Peacebuilding as Counterinsurgency in the Occupied Palestinian Territory." *Review of International Studies* 41, no. 1 (2015): 73–98.

Turner, Mandy, and Omar Shweiki, eds. *Decolonizing Palestinian Political Economy: De-development and Beyond*. New York: Palgrave-McMillan, 2015.

US Agency for International Development. "Fragile States Strategy." 2005. http://www.usaid.gov/policy/2005_fragile_states_strategy.pdf.

US Embassy of Israel. "Text of Cairo Conference Declaration." November 14, 1996. www.usembassy-israel.org.il/publish/press/summit/es111115.html.

Weber, Max. *Economy and Society. An Outline of Interpretive Sociology*. Berkeley: University of California Press, 1978.

Wimmer, Andreas, and Nina Glick-Schiller. "Methodological Nationalism and Beyond: Nation–State Building, Migration and the Social Sciences." *Global Networks* 2, no. 4 (2002): 301–34.

World Bank. *Over the Horizon: A New Levant*. Washington, DC: World Bank Group, 2014, https://openknowledge.worldbank.org/handle/10986/20491.

———. *Strengthening Governance: Tackling Corruption. The World Bank Group's Updated Strategy and Implementation Plan*. Washington, DC: World Bank, 2012.

———. *The Underpinnings of the Future Palestinian State: Sustainable Growth and Institutions*. Washington, DC: World Bank, 2010.

2

The Gaza Strip

Humanitarian Crisis and Lost Statehood

Tareq Baconi

The Oslo Accords defined a moment of transition in which the Palestinian liberation project moved from a focus on armed struggle and revolution towards negotiation and state-building under occupation. While many were initially hopeful about the Oslo Accords, one of the unexpected effects of these agreements was the split of the Palestinian movement into two projects: one that broadly remained committed to the principles of liberation as first articulated by the Palestine Liberation Organization (PLO), and one that adopted a diplomatic path towards the partition of Mandatory Palestine. These two projects have manifested themselves in divisions between and within factions, the most explicit of which is the divide between Hamas, the Islamic resistance movement currently governing the Gaza Strip, and the Palestinian National Authority (PNA) in Ramallah. The Gaza Strip, as home to the Palestinian school of thought that remains committed to the PLO's purist vision of armed struggle for liberation, albeit in an Islamist guise, is in many ways today a microcosm of the Palestinian national movement. It demonstrates in contemporary fashion the costs and limitations of remaining committed to central tenets of the Palestinian struggle. In that sense, the Gaza Strip is also the lynchpin of the debate for determining the future of the Palestinian national movement.

The Palestinian people are currently undergoing a period of transition into a post-Oslo reality, the nature of which is yet to be determined. Many possible trajectories present themselves: a reorientation and strengthening of efforts to achieve self-determination within the context of a two-state model through internationalization efforts or multilateral diplomacy; a shift towards a rights-based movement and the launching of an anti-apartheid grassroots struggle; an armed uprising; or, most likely, a future that combines elements of all of the above. It is also probable that debates and introspection regarding the optimal path forward will be preempted by a tipping point that is at this moment unforeseen. The policies of an increasingly right-wing and messianic Israeli political establishment, backed by American support, are actively creating facts on the ground that could force Palestinians to react in one way or another, heightening their sense of uncertainty and instability.

Regardless of the future trajectory of the Palestinian national movement, policies that have now been imposed and institutionalized within the Gaza Strip must be contended with. The political reality that informs and justifies present attempts to separate and isolate the Gaza Strip is itself a symptom of a broader unwillingness to contend with the ongoing suffering of the Palestinian people, and their quest for a justice rooted in the catastrophic events of 1948. Past and contemporary political discourse, led primarily by Israel and the United States, seeks to avoid such a reckoning by adopting humanitarian, military, and/or economic means to assuage the need for a political resolution. Such efforts are clearest today in Gaza, where members of the international community deal with the strip variously as a humanitarian challenge or a terroristic security threat. Within such a framing, the political drivers that have given rise to the current situation in Gaza are effectively marginalized.

This has resulted in the emergence of a de facto reality where dealings with the question of Palestine are necessarily restricted to the West Bank, particularly the effort to address Israel's colonization of the territories there. Yet such a focus will not in any way settle the principle drivers of Palestinian nationalism. Rather, it is imperative to know the underlying factors that animate the status quo in the Gaza Strip, and Israel's disposition towards it, as these are representative of the core issues. To do so, one must also contend with the reality of Hamas. The fates of Hamas and the Gaza Strip over the past three decades have inadvertently come to be intertwined, and it is impossible to deal with one without understanding the other. During the present period of transition, as Palestinians rethink their visions of statehood and contemplate the future of their struggle, an understanding of this interplay between Hamas and Gaza, and the historical backdrop that has led us to the present moment in time, where two million Palestinians are sealed off by an unforgiving blockade, is essential.

HAMAS AND THE OSLO PROCESS

In late 1988, Palestinian leader Yasser Arafat convened the exiled leadership of the PLO in Algiers. The eruption of the First Intifada in the Occupied Territories had finally compelled Arafat to officially adopt policies the PLO had been contemplating for years. Since Arafat had taken over the chairmanship of the PLO, and his movement, Fatah, had come to dominate its leadership, the PLO's policies had been clear. PLO factions were conducting a revolutionary "global offensive" against Israel.[1] According to a 1967 statement by Fatah, armed struggle was central to this revolution. "Our correct understanding of the reality of the Zionist occupation confirms to us that regaining the occupied homeland cannot happen except through armed violence as the sole, inevitable, unavoidable, and indispensable means in the battle of liberation."[2] Fatah's statement goes on to describe the necessity of dismantling the "colonial base . . . of the Zionist occupation state" and asserts that its intellectual, social, political, military, and financial elements have to be destroyed before the Palestinian homeland can be liberated.[3]

Addressing the convened attendees in 1988, Arafat gave a speech that conclusively broke with this trajectory. Rejecting the use of armed struggle for liberation, Arafat declared the independence of the State of Palestine and invoked international resolutions that demonstrated the PLO's willingness to accept a state on the West Bank and the Gaza Strip, with East Jerusalem as the capital. Arafat's declaration signaled the PLO's readiness to concede the 78 percent of Palestinian land that had been lost in 1948 and to officially renounce terrorism.[4] With this long-anticipated about-face, the PLO transitioned to a diplomatic track that was focused on achieving statehood on the remaining 22 percent of "historic Palestine."[5]

The PLO's concessions were anathema for Hamas, the Islamic resistance movement that had been created in December 1987, only a few months prior to Arafat's speech. In its charter, Hamas stressed the indivisibility of the land of historic Palestine, referring to the land that had constituted the British Mandate, located between the Eastern Mediterranean and the River Jordan, over which Israel had been established. Hamas defined this territory as "an Islamic land entrusted to the Muslim generations until Judgement Day."[6] The charter proclaimed that "jihad for the liberation of Palestine is obligatory." No other path for liberation was viable. The movement dismissed diplomatic efforts as contrary to its ideology, primarily because they were premised on conceding parts of Palestine, but also because Hamas believed they were unlikely to serve Palestinian interests. Instead, jihad was defined not as a tactic but rather a holistic and effective strategy around which the Palestinian community could rally.[7]

With Hamas's charter and the PLO's strategic shift, 1988 became a turning point that heralded a new phase of Palestinian nationalism.[8] In that year, the PLO's resolve to sustain the use of armed force to liberate historic Palestine appeared to wane. Almost seamlessly, Islamic nationalism rose to carry the mantle forward. While the PLO had risen at a time of global revolutionary anticolonialism, Hamas emerged against a regional backdrop of resurgent Islamism. The lessons that Fatah and the PLO had learned regarding the limitations of armed struggle and their path towards pacification were not seen as relevant to Hamas, which believed that its success was predestined.[9] The movement's leaders contended that Hamas's Islamic character would offer a robust ideological framework through which to offset the worldly pressures that had hamstrung the PLO.

With Arafat's concession, the Palestinian national movement conclusively moved away from the notion of liberation through arms towards state-building in the pursuit of independence. This transition culminated with the signing of the Oslo Accords in 1993, which Hamas came out in full opposition against.[10] The Oslo Accords enshrined the mutual recognition of Israel and the PLO, without officially making any commitments to Palestinian statehood. A central product of the Oslo Accords was the creation of the PNA. It was established in 1994 as a temporary administrative body that could govern portions of the Palestinian territories for a transitional period of five years, when the conclusive settlement was to be reached.[11] Among other governing tasks, the PNA was held accountable for security issues, as coordination mechanisms were put in place between the nascent entity and the Israeli army. Security was framed as a litmus test for Palestinian readiness to self-govern and a prerequisite for further Israeli withdrawal.[12] While the PNA was restricted to administering the affairs of daily governance under occupation, responsibility for negotiations in the pursuit of liberation ostensibly continued to rest with the PLO.

The Oslo Accords precipitated what has become a chronic disagreement between the PLO and Hamas on the nature of the Palestinian national movement, one that continues to this day. Palestinians under occupation hoped the Oslo Accords would bring statehood.[13] Yet Hamas opposed the recognition of Israel on which the Oslo Accords were premised. It joined forces with Marxist and other nationalist groups to form a rejectionist front that called for the continuation of resistance.[14] As peace talks were launched, Hamas played the role of a typical spoiler movement, embracing armed operations to derail the talks, even though this put it at odds with public sentiment.[15] In response, thousands of Hamas members were arrested by the PNA and Israel, as security coordination mechanisms were initiated throughout the West Bank and Gaza.[16] Alongside its military operations, Hamas also contemplated participating in the PNA's presidential and legislative elections, which were set for 1996.[17] After extensive debate, however, the movement's consultative council decided to boycott the ballot box to avoid conferring legitimacy to the Oslo Accords.[18] Expectedly, Yasser Arafat and his party, Fatah, emerged victorious and consolidated their grip on the presidency and the legislature.[19]

The PLO and successive Israeli governments sustained peace talks even as it became evident that the five-year deadline for reaching a final settlement in 1999 would be missed. During this period, Israeli settlements continued to expand against a backdrop of growing Palestinian frustration, aggravated by Israeli closures and checkpoint policies that severely undermined the Palestinian economy, weakened its labor markets and physically separated the Gaza Strip from the West Bank.[20] During this time, the number of settlers reached more than 350,000, controlling almost 7 percent of the land on which three million Palestinians were living. Israeli settlers competed with Palestinians for access to land and resources, fragmented the Palestinian territories into increasingly isolated silos, and restricted freedom of movement, with severe implications on the overall economy. During the period of negotiations, unemployment rose from under 7 percent before the Oslo Accords to 25 percent in the West Bank and 38 percent in the Gaza Strip by 1996. In the five-year period of negotiations, Israel imposed 443 days of closure, preventing the movement of persons, goods, or capital between Israel and the Palestinian territories.[21] As the Palestinian economy sagged under the weight of the occupation, Palestinian quality of life suffered and discontent grew.[22]

AL-AQSA INTIFADA: PALESTINIAN RESISTANCE, ISRAELI UNILATERALISM, AND "WAR ON TERROR"

In September 2000, in the absence of prospects for a Palestinian state, the Occupied Territories erupted in the Second Intifada, what Hamas hailed as "the divine intervention" that had derailed the diplomatic process.[23] Unlike the first uprising, the Second Intifada rapidly militarized, as Palestinian mobilization was met with the full power of Israel's army. The military wings of both Hamas and Fatah reverted to armed resistance in order to pressure Israel to end its occupation. Arafat's role was widely interpreted as focused on leveraging arms to change the balance of power in the negotiations, and thereby as complementing, rather than supplanting, the diplomatic track that the PLO had committed to with Oslo. For Hamas, the reading was different. Hamas's leaders celebrated the Intifada, and early on articulated their vision for it. As Abdel Aziz al-Rantissi, a prominent Hamas leader, explained succinctly, "I am not saying that the Intifada will lead to the complete liberation of Palestinian land from the river to the sea. Still, this Intifada [can] . . . achieve the complete withdrawal from the West Bank, the [Gaza] Strip and Jerusalem without giving up on 80 percent of Palestine."[24] Hamas's statements indicated that its goal for the Intifada was focused on ending Israel's occupation, a disposition that carried with it an implicit recognition of the 1967 lines.[25]

While both Hamas and the PLO limited their immediate goals to the liberation of the Occupied Territories, Hamas was clear that this must come through force as the only way liberation could be unconditional. The movement's publications explained that diplomacy meant the "return of these lands with truncated sovereignty, subservience to the occupier, deformation of Jerusalem and without the rights of refugees."[26] Hamas rapidly became the central instigator of armed operations against Israel. Al-Qassam Brigades, Hamas's military wing, adopted what they referred to as a "Balance of Terror" approach: in return for their brutal and indiscriminate killing of the elderly, women, and children, "now, the Zionists also suffer from being killed . . . . Now Israeli buses have no one riding in them and Israeli shopping centers are not what they used to be."[27] Balancing terror was a tool for Hamas to deter Israeli attacks on the Palestinians by forcing Israel to anticipate inevitable retaliation.[28]

Yet Hamas's military strategy reflected a fundamental misunderstanding on its part regarding how Israel would react, particularly under Prime Minister Ariel Sharon, who was elected into power six months after the Intifada began, on

February 6, 2001. Sharon won with a landslide vote, a resounding mandate from the Israeli electorate to deal with the Palestinian question militarily. A deeply controversial figure within Israel itself, Sharon was also despised by Palestinians, as he had built a military and political career rooted in destroying Palestinian nationalism.[29] His ideal outcome for Israel entailed the pacification of the Palestinian territories and their inhabitants, subjugating them to Israeli rule without conferring any collective political rights. Sharon's election had far-reaching consequences. Hamas, as well as Palestinians more broadly, interpreted his victory to mean that the Israeli public was not looking for peace.[30]

Early on, Sharon sought American approval for Israel's heavy-handedness. Reaching out to the United States, Sharon noted that Israel was facing its own Al-Qaeda in the form of Palestinian armed resistance. Initially, Sharon's rhetoric failed to gather sympathy from the administration of George W. Bush.[31] However, after September 11, the war of attrition between Israel and the Palestinians that had marked the first year of the Second Intifada almost immediately shifted in Israel's favor. Overnight, the Second Intifada was presented as Israel's War on Terror. Arafat condemned Al-Qaeda's actions, as did Hamas, which deescalated its military front.[32] Nonetheless, in a post-9/11 Bush administration, Sharon's analogy carried a great deal of weight. Conflating what constituted "Islamic extremism," Hamas's bombs in Jerusalem were described as being another symptom of global "Islamic terrorism." Within the regional and international climate, any argument that Hamas was using armed struggle strategically to end Israel's illegal occupation of Palestinian land was circumvented, as Israel positioned its response to the Second Intifada as an existential battle. Even though Sharon held Arafat, and the PNA, directly responsible for the violence, Israel also dealt Hamas a powerful blow. Israel sustained a policy of targeted assassinations that removed all of Hamas's senior leadership, including those seen as pragmatic leaders who had been instrumental in negotiating ceasefires.

The War on Terror rhetoric justified, to the American administration, not only Israel's iron grip, but also its unilateral initiatives to reconfigure the structure of occupation. This was carried out through the construction of a wall, which Israelis refer to as the security fence and Palestinians as the apartheid wall, that physically separates the West Bank from Israel.[33] Simultaneously, Sharon announced Israel's unilateral disengagement from the Gaza Strip. This entailed withdrawing nine thousand Jewish settlers as a precursor to strengthening Israel's grip over areas that "constitute an inseparable part of the State of Israel," namely the West Bank. Such a disengagement promised to reduce Israel's exposure to Palestinian resistance from the coastal enclave, and save significant security expenditure, given that these few thousand settlers controlled up to 30 percent of the Strip.[34] The remaining 70 percent of the Gaza Strip housed 1.8 million Palestinians. More important than security was Sharon's plan to remove these Palestinian inhabitants from Israel's direct jurisdiction. This allowed the state to maintain its control over the territories of the West Bank and East Jerusalem, with their 2.7 million non-Jewish inhabitants, without the threat of altering Israel's character as a Jewish-majority nation.[35]

Sharon's initiative reflected a continuation of his use of the pretext of security to unilaterally consolidate Israel's grip on the territories while avoiding any form of political engagement with the Palestinians.[36] This goal was explicitly articulated by Sharon's top aide, Dov Weisglass, in an interview several months after the announcement of the disengagement plan. "The disengagement is actually formaldehyde," Weisglass told the Israeli newspaper *Haaretz*. "It supplies the amount of formaldehyde that is necessary so that there will not be a political process with the Palestinians."[37] Hamas understood these calculations and voiced early reservations regarding Israel's disengagement even while celebrating what it viewed as the ability of the resistance front to prompt an Israeli retreat.[38]

As Israel decimated the Palestinian uprising and political establishment, the Bush administration pushed for "democratization" in the Palestinian territories, another element of its War on Terror doctrine. After Arafat's death in 2004, the United States and Israel sought a new Palestinian leadership that might revert to the project of state-building and diplomacy that had been initiated under the Oslo Accords. The failure of Hamas's military strategy meant that the movement needed to consider other means to safeguard its ideology. The elections that the United States pushed for in 2006 inadvertently provided an entry point for Hamas into the Palestinian political establishment, which had to be rebuilt. This major reform and resuscitation of the Palestinian political system offered Hamas the impetus to seek an alternative to its military strategy, one that could safeguard the fixed principles that it viewed as central to the Palestinian struggle.[39] Like the PLO before it, Hamas defined these principles as the refusal to concede the land of historic Palestine, a commitment to the right of return of refugees, and the safeguarding of the right to resist in the face of an unyielding and lethal occupation.[40]

MARRYING RESISTANCE WITH POLITICS

The opportunity for Hamas to transition its ideology into the political sphere came in the form of planned presidential and legislative elections in 2006. Hamas's prospective engagement with the elections had to contend with a central tension: it disapproved of the premise of the PNA and the underlying Oslo Accords that had created it. As the movement considered engagement in the political process, it sustained its armed operations, in keeping with its perception that it could "marry" resistance with politics.[41] Musa Abu Marzouq, a Hamas leader, explained that Hamas's political aspirations entailed "preserving the program of resistance. Despite [armed struggle] being in an ebb and flow, the political framework should be the continuation of resistance, the refusal to undermine it, to remove its arms, or to shackle it with unfair security arrangements."[42] While the PLO's past entry into politics had been premised on concessions, Hamas tethered its possible engagement in politics to the failure of negotiations and underscored the need to reject any further concessions from the Palestinian side.[43]

After extensive deliberations throughout 2005, Hamas's consultative council gave the go-ahead for the movement to take part in the elections.[44] Hamas's leadership declared that the perceived demise of the peace process meant that its political participation could not be seen as conferring legitimacy onto the Oslo Accords, which it believed had been annulled by the developments of the Second Intifada.[45] Rather, Hamas held the goal of circumventing the PNA and what it felt was the focus on governance that had institutionalized Palestinian capitulation to the Israeli occupation. Hamas's leaders advocated instead for the resuscitation of the overarching institutions overseeing Palestinian liberation, namely the PLO.[46] It was on this basis that Hamas ran on a platform of "Change and Reform," a far-reaching agenda that presented its strategic trajectory for the liberation struggle alongside promises to tackle daily administrative challenges within the territories.

In a historic watershed that marked the culmination of its politicization, Hamas won 76 of the 132 seats of the legislative council, relative to Fatah's 43. As a senior leader in Beirut stated, "This is a peaceful coup on the present decrepit political reality, which was born out of defeat, corruption and acquiescence to rotten political solutions . . . . These results are an excellent political renewal, as if the Palestinian people are reborn, and it's a new birth for the project of resistance, for the development of a society of resistance, for a shaking-off of all the institutions."[47] Hamas's political emergence heightened Israeli worries by rupturing the prolonged subservience of Palestinian institutions to the occupation. This compliance had become concretized in the body of the PNA following the Oslo Accords. By resuscitating key demands that the PLO had conceded, including the goal of liberating historic Palestine, Hamas was attempting to take Palestinian nationalism back to a pre-Oslo period. The Oslo Accords had failed to achieve the goals that Palestinians aspired to, and had instead facilitated the continuation of Israel's occupation at significant cost to Palestinians. Hamas's efforts to undo the political structures created by Oslo challenged a status quo that had been made sustainable, if not beneficial, for Israel and its colonization of Palestinian territories.

Hamas's victory caused utter confusion within the Bush administration, given its focus on democracy promotion in Palestine and in Iraq, as test cases for the region. The most immediate reaction was trepidation regarding the place of a designated terrorist organization in public office. As Elliot Abrams, a senior member of the Bush administration, noted, "legally, we had to treat Hamas as we treated al Qaeda."[48] In high-level meetings within the White House shortly after Hamas's victory, it was quickly decided that the optimal response was to adopt a strategy that could both isolate Hamas and reassert Fatah's dominance.[49] The dual-pronged plan was to be implemented on several levels: military, financial, and diplomatic.[50] Concurrently, the Quartet, the international body composed of the United States, the United Nations, the European Union, and Russia, issued a statement noting "that it was inevitable that future assistance to any new government would be reviewed by donors against that government's commitment to the principles of nonviolence, recognition of Israel, and acceptance of previous agreements and obligations."[51]

The Quartet's conditions mirrored the prerequisites the PLO had been required to fulfill for diplomatic engagement almost two decades prior. Even though the PLO's acceptance of these conditions and the subsequent extensive peace talks had still not compelled Israel to relinquish its hold over the territories, the same demands were now put to Hamas. Until these demands were met, the United States and Israel launched what Hamas's publications referred to as an "iron-wall" strategy aimed at suffocating its government.[52] Such intervention precluded any engagement with Hamas despite the movement's efforts to show pragmatism, including offering a political agenda that called for "the formation of an independent and fully sovereign Palestinian state, with Jerusalem as its capital," on the West Bank and the Gaza Strip, and limiting resistance to the removal of the occupation beyond the 1967 borders.[53] In a pragmatic nod, Hamas's agenda stated that "the government will deal with [past] signed agreements with a high level of responsibility, in a manner that protects the interests of our people, preserves their rights and does not harm their fixed principles."[54] Addressing calls for more flexibility in dealing with the Quartet's conditions, Hamas's leader Khaled Meshal stated, "we have shown enough flexibility. We cannot say more than the official Arab and Palestinian position, which is to call for a Palestinian state on the land occupied in 1967. The problem is not with us. It is not with Hamas, as in the past it was also not with the official Palestinian and Arab positions. The problem has always been with Israel."[55]

Alongside such offerings, Hamas stressed the need to sustain resistance. Abu Marzouq explained, "We are in government, yes, but the government is not whole. We are a government under occupation. We cannot assume that we have a government similar to others in the world. Or as the Americans demand, that we act only as a government. Hamas's program in government is one which is aligned, which is compatible, with its program of resistance."[56] Through its political intervention, Hamas sought to reassess how Palestinians dealt with their occupation, namely by breaking from the trappings of self-governance, repoliticizing the PNA away from its administrative focus and dedication to endless peace talks, and rupturing the continuity that the incumbent leadership hoped to secure.[57] In essence, Hamas sought to reverse the institutional inertia that had pacified the Palestinian leadership, and to resuscitate the calls for liberation that had marked the PLO's early history—and to do so within the framework of its Islamist ideology.[58]

Hamas's politics of resistance created much discomfort to those invested in the peace process launched through the Oslo Accords, which called for governance and gradual state-building under occupation. Opposition to Hamas's vision of the Palestinian national movement, now endowed with a popular mandate by the democratic election, was seen as an existential threat to Fatah and the PNA, which remained wedded to the Oslo principles. Supported by the United States and Israel, and by the cover of the Quartet principles, domestic measures were taken within the Palestinian political establishment to stymie power-sharing and prevent Hamas's actual entry into a leadership position. Signaling an initial impetus to act pluralistically within the PNA, Hamas extended a formal request to Fatah to form a coalition government.[59] Yet, reflecting wider sentiment, Fatah leaders suggested it would be "shameful" for Fatah to even consider entering a coalition government with Hamas.[60]

Fatah's monopolization of the political establishment meant that Hamas faced enormous institutional inertia. This was exacerbated by the international community's overt and clandestine support of the incumbent. As discussions among factions progressed to forming a unity government, the PNA's leadership initiated measures to mitigate Hamas's entry into politics. In an extraordinary session, the outgoing legislature proposed and passed bills to expand the remit of the president's office, held by Mahmoud Abbas, who won the presidential elections in 2006, at the expense of the incoming cabinet in areas such as security and the judiciary. These measures reversed past American-led reforms and recentralized political power within the hands of the president.[61] Hamas's publications viewed these activities as part of an "international conspiracy" and called the extraordinary session "unconstitutional."[62] Articles condemned Abbas's authoritarian hold on power.[63] Leaders remarked that "when [the United States and Israel] pushed reforms on President Arafat, the goal was to pass the authority to the prime minister, particularly over the security forces. Now the time is to return the authority to the president once Hamas has come into government. That is illogical and unacceptable."[64]

For close to eighteen months, the parties pursued a plethora of initiatives aimed at sharing power. Yet Fatah insisted that, prior to sharing power, it was incumbent on Hamas to transition, as the PLO had done in the past, from "liberation through armed struggle" to "state-building towards independence." As a senior Fatah leader said, "If new parties come into power in Spain or Italy, they would still recognize their membership in NATO. Recognition does not have to come from the party—but the government would have to respect past agreements."[65] Fatah's leadership was working from the premise of continuity, on the basis that the PLO was an authoritative body, akin to a sovereign state, recognized through its adherence to past agreements. The PLO remained committed to the 1988 concessions and the Oslo Accords, despite their failure to lead to a Palestinian state, and they believed Hamas's politicking in the PNA was premised on an implicit embrace of the Oslo Accords. Hamas dismissed these "delusions." Citing the absence of sovereignty, repeated American and Israeli intervention, and the vacuous nature of past agreements given Israeli reservations, Hamas questioned the basis of international recognition.[66] Before past agreements could be upheld, Hamas insisted that the PLO must be reformed so that all political parties could have a say in

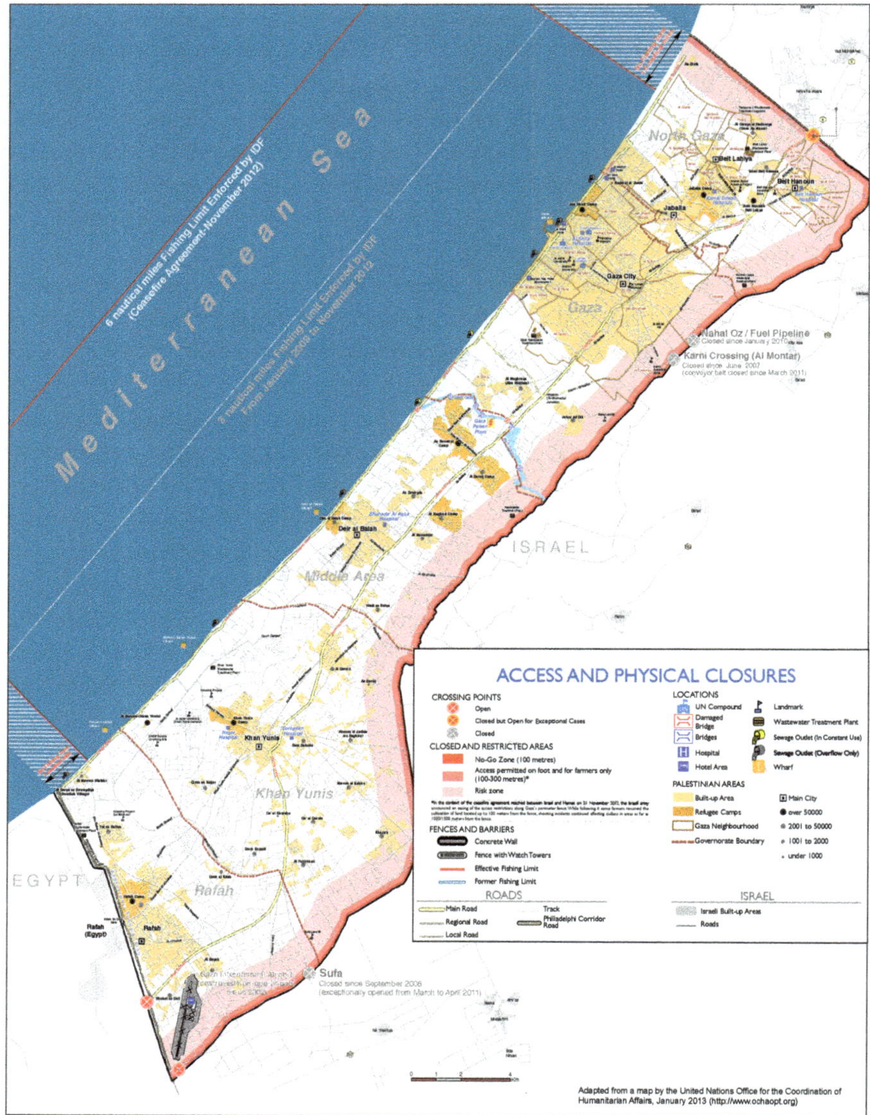

MAP 7. Gaza Strip, 2014. Source: Palestinian Academic Society for the Study of International Affairs.

reconstituting its manifesto. Widely understood but unspoken was Hamas's desire to reverse the trajectory that the PLO had taken under Fatah's tenure, including its recognition of Israel.[67]

Hamas's attempts to offer pragmatic concessions were consistently ignored in favor of military, financial, and diplomatic intervention. During the brief window between 2006 and 2007 when Hamas sought to claim its position as democratically elected government, more than six hundred Palestinians were killed. A brief episode in Palestinian democracy had ended in fratricide.[68] Foreign intervention and domestic authoritarianism ultimately facilitated military clashes between Hamas and Fatah, and paved the way for Hamas's violent capture of the Gaza Strip. Underlying such turmoil was an absence of any effort to deal with the political motivations underpinning Hamas's agenda. Like the PLO before it, Hamas's political vision, and with it the internationally sanctioned right of self-determination, right of return, and right to resist—demands that form the core of Palestinian nationalism—had effectively been neutralized.

THE FIG LEAF: GAZA AS TERRORIST HAVEN

On the eve of Hamas's takeover of Gaza in June 2007, a leaked report noted that a senior member of Israel's security establishment was quoted as being "happy" at the prospect of Hamas taking over the Gaza Strip, as that would then allow Israel to declare the coastal enclave a "hostile territory."[69] Although not an official position, this well encapsulates Israel's disposition towards the Gaza Strip after Hamas's takeover, a development which ruptured the Palestinian territories institutionally and politically. With that division, the international blockade that had been imposed on the Palestinian Authority (PA) following Hamas's entry into the political establishment morphed to focus primarily on the Gaza Strip, where Hamas's jurisdiction could be geographically delineated. All five crossings leading into the territory from Israel were shut, as was the Rafah border with Egypt, hermetically sealing the strip and preventing the movement of goods or people into or out of it.[70]

Israel cut fuel shipments by half and reduced imports into Gaza to the minimum amounts of food and medical supplies required for survival without sinking Gaza into a humanitarian catastrophe.[71] Food shortage and healthcare crises were felt almost instantly as poverty rates and unemployment soared. Palestinians in Gaza began experiencing electricity cuts of up to sixteen hours per day; half of Gaza's 1.8 million Palestinians were receiving water for only a few hours a week; unemployment rose to more than 50 percent; only 23 out of more than 3,900 industrial operations continued to function; and 70 percent of Gaza's agricultural land was no longer being irrigated.[72] Rapid economic deterioration was compounded by the fact that Gaza had suffered decades of de-development, whereby its economy had contracted and its infrastructure regressed as a result of Israel's isolationist policies towards the strip, which officially began following the Oslo Accords.[73]

Under international law, the blockade amounted to collective punishment and came at a horrific cost to Gaza's population.[74] Initially, as articulated by Israeli, US, and PNA politicians, the blockade was aimed at forcing the collapse of Hamas's government, and reunifying the Palestinian territories under a single leadership committed to negotiations with Israel. Yet rather than collapsing Hamas, the blockade allowed it to consolidate its grip and institutionalize a government that today oversees the affairs of the Gaza Strip in much the same way as the PNA does in the West Bank. In response to Hamas's entrenchment in the Gaza Strip, Israel gradually adopted a military doctrine referred to by its security establishment as "mowing the lawn."[75] This entails the intermittent use of military power to undercut any growth by the resistance factions in Gaza. Through three major military assaults and countless incursions since 2007, Israel has used overwhelming military might to break the spirit of resistance in Gaza, pacify Hamas, and work towards deterrence.[76]

Over the course of more than a decade, this dynamic has given rise to an equilibrium of belligerence between Hamas and Israel. Hamas relies on rocket fire as a negotiating tactic, to unsettle the status quo and pressure Israel to ease access of goods and people into the Gaza Strip by loosening the blockade. Israel employs military might to deter Hamas and prevent it from developing its military arsenal. This modus operandi has enabled both Israel and Hamas to pursue short-term victories at the expense of a longer-term resolution while they both bide their time. From Israel's perspective, resistance has been sufficiently managed so that Hamas's rule over the Gaza Strip can be tolerated, even abetted. Israeli politicians and the security establishment today speak of the need to "stabilize" Gaza under Hamas's rule and as a separate territory from the West Bank.[77] As a key member of Israel's security establishment noted, "Israel needs Hamas to be weak enough not to attack, but stable enough to deal with the radical terrorist groups in Gaza. This line may be blurry but the logic is clear. The challenge lies with walking this blurry line."[78]

Such policies have produced a situation whereby Israel is able to exercise effective control over the entirety of the Occupied Palestinian Territories without taking responsibility as an occupying force. Within the West Bank, the occupation has been outsourced to a compliant PA. Even as Israel maintains its settlement expansion throughout the territories, the PA is still held accountable for administering and governing the lives of Palestinians under Israel's occupation and for safeguarding Israel's security through extensive coordination mechanisms with the Israeli army. Even in the absence of an effective peace process, the Palestinian leadership in the West Bank remains rooted in the international legitimacy that was gained following the PLO's concessions in 1988 and the signing of the Oslo Agreement. The ongoing belief is that international law mechanisms and diplomacy will ultimately compel Israel to allow for the creation of a Palestinian state on the 1967 armistice line. As such, commitment to security coordination with Israel persists alongside state-building endeavors by the PNA, despite the absence of the effective sovereignty such tactics entail.

Within the Gaza Strip, Hamas remains ideologically committed to the notion of armed struggle for full liberation, despite the failure of this strategy as well to achieve any tangible gains for the Palestinian people. Hamas's ideology and its Islamist nature are often described by Israel, cynically or inadvertently, as the local manifestation of global terror networks.[79] Such demonization has succeeded in marginalizing the Gaza Strip and justifying the collective punishment inherent in besieging two million Palestinians. Operations carried out by the Israeli army against Gaza are then understood as a legitimate form of—most often preemptive—self-defense. By containing Hamas in the Gaza Strip, Israel has effectively cultivated a fig leaf that legitimates its policies of separation towards the strip. Those policies predate Hamas. As home to a high proportion of Palestinian refugees, Gaza had long been a foundation of resistance to Zionism and to Israel's ongoing military rule over Palestinians.[80] In the 1950s, decades before Hamas's creation, Israel designated Gaza a "*fedayeen*'s nest," in reference to the PLO fighters, and thus a territory that merited constant isolation and military bombardment in order to break the resistance.[81] Under Hamas's rule, Gaza moved from being a "*fedayeen*'s nest" to becoming a "hostile entity" and an "enclave of terrorism." Israel has leveraged Hamas's entrenchment in Gaza in a manner that allows it to act as an "effective and disengaged occupier," ensuring the containment and isolation of the Palestinians in Gaza without having to incur any additional cost for administration.[82]

The outcome is two administrative Palestinian authorities operating under an unyielding occupation. Whether there is a systematic Israeli separation policy for the West Bank and Gaza remains unclear, but Israel has nonetheless benefited from and reinforced this division.[83] More importantly, by reducing both strands of the Palestinian national movement from liberation to governance and stabilization, Israel has successfully avoided any engagement with the political drivers that continue to animate the Palestinian struggle. Despite their failed strategies, both Hamas and the PLO are driven by key Palestinian political demands that remain unmet and unanswered and that form the basis of the Palestinian struggle: achieving self-determination, dealing with the festering injustice of the refugee problem created by Israel's establishment in 1948, and exercising the right to use armed struggle to resist an illegal occupation.[84]

Hamas's takeover of Gaza marked the failure of Israel's efforts to centralize Palestinian decision-making within compliant structures such as the PA, which in effect allows Israel to maintain its occupation cost-free. Hamas's fate, and with it Gaza's, is emblematic of Israel's "decision not to decide" on the future of the Palestinian territories and its reliance on military superiority to dismiss the political demands animating the Palestinian national movement, choosing instead to continually manage rather than address the question of Palestine.[85] In this light, Hamas is the contemporary manifestation of demands that began a century ago. Israeli efforts to continue sidelining these demands, addressing them solely from a military lens, have persisted. Having moved from the terminology of "anti-guerilla warfare" to that of its own "war on terror," Israel merely employs contemporary language to wage a century-old war.

Argued in another way, the political reality that makes Gaza "a hostile entity" extends beyond that strip of land and animates the Palestinian struggle in its entirety. Gaza is one microcosm, one parcel, of the Palestinian experience.[86] Instead of addressing this reality or engaging with Hamas's political drivers, Israel has adopted a military approach that defines Hamas solely as a terrorist organization. This depoliticizes and decontextualizes the movement, giving credence to the persistent "politicide" of Palestinian nationalism, Israel's process of erasing the political ideology that animates Palestinian nationalism.[87] This approach has allowed successive Israeli governments to avoid taking a position on the demands that have been upheld by Palestinians since before the creation of the State of Israel.

GAZA AS HUMANITARIANISM AND THE GREAT MARCH OF RETURN

Under the administration of President Donald J. Trump, American foreign policy towards Israel and the Palestinian territories was clarified. Rather than commit to the two-state model, as historically understood by the international community, President Trump pursued drastic measures to formalize the one-state reality on the ground, and effectively terminated the prospect of a viable and sovereign Palestinian state. Over the course of little more than a year after Trump's inauguration in 2017, the United States recognized Jerusalem as Israel's capital; severely defunded the United Nations Relief and Works Agency (UNRWA), the main international body charged with providing social and economic services to Palestinian refugees; reduced financial support to the PA and to development organizations active throughout the territories; recognized Israel's annexation of the Syrian Golan Heights; and legitimized Israel's settlement enterprise, paving the way for its de jure annexation of up to 30 percent of the West Bank.

Alongside these measures, the Trump administration also pursued policies that focused specifically on the Gaza Strip, and that demonstrated the continued efforts to depoliticize and isolate the coastal enclave. One year into his administration, as reports gathered pace regarding the presence of a "deal of the century" that would presumably resolve the question of Israel/Palestine, the Trump administration hosted a closed, invitation-only conference in the White House. This was attended by politicians and businesspeople from the United States, Israel, and a host of Arab countries. The conference was aimed at promoting foreign investment within the Gaza Strip, ostensibly with the goal of alleviating the dire humanitarian suffering on the ground. Projects ranged from power generation plants that would mitigate the chronic electricity crisis in Gaza to sewage treatment and water desalination plants. These interventions expanded and built on a history of developmental projects, including those that continue to be promoted by economic bodies such as the Office of the Quartet and other development organizations that are active in the Gaza Strip. Alongside planning for these projects, a media campaign was carried out by the US mediators against Hamas, blaming the movement exclusively for the situation in the Gaza Strip, and failing to mention issues related to the blockade or Israel's occupation of the Palestinian territories.

Efforts to deal with Gaza in a humanitarian framing are not new, and with the current reality, they serve Israel's continued occupation of Palestinian territories in two ways. The first is by reducing the humanitarian suffering in the Gaza Strip without challenging the overall political context that is, in reality, the prime driver for that suffering: that of the blockade. Addressing Gaza's humanitarian misery is an urgent priority. Yet doing so in a manner that does not engage with the blockade makes this reality sustainable for much longer than it otherwise might be. With the international community and the private sector underwriting and profiting from the need for humanitarian intervention in Gaza, the structure of the blockade can firmly remain in place without Israel risking a catastrophic humanitarian crisis that would turn the world's opinion against its flagrant violation of international law. The second benefit follows directly from the first, and involves the formalization of policies of positioning Gaza as a challenge to be addressed independently of the rest of the Palestinian territories. With Gaza stabilized under Hamas's governance and with international intervention, Israel's ongoing annexation of the West Bank is free to continue apace with no accountability.

The combination of these two issues has given rise to the reemergence of a "state minus" discourse. This alludes to a "resolution" whereby Palestinians would be placated with measures that are symbolically akin to statehood but that lack constituent elements of true sovereignty. Past and present measures include demanding that the future Palestinian state remain demilitarized, or limiting Palestinian sovereignty to autonomous governance in specific jurisdictions. The Trump plan, released in January 2020, redefined Palestinian statehood to entail self-governance within around 168 urban silos in the Occupied Territories, almost entirely surrounded by Israeli territory and lacking any form of sovereignty. With Jerusalem having been recognized by the United States as the capital of Israel, with major territorial divisions throughout the West Bank as a result of illegal settlements, and with the severance of the Gaza Strip from the rest of the territories, the "state" on offer to the Palestinians through formal diplomatic channels entails a fraction of the 22 percent of historic Palestine that Palestinians had hoped to build their state on when the PLO first accepted the notion of partitioning the land in 1988. Such formulations, although touted as "resolutions," are little more than a continuation of Israeli efforts to manage, rather than resolve, the question of Palestine. With the current failed strategies of both Hamas and Fatah and the institutionalization of the division within the territories, Israel has been able to sustain a cost-free occupation while enjoying Jewish supremacy over the entirety of the land of historic Palestine.

Yet it would be a mistake to overemphasize the sustainability of this situation. The failure of the Palestinian political elite and the slow demise of the Oslo project have initiated a gradual reorientation on the level of the Palestinian grassroots that is possibly indicative of where the future of the Palestinian national consciousness resides. From the "prayer intifada" of the summer of 2017 in Jerusalem to the "return marches" carried out from Syria outside Israel's northern front, a significant, if sporadic, mobilization on the grassroots level has been slowly flourishing over the past few years. Such mobilization is taking place outside the context of the PLO or that of the Palestinian political establishment. Previous ruptures in the long history of the Palestinian struggle for self-determination suggest that such sporadic instances of popular resistance to Israel's occupation are likely to erupt in one form or another. They are a reminder of the political nature of the Palestinian question, which remains unaddressed.

One of the most significant of these mobilizations was, of course, the Great March of Return (GRM), in which Palestinian civil society in Gaza launched a mass movement that cut across political affiliations. The GRM was a popular initiative that mobilized under the single banner of "return": the demand for the return of the Palestinian refugees to homes from which they had been expelled or had fled in 1948. Although the immediate goal of the GRM was to pressure Israel to lift the blockade, the overarching vision under which it unfolded was one of return. As such, the GRM openly broke from the central tenants of peace-making that marked the Oslo period, which entailed the minutia of diplomatic negotiations around land swaps and the 1967 lines, and instead returned to the roots animating Palestinian nationalism, which remain anchored in the tragedy of al-Nakba. The effect of such discourse was to begin the process of reclaiming a Palestinian narrative that might move beyond the factional fragmentation that was the outcome of the Oslo Accords, the most prominent result of which is Gaza's geographic isolation. Furthermore, the fact that the GRM was initiated at a grassroots level demonstrates an inherent rejection, or impatience, with factional politics, and a recognition that the Palestinian political elite have become embroiled in a system of power dynamics that has failed to achieve freedom, equality, or justice for the Palestinians.

The initial hope that the GRM could be the harbinger of broader change within the Palestinian struggle dissolved as the movement was challenged by Israel's disproportionate, and tremendously lethal, use of force, as well as, eventually, by greater involvement from Hamas. Hamas's efforts to coopt the GRM threatened to subsume it into the very political reality it was hoping to break away from. Yet even with such risks, the protests can nonetheless be understood as a rejuvenated form of Palestinian political mobilization—and possibly, as the catalyst for the launching of the next, post-Oslo, phase of the Palestinian struggle. The inclusive discourse that marked the GRM's ideology and its rootedness in 1948 have the power to unite Palestinians across geographies in a single narrative based on the Palestinian historical experience of dispossession and exile. It is this kind of narrative that ultimately has the power to lead the Palestinians out of the current political stalemate that first the PLO, then Hamas, have led them into.

In rethinking the notion of Palestinian statehood, one must heed the demands being generated from the grassroots, given that the political elite no longer have the required legitimacy to lead the narrative. Once again, Gaza is leading the path by illuminating the power of defining a Palestinian vision that is rooted in Palestinian rights, like the right of return. These rights and the political demands that emerge around them are the ones that Israel continues to marginalize in the hope of managing rather than resolving the question of Palestine, often through the use of overwhelming military might. The Gaza Strip, while contained and safely isolated under Hamas's government, demonstrates through its marches that even in the face of the greatest adversity, the Palestinian people remain committed in their quest to achieve the justice they have been seeking for the past century. It is imperative to heed this call, and to root the future trajectory of the Palestinian struggle in this call for rights, embracing the power of this narrative to reunify the Palestinian people and dismantle the political structures that have been created to fragment them.

NOTES

1. The term comes from Paul Thomas Chamberlin, *The Global Offensive: The United States, the Palestine Liberation Organization, and the Making of the Post-Cold War Order* (Oxford: Oxford University Press, 2012). For more on Palestinian politics during this time, see Edward Said, *The Politics of Dispossession: The Struggle for Palestinian Self-Determination, 1969–1994* (New York: Pantheon Books, 1994); and Amal Jamal, *The Palestinian National Movement: Politics of Contention, 1967–2005* (Bloomington: Indiana University Press, 2005).

2. Quoted in Yezid Sayigh, *Armed Struggle and the Search for State: Palestinian National Movement, 1949–1993* (Oxford: Oxford University Press, 1997), 212.

3. Sayigh, *Armed Struggle*, 212.

4. William B. Quandt, *Peace Process: American Diplomacy and the Arab Israeli Conflict since 1967.* (Berkeley: University of California Press, 2001), 245–90. For more on the PLO's diplomatic softening, see Rashid Khalidi, *The Iron Cage: The Story of the Palestinian Struggle for Statehood* (Boston: Beacon Press, 2006), 140–82; and Osamah Khalil, "Pax Americana: The United States, the Palestinians, and the Peace Process, 1948–2008," *The New Centennial Review* 8, no. 2 (2008): 1–42.

5. Yezid Sayigh, "Struggle within, Struggle Without: The Transformation of PLO Politics since 1982," *International Affairs* 65, no. 2 (1989): 247–71.

6. This Islamic endowment is referred to as *waqf*. In its charter, Hamas explains that this history allegedly goes back to the Caliph Umar ibn al-Khatab, who refused the division of the conquered lands in Iraq and Syria, choosing instead to endow them in perpetuity to future generations of Muslims.

7. For more on the use of violence as strategy rather than tactics, see Lawrence Freedman, "Terrorism as Strategy," *Government and Opposition* 42, no. 3 (2007): 314–39.

8. See Helga Baumgarten, "The Three Faces/Phases of Palestinian Nationalism, 1948–2005," *Journal of Palestine Studies* 34, no. 4 (2005): 24–48.

9. For more on the role of Islam in shaping such a worldview, see Hazem Kandil, *Inside the Brotherhood* (London: Polity Press, 2014). For more on the anticipated failure of secularism, see Mahmud Zahhar and Hussein Hijazi, "Hamas: Waiting for Secular Nationalism to Self-Destruct. An Interview with Mahmud Zahhar," *Journal of Palestine Studies* 24, no. 3 (1995): 81–88.

10. For more on the Oslo Accords and the subsequent decade of the peace process, see Laura Zittrain Eisenberg and Neil Caplan, *Negotiating Arab-Israeli Peace: Patterns, Problems, Possibilities* (Bloomington: Indiana University Press, 2010), 165–253; Ziad Abu-Amr, "The View from Palestine: In

the Wake of the Agreement," *Journal of Palestine Studies* 23, no. 2 (1994): 75–83; Baruch Kimmerling and Joel S. Migdal, *The Palestinian People: A History* (Cambridge, MA: Harvard University Press, 2003), 315–98; and Avi Shlaim, "The Oslo Accord," *Journal of Palestine Studies* 23, no. 3 (1994): 24–40.

11. Naseer H. Aruri and John J. Carroll, "A New Palestinian Charter," *Journal of Palestine Studies* 23, no. 3 (1994): 5–17.

12. Joseph Alpher, "Israel's Security Concerns in the Peace Process," *International Affairs* 70, no. 2 (1994): 229–41. For more on the security coordination, see Hillel Cohen, "Society-Military Relations in a State-in-the-Making: Palestinian Security Agencies and the 'Treason Discourse' in the Second Intifada," *Armed Forces and Society* 38, no. 3 (2012): 463–85; and Graham Usher, "Politics of Internal Security: The PA's New Intelligence Services," *Journal of Palestine Studies* 25, no. 3 (1996): 21–34.

13. This hope was misplaced. See Rashid Khalidi, "Beyond Abbas and Oslo," *New Yorker*, October 12, 2015.

14. This alliance, formed in 1991, was called the Ten Resistance Organizations. Despite the fact that its charter excoriated Communists and leftist groups, Hamas had no issues lauding them when they confronted the hegemony of the PLO. See Abd al-Qadir Yasin, *Hamas: Harakat al-Muqawamah al-Islamiyah fi Filastin* (Cairo: Sina lil Nashr, 1990), 71. For the impact of the Oslo Accords on Hamas, see Beverly Milton-Edwards, "Political Islam in Palestine in an Environment of Peace?" *Third World Quarterly* 17, no. 2 (1996): 206–10; and Wendy Kristianasen, "Challenge and Counterchallenge: Hamas's Response to Oslo," *Journal of Palestine Studies* 28, no. 3 (1999): 19–39.

15. Daoud Kuttab, "Current Developments and the Peace Process," *Journal of Palestine Studies* 22, no. 1 (1992): 100–7. In late 1993, polls indicated 73 percent of Palestinians favored negotiations and 60 percent supported the PLO. Only 17 percent supported Hamas; Beverly Milton-Edwards, *Islamic Politics in Palestine* (London: I.B. Tauris, 1996), 163. For more on Hamas's role as a spoiler movement, see Andrew Kydd and Barbara F. Walter, "Sabotaging the Peace: The Politics of Extremist Violence," *International Organization* 56, no. 2 (2002): 263–96; Ely Karmon, "Hamas's Terrorism Strategy: Operational Limitations and Political Constraints," *Middle East Review of International Affairs* 4, no. 1 (2000): 66–79; Claude Berrebi and Esteban F. Klor, "On Terrorism and Electoral Outcomes: Theory and Evidence from the Israeli-Palestinian Conflict," *Journal of Conflict Resolution* 50, no. 6 (2006): 899–925; and Stephen Stedman, "Spoiler Problems in Peace Processes," *International Security* 22, no. 2 (1997): 7–16. Polls indicated that Palestinian support for suicide bombing was very low. In November 1998, 75 percent of Palestinians opposed suicide bombing; in 1999, support for suicide bombing was under 20 percent and for Hamas under 12 percent; Mia Bloom, *Dying to Kill: The Allure of Suicide Terror* (New York: Columbia University Press, 2005), 25.

16. Between 1994 and 1995, the PA launched twelve arrest campaigns against Hamas, and made more than one thousand arrests. It also launched a system of highly controversial midnight trials and detention. See Khaled Hroub, "Harakat Hamas Bayn al-Sulta al-Filastiniyyeh wa Israel: Min Muthalath al-Ouwwa ila al-Mitraqa wa al-Sindan," *Majallat al-Dirasat al-Filastiniyyeh*, no. 18 (1994): 24–37.

17. Abu-Amr, "View from Palestine."

18. Hamas ultimately allowed members to run as independents. See Wael Abed Elhamid el-Mabhouh, *Opposition in the Political Thought of Hamas Movement, 1994–2006* (Beirut: Al Zaytouna Center, 2012); Tareq Baconi, "The Demise of Oslo and Hamas's Political Engagement," *Conflict, Security and Development* 15, no. 5 (2015): 503–20; Naim Ashhab, *Hamas: Min al-Rafd ila al-Saltah* (Ramallah: Dar al-Tanwir, 2006); and Naim Ashhab, *Imarat Hamas* (Ramallah: Dar al-Tanwir, 2006).

19. Lamis Andoni, "The Palestinian Elections: Moving toward Democracy or One-Party Rule?" *Journal of Palestinian Studies* 25, no. 3 (1994): 5–16; and Ahmad S. Khalidi, "The Palestinians' First Excursion into Democracy," *Journal of Palestine Studies* 25, no. 4 (1996): 20–28.

20. Sara Roy, "De-development Revisited: Palestinian Economy and Society since Oslo," *Journal of Palestine Studies* 28, no. 3 (1999): 64–82. See also Leila Farsakh, *Palestinian Labour Migration to Israel: Labour, Land, and Occupation* (New York: Routledge, 2005).

21. Leila Farsakh, "The Palestinian Economy and the Oslo 'Peace Process,'" *Trans Arab Research Institute*, http://tari.org/index.php?option=com_content&view=article&id=9&Itemid=11.

22. Sara Roy, "Palestinian Society and Economy: The Continued Denial of Possibility," *Journal of Palestine Studies* 30, no. 4 (2001): 5–20.

23. "Intifada of Arabs and Muslims," *Filastin al-Muslima*, November 23, 2000, 23–27.

24. Badr al-Din Mohammad, "Differences with the PA," *Filastin al-Muslima*, February 21, 2001, 20.

25. Hamas's focus on the Occupied Territories rather than Israel was conveyed to British and American interlocutors in private meetings. See Mark Perry, *Talking to Terrorists: Why America Must Engage with Its Enemies*, (New York: Basic Books, 2010), 130.

26. "Victory Waves on the Horizon," *Filastin al-Muslima*, December 19, 2000, 3.

27. "Al-Qassam Succeed," *Filastin al-Muslima*, April 12, 2001, 12. For insight into the impact this had on Israelis, see Ari Shavit, "Letter from Jerusalem: No Man's Land—The Idea of a City Disappears," *New Yorker*, December 9, 2002, 56–60.

28. Hamas and Israel became engaged in a "violent dialogue"; Mark Muhannad Ayyash, "Hamas and the Israeli State: A Violent Dialogue," *European Journal of International Relations* 16, no. 1 (2010): 103–23. For more on Hamas's discourse, see Tareq Baconi, "Politicizing Resistance: The Transformative Impact of the Second Intifada on Hamas's Resistance Strategy," in "Transformative Occupations in the Modern Middle East," special issue, *Humanity Journal* 8, no. 2 (2017): 311–33.

29. See Baruch Kimmerling, *Politicide: Ariel Sharon's War against the Palestinians* (London: Verso, 2003); Shlomo Ben-Ami, *Scars of War, Wounds of Peace* (Oxford: Oxford University Press, 2006): 285–312. For more on Ariel Sharon, see David Landau, *Arik: The Life of Ariel Sharon* (New York: Alfred and Knopf, 2013).

30. See "The Zionists Have Had their Say," *Filastin al-Muslima*, March 17, 2001.

31. Daniel E. Zoughbie, *Indecision Points: George W. Bush and the Israeli-Palestinian Conflict* (Cambridge, MA: MIT Press, 2014), 17.

32. See Charmaine Seitz, "Hamas Stands Down?" *Middle East Report* no. 221 (2001): 4–7.

33. The wall is an imposing eight meter-high, 703 kilometer-long concrete structure, fitted with electronic fences, barbed wire, and highly sophisticated surveillance equipment, that cut through Palestinian villages and unilaterally seized around 10 percent of the West Bank; Eyal Weizman, *Hollow Land: Israel's Architecture of Occupation* (London: Verso, 2007), 161–85. For more on the wall, see Ray Dolphin, *West Bank Wall: Unmaking Palestine* (London: Pluto Press, 2006); and Michael Sorkin, *Against the Wall: Israel's Barrier to Peace* (New York: New Press, 2005). On July 20, 2004, the International Court of Justice issued an advisory opinion ruling that the wall was illegal, to no effect; "The Legal Consequences of the Construction of a Wall in the Occupied Palestinian Territory," *International Court of Justice*, July 9, 2004.

34. Sara Roy, "Praying with Their Eyes Closed: Reflections on the Disengagement from Gaza," *Journal of Palestine Studies* 34, no. 4 (2005): 64–74, 66.

35. Sharon's disengagement plan entailed an ideological shift within Likud to accept the partition of the land of *Eretz Yisrael*, as a prerequisite to maintaining Israel's Jewish majority. See Jonathan Rynhold and Dov Waxman, "Ideological Change and Israel's Disengagement from Gaza," *Political Science Quarterly* 123, no. 1 (2008): 11–37.

36. Kimmerling, *Politicide*, 155–81.

37. Ari Shavit, "Top PM Aide: Gaza Plan Aims to Freeze the Peace Process," *Haaretz*, October 6, 2004.

38. Maha Abdel Hadi, "Plan to Withdraw," *Filastin al-Muslima*, March 25, 2004, 12–13; Ra'fat Murra, "Osama Hamdan Talks to *FM*," *Filastin al-Muslima*, March 25, 2004, 16; and Ibrahim al-Sa'id, "Snowball," *Filastin al-Muslima*, March 25, 2004, 14.

39. Author interviews with Hamas's leaders elucidated that its strategy was based on both fixed principles *(thawabet)* and variables *(motaghayerat)*. The movement's pragmatic nature is seen in its

ability to adapt its variables, for instance by restraining armed struggle or accepting engagement in the political establishment, as long as its fixed principles are left unharmed. For more, see Ismail Haniyeh's explanation in "Press Release for Ismail Haniyeh," *Palestine-Info*, June 10, 2004.

40. "Position of Palestinian Factions," *Filastin al-Muslima*, February 26, 2014, 32.

41. Author interview, Wassim Afifeh, 2015.

42. "Musa Abu Marzouq," *Filastin al-Muslima*, October 1, 2004, 54.

43. "Press Release for Rantissi," *Al-Noor*, March 1, 2004.

44. This decision was announced through the Cairo Declaration of 2005. "Doc. 29: Closing Statement, March 17, 2005," *al-Watha'iq al-Filastiniyyah*, 69.

45. Zahhar elaborated in an interview ahead of the 2006 legislative elections that Hamas had needed to wait until the failure of the Oslo Accords would be demonstrated before running. See Badr al-Din Mohammad, "Hamas's Political Vision," *Filastin al-Muslima*, December 5, 2005, 39.

46. See for instance "Press Release for Nazzal," *Al-Hayat*, September 18, 2004, IPS.

47. Ra'fat Murra, "After the Elections," *Filastin al-Muslima*, February 13, 2006, 45.

48. Elliott Abrams, *Tested by Zion: The Bush Administration and the Israeli-Palestinian Conflict* (Cambridge: Cambridge University Press, 2013), 163.

49. Zoughbie, *Indecision Points*, 104–12. For insight into the American administration's thinking, see Abrams, *Tested by Zion*, 163–77; and Condoleezza Rice, *No Higher Honor: A Memoir of My Years in Washington* (New York: Crown Publishers, 2011), 413–20.

50. Zoughbie, *Indecision Points*, 104–12; Perry, *Talking to Terrorists*, 135; and Sara Roy, *Hamas and Civil Society in Gaza: Engaging the Islamist Social Sector* (Princeton, NJ: Princeton University Press, 2011), 39–50. For investigative reporting on this, see John B. Judis, "Clueless in Gaza: New Evidence that Bush Undermined a Two-State Solution," *The New Republic*, February 19, 2013; David Rose, "The Gaza Bombshell," *Vanity Fair*, April 2008; and Alastair Crooke, "Elliott Abram's Uncivil War," *Conflicts Forum*, January 7, 2007.

51. "Statement on Palestinian Elections by Middle East Quartet," January 26, 2006, https://www .un.org/unispal/document/auto-insert-204634/. For more, see Khaled Elgindy, "The Middle East Quartet: A Post-Mortem," *Brookings Institution*, no. 25 (February 2012): 2–34.

52. See Ibrahim al-Said, "The Occupation Puts a Plan," *Filastin al-Muslima*, March 6, 2006, 26–27.

53. "Doc 69: The Political Program, March 20, 2006," *al-Watha'iq al-Filastiniyyah*, 160.

54. "Doc 69: The Political Program," 161.

55. "Interview with Meshal, June 13, 2006," *al-Watha'iq al-Filastiniyyah*, 479.

56. "Doc. 37: Interview with Abu Marzouq, February 2, 2006," *al-Watha'iq al-Filastiniyyah*, 88.

57. "Doc. 30: Letter from Hamas, January 30, 2006," *al-Watha'iq al-Filastiniyyah*, 63.

58. For more on Hamas's views of reformulating the Palestinian reality under occupation, from the political to the economic, see "Doc. 41: Meshal's Speech, February 7, 2006," *al-Watha'iq al-Filastiniyyah*, 96–97; "The New Government's Proposed Economic Agenda," *Filastin al-Muslima*, March 6, 2006, 34; "Doc. 13: Interview with Mahmoud al-Ramhi, January 19, 2006," *al-Watha'iq al-Filastiniyyah*, 43–44; and "Doc. 44: Interview with Osama Hamdan, February 13, 2006," *al-Watha'iq al-Filastiniyyah*, 106. Publications discussed how foreign aid was never aimed at producing a functioning economy, but was rather a cover to sustain the diplomatic process; Nasser Atyani, "International Aid," *Filastin al-Muslima*, March 6, 2006, 30. See also Yezid Sayigh, "Inducing a Failed State in Palestine," *Survival* 49, no. 3 (2007): 7–40; Mandy Turner and Omar Shweiki, eds., *Decolonizing Palestinian Political Economy: De-development and Beyond*, (London: Palgrave Macmillan, 2014); and Shir Hever, *The Political Economy of Israel's Occupation: Repression beyond Exploitation* (London: Pluto Press, 2010).

59. "Doc. 47: Interview with Said Sayyam, February 16, 2006," *al-Watha'iq al-Filastiniyyah*, 114–17.

60. "Doc. 24: Release for Dahlan, January 27, 2006," *al-Watha'iq al-Filastiniyyah*, 58. Following Hamas's victory, al-Aqsa Brigades issued a statement calling on Abbas and Fatah's senior leadership to resign rather than partake in a Hamas government. "Doc. 20: Al-Aqsa Bayan, January 26, 2006," *al-Watha'iq al-Filastiniyyah*, 53–54.

61. Abbas passed legislation to become the commander-in-chief of all armed forces; "A High Wire Act," *The Economist*, June 3, 2006. For an overview of the steps taken by Abbas's cabinet to centralize power, see Mariam Itani, *Conflict of Authorities between Fatah and Hamas in Managing the Palestinian Authority, 2006–2007* (Beirut: Al-Zaytouna, 2008). For Hamas's reporting, see Ibrahim Hamami, "One Year of Abbas's Presidency," *Filastin al-Muslima*, January 5, 2006, 36–38; and Samir Khweireh, "Priorities Are Now to End Corruption," *Filastin al-Muslima*, May 8, 2006, 47.

62. See "Conspiracy to Defeat Hamas," *Filastin al-Muslima*, March 6, 2006, 3; and Maha Abdel Hadi, "Political and Economic Siege," *Filastin al-Muslima*, May 8, 2006, 36.

63. "Conspiracy to Defeat Hamas," 3.

64. "Doc. 47: Interview with Said Sayyam, February 16, 2006," *al-Watha'iq al-Filastiniyyah*, 114–18. See also "Doc. 45: Press Release for Hamas, February 14, 2006," *al-Watha'iq al-Filastiniyyah*, 111–13.

65. "Doc. 123: Interview with Nabil Sha'ath, April 24, 2006," *al-Watha'iq al-Filastiniyyah*, 280.

66. For Hamas's take on PLO reform, see "Doc. 124: Interview with Musa Abu Marzouq, April 25, 2006," *al-Watha'iq al-Filastiniyyah*, 283–91. See also Kjorlien, "Hamas," 4–7.

67. For instance, "Doc. 13: Interview with Mahmoud al-Ramhi, January 19, 2006," *al-Watha'iq al-Filastiniyyah*, 44–45.

68. Zoughbie, *Indecision Points*, 127.

69. Zoughbie, *Indecision Points*, 127. For more, see "WikiLeaks: Possibility of Israeli-Palestinian Co-operation over Gaza," *The Telegraph*, December 20, 2010; and Barak Ravid, "Fatah Asked Israel to Help Attack Hamas during Gaza Coup, WikiLeaks Cable Shows," *Haaretz*, December 20, 2010.

70. For the blockade's immediate impact, see the collection of reports by the UN Office for the Coordination of Humanitarian Affairs at https://www.ochaopt.org/themes/articles/gaza-blockade.

71. Linda Butler, ed., "A Gaza Chronology, 1948–2008," *Journal of Palestine Studies* 38, no. 3 (Spring 2009): 98–121, 120. These policies depoliticized Gaza, separating it from the rest of the Palestinian conflict and presenting it solely as a humanitarian problem. See Ilana Feldman, "Gaza's Humanitarianism Problem," *Journal of Palestine Studies* 38, no. 3 (2009): 22–37.

72. UN Office for the Coordination of Humanitarian Affairs, "Gaza Humanitarian Situation Report: The Impact of the Blockade on the Gaza Strip: A Human Dignity Crisis," December 15, 2008, https://unispal.un.org/DPA/DPR/unispal.nsf/0/3E3505FD18CFB035852575220052C893.

73. See Sara Roy, *The Gaza Strip: The Political Economy of De-development* (Washington, DC: Institute for Palestine Studies, 1995); Sara Roy, *Failing Peace: Gaza and the Palestinian-Israeli Conflict* (London: Pluto Press, 2007), 79–102; and Avi Shlaim, "How Israel Brought Gaza to the Brink of a Humanitarian Catastrophe," *The Guardian*, January 7, 2009.

74. "UN Chief Ban Ki-Moon Calls for Israel to End 'Collective Punishment' Blockade of Gaza," *Haaretz*, June 29, 2016.

75. Efraim Inbar and Eitan Shamir, "Mowing the Grass in Gaza," *Jerusalem Post*, July 22, 2014. See also Mouin Rabbani, "Israel Mows the Lawn," *London Review of Books* 36, no. 15 (July 2014), https://www.lrb.co.uk/the-paper/v36/n15/mouin-rabbani/israel-mows-the-lawn.

76. Rashid Khalidi, "The Dahiya Doctrine, Proportionality, and War Crimes," *Institute for Palestine Studies*, no. 44 (2014–15): 5–13.

77. From author interviews with Israeli security analysts, June–August 2015. See also Anat Kurz and Shlomo Brom, eds., *The Lessons of Operation Protective Edge* (Tel Aviv: Institute for National Security Studies, 2014).

78. Yaakov Amidror, "Hamas's Irrational Rationale," *Israel Hayom*, July 21, 2017.

79. Israeli politicians, including Benjamin Netanyahu, frequently invoke the claim that Hamas, the Islamic State, and al-Qaeda are one and the same. For instance, see "Binyamin Netanyahu: ISIS and Hamas 'Branches of the Same Poisonous Tree,'" *The Guardian*, September 29, 2014.

80. For more on Israel's historic policies towards Gaza, see Jean-Pierre Filiu, *Gaza: A History*, trans. John King (Oxford: Oxford University Press, 2014), 57–125; and Ahmad S. Khalidi, "Al-Tahuwwlat al-Istratigiyyeh al-Askariyyeh wa al-Amniyyeh al-Israeliyyeh," paper presented at the Institute for Palestine Studies Conference in Ramallah, 2015.

81. Jean-Pierre Filiu, "The Twelve Wars on Gaza," *Journal for Palestine Studies* 44, no. 1 (2014): 53.

82. Gisha, "Disengaged Occupiers: The Legal Status of Gaza," *Gisha: Legal Center for Freedom of Movement* (January 2007).

83. Some Israeli analysts noted that Israel has not developed such a policy, mostly because it has no strategy towards Gaza, but has nonetheless actively reinforced it for their benefit. Others stressed that it is policy within Israel to deal with each of the entities, the Palestinian Authority and Gaza, separately. Author interviews with Israeli security analysts. See also Ilana Feldman, "Isolating Gaza," *Stanford University Press Blog*, July 28, 2014, https://stanfordpress.typepad.com/blog/2014/07 /isolating-gaza.html; and Gisha, "What Is the 'Separation Policy'?" *Gisha: Legal Center for Freedom of Movement* (May 2012).

84. For more on the right to armed struggle, see Richard Falk, "International Law and the al-Aqsa Intifada," *Middle East Research and Information Project*, no. 30 (2000), https://merip.org/2000/12 /international-law-and-the-al-aqsa-intifada/.

85. Avi Raz, *The Bride and the Dowry: Israel, Jordan and the Palestinians in the Aftermath of the June 1967 War* (New Haven, CT: Yale University Press, 2012), 44. See also Seth Anziska and Tareq Baconi, "The Consequences of Conflict Management in Israel/Palestine," *Norwegian Peacebuilding Resource Center* (January 12, 2016): 1–8.

86. For a useful resource, see the website Gaza in Context, www.gazaincontext.com.

87. At least since the eruption of the Second Intifada, successive Israeli leaders have chosen not to engage with Palestinian political demands and have dealt with Palestinians primarily through the prism of Israel's security. See Sylvian Cypel, *Walled: Israeli Society at an Impasse* (New York: Other Press, 2006).

BIBLIOGRAPHY

Abrams, Elliott. *Tested by Zion: The Bush Administration and the Israeli-Palestinian Conflict.* Cambridge: Cambridge University Press, 2013.

Abu-Amr, Ziad. "The View from Palestine: In the Wake of the Agreement." *Journal of Palestine Studies* 23, no. 2 (1994): 75–83.

Alpher, Joseph. "Israel's Security Concerns in the Peace Process." *International Affairs* 70, no. 2 (1994): 229–41.

Andoni, Lamis. "The Palestinian Elections: Moving toward Democracy or One-Party Rule?" *Journal of Palestine Studies* 25, no. 3 (1996): 5–16.

Anziska, Seth, and Tareq Baconi. "The Consequences of Conflict Management in Israel/ Palestine." *Norwegian Peacebuilding Resource Center*, January 12, 2016, pp. 1–8.

Aruri, Naseer H., and John J. Carroll. "A New Palestinian Charter." *Journal of Palestine Studies* 23, no. 3 (1994): 5–17.

Ashhab, Naim. *Hamas: Min al-Rafd ila al-Saltah*. Ramallah: Dar al-Tanwir, 2006.

———. *Imarat Hamas*. Ramallah: Dar al-Tanwir, 2006.

Ayyash, Mark Muhannad. "Hamas and the Israeli State: A 'Violent Dialogue.'" *European Journal of International Relations* 16, no. 1 (2010): 103–23.

Baconi, Tareq. "The Demise of Oslo and Hamas's Political Engagement." *Conflict, Security and Development* 15, no. 5 (2015): 503–20.

———. "Politicizing Resistance: The Transformative Impact of the Second Intifada on Hamas's Resistance Strategy." In "Transformative Occupations in the Modern Middle East," special issue, *Humanity Journal* 8, no. 2 (2017): 311–33.

Baumgarten, Helga. "The Three Faces/Phases of Palestinian Nationalism, 1948–2005." *Journal of Palestine Studies* 34, no. 4 (2005): 25–48.

Ben-Ami, Shlomo. *Scars of War, Wounds of Peace*. Oxford: Oxford University Press, 2006.

Berrebi, Claude, and Esteban F. Klor. "On Terrorism and Electoral Outcomes: Theory and Evidence from the Israeli-Palestinian Conflict." *Journal of Conflict Resolution* 50, no. 6 (2006): 899—925.

Bloom, Mia. *Dying to Kill: The Allure of Suicide Terror*. New York: Columbia University Press, 2005.

Butler, Linda, ed. "A Gaza Chronology, 1948–2008," *Journal of Palestine Studies* 38, no. 3 (Spring 2009): 98–121.

Chamberlin, Paul Thomas. *The Global Offensive: The United States, the Palestine Liberation Organization, and the Making of the Post-Cold War Order*. Oxford: Oxford University Press, 2012.

Cohen, Hillel. "Society-Military Relations in a State-in-the-Making: Palestinian Security Agencies and the 'Treason Discourse' in the Second Intifada." *Armed Forces and Society* 38, no. 3 (2012): 463–85.

Cypel, Sylvain. *Walled: Israeli Society at an Impasse*. New York: Other Press, 2006.

Dolphin, Ray. *The West Bank Wall: Unmaking Palestine*. London: Pluto Press, 2006.

Eisenberg, Laura Zittrain, and Neil Caplan. *Negotiating Arab-Israeli Peace: Patterns, Problems, Possibilities*. Bloomington: Indiana University Press, 2010.

Elgindy, Khaled. "The Middle East Quartet: A Post-Mortem." *Brookings Institution* 25, February 2012, https://www.brookings.edu/wp-content/uploads/2016/06/02_middle_east_elgindy_b-1.pdf.

el-Mabhouh, Wael Abed Elhamid. *Opposition in the Political Thought of Hamas Movement, 1994–2006*. Beirut: Al Zaytouna Center, 2012.

Falk, Richard. "International Law and the al-Aqsa Intifada." *Middle East Research and Information Project* no. 217 (Winter 2000), https://merip.org/2000/12/international-law-and-the-al-aqsa-intifada/.

Farsakh, Leila. "The Palestinian Economy and the Oslo 'Peace Process.'" *Trans Arab Research Institute*. http://tari.org/index.php?option=com_content&view=article&id=9&Itemid=11, 2000.

———. *Palestinian Labour Migration to Israel: Labour, Land and Occupation*. New York: Routledge, 2005.

Feldman, Ilana. "Gaza's Humanitarianism Problem." *Journal of Palestine Studies* 38, no. 3 (2009): 22–37.

Filiu, Jean-Pierre. *Gaza: A History*. Translated by John King. Oxford: Oxford University Press, 2014.

———. "The Twelve Wars on Gaza." *Journal for Palestine Studies* 44, no. 1 (2014): 52–60.

Freedman, Lawrence. "Terrorism as Strategy." *Government and Opposition* 42, no. 3 (2007): 314–39.

Gisha. "Disengaged Occupiers: The Legal Status of Gaza." *Gisha: Legal Center for Freedom of Movement*, January 2007, https://gisha.org/publication/1649.

———. "What is the 'Separation Policy'?" *Gisha: Legal Center for Freedom of Movement*, May 2012, https://gisha.org/publication/1662.

Hever, Shir. *The Political Economy of Israel's Occupation Repression beyond Exploitation.* London: Pluto Press, 2010.

Hroub, Khaled. "Harakat Hamas Bayn al-Sulta al-Filastiniyyeh wa Israel: Min Muthalath al-Quwwa ila al-Mitraqa wa al-Sindan." *Majallat al-Dirasat al-Filastiniyyeh*, no. 18 (1994): 24–37.

Itani, Mariam. *Conflict of Authorities between Fatah and Hamas in Managing the Palestinian Authority, 2006–2007.* Beirut: Al-Zaytouna, 2008.

Jamal, Amal. *The Palestinian National Movement: Politics of Contention, 1967–2005.* Bloomington: Indiana University Press, 2005.

Kandil, Hazem. *Inside the Brotherhood.* London: Polity Press, 2014.

Karmon, Ely. "Hamas's Terrorism Strategy: Operational Limitations and Political Constraints." *Middle East Review of International Affairs* 4, no. 1 (2000): 66—79.

Khalidi, Ahmad S. "Al-Tahuwwlat al-Istratigiyyeh al-Askariyyeh wa al-Amniyyeh al-Israeliyyeh." Paper presented at the Institute for Palestine Studies Conference in Ramallah, 2015.

———. "The Palestinians' First Excursion into Democracy." *Journal of Palestine Studies* 25, no. 4 (1996): 20–28.

Khalidi, Rashid. "The Dahiya Doctrine, Proportionality, and War Crimes." *Institute for Palestine Studies*, no. 44 (2014–15): 5–13.

———. *The Iron Cage: The Story of the Palestinian Struggle for Statehood.* Boston: Beacon Press, 2006.

Khalil, Osamah. "Pax Americana: The United States, the Palestinians, and the Peace Process, 1948–2008." *The New Centennial Review* 8, no. 2 (2008): 1–42.

Kimmerling, Baruch. *Politicide: Ariel Sharon's War against the Palestinians.* London: Verso, 2003.

Kimmerling, Baruch, and Joel S. Migdal. *The Palestinian People: A History.* Cambridge, MA: Harvard University Press, 2003.

Kristianasen, Wendy. "Challenge and Counterchallenge: Hamas's Response to Oslo." *Journal of Palestine Studies* 28, no. 3 (1999): 19–39.

Kurz, Anat, and Shlomo Brom, eds. *The Lessons of Operation Protective Edge.* Tel Aviv: Institute for National Security Studies, 2014.

Kuttab, Daoud. "Current Developments and the Peace Process." *Journal of Palestine Studies* 22, no. 1 (1992): 100–7.

Kydd, Andrew, and Barbara F. Walter. "Sabotaging the Peace: The Politics of Extremist Violence." *International Organization* 56, no. 2 (2002): 263–96.

Landau, David. *Arik: The Life of Ariel Sharon.* New York: Alfred and Knopf, 2013.

Milton-Edwards, Beverley. *Islamic Politics in Palestine.* London: I.B. Tauris, 1996.

———. "Political Islam in Palestine in an Environment of Peace?" *Third World Quarterly* 17, no. 2 (1996): 119–225.

Perry, Mark. *Talking to Terrorists: Why America Must Engage with Its Enemies.* New York: Basic Books, 2010.

Quandt, William B. *Peace Process: American Diplomacy and the Arab Israeli Conflict since 1967.* Berkeley: University of California Press, 2001.

Raz, Avi. *The Bride and the Dowry: Israel, Jordan and the Palestinians in the Aftermath of the June 1967 War.* New Haven, CT: Yale University Press, 2012.

Rice, Condoleezza. *No Higher Honor: A Memoir of My Years in Washington.* New York: Crown Publishers, 2011.

Roy, Sara. "De-Development Revisited: Palestinian Economy and Society since Oslo." *Journal of Palestine Studies* 28, no. 3 (1999): 64–82.

———. *Failing Peace: Gaza and the Palestinian-Israeli Conflict.* London: Pluto Press, 2007.

———. *The Gaza Strip: The Political Economy of De-development.* Washington, DC: Institute for Palestine Studies, 1995.

———. *Hamas and Civil Society in Gaza: Engaging the Islamist Social Sector.* Princeton, NJ: Princeton University Press, 2011.

———. "Palestinian Society and Economy: The Continued Denial of Possibility." *Journal of Palestine Studies* 30, no. 4 (2001): 5–20.

———. "Praying with Their Eyes Closed: Reflections on the Disengagement from Gaza." *Journal of Palestine Studies* 34, no. 4 (2005): 64–74.

Rynhold, Jonathan, and Dov Waxman. "Ideological Change and Israel's Disengagement from Gaza." *Political Science Quarterly* 123, no. 1 (2008): 11–37.

Said, Edward W. *The Politics of Dispossession: The Struggle for Palestinian Self-Determination, 1969–1994.* New York: Pantheon Books, 1994.

Sayigh, Yezid. *Armed Struggle and the Search for State: Palestinian National Movement, 1949–1993.* Oxford: Oxford University Press, 1997.

———. "Inducing a Failed State in Palestine." *Survival* 49, no. 3 (2007): 7–40.

———. "Struggle within, Struggle Without: The Transformation of PLO Politics since 1982." *International Affairs* 65, no. 2 (1989): 247–71.

Seitz, Charmaine. "Hamas Stands Down?" *Middle East Report*, no. 221 (2001): 4–7.

Shlaim, Avi. "The Oslo Accord." *Journal of Palestine Studies* 23, no. 3 (1994): 24–40.

Sorkin, Michael, ed. *Against the Wall: Israel's Barrier to Peace.* New York: New Press, 2005.

Stedman, Stephen. "Spoiler Problems in Peace Processes." *International Security* 22, no. 2 (1997): 5–53.

Turner, Mandy, and Omar Shweiki, eds. *Decolonizing Palestinian Political Economy: De-development and Beyond.* London: Palgrave Macmillan, 2014.

Usher, Graham. "The Politics of Internal Security: The PA's New Intelligence Services." *Journal of Palestine Studies* 25, no. 3 (1996): 21–34.

Weizman, Eyal. *Hollow Land: Israel's Architecture of Occupation.* London: Verso, 2007.

Yasin, Abd al-Qadir. *Hamas: Harakat al-Muqawamah al-Islamiyah fi Filastin.* Cairo: Sina lil Nashr, 1990.

Zahhar, Mahmud, and Hussein Hijazi. "Hamas: Waiting for Secular Nationalism to Self-Destruct. An Interview with Mahmud Zahhar." *Journal of Palestine Studies* 24, no. 3 (1995): 81–88.

Zoughbie, Daniel E. *Indecision Points: George W. Bush and the Israeli-Palestinian Conflict.* Cambridge, MA: MIT Press, 2014.

3

The Forgotten Palestinians

East Jerusalem and the Oslo Peace Process

Hania Walid Assali

According to the Palestine Liberation Organization's 1988 Declaration of Independence, East Jerusalem (the Arab side of the city) is the capital of the envisioned Palestinian state. The Oslo Accords, signed between the PLO and the government of Israel in the early 1990s, defined Jerusalem as one of seven "permanent status" issues, to be negotiated at a future point as part of negotiations on a permanent status agreement. Such negotiations subsequently started and broke down at several points, including in 1996 and 1999–2001. This effort peaked with the Camp David Summit of 2000 and the Taba Talks of 2001, both of which used the framework of the Oslo process and ultimately ended in failure. In 2012, the PLO again announced its state, with its capital as East Jerusalem, this time at the United Nations, to which it was admitted as a nonmember state. Despite having been recognized by 138 countries, the Palestinian state, let alone its capital, has failed to materialize.

Rather, twenty-eight years after the Oslo Accords—and more than twenty years beyond the timeline stipulated in the original accords—the negotiations over the permanent-status issues have completely broken down, and the Oslo process has been declared dead.[1] This failure has taken a particularly high toll on East Jerusalem and its approximately 330,000 Palestinian residents.[2]

This chapter explores how the Oslo Accords failed to lay the groundwork for East Jerusalem to become the future capital of the State of Palestine. It exposes how Israel consolidated its control over the eastern side of Jerusalem, in support of its goal of keeping the entire city as its unified capital and Judaizing it, in violation of international law.

Since 1991 Israel has effectively severed East Jerusalem from the West Bank, for which it was formerly a central hub. Throughout the Oslo years, Israel took myriad unilateral measures against both land and people aimed at making any future division of the city impossible. Israel's actions and sweeping statements clearly demonstrate not only that it does not intend to relinquish control over East Jerusalem, but also that it intends to transform it from an Arab urban space to a Jewish one. On the flip side, the Palestinian National Authority (PNA), established as part of the Oslo Accords, failed to counter Israel's unilateral measures. Palestinians in Jerusalem ended up feeling abandoned and left to fend for themselves with the scant political and social resources available to them.

Today, the demise of the peace process and the vanishing possibility for the two-state solution it envisioned requires us to examine anew how drastically the situation for Palestinians living in Jerusalem has changed in the decades since Oslo, and what can potentially be done about it. This need is all the more urgent in view of the United States's formal recognition in December 2017 of Jerusalem as the capital of Israel, US efforts to impose a regional "deal" to terminate the Israeli-Palestinian conflict, and the ongoing rapprochement between Israel, Saudi Arabia, and certain Gulf countries, notably the United Arab Emirates, which culminated with the signing of the Abraham Accords in August 2020. These accords normalize economic and diplomatic relationships between Israel and the United Arab Emirates and Bahrain.

To this end, this chapter is divided into four parts: first, it provides an overview of the status of the city and its Palestinian residents since 1967. Next, it focuses on the toll that the Oslo years have had on East Jerusalem as a *territory*. Third, it delves into the impact of these developments on the city's Palestinian *residents*. Finally, the chapter explores what may lie ahead for East Jerusalem and its Palestinian residents.

EAST JERUSALEM SINCE 1967: AN OVERVIEW

During the 1967 war, Israel occupied East Jerusalem, along with the rest of the West Bank, the Gaza Strip, the Golan Heights, and the Sinai Peninsula. After the war, Israel illegally annexed East Jerusalem, redrew its boundaries, and expanded them to include the maximum amount of territory, with the fewest number of Jerusalemite Palestinians, in order to ensure a Jewish majority in the city.[3] This expansion was formally approved by Israel's cabinet on July 26, 1967, and by the Knesset two days later. It brought the combined East and West Jerusalem area to a total of 108 square kilometers with a population ratio of 74.2 percent Jewish to 25.8 percent Palestinian Arab.[4] The newly expanded total area was comprised of 38 square kilometers of West Jerusalem, 6 square kilometers that had been the Jordanian-administered area of East Jerusalem, and 64 square kilometers of additional annexed land that belonged to twenty-eight adjacent Palestinian villages in the West Bank.[5]

Israel immediately proceeded to apply Israeli law to the total expanded municipal area. It issued Law and Administration Ordinance (Amendment No. 11) 5727 of 1967, which included language from Section 11B of Law and Administration

Ordinance No. 5708 of 1948. Section 11B reads as follows: "The law, jurisdiction and administration of the State shall extend to any area of *Eretz Israel* designated by the Government by order." By virtue of this provision, the Minister of the Interior ordered on June 28, 1967 the expansion of the municipal boundaries of the Jerusalem municipality and ensured the application of Israeli law within it.

Israel did not, however, explicitly state in any of the above amendments that it was annexing East Jerusalem, nor did it affirm that it was applying its sovereignty over East Jerusalem. Israel simply started applying Israeli law to East Jerusalem. It went for a de facto rather than a declared annexation, hoping to stay under the radar and avoid international condemnation—and hoping that the de facto annexation would become a fait accompli somewhere down the line.[6] In 1980, Israel passed Law no. 5740, Jerusalem, Capital of Israel, which states that Jerusalem is the complete and united capital of Israel. UN Security Council Resolution 478 in 1980 affirmed that this law constitutes a violation of international law, declared its enactment null and void, and decided not to recognize it.[7] The annexation of East Jerusalem is illegal under international law in light of the inadmissibility of territory acquired through the use or threat of use of force, as codified into article 2(4) of the UN Charter and reiterated in UN General Assembly Resolution 2253 and UN Security Council Resolution 242. Accordingly, the international community has never recognized the annexation and has continuously declared it null and void. The only exception came from the Trump US administration, which broke with the international consensus and all diplomatic precedents and recognized Jerusalem as Israel's capital in December 2017.

Israel, however, had little concern for the international illegality of its territorial annexation of East Jerusalem. Its major interest was rather in devising legal, urban, and demographic strategies that would enable it to incorporate the city without its Palestinian population. Israel considered the Palestinians of East Jerusalem a liability that needed to be contained if not dissolved. In June 1967, just after occupying East Jerusalem and annexing it, Israel conducted a census in the annexed area. It declared that Palestinians who happened to be absent at that time had lost the right to return to their homes. Only Palestinians who were present in their homes in East Jerusalem during the census were given the status of "permanent residents." This status was given to them on the basis of the Entry into Israel Law enacted in 1952, even though East Jerusalemites had not "entered" "Israel"; rather, Israel "entered" the area where they lived by means of belligerent occupation.

It is important to try to understand why East Jerusalemites were granted permanent residency, in contrast to the Palestinians who remained in 1948 and on whom Israeli citizenship was imposed in 1952, and those present in the West Bank and the Gaza Strip (WBGS) after the 1967 war, who were given identification cards by the Israeli authorities. Elements of an answer are cited in a 2012 book by Ir Amim's publication: "In June 1967, during discussions to determine the legal framework required to apply Israeli law to the area, officials considered

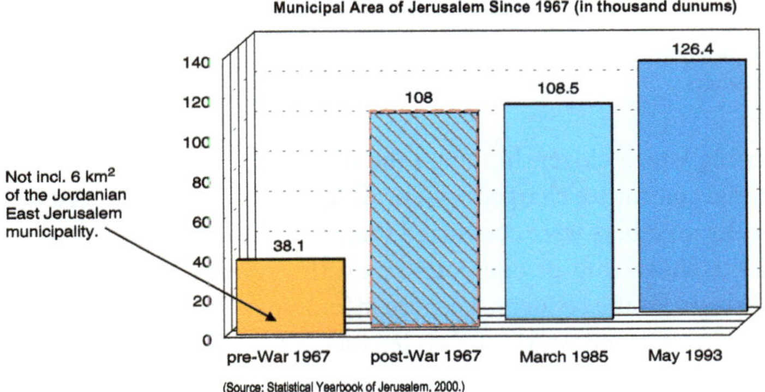

MAP 8. Municipal boundaries of Jerusalem, 1947–2000. Source: Palestinian Academic Society for the Study of International Affairs.

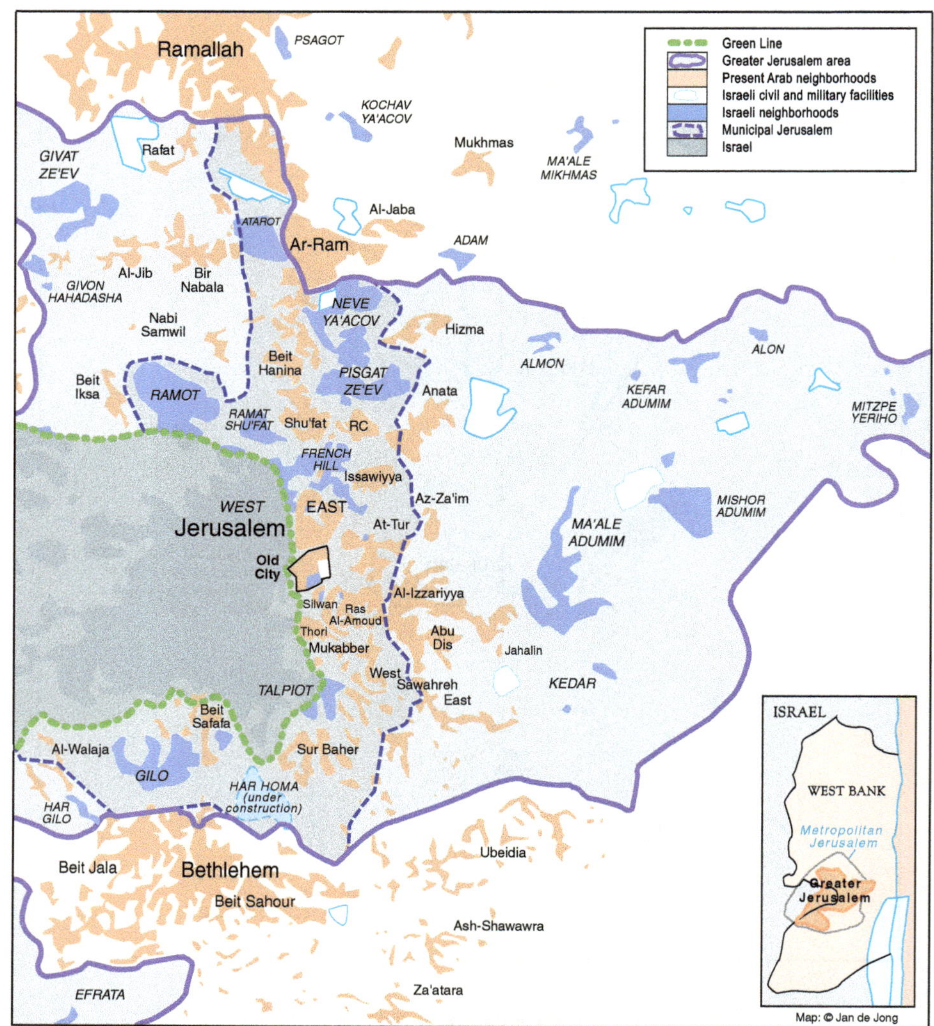

MAP 9. Greater and metropolitan Jerusalem, 2000. Source: Palestinian Academic Society for the Study of International Affairs.

the idea of imposing Israeli citizenship upon the residents of the annexed territory. The ministerial committee charged with drafting the unification procedures rejected the idea. Its members were convinced that the rules of international law forbade forcing the citizenship of one country on the citizens of another. An opposing proposal—to let the residents keep their Jordanian identity cards—was also ruled out. In the end, the Arabs of East Jerusalem became Israeli residents with Jordanian citizenship."[8] Meanwhile, Israel worked on maintaining a Jewish demographic majority in the city. In 1973, the Gafni Committee recommendation on "development rates" for Jerusalem was adopted by the Israeli government, calling for the percentages of Jews and Arabs to be preserved at their levels of 1972, that is, at 73.5 percent Jews and 25.5 percent Palestinians.[9] Granting East Jerusalemites residency rather than citizenship was a means of controlling the Palestinian population growth in the city since residency, by definition, requires constant verification and is subject to revocation.

The 1952 Entry into Israel Law, though, does not explicitly provide for a permit for permanent residency to expire if the permit holder leaves Israel and settles abroad. Provisions to that effect exist in Amendment 2 of the Entry into Israel Law Regulations no. 5734 of 1974.[10] In 1985, that amendment was introduced into Section 11(c) and Section 11A. Section 11(c) states that the validity of a permanent residency expires if the permit holder leaves Israel and settles in another country. Section 11A states that a person shall be considered as having settled in another country if any one of the following applies: (1) s/he stayed outside Israel for a period of at least seven years; (2) s/he received temporary residency in that country; or (3) s/he received citizenship of that country by way of naturalization.

Jerusalem in the Oslo Accords

As noted, the first Oslo Accord (officially called the Declaration of Principles on Interim Self-Government Arrangements, or the Declaration of Principles [DOP], and known simply Oslo I) relegated negotiation over Jerusalem—as a permanent-status issue—to a later stage. Article V2 of Oslo I stipulates that "Permanent status negotiations will commence as soon as possible, but not later than the beginning of the third year of the interim period, between the Government of Israel and the Palestinian people representatives."[11] Article V3 continues, "It is understood that these negotiations shall cover remaining issues, including: Jerusalem, refugees, settlements, security arrangements, border, relations and cooperation with their neighbors, and other issues of common interest." While Article IV specifies that "the two sides view the West Bank and the Gaza Strip as a single territorial unit, whose integrity will be preserved during the interim period," it was not specified if that territorial unit includes East Jerusalem.

The 1995 second Oslo Accord excluded Jerusalem from the jurisdiction of the new Palestinian Authority. Chapter 3, Article XVII stipulated that "the jurisdiction of the Council will cover West Bank and Gaza Strip territory, except for issues that will be negotiated in the permanent-status negotiations."[12]

The Oslo Accords also did not provide any protection to the territorial integrity of East Jerusalem or its Palestinian residents. As far as the latter, the Oslo Accords afforded them only the right to participate in the election process of the Palestinian Legislative Council (PLC).[13] However, this "right to representation" is in fact superfluous, because, as noted, the PNA and the PLO were given no jurisdiction over East Jerusalem. The lack of protection for either East Jerusalem as an urban space or its Palestinian residents meant that Israel had a free hand to tighten its grip over East Jerusalem, especially as negotiations continued to drag on.

ISRAEL'S CONSOLIDATION OF TERRITORIAL CONTROL IN THE WAKE OF OSLO

Since the Oslo Accords were signed, Israel has taken several unilateral actions to sever East Jerusalem from its hinterland. These included severing Jerusalem from its natural hinterland, the West Bank, via restricting entry and constructing the Separation Wall as well as expanding Jewish settlements and targeting the heart of East Jerusalem—the Old City and its surrounding basin.[14]

Settlement Activity and Urban Planning

As early as 1968 Israel started building settlements to create facts on the ground, focusing first on the Arab areas of what it had declared to be "municipal Jerusalem" in 1967, on land confiscated from the West Bank. Between 1968 and 1977, Israel built eight settlements hosting 33,300 settlers, compared with only 4,300 in the rest of the West Bank.[15] In 1982, a document prepared for Mayor Teddy Kollek's international advisory council, the Jerusalem Committee, stated that the ring of settlements surrounding Jerusalem would provide a necessary buffer against any political or military pressure to make a compromise on Jerusalem. This document added that "the overriding, undisputed principle underlying Jerusalem's planning is the realization of her unity. . . . [by] building up the city in such a way as to preclude the bi-polar emergence of two national communities and forestall any possibility of re-dividing it along such lines."[16] By 1986, a total of 103,9000 settlers lived in eleven settlements in East Jerusalem, equaling the number of Palestinians living in what was defined as "municipal Jerusalem."[17]

Israel's settlement ideology sought the "Judaization" and "de-Arabization" of the city, as well as the isolation of Jerusalem from the West Bank and the fragmentation of the Palestinian neighborhoods within the city.[18] By 1993, just as the Oslo Accords were negotiated, a total of 137,400 settlers lived in settlements around Jerusalem and Israel had no intention to stop their development.

During the Oslo years, Israel built two new settlements (one of them Har Homa) around Jerusalem on confiscated West Bank land, and there was a surge of new hardcore religious settlements in the heart of Palestinian neighborhoods, in concentrated outposts in the so-called "visual basin of the Old City." Moreover, in 1995, just as Israel was negotiating the Oslo II agreement and supposedly deferring any action on Jerusalem to permanent-status negotiations, the Rabin government officially adopted the Greater Jerusalem Master Plan.[19] This plan incorporated Jewish settlements in the West Bank that are not part of municipal Jerusalem. The plan's strategic aim was to secure Israeli domination over the entire central portion of the West Bank and prevent the establishment of a viable Palestinian state. It was revived in 2000, at the Camp David Summit. According

Number of Israeli settlers in West Bank and East Jerusalem Settlements, 1972–2017

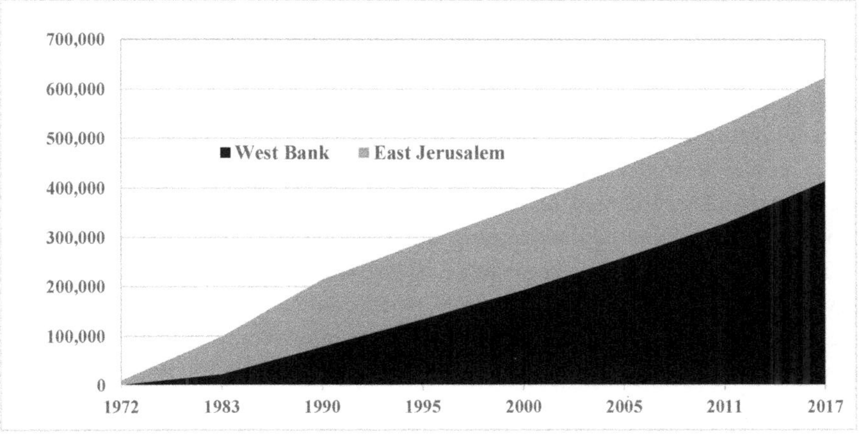

Source: ICBS, Statistical Abstract of Israel, various years and Btselem.

FIGURE 1. Number of Israeli settlers in West Bank and East Jerusalem settlements, 1972–2017. Source: Israeli Central Bureau of Statistics, *Statistical Abstract of Israel*, and B'Tselem, "Statistics on Settlements and Settler Population," last updated January 16, 2019, at https://www.btselem .org/settlements/statistics.

to Jeff Halper, during Camp David, the then-Israeli Prime Minister Ehud Barak believed that "expanding Jerusalem outward to include the outer settlement ring would make the division of the city not only impossible but also advantageous to Israel: expanding Israel's territorial control and boosting its demographic majority in order to neutralize the demographic and political costs of 'conceding' parts of East Jerusalem."[20]

The Greater Jerusalem plan, which expanded the boundaries of Jerusalem to a diameter of one hundred miles was in essence an annexationist plan and remains so today. This plan was submitted in two bills to the Knesset in 2017.[21] The Rabin government also adopted the Metropolitan Jerusalem Plan, which extended the total area to 950 square kilometers, in the same year. Both plans' strategic aim was to secure Israeli domination over the entire core of the West Bank and prevent the establishment of a viable Palestinian state.[22]

By 2018, East Jerusalem had fifteen Israeli settlements with 213,000 Israeli settlers living in an estimated sixty thousand housing units. About three thousand Israeli settlers live in the heart of Palestinian neighborhoods in outposts concentrated in the so "visual basin of the old city" area, which includes the Muslim and Christian quarters of the Old City, Silwan, Sheikh Jarrah, At-Tur (Mount of Olives), Wadi Al-Joz, Ras Al-'Amud, and Jabal Al-Mukabber. Settlement blocks surrounding municipal Jerusalem house over 100,000 Israeli settlers who are thus incorporated within "Greater Jerusalem."[23]

Another important tool that Israel used to advance its goals in East Jerusalem is urban planning. Israel's plans are aimed at creating "urban facts which would make any future division of the city practically impossible."[24] Israel discriminates against Palestinians through the master plans and town planning schemes that it formulates for the city of Jerusalem, and "East Jerusalemites are unable to receive permits to build or renovate their homes; and if they build without permits, Israeli authorities demolish their homes."[25] Moreover, Israeli laws "limit the election of certain positions in Jerusalem solely to Israeli citizens; for example, 'a person who is not an Israeli citizen' cannot serve as a board member or executive member of the Jerusalem Development Authority. The Jerusalem Development Authority has broad powers concerning the planning and development of Jerusalem."[26]

Indeed, Israel's intentions regarding East Jerusalem, irrespective of which Israeli government is in power, have not changed since 1967. Less than three years after the signing of Oslo I, Israeli Prime Minister Benjamin Netanyahu began to use the words "undivided" and "eternal" in relation to Jerusalem. In his speech to a joint session of the US Congress in Washington, DC on July 10, 1996, the newly elected Netanyahu said, "There have been efforts to redivide this city by those who claim that peace can come through division—that it can be secured through multiple sovereignties, multiple laws and multiple police forces. This is a groundless and dangerous assumption, which impels me to declare today: There will never be such a re-division of Jerusalem. Never. We shall not allow a Berlin Wall to be erected inside Jerusalem. We will not drive out anyone, but neither shall we be driven out of any quarter, any neighborhood, any street of our eternal capital."[27]

Closure, Checkpoints, and the Separation Wall

In January 1991, in the wake of the First Intifada and during the Gulf War, Israel revoked the general exit permit for residents of the Occupied Territories wishing to enter Jerusalem, marking the beginning of the permanent closure policy.[28] On March 30 1993, during Israeli Prime Minister Yitzhak Rabin's term and following a series of stabbings, Israel imposed an overall closure on the Occupied Territories "until further notice." To enforce the closure, Israel set up military checkpoints along the Green Line separating the West Bank from Jerusalem. Permits for Palestinians from the West Bank to enter Jerusalem for any reason were issued only sparingly.[29]

Israel also began curtailing the activities of Palestinian institutions in East Jerusalem. From 1967 to 1995, Jerusalem had been "the home for Palestinian newspaper publishers, the main printing presses and publishing houses, the best hospitals, the most important schools, the largest and most important commercial market, the center for trade union associations, and so on. It was the undisputed economic center and the center of the national movement and its official and unofficial leadership and institutions."[30] In October 2000, as the Second Intifada erupted in the wake of Ariel Sharon's deliberate provocation in the form of visiting the Al-Aqsa mosque surrounded by a phalanx of Israeli soldiers, then-Israeli Prime Minister Ehud Barak approved plans to establish more permanent checkpoints and barriers across the entire West Bank to stop Palestinians from entering Israel.[31] In March 2001, Sharon's government ordered the closure of the Orient House, the historic building and institution that had served as the unofficial PLO headquarters in Jerusalem in the late 1980s and early 1990s and was a center for Palestinian national work, diplomatic relations, community support, and cultural and economic development projects in East Jerusalem.[32] The closure of the Orient House happened less than four months after the sudden death of the Palestinian East Jerusalemite leader Faisal Hussayni in a hotel in Kuwait. Under his leadership, the Orient House had become the Palestinian political center of East Jerusalem. Its closure marked the end of the leadership role that Jerusalem had enjoyed in Palestinian life up until 1995, when the late Yasser Arafat set up the PNA headquarters in Ramallah. Israel also closed other Palestinian organizations in the city, notably the chamber of commerce. Several of those Palestinian institutions that had not been closed by Israel were left with no choice but to relocate to Ramallah, especially after Israel closed the city to the West Bank and then started the construction of the Separation Wall in 2002.

In 2002, Israel started construction of the Separation Wall, designed to include as many Israeli settlements while excluding as many Palestinian neighborhoods as possible. The total length of the Separation Wall total is 712 kilometers, of which only 15 percent run along the Green Line. The length of the wall in Jerusalem reaches approximately 140 kilometers, of which only four kilometers runs along the Green Line. Its route severs entire Palestinian neighborhoods from the city, not only minimizing their development potential but also keeping large areas of open space areas as reserves for the future expansion of Jewish settlements. Today 140,000 Palestinian East Jerusalemites live in neighborhoods that lie beyond the wall and as a result do not receive any municipal services from the Jerusalem municipality. The Jerusalem municipality does not provide services to these neighborhoods because they are located on the other side of the Separation Wall, although legally their residents live in the municipality of Jerusalem. On the other hand, the Palestinian National Authority (PNA) does not provide services to these residents because it has no jurisdiction to do so. "These neighborhoods have remained a sort of 'no man's land' in which the warning of an impending humanitarian disaster is screaming from the walls. . . . Police responsibility for these neighborhoods resides with Israel, according to its own decision and made ironclad by the legal constraints [previously described]; as a result, on the day of reckoning, it is Israel that will be called upon to give a moral accounting both to itself and to the international community."[33]

On July 9, 2004, the International Court of Justice in the Hague published its advisory opinion on the Separation Wall. It held that both construction of the wall and the regime that Israel instituted to accompany it violate international law, and that Israel must tear it down and compensate the Palestinians who suffered losses as a result of its construction.[34] The checkpoints and illegal Separation Wall continue to infringe upon the fundamental rights of Palestinians to freedom of movement and to family unity.[35]

*Legal Entrenchments Aimed at Impeding Future Territorial
Concessions in Jerusalem*

Over the last ten years, Israel has enacted legislation aiming at creating legal barriers to conceding any East Jerusalem territory, in case the government of Israel was to reach an agreement with other parties or decide to do so unilaterally.[36] Thus, in 2000, Israeli Basic Law: Jerusalem, Capital of Israel, 5740–1980 was amended by the insertion of Sections 5, 6, and 7.[37] Section 5 states for the first time that "the jurisdiction of Jerusalem includes, as pertaining to this Basic Law, among other things, all of the area that is described in the appendix of the proclamation expanding the borders of municipal Jerusalem beginning 20 Sivan, 5727 (June 28, 1967), as was given according to the Municipalities Ordinance."

Section 6 specifies that "no authority that is stipulated in the law of the State of Israel or of the Jerusalem municipality may be transferred either permanently, or for an allotted period of time, to a foreign body, whether political, governmental, or any other similar type of foreign body." As for Section 7, it was inserted to entrench the above two sections. It states that Sections 5 and 6 cannot be modified except by a basic law passed by a majority of Knesset [Parliament] members (MKs).

In 2014, further entrenchment took place with Basic Law: Referendum, no. 5774–2014.[38] This law stipulates that Israel's sovereignty over part of its territory may not be waived unless the government has so decided, and its decision is ratified by a two-thirds majority of MKs as well as by a referendum. All these enactments are intended to render difficult, if not impossible, any future division of Jerusalem between Israel and the Palestinians.

In 2018, yet another entrenchment was undertaken by further amending Basic Law: Jerusalem, Capital of Israel, with the aim of impeding any future division of the city. The amendment stipulates that the government must obtain a super-majority of 80 of the 120 MKs in order to transfer to a foreign entity any "authority pertaining to the area of the Jerusalem Municipality." However, it is possible to change this statutory requirement for a super-majority through a simple majority vote by only sixty-one MKs. This same stipulations would also make it possible to change the city's municipal boundaries by a simple majority, rather than a super majority of MKs, as it did before. The Knesset thus paved the way for the realization of its goal to advance the Greater Jerusalem plan.[39] In 2017, two bill proposals were submitted in the Knesset with the aim of putting five settlement blocks under Jerusalem's municipal jurisdiction and of disconnecting from the Jerusalem municipality the Palestinian neighborhoods of Kufr Aqab and Shua'fat, which lie beyond the Separation Wall, placing them under a different municipal Israeli authority.[40] As of this writing, these proposals have not yet been passed, but their success is likely given the immunity that Israel continues to have.

Thus with the advent of the Oslo peace process, Israel finalized the process by which East Jerusalem became a forbidden city for all Palestinians from the West Bank and the Gaza Strip. For them, going to East Jerusalem—surrounded by

Jewish settlements and the Separation Wall—has become an unreachable dream. That said, in the eyes of international law and the international community, East Jerusalem is still an occupied territory.

DEMOGRAPHIC ENGINEERING: ACCELERATING PALESTINIAN EXPULSION FROM EAST JERUSALEM POST-OSLO

Alongside these sweeping changes in land, planning, and access, Israel implemented a variety of harsh policies and administrative measures to discourage demographic growth among Jerusalem's Arab population. Since 1967, Israeli leaders have adopted two basic principles in their rule of the Palestinian residents in East Jerusalem.[41] The first was to hinder by any means the growth of the Arab population and to force Arab residents to make their homes elsewhere. The second was to rapidly increase the Jewish population in East Jerusalem. The building of settlements was a key element for increasing the number of Israelis in East Jerusalem, as noted. Israel also introduced and enhanced administrative measures to deprive Palestinians of their residence rights.

The "Center of Life" Policy: The 1988 Mubarak Awad Case

In regulating the permanent residency of Palestinians in East Jerusalem, one case in particular became notorious for the ways in which Israel devised legalistic measures to curtail the rights of Palestinian residents of East Jerusalem to live in their city: the Mubarak Awad case of 1988.[42] Mubarak Awad, an East Jerusalemite, was born and raised in Jerusalem. In the 1970s, he left for the United States to study and work. In the 1980s, he returned to live in Jerusalem but was ultimately deported by the Israeli authorities. In his case, the Supreme Court of Israel ruled that eligibility for the right of residence and loss thereof are decided in accordance with the Entry into Israel Law of 1952 and with the Entry into Israel Regulations of 1974, issued in accordance with the 1952 law. The Court rejected the argument that Palestinian Jerusalemites have a special status that provides them with "quasi-citizenship" or "constitutional residency" that cannot be revoked by the Minister of the Interior.[43] Justice Aharon Barak held that "permanent residency" might also "automatically expire," either because it had surpassed its period of validity or because the premise on which it rests—actual permanent residency in Israel—had expired."[44] He went beyond the provisions of the 1974 regulations and held that "a permit for permanent residency, when granted, is based on a reality of permanent residency. Once this reality no longer exists, the permit expires of itself."[45] He thus went beyond the written law as it existed in the 1974 regulations and formulated a new principle, the "center of life" principle. Barak further stated, "Awad's acquisition of American citizenship signified that his 'center of life' is no longer [Israel]," regardless of the fact that "in his heart of hearts he aspired to return to [Israel]."[46]

After the Oslo Accords, the "center of life" principle came to be one of the most harmful policies for Palestinian residents of East Jerusalem. In the Shiqaqi case of June 1995, Fathiya Shiqaqi lost her permanent residency rights despite the fact that none of the situations specified in Section 11A of the Entry into Israel Law of 1952 applied to her. She had remained outside Israel for less than seven years and had not received citizenship or permanent residency in any foreign country. At the time of her case, she had been living with her husband and her children in Syria for six years after her husband was deported from Israel. In her case, Justice Goldberg stated, "The appearance of a new reality, changing the reality of permanent residency in Israel, is clearly indicated by circumstances other than those mentioned in regulation 11A of the [Entry into Israel Law]."[47]

After the Shiqaqi case, Israel started to apply the "center of life" principle introduced in the 1988 Awad case aggressively and across the board. By end of 1996, 739 Palestinian East Jerusalemites had their residencies revoked. By end of 1997, the total annual number jumped to 1,067. In 2006, the number reached 1,363, and in 2008, it skyrocketed to 4,577.[48]

The "center of life" principle was not utilized by the Israeli Ministry of the Interior until after the Oslo Accords, when Jerusalem had been defined as a permanent-status issue. Up until 1995, a Palestinian resident of East Jerusalem could lose his or her residency status only by settling outside Israel for a period of seven years without renewing the exit permit or by receiving the status of resident or citizen in another country. The Israeli Ministry of Interior regularly renewed exit permits and registered changes to family status. Also, before 1995, Palestinian East Jerusalemites who moved elsewhere in the WBGS were not required to have permits to exit and enter Jerusalem, and some even continued to receive the allotments from the National Insurance Institute that they had received prior to leaving the city.[49]

After 1995, the interpretation of the term "outside Israel" was expanded to include residency in the WBGS, effectuated through a directive issued by the legal advisor of the Ministry of the Interior to the East Jerusalem office. This meant that all Palestinian East Jerusalemites who had lived for a period of time in a foreign country or in the WBGS were liable to lose their rights as Jerusalem residents. This policy remained unclear on how much time spent outside Israel in a foreign country could cost a person his or her residency, and it has been applied arbitrarily.[50] Even worse, the Israeli Interior Ministry did not publicize it at the time and then applied it retroactively.[51] Between 1995 and 2017, Israel revoked the status of 11,555 Palestinians from East Jerusalem as opposed to 3,078 revocations during the period from 1967 till 1994.[52]

This "center of life" policy came to be known as "silent transfer" or "quiet deportation," intended to further reduce the Palestinian population in Jerusalem after the Oslo Accords. As a result of numerous legal challenges against this policy by various Arab and Israeli civil society organizations, though, the Sharansky Declaration was issued in 2000. Named after then-Minister of the Interior Natan

Sharansky, it provided for the reinstatement of residency status on a case-by-case basis under a rigorous set of criteria, including the period of absence of the residents, retention of connection with East Jerusalem during their absence, reasons for obtaining citizenship or residency in another country, and years of residency in East Jerusalem after return. However, this measure led to the reinstatement of the residency of only a few hundred East Jerusalem residents.

On March 14, 2017, the High Court of Justice issued the Al-Haq ruling, in which it recognized East Jerusalemites as "native-born residents." Al-Haq was nine years old when his family moved from Jerusalem to the United States. Years later, as a married adult, he wanted to move back to his native city and was told that he didn't have the right to do so. The Court ruled that Israel must consider the unique status of Palestinian East Jerusalemites as native-born when deciding whether to restore their residency status.[53] In this particular case, the High Court shifted away from the discriminatory legal precedents of the Awad and Shiqaqi cases. However, this ruling does not eliminate the possibility of revocation of residency of East Jerusalem residents according to the Awad precedent, as it adds weight in favor of restoring status only in cases of purportedly "expired" residency following a long stay abroad—excluding the WBGS—or the acquisition of foreign status. The most striking aspect of Israel's residency regulations is how deeply discriminatory they are: Israeli citizens, including Jewish settlers in East Jerusalem, can live anywhere in the world for as long as they wish without losing their citizenship or any of the rights it entails.

Special Complications Facing "Mixed" Families

In families where a Palestinian East Jerusalemite marries a Palestinian from the West Bank or Gaza, issues of family unification and child registration further complicate the picture. Until early 1990, Palestinian residents of the WBGS could live with their Palestinian East Jerusalemite spouses and children without needing special permits. As noted, in 1991, Israel started to require personal entry permits issued by the military commander for residents of the WBGS who wished to enter Jerusalem (or Israel generally). Initially such permits were issued with almost no restriction and for relatively long periods. Gradually, however, the issuance of permits tightened. Today, only a few permits are issued and according to unknown criteria. Palestinians from the WBGS without permits who choose to live long-term in Jerusalem with their spouses and families are under the constant threat of deportation. As of March 1993, when Israel started imposing a sweeping closure on the WBGS, it became extremely difficult for couples in which one spouse has a Jerusalem ID and the other has a West Bank or Gaza Strip ID to live together. Many resorted to filing for family unification, although they had been married for years. In 1996, Israel instituted a graduated procedure that stipulated that permanent residency status was to be given five years and three months from the day the family unification application was approved (rather than immediately upon approval, as was the case before 1996). In practice, the entire process lasts for much longer than stipulated, due to foot-dragging by the Ministry of the Interior.

In 2003, to the further detriment of Palestinian family life, the Israeli government issued the Citizenship and Entry into Israel Law (Temporary Order), 5763–2003, which has been renewed year after year since its enactment. Its main purpose is to prohibit Palestinians from the WBGS who are married to Palestinian East Jerusalem residents from applying for family unification and permanent residency (or naturalization in the case of those married to Palestinians holding Israeli citizenship). Palestinian East Jerusalem residents with mixed families were thus left with the following options: live separately in the unrealistic hope that their application would eventually be accepted; live "illegally" with their spouses in East Jerusalem and risk being penalized; or leave Jerusalem to live together and risk revocation of one spouse's Jerusalem ID. An additional option would be to maintain two households, one within the city's municipal boundaries and another in the West Bank or Gaza—an option that is open to only a few, given the cost of housing and the high levels of poverty in East Jerusalem.[54]

East Jerusalem residents with mixed families are also expected to navigate Israel's draconian residency regulations, which have been deliberately designed to be a legal labyrinth that few can comprehend. According to the Israeli human rights organization, HaMoked: "The fate of each man, woman and child is decided according to an endless web of legal sections, subsections, procedures and precedents; examinations of the family unification application submission date and the applicant's age at that time in relation to the enactment dates of the amendments to the Law, and so on. Within this tangle of legal complexities, the natural right of every person to family life is often trampled—a right which Israel is charged with upholding, under its own constitutional law and international law alike."[55]

Quality of Life Overall

By all measures, since the Oslo Accords, Palestinian East Jerusalemites have seen their daily lives become an increasingly constant struggle. They carry the heavy burden of having to continuously prove their connection to their city. They are required to submit endless documentation proving their residency every time they enter any government office.[56] And any visit to the Ministry of the Interior poses a significant risk, because the visit could easily trigger the Ministry's heavy investigation procedure into whether Jerusalem is indeed their "center of life." They do all that they can to avoid any such visits, but avoiding all arms of the government is nearly impossible in East Jerusalem, where all systems are interlinked and cross-checked against one another. As Jefferis elaborates:

> For instance, claiming national health benefits requires that an individual present residency documentation at the National Insurance Institute, where they are then often referred to the Ministry of Interior to obtain proof of residence. And where

permanent military checkpoints might be avoided by traveling different routes, the Israeli army often installs temporary or 'flying' checkpoints in East Jerusalem neighborhoods, requiring all those who pass to present their identity documentation. Soldiers often tell [Palestinian] East Jerusalemites that they must go to the Ministry of Interior to replace a worn out identity card, even where the card is still valid. When permanent residency is revoked, the individual is forced to attempt to continue to live without permission in Jerusalem, which carries enormous penalties if apprehended, or, if he has no other connection to another state, to flee to Gaza or the West Bank.[57]

Israel also infringes upon the freedom of Palestinian East Jerusalemites through a stringent and stifling taxation enforcement system that is linked and continuously cross-checked with their residency status. While they are entitled to receive social welfare benefits, including medical coverage, as are all Israeli citizens, these benefits are not proportionate to what they pay in taxes and fees.[58]

Political Representation

Palestinian East Jerusalemites have been effectively deprived of their political rights with the advent of the Oslo years, and especially the closure of the Orient House in 2001. Their freedom of expression and right to equality, including economic equality, depend on the goodwill of Israel, their occupier. The legislative body they are eligible to vote for (the Palestinian Legislative Council), is not allowed to promulgate laws or to act in East Jerusalem; the Knesset, Israel's legislative body, which legislates all aspects of their lives, is totally out of their reach as they are not allowed to participate in this body's elections.

Generally, most Palestinian East Jerusalemites remain in a political and legal limbo. They have Jordanian passports, which serve as travel documents, but they are not Jordanian citizens.[59] Likewise, they have Israeli identity cards, but they are not Israeli citizens; they are subject to Israeli law and are obliged to pay taxes to the Israeli authorities lest they lose their residency. They can obtain Israeli travel documents, but not Israeli passports. They self-identify as Palestinians, but they are not allowed to carry any formal papers officially identifying them as such. They are allowed to vote in PLC elections, but the PLC is not allowed to act in the place of their residence, that is, East Jerusalem. In sum, Palestinian East Jerusalemites have no real representation or effective mechanism for defending their political rights today. They effectively are stateless residents of an occupying state.

On the flip side, the PNA and the PLO have failed to sustain Palestinian Jerusalemites' presence and resilience in their city. This contention stands regardless of the limitations placed by the Oslo Accords on the PNA's presence and actions in East Jerusalem. The PNA's failure has meant that the Palestinian residents of East Jerusalem feel abandoned. They have been forced to fend for themselves through whatever institutions have survived, including a vast number of civil society NGOs that have emerged to try and fill the vacuum left by the PLO and PNA in East Jerusalem.[60]

WHAT LIES AHEAD: REDEEMING JERUSALEM?

The Palestinian people, and those in East Jerusalem in particular, find themselves at a standstill, with the most viable option being to exercise resilience and focus on self-preservation until the balance of power shifts and the time is ripe for all parties to reach a comprehensive, fair, and just solution. The formal recognition by the United States in December 2017 of Jerusalem as the capital of Israel, the American so-called "deal of the century," and the ongoing rapprochement between Israel, Saudi Arabia, and certain Gulf countries do not bode well for the Palestinian people, making the need for resilience and self-preservation all the more urgent. As bad as the past twenty-eight years have been, Palestinians in East Jerusalem have to prepare for worse to come. Recent developments—namely the Israeli municipal elections in Jerusalem in 2018 and the passage of the Israel nationality law in 2018—raise difficult questions that East Jerusalemites need to address; chiefly, how to protect their individual rights while still remaining part of a larger national Palestinian project, one that needs to be refined to ensure their effective, not rhetorical, participation.

The Israeli Municipal Elections in Jerusalem

In 2018, a few Palestinians in East Jerusalem began calling for participation in Jerusalem's municipal elections, held at the end of October 2018. For the first time since 1967, two Palestinian Jerusalemites stepped forward as candidates, Aziz Abu Sarah and Ramadan Dabash. Aziz Abu Sarah was the first to present his candidacy for mayor but withdrew it in September. He was caught between two fires—Israel trying to take away his residency rights and his people's anger at him for breaking ranks.[61] Palestinians have historically refused to participate in such elections in order not to bestow any legitimacy on Israel's annexation of the city. The Palestinian leadership has always rejected participation in Israeli municipal elections and the council of Palestinian muftis issued a religious ruling barring Muslim residents of Jerusalem from either running for office or voting in municipal elections.[62] Palestinian Christian leaders also issued similar pronouncements in 2018.[63] As for Ramadan Dabash, an engineer and one of the few Palestinian East Jerusalemites to receive Israeli citizenship, he continued in his candidacy only to receive 3,001 votes, several hundred of them from Jews.[64] According to neighborhood-level election results provided by the Jerusalem municipality, under 1 percent of eligible East Jerusalemite voters cast ballots.[65]

Using Israeli political channels to protect Palestinian individual rights is in fact futile. According to Ir Amim, an Israeli nonprofit that advocates for a shared Jerusalem, Palestinians do not believe that their political participation in municipal elections will "significantly reduce their systematic deprivation in every area of life. Their position is understandable because policy for Jerusalem is not made at City Hall but by the Israeli government, through the Ministerial Committee on Jerusalem Affairs, development authorities that answer directly to the Prime Minister's office and the Interior Ministry. Without the ability to vote on the national level and without political representation, the ability of Jerusalem Palestinians to affect their daily lives is minimal."[66] One Eastern Jerusalemite woman said: "I don't want to legitimize the Israeli occupation, and I am afraid of the Palestinian Authority. Our situation is terrible, but voting wouldn't make it any better. We Jerusalemite Palestinians are no one and we are nowhere."[67]

Applying for Israeli Citizenship

In the past few years, some Palestinian East Jerusalemites have applied for Israeli citizenship: "they consider themselves to be Palestinians, but request citizenship to guard their residency status."[68] Since 1967, applying for Israeli citizenship has been viewed by Palestinians as recognition of Israel's illegal "annexation" of East Jerusalem. Even if this view is changing slightly, the numbers who actually become citizens are minimal. Between 2014 and September 2016, of 4,152 East Jerusalemites who applied for citizenship, only 84 were approved and 161 were rejected. The rest of the applications are "pending"—formally, still being processed.[69] Most importantly, and regardless of the number of applications, there should be no doubt as to the fact that Israel will always ensure that these applications are approved at the lowest possible rate, in order to ensure its demographic majority and Jewish character of the city.[70] The outcome of all applications is ultimately at the discretion of the Minister of the Interior, who can deny citizenship even where all requirements are met.

In all cases, and notwithstanding any change in the Israeli position, applying for Israeli citizenship remains an individual undertaking that will not advance the cause of East Jerusalem and its Palestinian residents as a community and will only end up diluting their Palestinian identity—unless this comes as part of an agreed-upon comprehensive and just solution that maintains the identity of both East Jerusalem and its Palestinian residents and does not isolate them from the rest of their fellow Palestinians. This could potentially be part of a one-state solution scenario.

Palestinian Resistance

Palestinians in East Jerusalem have resisted Israel's oppressive rule in various ways. Before Oslo, they maintained, against all odds, their own schools and curricula, their own newspapers, their own NGOs, and a local leadership. The Orient House (also known as the Arab Studies Society) established by Faisal Husseini in the early 1970s was the main forum for catalyzing Palestinian resistance and vocalizing Palestinian political demands in Jerusalem and the whole of the Occupied Territories. It was the national address for local notables and grassroots organizations working to challenge Israel's encroachment upon their land. Husseini and other East Jerusalem notables were often the main spokespersons representing Palestinian demands as well as affirming the centrality of East Jerusalem as capital of a future Palestinian state. They garnered funds from the European Union and the Gulf, as well as from local Palestinians. Husseini played a key role in the Madrid peace negotiations between 1991 and 1993. During and after the First Intifada, Husseini and other East Jerusalemites also worked with the Israeli peace camp to find a viable formula for sharing Jerusalem as a capital of two states.[71]

After the signing of the Oslo Accords and the relegation of the question of Jerusalem to the permanent-status negotiations, Faisal Husseini and the Orient House continued to act as the unofficial representatives of the PLO/PNA in the city. They led major campaigns opposing Israel's construction of the Har Homa settlement on Abu Ghuneim and generated funds to prevent both Israeli eviction of East Jerusalemites from their homes and Israeli encroachment on the Al-Aqsa mosque. The death of Husseini in 2001 and the closing of the Orient House signaled Israel's determination to destroy any Palestinian political and national claim to the city.

Indeed, since 2000, East Jerusalemites have had to fend for themselves, as the PNA had limited physical and financial access to them because of the conditions Israel imposed during negotiations. Although the PNA created a Ministry for Jerusalem Affairs and continued to have a representative for the city, its main energy was channeled into state-building in the West Bank and preserving its own existence in Ramallah. Palestinians and their NGOs in East Jerusalem found themselves devoid of any political forum in which to their individual struggles with the Palestinian national struggle. Often they found themselves reliant on their own NGOs, such as Al-Haq, the Jerusalem Legal Aid and Human Rights Center (JLAC), and the Civic Coalition for Palestinian Rights in Jerusalem (CCPRJ), and on Israeli peace activist organizations, such as HaMoked and the Israeli Committee against House Demolitions (ICAHD), to protest Israeli government home demolitions and confiscation orders.[72] The Palestinian NGOs and associations in East Jerusalem have found themselves increasingly pushed to address the growing humanitarian needs in the city. Their success remains a function of the aid they receive from international donors and their compliance with the donors' agendas.[73] Above all, their work continues to be challenged by Israel. Perhaps the clearest example of the limits of Palestinian steadfastness, and extent of Palestinian despair, in East Jerusalem was the wave of knife stabbings between 2016 and 2017, which led to the death of the assailants while petrifying Israeli soldiers and civilians. These attacks were neither nationally planned nor coordinated, reflecting a certain atomization of Palestinian resistance. They also remind everyone that Israel cannot ignore the Palestinians and their rights indefinitely as revealed by their demonstration against Israeli attempted evictions from their homes in Sheikh Jarrah in April-May 2021.

The Way Forward

Palestinian East Jerusalem needs immediate, creative, proactive, and efficient action from the Palestinian leadership, the PNA, and the PLO. Major funding is required to sustain Palestinian presence in the city. The PNA has formulated several plans defining its strategy in East Jerusalem, but these have not been properly implemented, especially as the insufficient funding allocated to them is often inefficiently channeled.[74] Meanwhile, on January 15, 2018 the PLO Central Council adopted a resolution, subsequently confirmed by the Palestinian National Council meeting held from April 30 to May 3, 2018 in Ramallah, calling for "the recomposition of the Palestinian Jerusalem Municipality in accordance with the best democratic and representative ways possible."[75] On the PNA's Council of Ministers website, for example, the Ministry of Jerusalem Affairs offers its services to help those affected "by the policies of the occupation, construction violations, total and partial demolition of the buildings, providing support for the engineering clinic, legal clinic, humanitarian assistance, and strengthening the steadfastness of the merchants in the Old City."[76] These are all good "reactive" assistance measures, but what is actually needed are *proactive* measures solidifying the Palestinian presence on the ground and countering Israel's policies targeting the land and the people of East Jerusalem.

Proactive Protection of East Jerusalem Land and Property

A task force aimed at preemptively protecting Arab property in East Jerusalem from being dispossessed through ambiguous transactions is urgently needed to protect against such aggressions within and outside of the Old City walls by both the Israeli government and right-wing Israeli-Jewish settler organizations such as Ateret Cohanim. A very recent publication of the NGO Peace Now, entitled "Annex and Dispossess: Use of the Absentees' Property Law to Dispossess Palestinians of their Property in East Jerusalem," reveals the collaborative efforts, dating from the early 1980s, between the Israeli government and settlers in dispossessing Arab property in East Jerusalem and the unbearable ease with which properties were deemed "absentees' property."[77]

Attacks and aggressions on Arab property in East Jerusalem have been made worse by right-wing organizations such as Ateret Cohanim, which was founded in 1978 with the primary goal of "seizing-acquiring" as much land and as many buildings as possible in order to settle as many Jews as possible in the Muslim and Christian Quarters of the Old City and beyond.[78] Such organizations are extremely well organized and funded. They are able to infiltrate Palestinian society searching for potential "deals." For example, recently, the PNA arrested Issam Akel, a resident of East Jerusalem who holds US citizenship, on the suspicion that he sold his home in the Old City to a right-wing Jewish association. The PNA's appointed Jerusalem District Governor, Adnan Ghaith, was apparently involved in Akel's arrest and was subsequently himself arrested by the Israeli police.[79] The actions of such aggressive organizations need to be exposed, defended against, and, if possible, halted. A task force to work to this end will require major funding. The task force should be very active and highly involved in defending Arab property in addition to to preemptively protecting Arab property in East Jerusalem by all possible legal means.

Proactive Protection of Palestinian East Jerusalemites

All possible efforts must be exerted to defend against the Israeli government's revocation of Palestinians' residency status, on both the individual and on collective levels. Palestinian East Jerusalemites need a support system for defending their individual cases in Israeli courts. On the collective level, several organizations (both Arab and Israeli) offer legal assistance and advocacy in general, among them the Jerusalem Legal Aid and Human Rights Center, the Alternative Information Center, the Civic Coalition for Palestinians Rights in Jerusalem, and the Israeli Coalition against House Demolition. Their work is excellent, but their capacities are limited. More resources and advocacy are needed so that individual cases become a collective cause. This collective cause could then be put in front of all possible international forums to influence international public opinion and raise awareness about the unjust treatment of Palestinian East Jerusalemites. Israel's treatment of Palestinians in East Jerusalem violates multiple internationally recognized human rights, including several rights codified in the International Covenant on Civil and Political Rights and the International Covenant on Economic, Social, and Cultural Rights.[80] And although the systematic reporting of any such violations to the relevant international bodies will not result in any enforcement, it will nonetheless greatly contribute to rallying support among these bodies and in the international public sphere in general.

East Jerusalem and its Palestinian residents are an integral part of the Palestinian cause in its just call for liberation and self-determination. They remain key to any peaceful resolution of the Israeli-Palestinian conflict. Jerusalem has been declared the capital of a Palestinian state, a declaration supported by international law. The failure of all peace negotiations conducted between Israel and the Palestinians since 2000 has been attributed largely to the Israeli unwillingness to share Jerusalem. The US decision to move its embassy to Jerusalem might have boosted Israeli claims in the court of public opinion, but it did not make them legal or internationally acceptable.

The current conglomeration of events does not bode well for Palestinians in general and for Palestinians in Jerusalem in particular. Israel's annexationist plans loom on the horizon, with the Greater Jerusalem bill still on hold in the Knesset. Israel has also been increasingly targeting Al-Aqsa mosque in particular and the Old City in general. All this needs to be countered effectively. The PNA and PLO as leaders of the Palestinian people have to stand firmly by East Jerusalem and its Palestinian residents, in concrete, proactive actions taken on the ground, not in rhetoric. They are in dire need of support from their leadership, the Arab world, and all freedom-loving peoples.

Israel's policies of closure, silent transfer, impoverishment, and deinstitutionalization continue to suffocate Palestinians in East Jerusalem and to render them increasingly dependent on the Israeli authorities. Nonetheless, they remain resilient and steadfast as they have been since 1967. Their resilience continues to be repeatedly tested, for example recently in the summer of 2017 when Israel planted metal detectors at the entrances of the Al-Aqsa mosque and ended up removing them several days later.[81] In April 2021, Palestinian youth demonstrated again against Israeli right-wing groups, who were shouting "Death to the Arabs" in the Old City. Palestinians in East Jerusalem, especially the younger generation, have become more resilient and street smart and know how to navigate the Israeli system with the least harm possible while maintaining their identity. Clinging to their city against all odds, Palestinian East Jerusalemites are *morabitoun* (here to stay) and therein lies their strength.

NOTES

1. Joseph Dana, "Twenty-Five Years on, the Oslo Accords Are Dead. They Only Served to Advance, Entrench and Protect Israel's Occupation," *The National*, September 6, 2018.

2. There has been no recent official count of the population of Palestinian residents of East Jerusalem, but 330,000 is the number used by the most recent publications, such as Michael Omer-Man, "Who Gets to Vote in Israel's Version of Democracy," *+972 Online Magazine*, January 3, 2019. See also Nazmi Al-Jubeh, "Jerusalem: Fifty Years of Occupation," *The Jerusalem Quarterly* 72 (2017): 1–19, 16. The Israeli Central Bureau of Statistics in 2020 tallied 390,000 non-Jews in Jerusalem, most of them Arabs. For further details see https://www.cbs.gov.il/he/publications/doclib/2020/2.shnatonpopulation/sto2_15x.pdf.

3. Passia, *Jerusalem and Its Changing Boundaries* (Jerusalem: Passia Academic Society for the Study of International Affairs, 2018), 7.

4. Michael Dumper, *Jerusalem Unbound: Geography, History and the Future of the Holy City* (New York: Columbia University Press, 2014), 4.

5. The entire area added to what had formerly been Jordanian East Jerusalem, as described here, has since come to be called East Jerusalem.

6. Shmuel Berkowitz, "The Status of Jerusalem in International and Israeli Law," Jerusalem Center for Public Affairs, n.d., http://jcpa.org/the-status-of-jerusalem-in-international-and-israeli-law/; Ian Lustick, "Has Israel Annexed East Jerusalem?" *Middle East Policy* 5, no. 1 (1997): 36.

7. In response, UN Security Council Resolution 478 in 1980 affirmed that the enactment of this law constitutes a violation of international law, declared the enactment null and void, and decided not to recognize it. United Nations Security Council, "Resolution 478," S/RES/478, August 20, 1980, https://unispal.un.org/DPA/DPR/unispal.nsf/0/DDE590C6FF232007852560DF0065FDDB.

8. Ir Amim, *Permanent Residency: A Temporary Status Set in Stone* (Jerusalem: Ir Amim, 2012), 33, http://www.ir-amim.org.il/sites/default/files/permanent%20residency.pdf; citing Uzi Benziman, *Jerusalem: A City without a Wall* (New York: Schocken Books, 1973).

9. HaMoked Center for the Defence of the Individual, "The Status of Palestinians in East Jerusalem: Timeline: 1967–2018," HaMoked, 2018.

10. HaMoked Center for the Defence of the Individual, "Excerpt: Regulations 11–12 of the Entry into Israel Regulations, 5734-1974," HaMoked, 2018, http://www.hamoked.org/files/2018/3050_eng.pdf.

11. United Nations General Assembly Security Council, "Declaration of Principles on Interim Self-Government Arrangements." A/48/486 S/26560, September 13, 1993, https://peacemaker.un.org/sites/peacemaker.un.org/files/IL%20PS_930913_DeclarationPrinciplesnterimSelf-Government%28Oslo%20Accords%29.pdf.

12. United Nations General Assembly Security Council, "Annex: Israeli-Palestinian Interim Agreement on the West Bank and the Gaza Strip," A/51/889 S/1997/357, September 28, 1995, https://peacemaker.un.org/sites/peacemaker.un.org/files/IL%20PS_950928_InterimAgreementWestBankGazaStrip%28OsloII%29.pdf.

13. The right to participate in the PNC election process appears in Annex I of Oslo I and Article II of Oslo II.

14. The area referred to as the "Visual Basin of the Old City" comprises the Muslim and Christian Quarters of the Old City and the following surrounding areas outside the Old City walls: Silwan, Sheikh Jarrah, At-Tur (Mount of Olives), Wadi Al-Joz, Ras Al-'Amud, and Jabal Al-Mukabber.

15. Leila Farsakh, *Palestinian Labour Migration to Israel: Labour, Land and Occupation* (London: Routledge Press, 2005), 61.

16. Wendy Pullan, "The Space of Contested Jerusalem," *The Jerusalem Quarterly* 39 (Autumn 2009): 39–50, 43.

17. Farsakh, *Palestinian Labour Migration to Israel*, 63.

18. Farsakh, *Palestinian Labour Migration to Israel*, 61–65.

19. Jeff Halper, "The Three Jerusalems: Planning and Colonial Control," *The Jerusalem Quarterly* 15, no. 3 (2002): 6–17.

20. Halper, "The Three Jerusalems," 11.

21. Al-Haq, "The Occupation and Annexation of Jerusalem through Israeli Bills and Laws," Al-Haq website, March 5, 2018, http://www.alhaq.org/advocacy/6263.html.

22. According to Halper, the "Metropolitan Jerusalem Plan"—which includes an area of 950 square kilometers with boundaries that stretch from Beit Shemesh in the west, up through Kiryat Sefer until and including Ramallah, then southeast through Ma'aleh Adumim almost to the Jordan River, then turning southwest to encompass Beit Sahour, Bethlehem, Efrat, and the Etzion Bloc, and then west again through Beitar Illit and Tsur Hadassah back to Beit Shemesh—was "designed as a regional infrastructure of control rather than a region to be annexed to Israel." See Halper, "The Three Jerusalems," 14.

23. International Peace and Cooperation Center, *Conflict in Jerusalem: Urbanism, Planning, and Resilience Palestinian Community Initiatives to Promote Urban Rights* (Jerusalem: IPCC, 2018).

24. Francesco Chiodelli, "The Jerusalem Master Plan: Planning into the Conflict," *The Jerusalem Quarterly* 51 (Autumn 2012): 5–20.

25. Eeta Prince-Gibson, "Why There's No Protest Vote in Jerusalem," *Foreign Policy*, November 19, 2018, https://foreignpolicy.com/2018/11/19/why-theres-no-palestinian-protest-vote-in-jerusalem-israel-municipal-palestinian-authority-ramadan-dabash-aziz-abu-sarah/.

26. Ir Amim, *Permanent Residency*, 7.

27. "PM Netanyahu: Speech to US Congress," Israeli Ministry of Foreign Affairs, July 10, 1996, https://mfa.gov.il/mfa/mfa-archive/1996/pages/pm%20netanyahu-%20speech%20to%20us%20congress-%20july%2010-%201996.aspx.

28. B'Tselem, *Divide and Rule: Prohibition on Passage Between the Gaza Strip and the West Bank* (Jerusalem: B'Tselem, 1998), 5.

29. B'Tselem, *Divide and Rule*, 5.

30. Al-Jubeh, "Jerusalem: Fifty Years of Occupation."

31. On the closure policy, see International Peace and Cooperation Center, *Conflict in Jerusalem*.

32. The Orient House was ordered temporarily closed for six months on August 9, 2001, along with nine other Palestinian organizations, notably the Chamber of Commerce. The six-month closure has been repeatedly renewed up until the day of this writing. Al-Jubeh, "Jerusalem: Fifty Years of Occupation."

33. Ir Amim, *Permanent Residency*, 19.

34. United Nations, "ICJ Advisory Opinion on the Legal Consequences of the Construction of a Wall in the OPT," General List No. 131, July 9, 2004, https://www.un.org/unispal/document/icj-advisory-opinion-on-the-legal-consequences-of-the-construction-of-a-wall-in-the-opt-icj-document.

35. Israel currently maintains twelve full checkpoints and one partial one for those wishing to enter Jerusalem from the West Bank. For further details see Passia, *Jerusalem and Its Changing Boundaries*.

36. Berkowitz, "The Status of Jerusalem."

37. An unofficial translation of this law from Hebrew is available at http://knesset.gov.il/laws/special/eng/BasicLawJerusalem.pdf.

38. An unofficial translation of this law from Hebrew is available at http://knesset.gov.il/laws/special/eng/BasicLawReferendum.pdf. This law applies to the entire territory of the state of Israel within the boundaries of the "Green Line" (according to the demarcation lines as set out in the Armistice Agreements signed in 1949), as well as East Jerusalem and the Golan Heights. There would be no need to hold a referendum if there were a super-majority of eighty Knesset members.

39. Moien Odeh, "Israel's Greater Jerusalem Bill," *Jurist*, March 5, 2018, www.jurist.org/commentary/2018/03/israels-greater-jerusalem-bill/.

40. These include Ma'aleh Adumim, Gush Etzion, Efrat, Beitar Illit, and Givat Ze'ev, which together house about 150,000 settlers.

41. Halper, "The Three Jerusalems."

42. A nonbinding translation of the original Hebrew High Court of Justice ruling on the Mubarak Awad case can be found at http://www.hamoked.org/files/2010/1430_eng.pdf.

43. Usama Halaby, "Stop Ethnic Cleansing in Jerusalem," *Article 74*, July 3, 1997, http://www.badil.org/phocadownload/Badil_docs/Article_74/1997/art21e.htm.

44. Danielle C. Jefferis, "The 'Center of Life' Policy: Institutionalizing Statelessness in East Jerusalem, *The Jerusalem Quarterly* 50, (Winter 2012): 94–103, 98.

45. Although Barak acknowledged that "it is often difficult to point to a specific point in time at which a person ceased from permanently residing in a country and that there is certainly a span of time in which a person's center of life seemingly hovers between his previous place of residency and his new place of residence," he nonetheless did not clear this ambiguity in his ruling. Jefferis, "The 'Center of Life' Policy," 98.

46. Jefferis, "The 'Center of Life' Policy," 98.

47. Jefferis, "The 'Center of Life' Policy," 98.

48. HaMoked Center for the Defence of the Individual, "Ministry of Interior Response to HaMoked's Freedom-of-Information Request: In 2017, Israel Revoked the Permanent Residency Status of 35 East Jerusalem Palestinians," HaMoked, April 10, 2018, http://www.hamoked.org/Document.aspx?dID=Updates1975.

49. B'Tselem and HaMoked, *The Quiet Deportation Continues: Revocation of Residency and Denial of Social Rights of East Jerusalem Palestinians* (Jerusalem: B'Tselem and HaMoked, 1998), 9.

50. Jefferis, "The 'Center of Life' Policy," 1.

51. B'Tselem and HaMoked, *The Quiet Deportation Continues*.

52. HaMoked, "Ministry of Interior Response to HaMoked's Freedom-of-Information Request."

53. A summary of this ruling is available at http://www.hamoked.org/Document.aspx?dID=Updates1850.

54. Tamara Tawfiq Tamimi, "Revocation of Residency of Palestinians in Jerusalem: Prospects for Accountability," *The Jerusalem Quarterly* 72 (Winter 2017): 37–47.

55. HaMoked: Center for the Defence of the Individual, "The Status of Palestinians in East Jerusalem: Timeline: 1967–2018," HaMoked, 2018, http://www.hamoked.org/Timeline.aspx?pageID=timeLineNews.

56. Required documentation could include home ownership papers or rent contracts; electricity, water, and telephone bills; receipts for payment of municipal taxes; salary stubs; proof of receipt of medical care; and certificate of children's school registration. The Ministry demands these documents *each time* the individual submits any request. Even where documentation had already been submitted for one type of application, the Ministry still requires the family to provide the same documentation again for each subsequent request, even for a simple change of address.

57. Jefferis, "The 'Center of Life' Policy," 99.

58. Ir Amim, *Permanent Residency*, 44.

59. On July 31, 1988, Jordan renounced its claims to the West Bank (with the exception of guardianship over the Muslim and Christian holy sites in Jerusalem) and recognized the Palestine Liberation Organization as "the sole legitimate representative of the Palestinian people." This decision is known as the "Jordanian disengagement." After this date, Palestinians holding Jordanian passports were no longer Jordanian nationals.

60. Safa Dhaher, *The Impact of the Current Situation on the Human Rights of the Vulnerable Palestinian Groups in East Jerusalem* (Ramallah: Heinrich-Böll-Stiftung, 2017).

61. Nir Hasson, "Palestinian Resident of East Jerusalem Withdraws from Jerusalem Mayoral Race," *Haaretz*, September 25, 2018.

62. Jack Khoury, "Palestinian Muftis Bar Participation in Jerusalem Elections," *Haaretz*, July 31, 2018.

63. Prince-Gibson, "Why There's No Protest Vote in Jerusalem."

64. Prince-Gibson, "Why There's No Protest Vote in Jerusalem."

65. Prince-Gibson, "Why There's No Protest Vote in Jerusalem."

66. Ir Amim, *Permanent Residency*, 7.

67. Prince-Gibson, "Why There's No Protest Vote in Jerusalem."

68. Dov Lieber, "Israel Almost Entirely Halts Citizenship Approvals for East Jerusalemites," *The Times of Israel*, September 26, 2016.

69. Lieber, "Israel Almost Entirely Halts Citizenship Approvals."

70. Nir Hasson, "The Plan to 'Israelize' Jerusalem has 300,000 Problems," *Haaretz*, May 13, 2018.

71. Hillal Cohen, "Palestinian Armed Struggle, Israel's Peace Camp, and the Unique Case of Fatah-Jerusalem" *Israel Studies* 18, no. 1 (2013): 101–23; Dumper, *Jerusalem Unbound*.

72. Cohen, "Palestinian Armed Struggle," 114–16.

73. ICAHD stands for Israeli Committee against House Demolition; Dhaher, *Impact of the Current Situation.*

74. Al-Jubeh, "Fifty Years of Occupation," 20.

75. The Palestinian Jerusalem municipality referred to here is the one that was in place before the 1967 war. Walid Salem, "The East Jerusalem Municipality: Palestinian Policy Options and Proposed Alternatives," *The Jerusalem Quarterly* 74 (Summer 2018): 120–36.

76. Salem, "The East Jerusalem Municipality."

77. See Peace Now, "Annex and Dispossess: Use of the Absentees' Property Law to Dispossess Palestinians of their Property in East Jerusalem," July 2020, http://peacenow.org.il/wp-content/uploads/2020/07/Abestnetee_Property_East_Jerusalem_ENG.pdf.

78. Sue Surkes, "Supreme Court Rules for Jewish Group in Battle Over Old City Church Leases," *The Times of Israel*, June 13, 2019.

79. Nir Hasson, "Israeli Security Forces Raid PA Offices in West Bank Over Sale of Jerusalem Home to Jews," *Haaretz*, November 4, 2018.

80. See Tamimi, "Revocation of Residency of Palestinians;" Jefferis, "The 'Center of Life' Policy."

81. Jesse Rosenfeld, "With al-Aqsa Protests, a Popular Mass Movement Is Again Taking the Lead in Palestinian Resistance," *Intercept*, August 3, 2017.

BIBLIOGRAPHY

Al-Jubeh, Nazmi. "Jerusalem: Fifty Years of Occupation." *The Jerusalem Quarterly*, trans. Zahra Khalidi, 72 (Winter 2017): 7–25. Originally published under the same title in *Majallat al-Dirasat al-Filastiniyya* 111 (Summer 2017): 140–59.

Berkowitz, Shmuel. "The Status of Jerusalem in International and Israeli Law." Jerusalem Center for Public Affairs, n.d. http://jcpa.org/the-status-of-jerusalem-in-international-and-israeli-law/.

B'Tselem. *Divide and Rule: Prohibition on Passage between the Gaza Strip and the West Bank*. Jerusalem: B'Tselem, 1998.

B'Tselem and Ha Moked. *The Quiet Deportation Continues: Revocation of Residency and Denial of Social Rights of East Jerusalem Palestinians*. Jerusalem: B'Tselem and HaMoked, 1998.

Chiodelli, Francesco. "The Jerusalem Master Plan: Planning into the Conflict." *The Jerusalem Quarterly* 51 (Autumn 2012): 5–20.

Cohen, Hillal. "Palestinian Armed Struggle, Israel's Peace Camp, and the Unique Case of Fatah-Jerusalem." *Israel Studies* 18, no. 1 (2013): 101–23.

Dhaher, Safa. *The Impact of the Current Situation on the Human Rights of the Vulnerable Palestinian Groups in East Jerusalem*. Palestine and Jordan: Heinrich-Boll Stiftung, February 2017.

Dumper, Michael. *Jerusalem Unbound: Geography, History and the Future of the Holy City*. New York: Columbia University Press, 2014.

Farsakh, Leila. *Palestinian Labour Migration to Israel: Labour, Land and Occupation*. London: Routledge, 2005.

Halper, Jeff. "The Three Jerusalems: Planning and Colonial Control." *The Jerusalem Quarterly* 15, no. 3 (2002): 6–17.

HaMoked: Center for the Defence of the Individual. "Excerpt: Regulations 11–12 of the Entry into Israel Regulations, 5734–1974." Nonbinding translation from the original Hebrew document, HaMoked, 2018. http://www.hamoked.org/files/2018/3050_eng.pdf.

———. "Ministry of Interior Response to HaMoked's Freedom-of-Information Request: In 2017, Israel Revoked the Permanent Residency Status of 35 East Jerusalem Palestinians." HaMoked, 2018. http://www.hamoked.org/Document.aspx?dID=Updates1975.

———. "The Status of Palestinians in East Jerusalem: Timeline: 1967–2018." HaMoked, 2018. http://www.hamoked.org/Timeline.aspx?pageID=timeLineNews.

International Peace and Cooperation Center. *Conflict in Jerusalem: Urbanism, Planning, and Resilience Palestinian Community Initiatives to Promote Urban Rights*. Jerusalem: IPCC, 2018. http://fespal.org/wp-content/uploads/2018/11/FES-IPCC-Publication-18-Nov-2018-1-ilovepdf-compressed-1.pdf.

Ir Amim. *Permanent Residency: A Temporary Status Set in Stone*. Jerusalem: Ir Amim, 2012. http://www.ir-amim.org.il/sites/default/files/permanent%20residency.pdf.

Jefferis, Danielle C. "The 'Center of Life' Policy: Institutionalizing Statelessness in East Jerusalem." *The Jerusalem Quarterly* 50 (2012): 94–103.

Lustick, Ian. "Has Israel Annexed East Jerusalem?" *Middle East Policy* 5, no. 1 (1997): 34–45.

Passia. "Factsheet: Jerusalem." Passia website, 2018. http://passia.org/media/filer_public/11/c6/11c6b133-89f5-4309-b6a9-f904e959866a/jerusalem.pdf.

———. *Jerusalem and Its Changing Boundaries*. Jerusalem: Passia Academic Society for the Study of International Affairs, 2018.

Peace Now, "Annex and Dispossess: Use of the Absentees' Property Law to Dispossess Palestinians of their Property in East Jerusalem," July 2020, http://peacenow.org.il/wp-content/uploads/2020/07/Abestnetee_Property_East_Jerusalem_ENG.pdf.

Pullan, Wendy. "The Space of Contested Jerusalem." *The Jerusalem Quarterly* 39 (Autumn 2009): 39–50. https://www.palestine-studies.org/sites/default/files/jq-articles/39_the_space_2.pdf.

Salem, Walid. "The East Jerusalem Municipality: Palestinian Policy Options and Proposed Alternatives." *The Jerusalem Quarterly* 74 (Summer 2018): 120–36.

Schmitt, Kenny. "Ribat in Palestine: The Growth of a Religious Discourse alongside Religious Practice." *The Jerusalem Quarterly* 72 (Winter 2017): 26–36.

Tamimi, Tamara Tawfiq. "Revocation of Residency of Palestinians in Jerusalem: Prospects for Accountability." *The Jerusalem Quarterly* 72 (Winter 2017): 37–47.

United Nations. "ICJ Advisory Opinion on the Legal Consequences of the Construction of a Wall in the OPT—ICJ document." General List No. 131. July 9, 2004. https://www.un.org/unispal/document/icj-advisory-opinion-on-the-legal-consequences-of-the-construction-of-a-wall-in-the-opt-icj-document/.

United Nations General Assembly Security Council. "Annex: Israeli-Palestinian Interim Agreement on the West Bank and the Gaza Strip." A/51/889 S/1997/357. September 28, 1995. https://peacemaker.un.org/sites/peacemaker.un.org/files/IL%20PS_950928_Interi mAgreementWestBankGazaStrip%28OsloII%29.pdf.

———. "Declaration of Principles on Interim Self-Government Arrangements." A/48/486 S/26560. September 13, 1993. https://peacemaker.un.org/sites/peacemaker.un.org/files /IL%20PS_930913_DeclarationPrinciplesnterimSelf-Government%28Oslo%20Accords %29.pdf.

United Nations Security Council. "Resolution 478." S/RES/478. August 20, 1980. Available at United Nations Information System on the Question of Palestine, https://unispal .un.org/DPA/DPR/unispal.nsf/0/DDE590C6FF232007852560DF0065FDDB.

4

The State, the Land, and the Hill Museum

Hanan Toukan

How are we to think about a museum that represents a people who not only do not exist on conventional maps but who are also in the process of resisting obliteration by one of the most brutal military complexes in the world? What is, and what can be, the role of a museum in a violent colonial context compounded by the twin effects of imperialism and capitalism? Whom does the museum speak for in such a context? And what can or should it say to a transterritorial nation while physically located in a supposed state-to-be that has no real prospect of gaining control over its land, water, or skies through current international diplomatic channels?

Four interrelated phenomena are central to thinking through these questions in relation to the Palestinian Museum, which opened in 2016 in the university town of Birzeit in the West Bank, on a hill that offers a breathtaking view of farms, terraced hillsides, and the Mediterranean Sea. First, one must acknowledge the convoluted, bureaucratic, and deceptive nature of the Oslo peace process and the new phase of colonization that it inaugurated in 1993. This predicament, which has been described as one of living in a "postcolonial colony," is largely defined by the paradox of living in a state without sovereignty in the West Bank and Gaza under the guise of a diplomatic process leading toward a two-state solution.[1] Under this regime, the Palestinian National Authority (PNA), established in 1994 as an outcome of the now unpopular Oslo Peace Accords, did not gain full sovereignty for itself or the Palestinian people it purportedly represents. Rather, it became the middleman of the Israeli occupation, managing security and repressing Palestinian dissent on behalf of Israel through its own internal military and intelligence apparatus, helping to intensify the Israeli colonial strategies of spatial segregation and economic control. At the same time, despite its increasing unpopularity, the PNA has continued to act as the recognized representative of a state-to-be in international diplomacy. This role has necessitated its cultural diplomacy and top-down identity formation in an attempt to rebrand Palestinians as nonviolent and modern global citizens residing within the 1967 borders—processes that are key to understanding how and why the Palestinian Museum has, from its inception, had to think about representing the story of the Palestinian people outside the limits of the diplomatically sanctioned, yet now probably defunct, two-state solution.

Second, one must take account of ongoing Israeli colonial practices of cultural exclusion and military domination. Supported by an architecture of bureaucratic hurdles and procedures, the Israeli occupation uses a carefully designed system of legalized, institutionalized, and normalized racial discrimination to debilitate the freedom of movement of objects, people, and ideas that a museum or any institution of knowledge production requires in order to function. As I demonstrate, the Palestinian Museum has had to maneuver around this in order to materialize.

Third, the Palestinian Museum has indirectly interrogated the European museum's Western-centric yet universalizing mission of acquiring, conserving, and displaying aesthetic objects as part of the project of constructing nation-states and indeed modernity itself. It is precisely because of the Palestinian Museum's restricted spatial reality that it is able to intervene in a global discussion concerned with the role of the museum in our world. This conversation centers on the question of how to make the museum—an institution historically bound up with the emergence of the nation-state and the notion of the public in eighteenth-century Europe—relevant to the global realities that shape its direction today.[2] The Palestinian Museum can be read as proposing answers to this question, first through its mission of being "a museum without borders," and second through its very process of construction, which drew on the land's historically terraced landscapes to create a structure embedded in the communities and histories it seeks to speak to and for.[3] Through this process, it arguably rethinks the "postcolonial museum" as an unstable yet dynamic memory-making institution, as much a living archive of violence as an affective encounter with the weight of the land and history.[4] In doing so, it intervenes in a global conversation about the sensorial dimensions of exhibition and collection practices in violent settings on the margins of the global South.

The final aspect that informs my reading of the Palestinian Museum is the wave of state-supported building and renovation of museums and other art institutions underway largely in the Arab Gulf states but also in Lebanon, Egypt, Kuwait, and to a lesser extent Jordan, from which the Palestinian Museum is arguably set apart by virtue of its status as an institution representing a transterritorial and stateless nation. Unlike the regional museum projects surrounding it, which offer clear instances of top-down globally attuned national identity formation, state-led societal development, and soft power and public diplomacy, the Palestinian

FIGURE 2. The Palestine Museum. Source: Iwan Baan, © the Palestinian Museum.

Museum prompts a rethinking and reworking of the vexed relationship between local Palestinian noncitizens and transterritorial Palestinian publics and their supporters, on the one hand, and the aesthetic form of an exhibition and the tastes of its varied global audiences, on the other.[5]

On the surface, it is easy to dismiss the beautifully landscaped, bunker-like, low and uneven twenty-four million dollar building that has become known as the Palestinian Museum as the vanity project of one organization and possibly even one person. The Welfare Association, better known by its Arabic name, Taawon, meaning cooperation, is Palestine's largest humanitarian and development nongovernmental organization, founded in 1983 by a group of Palestinian business and intellectual figures. It has spearheaded the project in its various iterations since its inception in 1997. Headed by Omar Al-Qattan, former chairman and acting director of the Palestinian Museum project, board member of Taawon, chairman of the Al-Qattan Foundation, and son of one of Palestine and the Arab world's most beloved businessmen and philanthropists, the late Abdel Mohsen Al Qattan, Taawon played a highly visible role in the making of the museum.[6] Taawon, which is highly respected regionally and locally in Palestine for its financial independence, especially from Western funders, and for its humanitarian work, is well known for how seriously it takes its self-proclaimed mission to "preserve the heritage of the Palestinians, supporting their living culture and building civil society."[7] The museum, one of Taawon's flagship projects, became a crucial site for the implementation of its heritage mandate. As with most of its humanitarian projects, Taawon relied heavily on private money donated by Palestinian business entities on the association's board, such as Arab Tech Jardaneh (a private practice of consulting engineers), Consolidated Contractors Company (one of the earliest Arab construction companies), Al-Hani Construction and Trading (based in Kuwait), Projacs International (the largest Pan-Arab project management firm), as well as the Bank of Palestine.

Yet as is always the case with the building of art institutions with private sector funds, questions concerning transnational financial ties, corporate ethics, and relationships with local cultural elites arise. The role of Taawon prompted those working closely with the project and others observing from afar to ponder how much the project was about global capitalist elite collusion with the local NGO sector rather than response to the needs of the Palestinian people. In this regard, people I interviewed or conversed with as part of my research raised a number of provocative questions: first, about the manner in which Taawon disbursed funds earmarked for the cultural sector to one museum as opposed to a wider range of cultural projects, arts organizations, and other activist initiatives already underway in Palestine; second, about how Taawon was seen to run the museum as if it were one of its mainstream NGO socioeconomic development projects, without the curatorial insight needed to get a museum of this kind off the ground; third, about how, in the eyes of some, especially those not working directly within the museum or in the art world, the opening of an empty museum in May 2016 made clear just how much it had been compromised by mismanagement; and finally, and perhaps most ominously, about what to make of the allegation that Taawon board members were getting returns on their in-kind donations to the museum in a context that has allowed big businesses to set the terms of cooperation for smaller and more local businesses.

Sentiments like these gathered from discussions about the Palestinian Museum are a reminder that even the most brilliantly conceived projects encounter friction when they leave the space of conception to become transformed into concrete projects. Specifically, how museums located at the nexus of the colonial/postcolonial divide reinvent their spaces and visual narrations, in contexts in which the divisions between public and private are opaque, and access to landscapes and architectures necessary for the movement of objects restricted, is fundamentally a question of the political economy of cultural production. Though the Palestinian Museum has been able to propose innovative museum practices, its ability to survive its near-impossible predicament of belonging to a "state" that is not in a position to defend itself will ultimately depend on the extent to which the transnational networks, including the financial ones, that it draws upon will allow it to experiment freely with different forms of knowledge production, narrations of memory, and cultural heritage preservation.

AN EMPTY MUSEUM?

If there is a blotch on the Palestinian Museum's image that metaphorically and visually represented some of the misgivings expressed about it, it was at its official opening on May 18, 2016, when there were no art objects in the building on display. The opening took place soon after the firing of Jack Persekian, the museum's chief curator and director since 2008, and one of the Arab region's most recognized contemporary arts curators, over "planning and management issues."[8]

The museum was supposed to have opened with Persekian's curated project "Never Part," which was to have featured illustrative material objects from the lives of Palestinian refugees all over the world. The "Never Part" team envisioned and worked towards an empty museum for the opening, but they wanted interventions from artists contemplating the emptiness of the building vis-à-vis Palestine's experience of having had its material culture confiscated, destroyed, or disappeared, to accompany this emptiness. The point was to reflect on Palestine's predicament—its lack of control over borders, waters, and skies—and to question the meaning of a museum, and the artifacts and collecting practices that supposedly define it, in the case of a people violently dispersed all over the globe and prevented from accessing their past and material present. In *Art Is Not What You Think It Is*, Claire Farago and Donald Preziosi demonstrate how the architecture of contemporary museums inspires active relationships between exhibitions and visitors, thereby provoking the potential that germinates in the built structure of the museum.[9] Accordingly, when artists and curators are invited to converse with the spaces of museums rather than contexts of art-in-architecture, unexpected capacities may be set in motion which go beyond the ordinary encounters of exhibitions and spectatorship, works and visitors. Persekian and his team, conversant in global art theory and practice, were working within a genealogy of modern and contemporary art that conceptualized and theorized the museum space as an artwork and a statement in and of itself.[10]

But having the museum empty for the official opening, which was scheduled to coincide with Nakba Day, did not go down well with the task force set up by Taawon to take charge of the museum project.[11] Less interested in the language of conceptual art and the contemporary global artscape's often experimental approach to engaging with the political, and more concerned with the Palestinian Museum's role as a local cultural institution that speaks to the transterritorial Palestinian reality of displacement, solidarity networks, and grassroots initiatives, Taawon might have seen in the proposed opening a shift in the role of the Palestinian Museum from borderless center for Palestinian culture and heritage to what they perceived as an overly abstract and theorized project conversing more with the global art sphere than the local cultural scene.[12] Being a grassroots organization, Taawon may also have been attuned to the fact that Palestinians, who lack sufficient access to their own artifacts but who value whatever material culture they are still in possession of as a means of historical narration, needed to see a museum that carried their name with objects in it, if only as a symbolic affirmation of their existence. Hence, even if the tradition of the empty museum (whether empty of audiences or artifacts) may have been an apt framework for highlighting the Palestinian condition in conceptual terms, in the Palestinian context, it takes on a different meaning.

When the Jewish Museum first opened without objects in Berlin in 1999 it was to highlight the eerily claustrophobic and uneven architecture of the zinc-clad building, which was meant to evoke feelings of fear, disorientation, and paranoia, even though the point of the museum was to celebrate Jewish contributions to the history of the city.[13] Its initial emptiness corresponded to the message being conveyed. In the case of the Palestinians, history has put them in the absurd position of perpetually having to convince the rest of the world of their very existence. In response, scholars, artists, and filmmakers working in and on Palestine, interested in countering orientalist tropes representing the Palestinian as terrorist, victim, or romantic revolutionary, are slowly building a formidable archive of the historical fact and experience of ongoing dispossession and displacement, but also continued survival on the land. By recording and proactively reorganizing existing oral and visual testaments of surviving witnesses they are reassembling the story of the Palestinian struggle into a coherent and introspective counternarrative that rejects the central tenets of the media and public discourse on Islam, Arabs, and the Palestinians. Even if it is difficult to access, cultural heritage and specifically material culture is the site where this reclamation of narrative is fought for most fiercely.

Ironically, notwithstanding Taawon's misgivings about the curatorial conceptualization of emptiness, the museum ended up being empty on the day of its opening, thanks to a series of internal developments that culminated in the dismissal of Persekian, officially attributed to differences over "planning and management."[14] Despite viewing the museum as incomplete, Taawon decided to move ahead with its opening to honor the promise they had made to open it on Nakba Day.[15]

It was difficult to ignore the ironies implicit in the opening of the empty museum in 2016 by the ever-unpopular Mahmoud Abbas, president of the PNA. This was especially true of mainstream Western media coverage. Headlines such as "Palestinian Museum Opens without Exhibits," "The Palestinian Museum Set to Open, Empty of Art," or, more provocatively, "Palestinian Museum Opening without Exhibits, but Creators Say That's No Big Deal" were predictably unkind.[16] Cynically hinting at a people with neither the capacity nor the cultural history required to fill such an expensive and well-designed building, the media latched on to the fact that the Palestinian Museum was empty. Conveniently, these same media outlets almost entirely ignored the reality of Palestinian existence as a dispossessed people with histories, memories, and material cultures scattered all over the world or stolen by their colonizers through the cultural appropriation of music, books, art, and food, or the seizure of objects and especially archives.[17]

This reality, in addition to the lack of control over the movement necessary for the travel of art objects—normally central to a museum's practice—makes compiling, acquiring, and exhibiting works an almost impossible feat.

In artist Khaled Hourani's 2009 art project "Picasso in Palestine," Pablo Picasso's 1943 portrait of his lover Françoise Gilot, *Buste de femme*, was exhibited on the grounds of the International Art Academy of Palestine (IAAP) in Ramallah. The bringing of Picasso's *Buste* to Ramallah, a collaborative effort between the IAAP and the Van Abbe museum in the Netherlands that began at the Middle East Summit held at the museum in 2008, was nearly three years in the making. In Hourani's project, the process of bringing one of Picasso's most famous works to Palestine included wrestling with the thorny politics of Oslo, international protocols defining museum loan traditions that normally deal only with sovereign states, the bureaucratic measures implementing so-called peace agreements, and Israel's control over checkpoints, airports, and international insurance requirements. The point of the intriguing, if overly elaborate and expensive, project was to highlight just how difficult it would be to bring artworks to Palestine.

ON THE POLITICAL ECONOMY OF MUSEUMS

Only a few months after the tumultuous official opening of the Palestinian Museum without art objects in it, in a much-discussed public speech as part of the Young Artists of the Year Award (YAYA), hosted annually by the Abdel Mohsen Qattan Foundation, Omar Al-Qattan reproached the failure of the Palestinian cultural and artistic milieu in the era of Oslo to produce any meaningful dialogue or questions about the demise of the Palestinian national project.[18] Having just returned from a trip to Gaza, Al-Qattan—also the director of the Al-Qattan Foundation, one of Ramallah's most prominent cultural institutions—seemed to be lashing out at the entire cultural scene. In fact, Al-Qattan expressed the discomfort that many, if not most members of the public, including writers, intellectuals, and artists, feel in the West Bank and Gaza about the extent to which cultural work and especially the visual arts have been able to engage with the collective Palestinian experience of oppression. In his words, he wanted to use the opportunity of the YAYA ceremony to address what he described as a "quickness, superficiality and general disengagement with historical and political subjects."[19]

Much has already been written about the debilitating and depoliticizing effects of the NGO-ization process created by international aid to the region—a process that has led to what is described by Palestinians as the collapse of the national liberation project. With globalization and transnational cultural markets becoming the norm in Palestine as elsewhere, artists and their institutions have not only been forced to readdress their role in the politics of the region and the transnational networks they need in order to survive, but also to present Palestine's plight and contributions to critical global conversations in the arts and activism more broadly. In Palestinian artist Khaled Hourani's words, "Artists started to reconsider the perception of arts, portraits, borders, artistic values, relations of artworks and exhibits, audience and arts dealers."[20] Whether, as a generation of artists, they were in fact able to do so without compromising on the core values of cultural resistance and the role of contemporary art in it is, today, a central and uncomfortable discussion in Palestinian cultural circles.

Interestingly, on the day of the official inauguration of the museum in 2016, the building was empty of artifacts but not of objects such as the materials needed for the construction of the museum like shovels, barrels, and piles of cement. As some critics of the museum quipped, the fact that the museum was not emptied of its construction materials was a visual reminder of precisely how tied up it was in global capital circulation and real-estate development, a marker of post-Oslo Palestine par excellence, rather than a representation of the dispossessed and oppressed people it supposedly represented.[21] This observation, which directly references the landscape dotted with cranes used to build the five-star hotels, restaurants, and upmarket housing that have come to define the "elite-driven production of space" in Ramallah in particular, prods us to think about the tensions between the provenance of the museum's capital and what it symbolizes.[22]

It is a fact that most of the investors in the Palestinian Museum were businessmen who made their money in the Arab Gulf. It is also believed that donations included in-kind contributions, revenue from which was channeled back into the construction, management, and development firms of some of the board's members. Adam Hanieh has shown how the internationalization of Gulf capital throughout the economies of the Middle East has been a central feature of regional capitalist development over the last two decades.[23] Palestinian class formation since Oslo has gone hand in hand with the internationalization of capital, a process that sits at the heart of the economic doctrine of neoliberalism. Hanieh posits that Palestinian class formation cannot be understood solely through the prism of Palestine's subordination to Israel. Important businesses based in the Gulf have played a critical role in restructuring society in ways that make it highly reliant and dependent on transnational capital in order to survive. Along these lines, Sherene Seikaly provides a fascinating account of a dynamic class of Palestinian capitalist entrepreneurs involved in both local and regional trade, enabling us to historicize today's class of museum investors.[24] Contemporary businesses are part of a longer genealogy of capital accumulation and investment in Palestine and the region at large. At the same time, they are only one component in a contingently linked cluster of people, technology, objects, and knowledge that circulate through the social and economic fields that museums inhabit.[25] This raises a question: Even if the presence of construction material and workers visually symbolized Ramallah's role in the normalization of the occupation, and provoked the ambivalent feelings that some felt toward the opening of an empty museum, might it still be possible to separate the function of the Palestinian Museum as resistant praxis from the context of its provenance?

LANDSCAPE AND ARCHITECTURE

Taking up a mere three thousand square meters of the forty thousand square meter plot on which it stands, the landscape in which the museum is set is as aesthetically and politically significant as the building and its artifacts. The visual and sensorial experience of standing in the foyer of the building is one of an affective encounter with the weight of history, the land, and continued presence on it. Indeed the topography of the land on which the museum is built and its terraced garden design was as significant to the conceptualization of the museum as the building itself. According to Lara Zureikat, the landscape architect, based in neighboring Amman, both understanding traditional practices of horticulture and working with the site's slopes and its existing plants were central to the Palestinian Museum's mission to respect the cultural and natural heritage of the landscape and its determination not to disrupt it yet again.[26] This is in reference, and contrast, to the Israeli occupation's practice of intercepting and intervening in the harmony of the landscape for settlement construction, surveillance, and wall-building purposes, intrusions which sever Palestinians' access to cultivable land.[27] Predictably, Zureikat, who is a Jordanian national, was prevented by Israel from visiting the site of the project. She and her team resorted to the use of satellite imagery and internet communication to finalize the project. This reveals how, from the beginning, the process of turning the museum into a material reality from an idea was imbricated with the museum's objective of building on the transterritorial reality of Palestinians by thinking imaginatively about modes of delivery.

The building is therefore physically and conceptually responsive to its landscape and built environment. In the words of Conor Sreenan, chief architect of the project, from the Dublin-based architecture firm Heneghan Peng, "It was the physical that introduced us to the geopolitical. We literally traced the existing topography and looked at the way that the landscape had been inhabited for 2000 plus years."[28] The idea, he explained, was not to be defined by the occupation but rather to take back control of the landscape.

The hills of the West Bank, on which illegal Jewish settlements sit, visually embody what settler-colonialism entails and the consequences it has had. Some of these include moving communities into territories acquired in war—a Zionist practice that predates the establishment of the Israeli state—in addition to settler violence against local Palestinian communities and the imposition of new demographic realities on the ground that will not only threaten the form but the very possibility of a future Palestinian state. The planting on the grounds of the museum of groves of apricot, pomegranate, mulberry, cypress, olive, walnut and fig trees, lemons and oranges, herbs like zaatar, mint, and other plants that Israel has appropriated as part of a policy of erasing the memory and identity of Palestinian people, are a step towards reclaiming what has been taken away.

But standing inside the small museum and looking out of the floor-to-ceiling windows that adorn an entire wall that overlooks the hills and the Mediterranean

Sea in the distance—which Palestinians are barred from reaching, thanks to Israeli-imposed restrictions on movement—the foundation on which Zionism stands is usurped, even mocked, if only momentarily. In other words, instead of directly confronting politics as such, the Palestinian Museum may in fact be aiming to create a platform from which to expand the meaning of the political to include not only critical thought and the collection and exhibition of dispersed art, but also to link the lived and built environments and peoples' relationships to each of these. With this in mind, even the sight of the unpopular Mahmoud Abbas cutting the ribbon on the opening day becomes more palatable.

THE ART INSTITUTION, THE STATE, AND DECOLONIZATION

The PNA complained about the museum's apparent appropriation of what it saw as the state's role of cultural patronage, most visibly in the name the museum chose for itself: the Palestinian Museum. Despite this point of contention, Taawon felt the need to be courteous and to invite the president because in the end, as Al-Qattan explained, "we need to work with the existing bureaucratic structure and engage it, regardless of who is in power. We cannot function in isolation."[29] Al Qattan's reasoning might sit uncomfortably with activists who see resisting colonial violence as a fundamentally confrontational act that requires tackling head-on the PNA's role as middleman of the occupation. Yet it is perhaps the only way in which to get a grand project of this kind off the ground in colonized Palestine today. The question that this reality begs is whether a museum of this kind was needed and whether Taawon would have done better to distribute its millions to the multitude of artists, writers, filmmakers, collectives, activists, and smaller-scale arts organizations that are working laboriously to collect and document Palestine's history and cultural heritage—a question I heard on numerous occasions in the field.

Rasha Salti and Kristine Khouri's *Past Disquiet: Narratives and Ghosts from the International Art Exhibition for Palestine, 1978* revisits the making of the International Art Exhibition for Palestine, which opened in Beirut in the spring of 1978 and which comprised some two hundred works donated by artists in solidarity with Palestine from nearly thirty countries. Following the exhibit's inauguration in Beirut, and after parts of it had traveled to Japan, Norway, and then Iran some years later, the Israeli Army invaded Beirut in the summer of 1982 with the aim of flushing out the PLO. The building where the collection was stored was bombed, along with the offices of the PLO's Office of Unified Information where most of the archive of the exhibition would have been stored. Salti and Khouri's painstakingly curated exhibition traces the sheer challenge of locating the works, archives, stories, and memories today scattered all over the globe, but which were intended as a seed collection for a museum-in-exile until the moment it could "return" to a free Palestine.[30]

Palestinian artist Nasser Soumi has been working since the mid-1990s to recover some of this lost cultural history by navigating the labyrinth of facts, urban legends, hints, clues, and social tensions that cluster around some of the disappeared paintings that featured in the show. When I recently asked him about his evident personal need to do so in the face of challenges he has faced from colleagues as well as the PNA that point to the impossibility of such collecting practices, he replied that Palestinians need some semblance of an art institution especially as their so-called state refuses to look for the story of resistance in places where it is not in control.[31] For him, finding these works and knowing their story is a way for Palestinians to reclaim part of their lost archive.

These histories and artistic initiatives point to the importance of a site around which an oppressed people fighting for liberation may gather to (re)present their narratives, (re)negotiate their strategies of protest in the face of oppression, and reflect on their colonial pasts and presents by referencing objects and ideas that are accessible to them in physical or virtual form. From its plans to set up a virtual museum and online archival platforms to its construction of satellite museums (in Chile, the United States, United Kingdom, Jordan, and Lebanon) and its novel incorporation of landscape and topography into its programmatic definition and practices, the Palestinian Museum has committed itself in both concept and practice to ongoing anticolonial and decolonization processes.[32] Its space is, then, equally a potential launch pad for interventions into, discourses on, and practices of decolonization, and specifically the "de-Westernizing" of knowledge production in a changing postcolonial world, by calling into question the principles that sustain the current dominant knowledge-production system, particularly in respect to art and museums.[33]

To appreciate what a significant institution the Palestinian Museum is, despite its precariousness, we need to revisit Palestinian historian Beshara Doumani's original conception of the project and the strategic plan he envisioned for it. Doumani was invited by Taawon in 2010 to submit a proposal for a museum to the organization's Palestinian Museum Task Force. To this day, the museum continues to use his original proposal as the blueprint for ongoing development of the project, even if it has been modified somewhat along the way. Doumani envisioned the museum as "postterritorial" in its need to encompass Palestinians who are scattered transterritorially and unable to access their homeland, and as "a mobilizing and interactive cultural project that can stitch together the fragmented Palestinian body politic by presenting a wide variety of narratives about the relationships of Palestinians to the land, to each other and to the wider world."[34] His starting point wasn't the geographical locale of the West Bank and Gaza—even if the museum building would be situated near Ramallah, the purported capital of a future Palestinian state—but rather the dispersed and divided Palestinian population brought together through online technology.[35] This population is composed of Gazans under siege, Jerusalemite Palestinians walled off from the rest of their people,

Palestinians living in the West Bank who are intercepted, harassed, enclosed, and surrounded by a complex of Israeli checkpoints, as well the Palestinian citizens of Israel and all those living as refugees in neighboring Arab countries and as exiles in the rest of the world.

Doumani, like Soumi and others who witnessed or remember Israel's destruction of the Palestine Office of Unified Information, sees the importance of investing in the materiality of cultural practices, even if they will always be under existential threat and part and parcel of global capital circuits. In reality, the multimillion dollar investment project that is the museum can neither be defended nor easily rebuilt, should Israel decide to destroy it at any point. The museum, like other initiatives in Palestine, whether "state"- or civil society-led, is vulnerable to the closures, looting, and destruction to which all Palestinian cultural heritage has always been subject. This destruction is a possibility that financial investors have had to contend with. Sreenan describes the stoic perseverance of financial and other investors in the project during the dark days of the Gaza slaughter by Israel in 2014 as "possibly one of the most graceful acts of resistance one could ever witness."[36]

Hence the question of the museum's role vis-à-vis the power structures it has to counter in the case of Israel and contend with in the case of the PNA was never about whether its construction would in and of itself be a compromise with the post-Oslo configuration of power. Rather, it was always about how it would negotiate with these power structures in order to position itself as a space of critique, resistance, and decoloniality in the convoluted colonial context of post-Oslo Palestine. As Doumani puts it, complicating the issue, "How this is done, of course, is of utmost importance."[37]

IN THE COMPANY OF OTHER MUSEUMS

The Palestinian Museum was first envisioned as a commemorative structure built around a single chronological narrative that begins in 1948. As it developed, it became clear to all those involved that in distancing itself from 1948 as the starting point of a chronological historical narrative, the museum would reject the standard Zionist line that the notion of a Palestinian people was constructed only after the establishment of the state of Israel in 1948. By beginning in the eighteenth century, it was agreed, the museum would better reflect the reality of the Palestinians as a dispersed people with urban, rural, and intellectual histories who were in existence well before Zionists began to arrive in Palestine and violently established their state. In this, the Palestinian Museum positions itself as a counternarrative not only to Israeli self-deception about the persecuted Jews of Europe having arrived to a land without a people, but also to the PNA's framing of the Palestinians as a people whose existence is articulated solely in opposition to Israel, as is evident in the museum projects in which it is involved.[38]

In both the Al-Birweh Park/Mahmoud Darwish Museum and the Yasser Arafat Museum in Ramallah (opened in 2014 and 2016 respectively), the PNA wrests control over narration from the people it governs in the name of figures who were dominant players (and narrators) in the Palestinian resistance movement and, in the case of Arafat, the Palestinian state formation project in the aftermath of the Oslo Accords. In other words, unlike the Palestinian Museum, the emphasis in the PNA's new multimillion-dollar museum projects is more on state power and state-building than on agency, peoplehood, and transterritoriality. More crucially, by focusing on Arafat and Darwish as the main characters in a story about the Palestinian struggle, the resistance is reified and commodified in ways that are both fathomable on the international stage and productive of nostalgia for the local public. What is insinuated through the aesthetics and narratives of the museums is that these figures are part of the struggle for independence from Israel that has supposedly been achieved with the signing of Oslo. They are stories from a glorious past, relics from a bygone era, what Svetlana Boym has termed a "dictatorship of nostalgia" that reigns at the supposed end of a conflict.[39] Or alternatively, they are a chance to critique the past in order to imagine the future, as the director of the Yasser Arafat Museum suggested when I proposed my cynical reading to him.[40] Ultimately, the differing temporal orientations of the Darwish and Arafat museums, dedicated to the past as a way of thinking about the future, on the one hand, and the Palestinian Museum, focused on the continuing reality of colonization, on the other, are reflected in the way one affectively experiences each of the museums.

Both the PNA's museum projects are exercises in formal and institutional design that evoke the state's legitimacy. By commissioning the late Ja'afar Tuqan, one of the Arab world's most renowned modernist architects—known for his functionalism, simplicity, and minimalism, expressed in major institutional buildings such as mosques, government offices, banks, and schools throughout the Levant and the Arab Gulf over the past forty years—the PNA was asserting its role as the neutral state apparatus representing the public interest. In the case of the Mahmoud Darwish Museum, which is also the "temporary" mausoleum of Palestine's most loved poet, the small and darkened space that sits atop a mountain of stairs, and which holds most of Darwish's personal writings and belongings, could be an exhibition space visualizing state grandeur anywhere in the world.[41] Unlike the Palestinian Museum, there is nothing inside save for the writings and book covers of Darwish's publications encased on the walls that tells visitors where they are. Formally, this could be a minimalist exhibition anywhere. Yet, like the Palestinian Museum, the Darwish Museum also deploys indigenous plants and the terraced gardening typical of the landscape to emphasize Palestinian claims over the land.

The role of museums in contributing to visualizing national identity is clearly identified in postcolonial literature.[42] How political actors make use of these institutions as tools for the conduct of diplomacy or to claim a symbolic significance for the nation-state through the collections that are held within them are matters that relate to the political function of museums and the emotions they conjure up for the communities they represent.[43] Yet the building of Palestine's museums, whether by civil society and private capital or by the state, cannot be fully understood outside of the tide of museum-building in the region. Focusing on national identity, societal development, and international understanding, museums in the Arab Gulf states of Qatar and the United Arab Emirates have taken it upon themselves in recent years to redraw Arab and Muslim identity on the global map as part of a larger process of diversifying their oil-based economies by investing in other areas.[44] Though these efforts replicate the tools, modes, and ideas of Western museum construction and maintenance, Gulf states have been credited with taking the initiative to de-Westernize and decolonize Arab representations by delinking them from their original source: the Western museum and its historic relationship to the nation-state in the time of empire.

In the words of the decolonial theorist Walter Mignolo, writing about the Qatari Museum of Islamic Art in Doha, "What is happening is not merely an imitation of westernization, but an enactment of de-westernization in that western cultural standards are being appropriated and adapted to local or regional sensibilities, needs and visions. In the sphere of civilizations and museums, this is a significant departure."[45] The suggestion that he and others have made is that prosperous and stable Arab capitals like Doha, Dubai, Abu Dhabi, and Muscat have the capability to redraw the global cultural map by redefining the Arab capital in a manner that is neither "Eurocentric nor Europhobic; neither retrograde nativist nor rootless cosmopolitan."[46]

While there is something to these celebratory and hopeful takes on art infrastructure in the Gulf, what seems to be missing is an examination of how tied up these spaces are in regional geopolitics, economic diversification strategies, and military alliances with Western powers (evidenced not least by the location of military bases such as those of France in the United Arab Emirates or the United States in Qatar), even if they are seemingly de-Westernizing art discourses and collecting practices by rerouting the direction of travel and sales of each. Decolonial claims do not seem to factor in the corporate power that often shapes the conversations that take place in and about museums, even if these museums—especially as in the case of the Gulf museums—are able to reverse art market trends by paying more for artworks than traditional Western art patrons, such as the British Museum, are able to today. I would argue that this process by itself is not proof that a decolonial epistemic shift is occurring, in the absence of evidence of the production of one's own knowledge on one's own terms, outside of market constraints.

My reference to other museums in Palestine and the Arab region more generally is not intended to suggest that the Palestinian Museum is somehow more resistant or more worthy as a museum "for the people by the people." Instead, my point concerns the need to start a conversation about the content and form of museums in the region that do not fit the emerging Gulf museum format of massive, powerful symbols of capital defined by aesthetically minimalist, white-cube styles that are a means to assert global relevance and centrality. I want to ask how smaller "postcolonial" museums, like the Palestinian Museum, that are not commissioned as part of a larger national strategic plan, intervene in the space of "decoloniality" that the Gulf is ironically now celebrated as spearheading.

It is no coincidence that the financial patrons of the Palestinian Museum have made their money in the Gulf. It is also possible that future links between the Palestinian Museum and Gulf museums will be solidified through staff training and other professional and infrastructural development that will be needed as the Palestinian Museum grows. What these links will signify, and how they will shape the direction that the museum will take, warrant continuing scrutiny and discussion.

The Palestinian Museum's mission of wresting back the narratives, material culture, and memories that have been so crudely taken from the Palestinian people is a reminder of an integral element of decolonization. If we think of decolonization in the realm of museum curation as entailing not simply a decentering of the art market and the flows of art sales, as suggested in the decolonial claims of Mignolo and others, but also a forestalling of the violence of amnesia and narrative erasure that accompanies colonialism in Palestine, a new emancipatory definition of the term may be enunciated.[47] For all its faults and the criticism it might incur in the future, the Palestinian Museum is ultimately striving to seize control over its destiny not only from its oppressor Israel but also from hegemonic understandings and practices of statehood, peoplehood, space, time, and architecture. For that, it should be celebrated not only as a triumphant moment in the cultural history of the Palestinian people, but also as a genuinely emancipatory moment in the grand project of epistemic decolonization, for Palestinians and for other colonized peoples everywhere.

NOTES

This article is reprinted with the permission of the journal *Radical Philosophy*, where it first appeared in December 2018.

1. Joseph Massad, "The 'Post-colonial' Colony: Time, Space, and Bodies in Palestine/Israel," *The Pre-occupation of Postcolonial Studies*, eds. Fawzia Afzal-Khan and Kalpana Seshadri-Crooks (Durham, NC: Duke University Press 2000), 311–46.

2. See Eilean Hooper-Greenhill, *Museums and the Interpretation of Culture* (London and New York: Routledge, 2000)

3. See the Museum's website on this concept: palmuseum.org/about/the-building-2.

4. On the "postcolonial museum," see Alessandra De Angelis, Celeste Ianniciello, Mariangela Orabona and Iain Chambers, eds., *The Postcolonial Museum: The Arts of Memory and the Pressures of History* (Abingdon: Routledge, 2016); and Sonja Mejcher-Atassi and John Pedro Schwartz, eds., *Archives, Museums and Collecting Practices in the Modern Arab World* (Abingdon: Routledge, 2016), both of which have paved the way for a reconceptualization of objects and collections as "processes or practices and not just things." See also Elizabeth Edwards, Chris Gosden and Ruth B. Phillips, eds., *Sensible Objects: Colonialism, Museums and Material Culture* (Oxford: Berg, 2006).

5. See for instance Pamela Erskine-Loftus, Victoria Penziner Hightower, and Mariam Ibrahim Al-Mulla, eds., *Representing the Nation: Heritage, Museums, National Narratives and Identity in the Arab Gulf States* (Abingdon: Routledge, 2016); Hayfa Matar, "Museums as Signifiers in the Gulf," in *Cities, Museums and Soft Power*, eds. Gail Dexter Lord and Ngaire Blankenberg, 87–98 (Washington, DC: AAM Press, 2015). Peggy Levitt, *Artifacts and Allegiances: How Museums Put the Nation and the World on Display* (Oakland: University of California Press, 2015) offers a dynamic approach to understanding museums' roles as sites of cosmopolitanism in an increasingly transnationalized and global world.

6. The A.M. Qattan Foundation is an independent, not-for-profit developmental organization working in the fields of culture and education, with a particular focus on children, teachers, and young artists.

7. Taawon mission statement, accessed March 13, 2018, taawon.org.

8. "Jack Persekian, Director of Palestinian Museum, Resigns," *Artforum*, December 11, 2015, artforum.com/news/jack-persekian-director-of-palestinian-museum-resigns-56674.

9. Donald Preziosi and Claire Farago, *Art Is Not What You Think It Is* (Oxford: Wiley-Blackwell, 2012).

10. See for instance Steven Conn, *Do Museums Still Need Objects?* (Philadelphia: University of Pennsylvania Press, 2010); Edwards, Gosden, and Phillips, *Sensible Objects*.

11. *Nakba* is the Arabic word for catastrophe and Nakba Day (May 15) was officially designated by Yasser Arafat in 1998 as the official day of mourning to coincide with Israel's official celebration of its establishment in 1948.

12. For Al-Qattan's criticisms of the global art world's approach to cultural production, which he sees as "far too restricted, abstract, filled with jargon, falsely academic," see Shany Littman, "Even Empty, the New Palestinian Museum Is Making History," *Haaretz*, May 26, 2016, http://haaretz.com /israel-news/culture/.premium-1.721510.

13. Esra Akcan, "Apology and Triumph: Memory Transference, Erasure, and a Rereading of the Berlin Jewish Museum," *New German Critique* 37, no. 2 (2010): 153–79.

14. "Jack Persekian," *Artforum*; James Glanz and Rami Nazzal, "Palestinian Museum Prepares to Open, Minus Exhibitions," *The New York Times*, May 16, 2016, nytimes.com/2016/05/17/world/midd leeast/palestinian-museum-birzeit-west-bank.html.

15. Zina Jardaneh, chair of the board of the Palestinian Museum, interview with author, December 17, 2017.

16. "New Palestinian Museum Opens without Exhibits," *BBC News*, May 18, 2016, http://bbc .com/news/world-middle-east-36322756; William Booth, "Palestinian Museum Opening without Exhibits, but Creators Say That's No Big Deal," *Washington Post*, May 18, 2016; 'Palestinian History Museum Opens without Any Exhibits," *Associated Press*, May 19, 2016, ynetnews.com /articles/0,7340,L-4805141,00.html.

17. See for instance Hannah Mermelstein, "Overdue Books: Returning Palestine's 'Abandoned Property' of 1948," *Jerusalem Quarterly* 47 (Autumn 2011): 199–228; Gish Amit, "Ownerless Objects? The Story of the Books Palestinians Left behind in 1948," *Jerusalem Quarterly* 33 (Winter 2008): 7–20; Sarah Irving, "'Endangered Archives' Program Opens Up Priceless Palestinian Heritage," *Electronic Intifada*, May 13, 2014, electronicintifada.net/blogs/sarah-irving/endangered-archives-program-opens-pricless-palestinian-heritage.

18. The Young Artists of the Year Award, named after the late artist Hassan Hourani, is one of the most important events in the visual arts calendar of Palestine and has been organized on a biannual basis by the A.M. Qattan Foundation since 2000. For some who were present at the YAYA ceremony, Al Qattan's words seemed harsh generalizations that overlooked the real achievement of getting Palestine onto the world cultural map. For others, Al-Qattan seemed to be pushing his audience to think honestly and critically about the global political economy of arts production that Palestinian artists, like artists elsewhere, have had to negotiate with, often at the expense of effacing local historical

and ongoing processes of resistance. See Tarek Hamdan, "Omar Al-Qattan: Bakae'ya Muta'akhira . . . Walakin" [Omar Al-Qattan: A belated jeremiad . . . or not], *Al Akhbar*, October 16, 2016. Al-Qattan offered a detailed response to the *Al-Akhbar* piece, which he saw as wrongfully representing his statement: "Omar Al-Qattan: (Cultural) Palestine Will Not Die," A.M. Qattan Foundation, December 6, 2016, qattanfoundation.org/en/qattan/media/news/omar-al-qattan-cultural-palestine-will-not-die.

19. Interview with author, December 20, 2017.

20. Khaled Hourani, "Globalisation Questions and Contemporary Art's Answers: Art in Palestine," in *Globalisation and Contemporary Art*, ed. Jonathan Harris, 297–306 (Oxford: Wiley-Blackwell, 2009), 301.

21. Lara Khalidi, an independent curator from Palestine, takes up this point in her paper "The Museum before the Museum," presented at Harvard Graduate School Quincy School of Design, November 6, 2017.

22. Nasser Abourahme, "The Bantustan Sublime: Reframing the Colonial in Ramallah," *City* 13, no. 4 (2009): 499–509.

23. Adam Hanieh, *Capitalism and Class in the Gulf Arab States* (New York: Palgrave Macmillan, 2011). See also chapter 1 of this volume.

24. Sherene Seikaly, *Men of Capital: Scarcity and Economy in Mandate Palestine* (Stanford, CA: Stanford University Press, 2016).

25. Levitt, *Artifacts and Allegiances*, 8.

26. Lara Zureikat, phone interview with author, November 23, 2017.

27. Eyal Weizman, *Hollow Land: Israel's Architecture of Occupation* (London: Verso, 2012), 120.

28. Conor Sreenan, Skype interview with author, December 5, 2017.

29. Omar Al-Kattan, phone interview with author, December 17, 2017.

30. For the curators' description of the project and its content, see Kristine Khouri and Rasha Salti, "Past Disquiet: From Research to Exhibition," *Artl@s Bulletin* 5, no. 1 (2016), article 8.

31. This conversation was part of an exchange I had with Soumi and others on a panel titled "Before the Museum," for which I was invited to be the discussant, as part of the symposium Shifting Ground: The Underground Is Not the Past, held at the Khalil Sakakini Cultural Centre as part of the Tamawuj chapter of the thirteenth Sharjah Biennial, held in Ramallah August 10–14, 2017.

32. For instance, the Museum is currently running two projects, "Palestinian Journeys" and the "Palestinian Museum Digital Archive," that constitute a large part of the open-access digital platform that will collect, organize, and archive Palestinian history in Palestine. See palmuseum.org/projects/e-platforms-1.

33. For an earlier take on the changing scope and content of the decolonization process, see Jan Nederveen Pieterse and Bhikhu Parekh, eds., *The Decolonisation of Imagination: Culture, Knowledge and Power* (London: Zed Books, 1995).

34. Ursula Biemman, "A Post-Territorial Museum: Interview with Beshara Doumani," *Arte East Quarterly*, Spring 2010, arteeast.org/quarterly/a-post-territorial-museum/?issues_season=spring&issues_year=2010.

35. I am not suggesting that this approach is the Palestinian Museum's alone. Since the late 1990s many museums have invested in an online presence and incorporated a wide range of web-based formats into their programs and exhibits in order to enable access by a global public.

36. Conor Sreenan, Skype interview with author, December 5, 2017.

37. Beshara Doumani, informal discussion with author, Providence, RI, December 4, 2017.

38. I want to stress here that this counternarrative is extremely important and necessary insofar as it responds to Israel's military and Zionist discursive narrative, which attempts to erase the Palestinian people. However, there is a need to go beyond the defensive. As Doumani puts it, "How can Palestinians take control of and shape their own narratives, but not in a defensive mechanical way that simply responds to how they are represented by others?" Biemman, "A Post-Territorial Museum."

39. Svetlana Boym, *The Future of Nostalgia* (New York: Basic Books, 2002), 354.

40. Mohammad Halayka, interview with author, Ramallah, May 23, 2018.

41. Both the mausoleums of Yasser Arafat and Mahmoud Darwish are generally regarded as temporary in anticipation of the day when they can be transplanted to Jerusalem, the occupied capital city that Palestinians, like Israelis, perceive as theirs.

42. Rodney Harrison and Lotte Hughes, "Heritage, Colonialism and Postcolonialism," in *Understanding the Politics of Heritage*, ed. Rodney Harrison, 243–67 (Manchester: Manchester University Press, 2010).

43. Clive Gray, *The Politics of Museums* (Basingstoke: Palgrave Macmillan, 2015); Melissa Nisbett, "New Perspectives on Instrumentalism: An Empirical Study of Cultural Diplomacy," *International Journal of Cultural Policy* 19, no. 5 (2013): 557–75. It is also interesting to take note of a roundtable discussion conducted between Jack Persekian, the former director of the Palestinian Museum, curator Lara Khalidi, and artist Yazan Khalil, on the nature of a museum in the context of a state that does not exist. Khalidi questions whether Palestinians are able to creatively take advantage of their nonstate status to interrogate other forms of political existence that the museum could experiment with. The one point that Persekian goes back to is that the museum is a civil society project that does not intend to represent the state but rather, works in parallel to it. See Welfare Association and the Palestinian Museum, *Muqaddima fi al Mathaf al Falastinya* (Ramallah: Welfare Association and the Palestinian Museum, 2014), 10–14.

44. Suzi Mirgani, "Introduction: Art and Cultural Production in the GCC," *Journal of Arabian Studies*, 7, no. 1 (2017): 1–11.

45. Walter Mignolo, "Enacting the Archives, Decentering the Muses: The Museum of Islamic Art in Doha and the Asian Civilisations Museum in Singapore," *Ibraaz* 006 (2013): 11–12, ibraaz.org/usr/library/documents/main/enacting-the-archives.pdf.

46. Hamid Dabashi, "Rethinking the Arab Capital through Art," *Al Jazeera*, April 10, 2017, aljazeera.com/indepth/opinion/2017/04/rethinking-arab-capital-art-170409105111270.html; Hamid Dabashi, "What Are the Saudis Afraid Of?" *Al Jazeera*, December 17, 2017, www.aljazeera.com/indepth/opinion/saudis-afraid-171217082544270.html.

47. Mignolo's understanding of decoloniality (as opposed to decolonization) is closely linked to the process of "delinking" as he expounds it in "Delinking: The Rhetoric of Modernity, the Logic of Coloniality and the Grammar of De-coloniality," *Cultural Studies* 21, no. 2–3 (2007): 449–514, 453. Here he refers to a process that leads to decolonial epistemic shifts that in turn propose alternative universalities or what he terms "pluri-versality" as a universal project.

BIBLIOGRAPHY

Abourahme, Nasser. "The Bantustan Sublime: Reframing the Colonial in Ramallah." *City* 13, no. 4 (2009): 499–509.

Akcan, Esra. "Apology and Triumph: Memory Transference, Erasure, and a Rereading of the Berlin Jewish Museum." *New German Critique* 37, no. 2 (2010): 153–79

Amit, Gish. "Ownerless Objects? The Story of the Books Palestinians Left behind in 1948." *Jerusalem Quarterly* 33 (Winter 2008): 7–20.

Biemman, Ursula. "A Post-Territorial Museum: Interview with Beshara Doumani." *Arte-East Quarterly*, Spring 2010. arteeast.org/quarterly/a-post-territorial-museum/?issues_season = spring&issues_year = 2010.

Boym, Svetlana. *The Future of Nostalgia*. New York: Basic Books, 2002.

Conn, Steven. *Do Museums Still Need Objects?* Philadelphia: University of Pennsylvania Press, 2010.

De Angelis, Alessandra, Celeste Ianniciello, Mariangela Orabona, and Ian Chambers, eds. *The Postcolonial Museum: The Arts of Memory and the Pressures of History*. Abingdon: Routledge, 2016.

Edwards, Elizabeth, Chris Gosden, and Ruth B. Phillips, eds., *Sensible Objects: Colonialism, Museums and Material Culture*. Oxford: Berg, 2006.

Erskine-Loftus, Pamela, Victoria Penziner Hightower, and Mariam Ibrahim Al-Mulla, eds. *Representing the Nation: Heritage, Museums, National Narratives and Identity in the Arab Gulf States*. Abingdon: Routledge, 2016.

Gray, Clive. *The Politics of Museums*. Basingstoke: Palgrave Macmillan, 2015.

Hanieh, Adam. *Capitalism and Class in the Gulf Arab States*. New York: Palgrave Macmillan, 2011.

———. "The Oslo Illusion." *Jacobin*, April 2013. jacobinmag.com/2013/04/the-oslo-illusion.

Harrison, Rodney, and Lotte Hughes. "Heritage, Colonialism and Postcolonialism." In *Understanding the Politics of Heritage*, edited by Rodney Harrison, 243–67. Manchester: Manchester University Press, 2010.

Hooper-Greenhill, Eilean. *Museums and the Interpretation of Culture*. London: Routledge, 2000.

Hourani, Khaled. "Globalisation Questions and Contemporary Art's Answers: Art in Palestine." In *Globalisation and Contemporary Art*, edited by Jonathan Harris, 297–303. Oxford: Wiley-Blackwell. 2009.

Khalidi, Lara. "The Museum before the Museum." Paper presented at Harvard Graduate School Quincy School of Design, November 6, 2017.

Khouri, Kristine, and Rasha Salti. "Past Disquiet: From Research to Exhibition." *Artl@s Bulletin* 5, no. 1 (2016), article 8.

Levitt, Peggy. *Artifacts and Allegiances: How Museums Put the Nation and the World on Display*. Oakland: University of California Press, 2015.

Massad, Joseph. "'The 'Post-colonial' Colony: Time, Space, and Bodies in Palestine/Israel." In *The Pre-occupation of Postcolonial Studies*, edited by Fawzia Afzal-Khan and Kalpana Seshadri-Crooks, 311–46. Durham, NC: Duke University Press 2000.

Matar, Hayfa. "'Museums as Signifiers in the Gulf." In *Cities, Museums and Soft Power*, edited by Gail Dexter Lord and Ngaire Blankenberg, 87–98. Washington, DC: American Alliance of Museums Press, 2015.

Mejcher-Atassi, Sonja, and John Pedro Schwartz, eds. *Archives, Museums and Collecting Practices in the Modern Arab World*. Abingdon: Routledge, 2016.

Mermelstein, Hannah. "Overdue Books: Returning Palestine's 'Abandoned Property' of 1948." *Jerusalem Quarterly* 47 (Autumn 2011): 199–228.

Mignolo, Walter. "Delinking: The Rhetoric of Modernity, the Logic of Coloniality and the Grammar of De-coloniality." *Cultural Studies* 21, no. 2–3 (2007): 449–514.

———. "Enacting the Archives, Decentering the Muses: The Museum of Islamic Art in Doha and the Asian Civilisations Museum in Singapore." *Ibraaz* 006 (November 2013). ibraaz.org/usr/library/documents/main/enacting-the-archives.pdf.

Mirgani, Suzi. "Introduction: Art and Cultural Production in the GCC." *Journal of Arabian Studies* 7, no. 1 (2017): 1–11.

Nederveen Pieterse, Jan, and Bhikhu Parekh, eds. *The Decolonisation of Imagination: Culture, Knowledge and Power*. London: Zed Books, 1995.

Nisbett, Melissa. "New Perspectives on Instrumentalism: An Empirical Study of Cultural Diplomacy." *International Journal of Cultural Policy* 19, no. 5 (2013): 557–75.

Preziosi, Donald, and Claire Farago. *Art Is Not What You Think It Is*. Oxford: Wiley-Blackwell, 2012.

Seikaly, Sherene. *Men of Capital: Scarcity and Economy in Mandate Palestine*. Stanford, CA: Stanford University Press, 2016.

Welfare Association and the Palestinian Museum, *Muqaddima fi al Mathaf al Falastinya*. Ramallah: Welfare Association and the Palestinian Museum, 2014.

Weizman, Eyal. *Hollow Land: Israel's Architecture of Occupation*. London: Verso, 2012.

5

Defending Palestinian Rights
in the Trump Era and Beyond

Yousef Munayyer

This chapter explores the challenges and opportunities presented for Palestinian rights work in the United States in the era of Donald Trump and beyond. It argues that Trump's election paradoxically enhanced the momentum for American support for Palestinian rights and for the Boycott, Divestment, and Sanctions (BDS) movement that seeks to hold Israel accountable for its treatment of Palestinians. Generating greater support for Palestinian rights in the United States remains a function of the nature of US-Israel special relations as much as the ability of Palestinian activists to expose the intersections between the Palestinian struggle and the struggle against racism in the United States more generally. Palestinian rights advocacy also remains tied to the ability of the Palestinian national movement to reframe the Palestinian struggle from one that is confined to implementing a defunct two-state solution to one that affirms and protects their rights, irrespective of whatever solution is proposed. By reviewing the history of activism for Palestine in the United States over the past two decades, and the opportunity that Obama's election in particular opened for talking about race and equal rights, this chapter explains why a rights-based approach for defending Palestinian rights has greater prospects for success today than ever before.

POLITICAL ACTIVISM FOR PALESTINIANS IN
THE UNITED STATES SINCE 2001

Advocacy for the Palestinian cause in the United States has a long history. Before the 1967 war, organizations such as the Arab National League and the Institute for Arab American Affairs focused on representing the Palestinian cause as part of the Arab struggle for independence from Western domination.[1] After the 1967 war, new organizations emerged, such as the Organization of Arab Students, the Arab American University Graduates, and eventually the American Arab

Anti-Discrimination Committee and the Arab American Institute.[2] These organizations focused their work on explaining the Palestinian plight to an American public and media that portrayed Palestinians through a stereotypical, simplistic lens—as terrorists. Some of these organizations also tried to lobby and generate support in the US Congress for a Palestinian state on the West Bank and Gaza in light of the Palestine Liberation Organization's declaration of independence, its recognition of Israel, and UN Security Council Resolution 242 in 1988. The advocacy work of these organizations, though, often came up against a special glass ceiling: despite an organized effort at the grassroots level, impact on policy was limited by influential pro-Israel interest groups who had developed strong relationships with policymakers.

With the collapse of the Camp David negotiations in 2000 and the eruption of the Second Intifada, a number of activist organizations came together to create the US Campaign for Palestinian Rights (USCPR).[3] Founded in 2001, this campaign became a coalition of over three hundred member groups across the United States working for Palestinian rights. It includes organizations large and small of various identities and in various locations across the country. At first, USCPR focused its efforts on ending American military aid to Israel by trying to impact policy makers in Washington, DC. With the advent of the Boycott, Divestment, and Sanction movement in 2005, USCPR took a new approach—one that sought new alliances and aimed at generating a grassroots approach that was seen as having more potential to succeed in impacting American policy on Palestine.

THE BDS CALL AND THE MOVEMENT FOR
PALESTINIAN RIGHTS IN THE UNITED STATES

The movement for Palestinian rights is a global one, and it is not new. Its growth in the United States has been shaped both by the political objectives set by the Palestinian national movement as well as by the nature of US-Israel relations. The US-Israel relationship is the single most important relationship with a country or group of countries that Israel has. Often referred to as a "special" relationship, the US-Israel relationship has paradoxically become the backbone of Israel's human rights abuses against the Palestinians. Without American support, it is hard to imagine how Israel could continue its extensive violations of Palestinian human rights with impunity. The traditional channels of advocacy, particularly as they relate to lobbying Congress and/or the White House, were thus extremely difficult for Palestinians to access and navigate. For this reason, the work of the USCPR has been very challenging. Whereas pro-Israel advocacy groups like American Israel Public Affairs Committee (AIPAC), the Anti-Defamation League (ADL), the American Jewish Committee, and many others, have invested heavily in developing and maintaining relations between Washington and Tel-Aviv for decades, such access to US government circles was very difficult for pro-Palestinian advocates.

No matter how many letters were written to Congress, how many members of Congress or their staff privately told Palestine rights advocates, "I agree with you, but if I do anything on this, it will cost me dearly," how many phone calls were made by constituents to members' offices—the efforts all came to naught. This had a very discouraging and demoralizing effect on activists engaged in Palestinian rights advocacy.

The Palestinian call for BDS, adopted by over 170 organizations in the West Bank and Gaza in 2005, provided a unique opportunity for Palestinian advocacy work in the United States.[4] While the idea of divestment had existed before 2005 and indeed, divestment campaigns were being organized and even won in campuses prior to the 2005 call, the call was the first time that the use of these tactics in a Palestinian-led framework was formalized, thanks to its endorsement by over 170 civil society organizations in the West Bank and Gaza. It is no exaggeration to say that the embrace of these tactics by Palestinian rights activists in the United States had a revolutionary impact on the movement. The call gave activists new ways to organize, new spaces in which to organize, new targets, and, most importantly, an opportunity to win. Within USCPR and outside it, activists started thinking that it was perhaps too difficult at the moment to get the US government to address its complicity in Israeli abuses—but what about the complicity of various levels of society below the government level? There was a push for highlighting how individual, community, organizational, institutional, and local government complicity in Israel's violation of Palestinian rights could be articulated in specific campaigns aimed at specific targets. These campaigns could operate in an arena with far less competition than in the halls of Congress, making success far more achievable. This quickly translated to optimism, engagement, buy-in, commitment, and the desire to do more campaign-related work. An effort that had become debilitating and discouraging visibly became dynamic, energizing, and empowering instead.

This grassroots approach also disarmed Israel and its advocates of the ability to discredit their opponents as "terrorists," which had become a particularly potent weapon in post-9/11 America. Those organizing and advocating boycott campaigns were engaged in explicitly nonviolent action. Further, boycott campaigns helped shift the focus away from a nationalist framing of the conflict that pitted Israelis against Palestinians—a framing that posed a number of challenges, including that uncommitted Americans might be reluctant to take sides. Now, the conflict began to be framed as about the average American's own complicity in Israel's human rights abuses against Palestinians.

For all these reasons, BDS campaigns have seen numerous successes in the past twelve years, as can be seen from the list of "BDS Wins" on the USCPR website.[5] The sheer diversity of victories is impressive: corporate divestment victories, church divestment victories, cultural boycott victories, university boycott victories, professional association victories, and the list goes on. As well, the pace of victories has accelerated over time. In the early years after the BDS call, victories were less prevalent, but in recent years, they have been increasingly frequent. The USCPR used to spend more time helping groups start campaigns; now, self-starting campaigns take off around the country, sometimes thanks to preexisting resources but often also out of the initiative of local organizers, without any support from the USCPR. Now much more of the USCPR's time is spent coordinating and providing support for campaigns that are up and running on their own.

The rights-based activist approach for defending the Palestinian cause in the United States has proved to be more productive than the pre-2000 efforts, which focused on the Palestinian demand for a state. Instead of confining itself to explaining and defending the Palestinian quest for a separate independent state in the West Bank and Gaza, a cause which is hard for outsiders to identify with, the USCPR opted to advocate for restoring denied human rights. This approach proved far easier for people, particularly Americans, to identify with and support. Furthermore, the rights-based approach exposed the pernicious nature of nationalism and specifically what Zionism, an ethnic nationalism, meant for Palestinians. At a moment when a growing political divide is emerging around the world between ethnic nationalism and multiculturalism, this rights-driven approach highlights the dangers of ethnic nationalism and the importance of defending the Palestinians' struggle for equal rights.

THE ZIONIST WHITE SUPREMACIST: FROM BALFOUR TO TRUMP

Revisiting the Balfour Declaration through the lens of the current moment allows us to understand how the tension between ethnic nationalism and multiculturalism has lain at the foundation of the question of Israel/Palestine from the outset until the present day.

Though he may be most known for aiding the Zionist cause in 1917, it is often overlooked that Arthur Balfour, prime minister of the United Kingdom from 1902 to 1905, was a white supremacist. He made that clear in his own words. In 1906, the British House of Commons was engaged in a debate about the native Black population in South Africa. Nearly all the members of Parliament agreed that the disenfranchisement of Blacks in South Africa was evil. But not Balfour, who was virtually the sole parliamentarian to argue for it, using these words: "We have to face the facts. Men are not born equal, the white and black races are not born with equal capacities: They are born with different capacities which education cannot and will not change."[6]

But Balfour's troubling views were not limited to Africa. In fact, despite his now-iconic support for Zionism, he was not exactly a friend to the Jews. In the late nineteenth century, pogroms targeting Jews in the Pale of Settlement in imperial Russia had led to waves of Jewish flight westward, to England and the United States. This influx of refugees led to an increase in British anti-immigrant racism and outright anti-Semitism—themes not unfamiliar to us today. Support for political action against immigrants grew as the English public demanded immigration control to keep certain immigrants, particularly Jews, out of the country.

In 1905, while serving as prime minister, Balfour presided over the passage of the Aliens Act. This legislation imposed the first restrictions on immigration into Great Britain, and it was primarily aimed at restricting Jewish immigration.

It may seem astonishing that Balfour, whose support of the Zionist cause has made him a hero among Jews, would have implemented anti-Jewish laws. But the truth is that his support of Zionism stemmed from the exact same source as his desire to limit Jewish immigration to Britain. Both can be traced back to his white supremacist beliefs. Balfour lived in an era of stirring nationalism, highly defined by ethnoreligious identity. Because of these sentiments, the early twentieth century was a time when ostensibly liberal Western nations struggled with the challenge of incorporating Jewish citizens into their fold. The Zionists provided Balfour with a solution to the challenges that Jewish citizens posed to his ethnonationalist vision, a solution that didn't force him to reckon with them. Instead of insisting that societies accept all citizens as equals, regardless of racial or religious background, the Zionist movement offered a different answer: separation. Balfour saw in Zionism not just a blessing for Jews, but for the West as well. As he wrote in 1919 in his introduction to Nahum Sokolow's *History of Zionism*, the Zionist movement would "mitigate the age-long miseries created for Western civilization by the presence in its midst of a Body which it too long regarded as alien and even hostile, but which it was equally unable to expel or to absorb."[7] By giving Jews a place to go to, Zionism seemingly solved two problems at once, in Balfour's mind. Balfour's support of Zionism was motivated to an extent by his desire to protect Britain from the negative effects, the "miseries," of having Jews in its midst. Rather than protecting the rights of one of its minorities, Britain could simply export them, or at least, not import any more. Needless to say, this view of Zionism is steeped in the same kind of white supremacy as Balfour's view of South Africa's Blacks. Yet, rather than solving the problem of how to handle a minority living in a white-majority country, the Balfour Declaration just shifted the same problem to a different geography.

For the tension between ethnonationalism and equality is equally present in Israel/Palestine. The Israeli state rules over the fate of millions of Palestinians who either have no right to vote, are treated as second-class citizens, or are refugees denied repatriation. Today, it is Israel that views Palestinians as a "demographic threat" and sees "the presence in its midst of a body which it too long regarded as alien and even hostile, but which it was equally unable to expel or to absorb," as Balfour put it.[8]

That Balfour's legacy of supremacy persists today is no accident. It has lent itself to an imperial project that allowed the Jewish national movement to assert its right to national self-determination while denying the same to the native non-Jews.

Remarkably, Balfour was unabashedly aware of the hypocrisy of his stance. "The weak point of our position of course is that in the case of Palestine we deliberately and rightly decline to accept the principle of self-determination," he wrote in a letter to the British prime minister in 1919.[9] "We do not propose even to go through the form of consulting the wishes of the present inhabitants of the country . . . the 700,000 Arabs who now inhabit that ancient land."[10]

Those Arabs, of course, made up approximately 90 percent of the population in 1919. Therein lies the fundamental problem that continues through this day, just over one hundred years later. Palestinians are denied the right to have rights because from the outset, their views, their human rights, and indeed their very humanity, were consistently seen as inferior to those of others. That was clear in Balfour's perspective and the British Mandate's policy. And it persists in one form or another in many of the policies of the state of Israel through this day.

Today as much as in 1917, the battle between ethnonationalism and equality, between particularism and universalism, has risen to the foreground, from Donald Trump's rise in the United States to Boris Johnson's Brexited Britain. The ideology that Trump rode into power favored a similar *herrenvolk* nationalism. It holds that a country is for a people, not for many peoples. Zionism fits this worldview very well. There is a crystalizing alignment taking place and it is happening globally. Israel, which has sold itself in the west as a liberal democracy, is fully and wholeheartedly aligning with reactionary right-wingers across the globe. Exposing this to those in liberal and progressive circles in the United States who have not yet taken a stand on Palestinian rights was one of the key tasks of activists for Palestine in the Trump era.

THE POLITICAL CONTEXT FOR PALESTINIAN RIGHTS BEFORE THE 2016 US ELECTION

To fully appreciate the meaning and gravity of the reactionary Trump political moment, it is crucial to understand the political moment it was reacting to and the growing partisan divide that developed in the United States. During the Obama era, despite his stalwart support for Israel, on par with or beyond that of his predecessors, an unprecedented shift in public opinion on Israel occurred in the United States. This shift followed largely partisan lines, itself a significant development given the prior American consensus regarding Israel; even when Republicans and Democrats couldn't agree on whether it was night or day, they always agreed on Israel. Now, suddenly, this was starting to change. Although the Democratic party, including under the Obama administration, remained a staunch supporter of Israel (indeed securing it the largest military financing agreement in history), the Republican party, together with right-wing Israelis, tried to portray itself as the only reliable ally of Israel. At the same time, Democrats began to be torn apart between a values-driven base, alienated by the horrors of apartheid on the ground in Palestine, and a traditional political and donor class who favored maintaining the bipartisan status quo.

This change took root for several reasons. The first was Obama the person. Barack Hussein Obama had been the first Black person elected as president of the United States. Many Israelis simply could not get past his middle name or the fact that his father was Muslim or that he had spent some time in Indonesia growing up or that he once had a dinner conversation with Edward Said and was acquainted with Rashid Khalidi. Obama was always viewed with suspicion in the highest levels of Israeli government. Michael Oren, the Israeli ambassador to the United States, wrote that "From the moment he entered office, Mr. Obama promoted an agenda of championing the Palestinian cause."[11] Oren, the representative of the Netanyahu government, would chalk this up to Obama's "ties to Indonesia and the Muslim villages of Kenya."[12] The right-wing Israeli government believed that Obama sympathized with the Palestinian narrative more than the Israeli narrative.

The second factor was Benjamin Netanyahu. Netanyahu's premiership in Israel essentially overlapped with Obama's presidency for all but a few months. Each government Netanyahu formed was a right-wing government, strongly supportive of settlement expansion, which caused friction with Obama's Washington as they spoke of advancing Israeli-Palestinian peace negotiations. This tension was evident from the outset of the relationship between the two leaders, and Netanyahu's way of dealing with it was to change the subject away from peace, settlements, and Palestinian rights to Iran.

The third factor is the Iran nuclear deal. Obama viewed the problems of the Middle East in a way that the Israelis did not like. He sought to stabilize it not through massive deployment, but through the pursuit of political agreements, and he saw an opening with Iran that allowed him to pursue the Joint Comprehensive Plan of Action or JCPOA, which would bring Iran in line with its commitments under the nuclear non-proliferation treaty. While this would result in an unprecedented inspections regime for Tehran's nuclear program, it would also mean that the Iranian government would be given a path out of the isolation that the international community had imposed on it. Netanyahu, and many in Israel, who see no option other than eventual regime change in Iran, viewed this as a mistake and worked as hard as possible to torpedo the Iran deal. On Obama's national security agenda, the Iran deal was seen as a significant policy achievement that advanced American national security interests while also keeping a promise Obama had made on the campaign trail about his willingness to talk to the Iranians and advance relations out of mutual respect. For Obama's opponents, some of whom accused the president of being too kind to adversaries of the United States and others who claimed he was not an American and was seeking to subvert the nation from the inside, the Iran deal was fuel for their fire. Many of Obama's supporters, though, not only agreed with the Iran deal for its national security objectives but also grew angry at the subtle, and not so subtle, allegations of treason against their president, which they often saw as racially coded or motivated by racism. Obama's election reflected a growing shift in approaching questions of race and white entitlement, the initial manifestations of a minority-majority America. Though when it came to policy, the Obama administration was not very different than others toward Israel, the idea of America that an Obama victory portended clashed with the very ethos of Israel, which is rooted in ethnonationalism and is maintained through discrimination. The partisan divide between Democrats and Republicans grew just as these ideas were coming into sharper contrast.

NARRATIVES OF RACE, BELONGING, AND
MULTICULTURALISM IN THE UNITED STATES

Pro-Israel advocacy in America has always relied not just on Jewish Zionist voices or institutions but also on Evangelical Zionists, a demographic that has for generations been the base of the Republican Party. But it was more recently, during the two Bush administrations between 1988 and 2008, that this constituency really started to flex its muscles.[13] The confluence of multiple American wars in Muslim countries, 9/11, the "War on Terror," and the Second Intifada all helped consolidate a "clash of civilizations" narrative that dominated the political discourse on the right and beyond. The discourse was clear about the axes of good and evil: predominantly white, Judeo-Christian civilization was on former side; Islam, on the latter.

The election of Barack Obama, the first African American US president, brought to the fore the first physical manifestation of the minority-majority divide in American politics and future. Among the immediate reactions to Obama's triumph were birtherism, the Tea Party, and a narrative that undergirded both: "Obama isn't one of us." These reactionary movements shared this core analysis with a more intellectual-seeming group. In right-wing neoconservative circles, the same narrative was congealing around Obama and one core issue: Israel. Obama, they would argue, was out of step with tradition, an outsider to the realm of the special relationship between the United States and Israel, and one whose intentions could not be trusted. Take, for example, a book published in 2009 by National Review writer Michael Ledeen, called *Obama's Betrayal of Israel*. For others, one question loomed large: Does Obama feel it in the *kishkes* for Israel?[14]

Obama, of course, was as pro-Israel as any of his predecessors; he also received the support of the majority of Jewish American voters, who rank Israel as their fifth most important issue.[15] But that didn't stop certain pro-Israel voices on the right, like Charles Krauthammer, who trumpeted, "It's Obama vs. Israel."[16] Searching for the source of Obama's hatred of Israel, Krauthammer wondered if it stemmed from Obama's penchant for "appeasing enemies while beating up on allies" or from his desire to "heal the breach between Christianity and Islam . . . and has little patience for this pesky Jewish state."

Over in *The Weekly Standard*, Bill Kristol argued that Obama was angry, "accelerating both his appeasement of Iran and his attacks on Israel." But there was good news: "The Republican Party and the conservative movement—and most of the American people—stand with Israel and against President Obama."[17] Kristol also set up the Emergency Committee for Israel, a right-wing attack operation intended to counterbalance J Street, the moderate-in-comparison American Jewish Zionist advocacy group, which was seen as giving Obama Jewish cover. The emergency? It was Hussein Obama, as robocalls supporting Netanyahu's reelection in Israel called him.[18] After the 2016 election, the Emergency Committee for Israel changed its name to the Committee for Israel. It literally declared the emergency over once the first Black president was replaced by the white-supremacist-in-chief, Donald Trump. According to Bret Stephens, Obama not only "betrayed" Israel, but also systematically failed to oppose everyone from the Iranian regime to Bashar al-Assad to Russia to the Muslim Brotherhood. Stephens wrote that the "most betrayed" by Barack Hussein Obama, the first African American president, was "Americans."[19]

The narrative flowed back and forth between these voices and others on the right, like Robert Spence, Dick Cheney, Sean Hannity and Alan West, who wrote for example, "The barbarians are indeed at the gate, but there are also traitors within our ranks. If Barack Obama goes to the UN Security Council and drops the veto support for the two-state solution—I believe we will see the latter enable the former."[20]

Likewise, Mike Huckabee and Newt Gingrich, two of President Trump's early supporters, helped carry the tune of dog whistles. Gingrich argued that Obama "is so outside our comprehension" that understanding him required knowing "Kenyan, anticolonial behavior."[21] Mike Huckabee told Fox News viewers that everything Obama "does is against what Christians stand for, and he's against the Jews in Israel. Furthermore, argued Huckabee, "The one group of people that can know they have his undying, unfailing support would be the Muslim community. And it doesn't matter whether it's the radical Muslim community or the more moderate Muslim community."[22]

Casting Obama as a traitor to the orthodox "Judeo-Christian" position on Israel had a deeper impact than these pundits reckoned with. This framing is well illustrated in an article written by Jennifer Rubin in *The Washington Post* with the headline, "Why It's Correct to Label the Obama Administration 'Anti-Israel.'" Rubin concluded that the Obama administration was "the most anti-Israel in history," a "disloyal, unhelpful ally." Her article, which was typical of her output regarding Obama throughout the eight years of his presidency, had a ripple effect. The piece was amplified on the online magazine Breitbart News, which Steve Bannon, its cofounder and later a chief strategic advisor to Donald Trump, called the "platform of the alt-right."[23]

In other words, the white supremacist base saw no contradiction between Rubin's analysis of Obama and Israel and their own weltanschauung. And this is exactly the point—not only did these pundits not contradict the ideological undercurrent of the alt-right, they provided a piece of the paradigm, with their insistence over and over on an "us-versus-them mentality."

The fight over the Iran deal, during which much of this narrative swirled, put Israel, Republicans, Islamophobes, and racists of various stripes on one side and the president, Democrats, and multiculturalists on another. It came to a climax when the Israeli Prime Minister Benjamin Netanyahu secured an invitation to speak before a joint session of the American Congress through the Republican speaker of the house, circumventing the White House, purely for the purpose of lobbying against the US president's agenda. This meant that the Republican speaker of the house was cooperating with a foreign leader in an effort to derail the signature foreign policy objective of the American president. As a result, a stunning sixty members of Congress, senators and representatives alike, almost all Democrats, chose to skip the speech of Benjamin Netanyahu and held press conferences instead explaining why they had done so. Many of them were members of the Congressional Black Caucus. Speeches of Israeli prime ministers before the American Congress had become known for featuring more standing ovations than the annual State of the Union Address delivered by the president. So for sixty members of Congress to skip out of this high-profile address was stunning rebuke for Netanyahu and a sign of the changing times.

This brings us to the fourth factor that can help explain the unprecedented shift in public opinion on Israel occurring in the United States: what Obama represented, and the challenge this was to many Americans, as the 2016 election of Trump showed. Barack Obama represented a changing America, a majority-minority country that was headed in the direction of more people of color assuming decision-making roles. Obama represented an ethos that would be at the center of the political battle boiling in the next election. That ethos is one of civic belonging; one that prioritizes democracy over identity. American is an idea, not a color, ethnicity, or religion. America does not cease to exist if it no longer has a white Christian majority. The same cannot be said for the Israeli ethos, however. This is an ethos that prioritizes identity over democracy. Obama represented an America that was becoming more demographically diverse and was embracing this diversity. Israel, on the other hand, considers demographic changes existential threats, a view Trump and his allies propagate with regards to the United States as well.

THE ELECTION OF TRUMP IN 2016

The 2016 US Presidential election was probably the most covered and most followed political contest in modern history. It was a campaign unlike any other, pitting the most insider of insiders, Hillary Clinton, against the most unorthodox of outsiders, Donald J. Trump. Neither of them was particularly good on Palestine or a friend to the BDS movement. Hillary Clinton made a commitment on the campaign trail to combat the BDS movement, in large part as a response to her major donor, Haim Saban, who has made fighting BDS a priority. Donald Trump's pro-Israel bona fides were laid out at the annual AIPAC conference and in many statements before or after.[24]

While activists for Palestine in the United States were not expecting much from Trump, most began thinking about how advocacy work for Palestine would change under his presidency. Trump rode to power on a wave of nativist, xenophobic white nationalism that would continue to be empowered after his victory. Trump won despite making attacking the press a cornerstone of his campaigning and despite his pernicious policies towards immigrants and refugees. Some of his key advisors had a "clash of civilizations" mindset that advocated for eternal war with Islam. Some think tanks friendly to Trump had made combating BDS a priority, including through attacking Muslim American organizations that practiced BDS, like American Muslims for Palestine, which is part of the USPCR, and was subjected to hostile legal targeting.

THE NETANYAHU/TRUMP BROMANCE

Despite uttering words about neutrality between Israel and Palestine early on in his campaign, candidate Trump soon made very clear he would veer further right than any previous major-party presidential candidate before him on this issue. Not only did he state he would recognize Jerusalem as Israel's capital, but he brought onto his team as advisers on the matter two right-wing pro-Israel advocates, David Friedman and Jason Greenblatt.[25] Both would later play key roles in the Trump administration's relations with Israel, the former as US ambassador to Israel and the latter as Middle East peace envoy.

While Trump continued to attack minorities, he also continued to embrace Israel and in particular Benjamin Netanyahu even before officially taking office. This was clearly seen in December 2016, when he was president-elect and the UN Security Council was voting on a resolution to condemn settlements, which Obama had ultimately permitted to pass by withholding the US veto. Netanyahu worked to stop the resolution, and when the White House refused to commit to veto it, Netanyahu called Trump. Trump then called Egypt's Sisi, whose ambassador had introduced the resolution, and Egypt withdrew it. However, four other countries were prepared to move ahead with it, and the vote ultimately happened with a US abstention. Trump, as always, let his thoughts be known to the world on Twitter, slamming the Obama administration for throwing Israel under the bus and promising that things would be different after January 20, inauguration day. During this time, he also promised to move the US embassy to Jerusalem. Netanyahu promptly thanked him for his support and tweeted that he looked forward to the new relationship.[26] When President Trump made clear he wanted to pursue an even bigger wall to prevent immigrants from coming into the United States from

Mexico, Netanyahu tweeted that Israel had built a wall and walls work. Trump would soon cite him in a TV interview.[27] Shortly after Trump's inauguration on January 20, it was announced that Netanyahu would be the first foreign leader to officially visit the White House after Prime Minister Theresa May of the United Kingdom. Netanyahu's trip was planned for February 15.

THE LOVEFEST DROVE THE WEDGE FURTHER

Early in his presidency, Trump was a remarkably unpopular figure in the United States and only becoming more despised, particularly among Democrats, including those who did not support Palestinian rights or BDS. Being in opposition to Trump was where all the energy, power, and dynamism was. Being able to brand Israel and Benjamin Netanyahu as Trump allies was a way to continue to open eyes to their pernicious alliance in progressive and liberal circles in the United States. The two leaders were largely doing this work on their own. But activists made highlighting their partnership a central part of their advocacy during this time.

Further, the Trump/Netanyahu love affair sent a shock through much of the American Jewish community, which votes overwhelmingly liberal. Trump's campaign brought all sorts of white nationalists out of the woodwork, leading to a spike in both Islamophobic and anti-Semitic incidents. Yet at the press conference between both leaders, the leader of the "state of the Jewish people" provided backing when Trump faced a question about his campaign's role in fueling anti-Semitism. This rubber-stamping attitude was once again on display when Netanyahu's government retracted a statement condemning an anti-Semitic ad targeting George Soros, an Israel critic and philanthropist, in Hungary. Or when Netanyahu's son Yair and the head of the Israeli American Coalition, Adam Milstein, shared social media memes attacking Israeli critics using anti-Semitic tropes.

Netanyahu's coddling of global right-wingers has been a constant theme in his foreign policy, and it only intensified during the Trump era. Netanyahu provided cover for the Polish government after it passed a law criminalizing suggestions that Poland had any complicity in Holocaust deaths and drew rebuke from the Holocaust museum in Israel.[28] He similarly was criticized for providing cover for Lithuania, despite the fact that it continues to honor Nazi collaborators.[29] In recent years, Netanyahu also gave a speech in which he blamed a Palestinian, not Hitler, for inspiring the Holocaust.[30] He welcomed a visit to Israel by the right-wing Rodrigo Duterte of the Philippines, who compared himself favorably to Hitler.[31]

When the US embassy was opened in Jerusalem on May 14, 2018, evangelical Christian pastors who have anti-Semitic track records spoke at the ceremony and were warmly welcomed by Israeli officials. More recently, Netanyahu has embraced newly elected Brazilian President Jair Bolsonaro, an outspoken supporter of military rule and torture, who also pledged to move Brazil's embassy to Jerusalem and close the Palestinian diplomatic office in Brazil. Netanyahu is shrewdly calculating that he can advance Israel's diplomatic agenda—thwarting accountability for Israel's historic denial of Palestinian rights—around the world, using the far right as a conduit. This alignment between Zionists and right-wing bigots, anti-Semites, and white supremacists has a long history.

TRUMP'S ANTI-DEMOCRAT AND ANTIDEMOCRACY MIDDLE EAST POLICY

The Trump administration's embrace of Benjamin Netanyahu and the Israeli right has catalyzed the process of making the issue of Israel a partisan one in the United States and helped turn away many Democrats, but Trump has also pursued what can be called an antidemocracy policy when it comes to Israel/Palestine. This approach sought to normalize Israeli apartheid, wherein millions of Palestinians are denied the right to vote, by having unelected Gulf Arab leaders recognize Israel despite the overwhelming opposition of Arab publics.[32]

In the beginning of 2020 and after several years of waiting, the Trump administration finally released its peace plan. Before doing so, however, it began laying the groundwork with regional allies, most notably Israel, the United Arab Emirates, Saudi Arabia, and Bahrain. This coordination was rooted in what seemed to be the pursuit of a new strategy of using the common interest of an adversarial Iran to bring Israel and Gulf states together. Doing so, despite the fact that Arab publics opposed the idea, would foster normalized relations between Israel and the Gulf states. This would in turn break the Arab consensus around the Arab Peace Initiative and upend the established sequence of land for peace, weakening what little leverage the Palestinians had and pressing them to accept an apartheid-like outcome instead of an independent state.

When it was revealed, the Trump peace plan followed the antidemocracy theme by looking favorably on Israeli annexation of 30 percent of the West Bank while still referring to a nonsovereign, disconnected land archipelago as a Palestinian state.[33] The first stage of the plans' release was programmed to coincide with an economic conference hosted in Manama, Bahrain, in which no Palestinians were officially involved. The political parameters were then released by the administration in January 2020.

The Manama conference in June 2019, which followed the Trump administration's support for the unprecedented Saudi- and Emirati-led marginalization of Qatar two years earlier, made it clear to many that the Trump administration was hoping to work with select Gulf monarchies to press the Palestinians into accepting an apartheid-like solution. While the Trump plan was roundly rejected in the Arab world officially and was met with an Arab League affirmation of the Arab Peace Initiative, that consensus began to shake when the United Arab Emirates announced it would pursue normalized relations with Israel in August 2020. The signing of the Abraham Accords in August 2020 between Israel and the United

Arab Emirates and Bahrain made official this normalization, to the detriment of Palestinian rights. The Trump administration's overall approach toward the region, as well as its specific initiatives to push Gulf autocracies to help legitimize Israel's ongoing violations of international law and human rights, offer observers a clear contrast between Trump and Israel on the one hand, and the values of rights, pluralism, and equality on the other.

AN AGENDA FOR CHANGE: CHALLENGES AND OPPORTUNITIES IN BUILDING TOWARD THE "S" IN BDS

While the movement for Palestinian rights has had success over the past twelve years, in many BDS campaigns much work remains as far as getting to the "S"— the sanctions. Getting the US government to level sanctions on Israel would be a game-changer, and the US campaign among others has not shied away from this objective. Rather, it has sought to assess what it would take to achieve this goal, to be realistic about the time it will take, and to build the popular or grassroot support necessary to march down this path and do so unapologetically. The question for activists on Palestine during the Trump era was how to work most effectively toward this ultimate goal. Below I outline what I see as current and future challenges and opportunities for this effort.

Intersectionally Organize

During the summer of 2014, Israel bombarded Gaza for fifty-five days, killing well over two thousand Palestinians, most of whom were civilians.[34] The war on Gaza received massive coverage in the United States, albeit primarily filtered through a pro-Israel lens, and was the lead story on almost every day of the summer and in every newscast. But what may be less known outside the United States is that on August 9, just as the war in Gaza was beginning to wind down, Michael Brown, an unarmed eighteen-year-old African American from Ferguson, Missouri was shot to death by a white police officer allegedly while he had his hands up and was turning around to face the officer. He was shot six times in the front. The case ignited long-simmering tensions between the city's majority-black population and the majority-white city government and police. The US media recentered its focus from Gaza to police brutality in the United States and the legacy of racism in American institutions, especially in law enforcement. But the fact that Brown's murder came during the war on Gaza meant that activists in the United States following the news on both traditional and social media were confronted by a striking juxtaposition between state violence aimed at upholding a system of injustice across the world, on the one hand, and right here at home, on the other. As protesters gathered in the streets of Missouri only to be met with harsh police response, activists from Palestine sent messages with tips on how to mitigate the influence of tear gas. Others circulated images of the identical tear gas canisters being used six thousand miles apart, made by the same corporation in Pennsylvania. Palestinian *keffiyahs* could be seen in the streets of Ferguson during protests. The connections were just too striking to ignore.

This episode highlights one of many intersectional organizing opportunities that offer a path to building coalitions with groups and movements who are unaware of activism on Palestine and can, in turn, benefit from support from Palestine activists. There are intersections with Palestinian rights issues and various other prominent issues in the United States, including some that came to the fore after Trump's election. For example:

- The same company that helped build Israel's Separation Wall in the West Bank and helped cage Gaza behind a wall was considered to be the frontrunner for the contract to expand Trump's wall to keep immigrants out along the southern border with Mexico.[35]
- The security systems company G4S, which has long been a BDS target, is deeply enmeshed in the American prison-industrial complex.[36]
- Since the 1990s, police exchange programs—many of them organized, facilitated, and funded by the pro-Israel Anti-Defamation League (ADL)—have been organized to take American law enforcement officers to Israel to "build bonds between two peoples fighting terror." But American police already have a tremendous and deadly problem with profiling and brutality and need not learn from Israeli police, who openly and unabashedly embrace racial profiling as a policing tactic.[37]

The opportunities to create alliances and to build support for the issue of Palestinian rights as belonging within the fold of progressive and liberal priorities continued to grow, as can be seen in Michelle Alexander's column in *The New York Times* ahead of Martin Luther King Jr. Day in 2019. An esteemed author on racial justice, she used her column to issue a clarion call for solidarity with the Palestinian people. She wrote:

Reading King's speech at Riverside more than 50 years later, I am left with little doubt that his teachings and message require us to speak out passionately against the human rights crisis in Israel-Palestine, despite the risks and despite the complexity of the issues. King argued, when speaking of Vietnam, that even "when the issues at hand seem as perplexing as they often do in the case of this dreadful conflict," we must not be mesmerized by uncertainty. "We must speak with all the humility that is appropriate to our limited vision, but we must speak." And so, if we are to honor King's message and not merely the man, we must condemn Israel's actions: unrelenting violations of international law, continued occupation of the West Bank, East Jerusalem, and Gaza, home demolitions and land confiscations. We must cry out at the treatment of Palestinians at checkpoints, the routine searches of their homes and restrictions on their movements, and the severely limited access to decent housing, schools, food, hospitals and water that many of them face.[38]

While these changes offer important opportunities for the continued and successful growth of Palestinian rights advocacy in the United States, a number of important challenges must also be addressed.

Reform Anti-lobbying Culture

An unfortunate byproduct of the success of BDS tactics is that they have directed grassroots energy away from focused engagement with policy-makers in the federal government. As activists get used to working on divestment campaigns targeting a corporation or aiming for a resolution in this church or that university, they are honing organizing skills for those campaigns but not developing the lobbying skills needed for effective government engagement. As I noted earlier, BDS tactics provided something of a refuge for activists who were tired of getting nowhere with Congress, but here is the hard truth: there is no way to sanctions without going through Congress. This means that at some point, that engagement needs to happen, and the sooner it starts the better. This is not to say there is currently no engagement with lawmakers—there is, but there can be much more and there will have to be much more for us to achieve the goals we have set. The anti-lobbying culture that has arisen as a byproduct of focused "B" and "D" work makes this more difficult, but the political ground for engagement is also ripe at this moment. A 2017 poll found that some 56 percent of Democrats, along with 41 percent of Americans overall, would support sanctions putting greater pressure on Israel over continued settlement expansion.[39] Addressing this anti-lobbying culture and correcting it will be a big task for political activism on Palestine in the United States in the years ahead.

It is also important to be clear that while Democrats might have more support among their base for moving in the direction of sanctions over time, elected officials will still have to be pulled in this direction and will not be eager to go there willingly. Democrats, particularly establishment Democrats who have been in office for years, adjusted to a politics of bipartisan consensus of unquestioning support for Israel. That is starting to change and a younger generation of progressive Democrats seems less beholden to this older way of thinking and more in tune with their base.[40] Further, these newcomers, like Jamaal Bowman and Cori Bush, are winning in primary elections, while others like Rashida Tlaib, Ilhan Omar, and Alexandria Ocasio-Cortez are beating back primary challengers and were elected to congress in 2020. Importantly, this younger generation of progressives is succeeding electorally against candidates supported by significant pro-Israel campaign funds.[41] For these reasons, it is more important than ever for activists and organizers who turned out of frustration to boycott and divestment and away from engaging elected officials to refocus their energies in that direction and in this moment.

Lawfare

An additional challenge we have been confronting in the United States in recent years and increasingly today is "lawfare" efforts aimed at repressing the Palestinian rights movement by attempting to criminalize BDS tactics. We have seen multiple such pieces of legislation in state legislatures across the United States over the last several years. As of this writing, twenty-seven states have enacted such legislation since 2014.[42] The US Campaign has organized local coalitions to fight these bills, but not all have been successful. As a group of organizations with a relatively small capacity in comparison to the capacity of those opposing them, local BDS organizers must be careful not to get bogged down in fighting anti-BDS legislation to the point where it becomes all-consuming. Activists are triaging the situation and strategically addressing state legislation, while also working with other civil rights and liberties groups to educate activists about their rights, which is a key component to defeating the chilling effect these proposed laws are designed to have.

Former President Trump notwithstanding, the US Constitution is still the law of the land. By contrast with France, for example, where the state can take draconian steps against BDS activity, in the United States political boycotts are considered free expression that is protected under the first amendment to the Constitution. For this reason, anti-BDS laws in the United States can only go so far before crossing a constitutional line that would open them to a legal challenge. Anti-BDS law drafters have attempted to tiptoe right up to this line in some places, but elsewhere have crossed it. Some state laws require state contractors to sign an oath swearing they will not boycott Israel. In Texas, for example, this led to a schoolteacher and several others being forced to choose between their constitutional rights and their jobs.[43] Legal challenges have already begun in several states.

In the summer of 2017, an important battle began against a piece of proposed federal legislation called the Israel Anti-Boycott Act. As originally written, it could lead to civil and even criminal penalties for BDS-type activity, with up to a one million dollar fine and a twenty-year jail sentence. The act was cosponsored by Republican and Democratic senators in an attempt to provide a bipartisan veneer, but in reality it was overwhelmingly supported by Republicans. It was clear it would not have the support needed to pass, and so early on, one of its leading sponsors, Ben Cardin (D-MD) attempted to add it as an amendment to other legislation so it could be snuck through without debate. This attempt failed, and a public debate began.

The American Civil Liberties Union (ACLU) joined several organizations, including the USCPR, to defeat this legislation. This is very important for several reason. First, the ACLU is highlighting the unconstitutional nature of these bills, a view that had been expressed loudly by many but was taken seriously only once the ACLU weighed in. Second, the ACLU is a very well-respected organization, particularly in liberal circles, and the fact that they adopted this cause sent an important political message. Third, the ACLU was the key institutional leader opposing Trump policies that violate human rights, such as the Muslim ban, for example. Once the ACLU weighed in, senators came under increased pressure to end their sponsorship of the legislation, and many expressed a willingness to amend it. Ultimately, enough pressure from a progressive coalition was generated to prevent the passage of such legislation in the 115th Congress and the Israel Anti-Boycott Act expired in December 2018. Further efforts in the 116th Congress to pass legislation that criminalized boycotts for Palestinian rights have also come under opposition from progressive actors and are unlikely to pass if they continue to include components violating First Amendment freedoms. This consensus has become so significant within the party that the latest party platform, adopted in 2020, included language specifically committing to uphold first amendment freedoms around boycott efforts.

Legislation is just one part of a repressive effort supported by a network of actors aiming to silence criticism of Israel. These authoritarian tactics belie Israel's image with American audiences as a "democratic ally." Continuing to expose these repressive efforts in partnership with institutions that have been leaders in protecting free expression will be an important feature of the work moving forward. As of this writing, repressive laws aimed at intimidating Palestinian rights activism have been successfully challenged in Kansas and Arizona, where federal courts have sided with the plaintiffs against the states whose legislatures passed anti-BDS bills.

Political progress was also made at the federal level after the shift in power in the House of Representatives in 2018. At the end of 2018, as power was changing hands, there was an effort to rush federal anti-BDS legislation through Congress by attaching it to a spending bill urgently needed to avoid a government shutdown.[44] But thanks to pressure created by advocacy groups, including the ACLU and others the *New York Times* editorial board came out against the legislation as did leading Democratic senators Bernie Sanders and Diane Feinstein.[45]

The legislation, the Israel Anti-Boycott Act, did not make it into the emergency spending measure but the high public drama around it encouraged Republican senators to try to force Democrats into choosing between siding with Israel or their base soon thereafter. With a new Congress sworn in at the start of the year, including members Rashida Tlaib and Ilhan Omar, who openly supported BDS, the opportunity for Republicans to use Israel as a political cudgel was heightened. The first piece of legislation considered by the Senate, Bill S.1., included four elements, among them anti-BDS legislation, seen as unconstitutional. Just weeks after the Israeli Anti-Boycott Act controversy, the stage was set again for another political fight over the constitutional right to boycott Israel. While S.1 ultimately passed the Senate, half the Democratic caucus in the Senate voted against it, including almost all the senators who sought the Democratic nomination for president in 2020. In the House, where Democrats had now come into control, the anti-BDS components of S.1. were dead on arrival after the progressive caucus extracted private concessions from House Speaker Nancy Pelosi not to bring forward legislation that would divide Democrats. While the party would not support BDS, and indeed opposed it on record, it also would not support efforts to unconstitutionally confront BDS activism. By the summer of 2020, that position had made it into the Democratic party platform.

Building Congressional Support

There is a need to continue to build support in Congress for standing up for Palestinian rights. In recent years, important gains have been made in this area, even though the energy of the movement has been more campaign-focused and not as focused on engaging government. In 2016, for example, nineteen members of Congress, led by Representative Betty McCollum, signed on to a letter to the Secretary of State demanding that steps be taken to protect Palestinian children whose rights are abused by Israeli policies. The letter even called for holding Israeli military units accountable under the Leahy Law, a provision that would deny aid or training to those units. Other letters have focused on supporting human rights defenders facing falsified charges or calling for investigations into extrajudicial killings.

This may seem unremarkable, but consider that even just ten years ago, it was difficult to get five members of Congress to sign a "Dear Colleague" letter urging continued support for humanitarian aid to Gaza through UN Relief and Works Agency. Much has changed in these ten years. Over time, multiple "Dear Colleague" letters have rallied progressive and liberal members of Congress concerned about Palestinian rights. After the letter-writing of the past decade, it was possible to introduce legislation supportive of Palestinian rights. That happened in late 2017, when Representative McCollum introduced HR 4391, which would condition aid to Israel on its treatment of Palestinian children. Some thirty-one members of Congress have since joined this legislation as cosponsors. While these letters and bills are important on their own, they are also vehicles for building and broadening congressional support.

By way of historical comparison, the first comprehensive bill for sanctions against South Africa was introduced in 1972, but it took a full fourteen years before it could pass. Today with unprecedented numbers of representatives and senators taking steps to defy the intimidation of pro-Israel lobby groups, there is newfound energy to redouble efforts and continue to build. As the number of people supporting Palestinian rights grows, more members feel safe joining. Activists are working to build a core, first among progressive Democrats and then into the mainstream of American politics, of Americans who support Palestinian rights— because Palestinian rights are as important as the rights of any other people or group.

THE LONG WALK

American policy is central when it comes to Israel-Palestine because American support for Israel enables it to act oppressively and with impunity. For many reasons, America's policy toward Israel is a function of a unique set of foreign and domestic interests that have established a long-standing orthodoxy. Today, that orthodoxy is starting to shake as a rights-based advocacy for Palestinians meets an America at a crossroads. Rights-based advocacy approach is uniquely positioned to gain the greatest traction in this American political moment and perhaps beyond.

While the conditions that can create change in US policy are increasingly beginning to assemble, there should be no doubt that the road ahead remains a lengthy one. Activists and advocates for Palestinian freedom can take comfort in the fact that the rights-based approach, as opposed to nationalist advocacy for partition or statehood, is the shortest path toward the goal because it is most likely to permit the formation of coalitions and alliances in a changing America. As the contrast between the values of freedom, justice, and equality and what Israel is doing to the Palestinian people continues to grow increasingly stark, Americans across the political spectrum will begin to reevaluate US support for Israel. Energy dedicated to sharpening that contrast for American audiences will likely help make the long walk to freedom shorter.

NOTES

1. Hani J. Bawardi, *The Making of Arab Americans: From Syrian Nationalism to US Citizenship* (Austin: University of Texas Press, 2014).

2. Pamela E. Pennock, *The Rise of the Arab American Left: Activists, Allies, and Their Fight against Imperialism and Racism, 1960s–1980s* (Chapel Hill: University of North Carolina Press, 2017).

3. USCPR's original name was the US Campaign to End the Israeli Occupation.

4. "Palestinian Civil Society Call for BDS," Palestinian BDS National Committee, July 9, 2005, https://bdsmovement.net/call.

5. "US BDS Wins," US Campaign for Palestinian Rights, last modified June 2019, https://uscpr .org/campaign/bds/bdswins/.

6. *Parliamentary Debates*, Commons (July 31, 1906).

7. Michael J. Cohen, *Britain's Moment in Palestine: Retrospect and Perspectives, 1917–1948* (London: Routledge, 2014), 11.

8. Cohen, *Britain's Moment in Palestine*, 11.

9. Arthur Balfour, quoted in Gudrun Krämer, *A History of Palestine: From the Ottoman Conquest to the Founding of the State of Israel* (Princeton, NJ: Princeton University Press, 2008), 167.

10. Walid Khalidi, *From Haven to Conquest: Readings in Zionism and the Palestine Problem until 1948* (Beirut: Institute for Palestine Studies, 1971), 208.

11. Michael B. Oren, "How Obama Abandoned Israel," *Wall Street Journal*, June 16, 2015, https:// www.wsj.com/articles/how-obama-abandoned-israel-1434409772.

12. Michael Oren, "How Obama Opened His Heart to the 'Muslim World,'" *Foreign Policy* (blog), June 19, 2015, https://foreignpolicy.com/2015/06/19/barack-obama-muslim-world-outreach-conse quences-israel-ambassador-michael-oren/.

13. Howard J. Gold and Gina E. Russell, "The Rising Influence of Evangelicalism in American Political Behavior, 1980–2004," *Social Science Journal* 44, no. 3 (2007): 554–62, https://doi.org/10.1016/j .soscij.2007.07.016.

14. Jeffrey Goldberg, "The Kishke Debate," *The Atlantic*, October 23, 2012, https://www.theatlantic .com/politics/archive/2012/10/the-kishke-debate/263981/.

15. Ron Kampeas, "How Barack Obama Won over Jewish Voters—While Irking Pro-Israel Establishment," *Jewish Forward*, January 18, 2017, https://forward.com/news/360276/how-barack-obama -won-over-jewish-voters-while-irking-pro-israel-establishme/.

16. Charles Krauthammer, "It's Obama vs. Israel," *New York Daily News*, March 18, 2010, https:// www.nydailynews.com/opinion/obama-israel-article-1.173095.

17. William Kristol, "Obama's Israel Problem," *Washington Examiner*, January 29, 2015, https://www.washingtonexaminer.com/weekly-standard/obamas-israel-problem.

18. Niv Elis, "Pro-Likud Campaign Call Warns Voters of 'Hussein Obama,'" *Jerusalem Post*, March 15, 2015, https://www.jpost.com/Israel-Elections/Pro-Likud-campaign-call-warns-voters-of-Hussein-Obama-393987.

19. Bret Stephens, "Obama's Fitting Finish," *Wall Street Journal*, December 26, 2016.

20. Robert Spencer, "Why Obama Is the Worst President in U.S. History," *Jihad Watch*, January 23, 2017, https://www.jihadwatch.org/2017/01/robert-spencer-why-barack-obama-is-the-worst-president-in-u-s-history. Sean Hannity, "Is President Obama Betraying Israel?" *Fox News*, March 2, 2015, https://www.foxnews.com/transcript/is-president-obama-betraying-israel. Allen West, "Obama Set to Betray Israel Again; When Will American Jews Wake Up?" AllenBWest.com, March 31, 2015, https://web.archive.org/web/20170904124901/; https://www.allenbwest.com/2015/03/31/obama-set-to-betray-israel-again-when-will-american-jews-wake-up/.

21. Newt Gingrich, quoted in Eric Kleefeld, "Gingrich Promotes Right-Winger D'Souza's Description of Obama as 'Kenyan Anti-Colonial,'" *Talking Points Memo*, September 13, 2010, https://talkingpointsmemo.com/dc/gingrich-promotes-right-winger-d-souza-s-description-of-obama-as-kenyan-anti-colonial.

22. Mike Huckabee, quoted in Michael W. Chapman, "Huckabee: Obama 'Against What Christians Stand For,' Against 'Jews in Israel,' Has 'Undying' Support for Muslims," CNSNews.com, February 10, 2015, https://www.cnsnews.com/blog/michael-w-chapman/huckabee-obama-against-what-christians-stand-against-jews-israel-has-undying.

23. "Washington Post Columnist: Why It's Correct to Label the Obama Administration 'Anti-Israel,'" *Breitbart Jerusalem*, January 22, 2016, https://www.breitbart.com/national-security/2016/01/22/washington-post-columnist-why-its-correct-to-label-the-obama-administration-anti-israel/.

24. "Read Donald Trump's Speech to AIPAC," *Time*, March 21, 2016, https://time.com/4267058/donald-trump-aipac-speech-transcript/.

25. Jason D. Greenblatt, "Joint Statement from Jason Dov Greenblatt and David Friedman, Co-Chairmen of the Israel Advisory Committee to Donald J. Trump," *Medium*, November 2, 2016, https://medium.com/@jgreenblatt/joint-statement-from-jason-dov-greenblatt-and-david-friedman-co-chairmen-of-the-israel-advisory-edc1ec50b7a8.

26. "Trump Urges Israel to 'Stay Strong' till January 20," *Times of Israel*, December 28, 2016, https://www.timesofisrael.com/trump-urges-israel-to-stay-strong-till-january-20/.

27. William Booth, "Israel's Netanyahu Applauds Trump's Plan for Wall; Mexico Not Pleased," *Washington Post*, January 27, 2017, https://www.washingtonpost.com/news/worldviews/wp/2017/01/29/israels-netanyahu-applauds-trumps-plan-for-wall-mexico-not-pleased.

28. Isabel Kershner, "Yad Vashem Rebukes Israeli and Polish Governments over Holocaust Law," *New York Times*, July 5, 2018, https://www.nytimes.com/2018/07/05/world/middleeast/israel-poland-holocaust.html.

29. "Despite Honors for Collaborators, PM Praises Vilnius for Holocaust Remembrance," *Times of Israel*, August 4, 2018, https://www.timesofisrael.com/despite-honors-for-collaborators-pm-praises-vilnius-for-holocaust-remembrance/.

30. "Netanyahu: Hitler Didn't Want to Exterminate the Jews," *Haaretz*, October 21, 2015, https://www.haaretz.com/israel-news/netanyahu-absolves-hitler-of-guilt-1.5411578.

31. "Jewish Leaders React to Rodrigo Duterte Holocaust Remarks," *BBC*, September 30, 2016, https://www.bbc.com/news/world-asia-37515642.

32. For detailed polls on this issue, see Arab Center for Research and Policy Studies, *The Arab Opinion Index 2018*, https://www.dohainstitute.org/en/Lists/ACRPS-PDFDocumentLibrary/2017–2018%20Arab%20Opinion%20Index%20Main%20Results%20in%20Brief%20-%20final%20(002).pdf.

33. I define this as antidemocratic insofar as it advances a racist understanding of the conflict, privileging Israeli right-wing interests and vision, rather than any adherence to international law or human rights when it comes to the Palestinians.

34. United Nations Human Rights Council, "The United Nations Independent Commission of Inquiry on the 2014 Gaza Conflict," United Nations Human Rights Council, June 24, 2015, https://www.ohchr.org/EN/HRBodies/HRC/CoIGazaConflict/Pages/ReportCoIGaza.aspx.

35. Jonathan Ferziger, "Israeli Company That Fenced in Gaza Angles to Help Build Trump's Mexico Wall," *Bloomberg News*, January 29, 2017, https://www.bloomberg.com/news/articles/2017–01–29/israel-s-magal-pushes-for-mexico-wall-deal-as-trump-buoys-shares.

36. Jamilah King, "Angela Davis on Palestine and the Prison Industrial Complex," *Colorlines*, July 22, 2014, https://www.colorlines.com/articles/angela-davis-palestine-and-prison-industrial-complex.

37. Noah Habeeb and Craig Willse, "US and Israeli Police Are Sharing Violent and Repressive Tactics," *Truthout*, December 11, 2018, https://truthout.org/articles/us-and-israeli-police-are-sharing-violent-and-repressive-tactics/.

38. Michelle Alexander, "Time to Break the Silence on Palestine," *New York Times*, January 19, 2019, https://www.nytimes.com/2019/01/19/opinion/sunday/martin-luther-king-palestine-israel.html.

39. Shibley Telhami and Stella Rouse, "American Attitudes on the Israeli-Palestinian Conflict" University of Maryland Critical Issues Poll, 2017, https://sadat.umd.edu/sites/sadat.umd.edu/files/american_attitudes_on_israel-palestine.pdf.

40. Catie Edmondson, "A New Wave of Democrats Tests the Party's Blanket Support for Israel," *New York Times*, October 7, 2018, https://www.nytimes.com/2018/10/07/us/politics/democrats-israel-palestinians.html.

41. Matthew Kassel Jacob Kornbluh, "Money in Politics Is Not Like It Once Was: Will Pro-Israel Donors Adapt?" *Jewish Insider*, August 17, 2020, https://jewishinsider.com/2020/08/money-in-politics-is-not-like-it-once-was-will-pro-israel-donors-adapt/.

42. "Anti-Boycott Legislation around The Country," *Palestine Legal*, 10, 2019, https://palestinelegal.org/righttoboycott.

43. Jacey Fortin, "She Wouldn't Promise Not to Boycott Israel, So a Texas School District Stopped Paying Her," *New York Times*, December 19, 2018, https://www.nytimes.com/2018/12/19/us/speech-pathologist-texas-israel-oath.html.

44. Emily Cochrane, "Lawmakers Consider Adding Measure Protecting Israel to Languishing Spending Bills," *New York Times*, December 17, 2018, https://www.nytimes.com/2018/12/17/us/politics/israel-boycotts-government-shutdown.html.

45. Kate Ruane, "Congress Is Trying to Use the Spending Bill to Criminalize Boycotts of Israel and Other Countries," American Civil Liberties Union (blog), December 10, 2018, https://www.aclu.org/blog/free-speech/rights-protesters/congress-trying-use-spending-bill-criminalize-boycotts-israel-and, Editorial Board, "Curbing Speech in the Name of Helping Israel," *New York Times*, December 18, 2018, https://www.nytimes.com/2018/12/18/opinion/editorials/israel-bds.html. Senator Bernie Sanders, "Sanders, Feinstein Oppose Inclusion of Israel Anti-Boycott Act in Appropriations Bill," press release, December 19, 2018, https://www.sanders.senate.gov/press-releases/sanders-feinstein-oppose-inclusion-of-israel-anti-boycott-act-in-appropriations-bill/.

BIBLIOGRAPHY

Arab Center for Research and Policy Studies. *The Arab Opinion Index 2018*. https://www.dohainstitute.org/en/Lists/ACRPS-PDFDocumentLibrary/2017–2018%20Arab%20Opinion%20Index%20Main%20Results%20in%20Brief%20-%20final%20(002).pdf.

Bawardi, Hani J. *The Making of Arab Americans: From Syrian Nationalism to US Citizenship*. Austin: University of Texas Press, 2014.

Cohen, Michael J. *Britain's Moment in Palestine: Retrospect and Perspectives, 1917–1948*. London: Routledge, 2014.

Gold, Howard J., and Gina E. Russell. "The Rising Influence of Evangelicalism in American Political Behavior, 1980–2004." *Social Science Journal* 44, no. 3 (2007): 554–62. https://doi.org/10.1016/j.soscij.2007.07.016.

Khalidi, Walid. *From Haven to Conquest: Readings in Zionism and the Palestine Problem until 1948* Beirut: Institute for Palestine Studies, 1971.

Krämer, Gudrun. *A History of Palestine: From the Ottoman Conquest to the Founding of the State of Israel*. Princeton, NJ: Princeton University Press, 2008.

Louis, Willian Roger. *Ends of British Imperialism: The Scramble for Empire, Suez, and Decolonization*. London: I.B. Tauris, 2006.

Pennock, Pamela E. *The Rise of the Arab American Left: Activists, Allies, and Their Fight against Imperialism and Racism, 1960s–1980s*. Chapel Hill: University of North Carolina Press, 2017.

Porter, Bernard. *Critics of Empire: British Radicals and the Imperial Challenge*. London: I.B. Tauris, 2008.

Telhami, Shibley, and Stella Rouse. "American Attitudes on the Israeli-Palestinian Conflict." University of Maryland Critical Issues Poll, 2017. https://sadat.umd.edu/sites/sadat.umd.edu/files/american_attitudes_on_israel-palestine.pdf.

United Nations Human Rights Council. "The United Nations Independent Commission of Inquiry on the 2014 Gaza Conflict." United Nations Human Rights Council. June 24, 2015. https://www.ohchr.org/EN/HRBodies/HRC/CoIGazaConflict/Pages/ReportCoIGaza.aspx.

Decolonizing beyond Partition

6

Transitional Justice in Palestine/Israel

Whose Justice? Which Transition?

Nadim Khoury

This chapter examines the significance of transitional justice in Palestine/Israel.[1] Transitional justice is the process of dealing with past wrongs in order to shift towards a new democratic regime. While the concept has gained little attention in mainstream debates on Palestine/Israel, it touches upon crucial aspects to ending the conflict, such as dealing with historical injustices, decolonization, and the proposed one-state and two-state solutions. The chapter makes two claims. First, it argues that transitional justice has gained appeal within the Palestinian camp as a way to devise political alternatives to the Oslo peace process. In this case, it is a tool used to counter the fragmentation of the Palestinian people, reckon with past wrongs, and provide venues for political reconciliation with Israeli Jews. Transitional justice, however, can further a variety of political ends or solutions. After examining the various ways in which transitional justice is discussed in Palestine/Israel, the chapter identifies deep disagreements over key issues, including what counts as a historical injustice; what mechanisms we should employ to deal with historical injustices; what are the goals we are transitioning to; and what is the nature of the transition that is supposed to take place. Disagreement over these issues means that transitional justice can serve a range of ends: to devise alternatives to the Oslo agreements, to justify measures that are in line with them, or even to negate Palestinian demands for justice. The chapter concludes with a precautionary note. In the context of Palestine/Israel, transitional justice is a deeply contested concept and its potential as a tool to devise real alternatives to the failed peace process depends on whether or not it is incorporated into a larger political project that seeks to establish equality and justice for all Palestinians.

WHAT IS TRANSITIONAL JUSTICE?

According to the United Nations, transitional justice is "the full range of processes and mechanisms associated with a society's attempt to come to terms with a legacy of large-scale past abuses, in order to ensure accountability, serve justice and achieve reconciliation."[2] The definition is wordy, but it is comprehensive. Transitional justice occurs when societies transition away from regimes responsible for large-scale abuses (e.g., dictatorship, apartheid) and move towards establishing accountable democratic regimes. These transitions rely on a variety of mechanisms, such as truth commissions, criminal trials, and apologies, whose purpose is to enable political reconciliation among competing parties in order to create a peaceful present and future.

Transitions rely on two kinds of justice: retributive and restorative.[3] Retributive transitional justice grants legitimacy to new democratic regimes by *punishing* the perpetrators of the old regime. Germany after WWII is good example in this regard, as the criminal trials at Nuremburg punished the leaders of the old regime, established a new jurisprudence, and created an official record of Nazi horrors. Nationally, these trials enabled a transition towards a new and democratic (West) Germany, and internationally they laid the basis of our contemporary international criminal justice system on which retributive transitional justice relies (with legal frameworks such as crimes against humanity, genocide convention, international tribunals, etc.).[4]

Retribution, however, is not a one-size-fits-all recipe. In the case of South Africa, for example, retribution would have hindered a peaceful transition towards democracy, as Thabo Mbeki acknowledges: "Within the ANC [African National Congress], the cry was to 'catch the bastards and hang them.' But we realized that you could not simultaneously prepare for a peaceful transition while saying we want to catch and hang people. So we paid a price for the peaceful transition. If we had not taken this route, I do not know where the country would have been today. Had there been a threat of Nuremberg-style trials over members of the apartheid security establishment we would never have undergone the peaceful change."[5]

The price that South Africa paid was indeed costly. The perpetrators were not punished but offered amnesty in exchange for the public acknowledgment of their crimes. Not all South Africans were happy with this decision, but the ANC deemed it necessary to guarantee a peaceful transition out of the apartheid regime. Therefore, it privileged truth commissions rather than criminal trials to pave the way towards a democratic South Africa. Truth commissions are government-appointed bodies mandated to unearth large-scale human rights abuses. Unlike criminal courts, they are extrajudicial and cannot pass sentences.[6] More fundamentally, they rely on a restorative conception of justice that is premised on public mediation between victims and perpetrators. In truth commissions, victims are given ample space to voice their narratives, receive validation for their stories, and demand reparations. This is unlike in criminal courts where victims are heard only to testify and provide evidence. Truth commissions, moreover, do not punish the perpetrators, but give them the opportunity to acknowledge their crimes, so that they can be restored as "active, full and creative members of the new order."[7] In South Africa, the work of restorative justice was colossal. Over a period of seven years, the Truth and Reconciliation Commission gathered the testimony of 21,000 victims and received 7,112 amnesty applications—849 of these were granted while 5,392 were denied.

The aim of both modes of transitional justice (retributive and restorative) and the variety of mechanisms they employ (criminal trials, truth commissions, apologies, commemoration, reparations, etc.) is political reconciliation.[8] In the context of the Israeli-Palestinian conflict, and international politics more generally, the term reconciliation has remained vague and confusing, especially given the reluctance of some peace negotiators to deal with the historical roots of conflict. In this regard, Nadim Rouhana calls for making a clear distinction between conflict settlement, conflict resolution, and reconciliation.[9] Conflict settlement, he argues, is a negative peace that is geared towards stopping conflict rather than seeking justice between the warring parties. It is used interchangeably with a victor's peace because it results from a military victory and serves to consolidate the interests of the victor. This limits peace negotiations to technical and military issues that are addressed by high officials and excludes the rest of society. Unlike conflict settlement, conflict resolution seeks to resolve conflict rather than contain it. The goal is a sustainable peace grounded in a principled solution that promotes reciprocity and formal equality between the fighting entities.[10] The cooperation it fosters, moreover, is not limited to foreign policy and military officials, but includes other strata of society such as business elites and civil society actors—what is usually referred to as track-two diplomacy.

Political reconciliation departs both from conflict settlement and conflict resolution, because it is a more transformative enterprise: "Reconciliation is defined as a process that brings about a genuine end to the existential conflict between the parties and transforms the nature of the relationship between the societies through a course of action that is intertwined with psychological, social, and political change."[11] Reconciliation does not mean that everybody will be *reconciled*. No political program can achieve such a goal, not in stable societies or in divided ones. Rather, the goal is to live *in reconciliation*—that is, to create structural and objective conditions that have the capacity to transform people's subjective and psychological predispositions towards one another while ensuring their political equality. Dealing with historical injustices is central to creating such conditions, and it is one important factor that distinguishes reconciliation from conflict settlement and conflict resolution. Moreover, reconciliation seeks the involvement of more than officials and social elites. It encourages the participation of victims, perpetrators, and the affected members of both communities.[12] The focus on victims is particularly noteworthy.[13] The guiding principles of the United Nation's approach to transitional justice, for example, stress "the centrality of victims in the design and implementation of transitional justice processes and mechanisms."[14] In theory, this means that political reconciliation is more of a victims' rather than victor's peace. In practice, however, things are far from being so clear-cut, as is evidenced by the mixed record of transitional justice over the last thirty years.

TRANSITIONAL JUSTICE AND THE OSLO PEACE PROCESS

The Israeli-Palestinian peace process contains elements of both conflict resolution and conflict settlement. Aspects of conflict resolution are evidenced in nominal references to international law, as well as attempts to set up democratic institutions and foster economic cooperation between Israel and the Palestinian authority. The terms and conditions of the peace process, however, were set by the stronger party, which is why the process is much closer to the realpolitik of conflict settlement.[15] What is clear is that the Oslo peace process did not qualify as a process of political reconciliation, especially since there was no serious engagement with the past. "Both leaderships eschewed discussions of the past," argues Ron Dudai, "and transitional justice mechanisms were never proposed."[16]

Avoiding the past was a deliberate policy on both sides, especially in the early stages of the negotiations. "We decided not to deal with past accounts," Yitzhak Rabin told the Israeli Knesset on April 18th, 1994, but "to try and create a new and better future for both peoples."[17] Israeli negotiator Uri Savir put it more bluntly: "never again would we argue about the past . . . . Discussing the future would mean reconciling two rights, not readdressing ancient wrongs."[18] "We focused our attention on the present and the future," writes Palestinian negotiator Ahmed Qurei, "trying to gauge the extent to which we had a common ground."[19] The focus was therefore given to "immediate" issues such as mutual recognition, the creation of a Palestinian authority, and a progressive withdrawal of Israeli occupying forces. It left the final-status issues, namely the status of Jerusalem, borders, and Palestinian refugees, to a later stage.

The negotiations at Camp David in 2000 were supposed to address these final-status issues, but they failed to bring about any resolution. One year later in Taba, the refugee issue made some progress and a consensus emerged around monetary compensation as the primary response to the problem of Palestinian refugees.[20] Disagreements remained, however, regarding what losses would be compensated, the amount for which they would be compensated, the party who would bear the costs of such compensation, as well as how the refugee issue would be narrated. Compensation, of course, was not a new solution. United Nations General Assembly Resolution 194, issued in December 1948, already offered refugees the option of monetary compensation if they decided not to return to their homes in what became Israel. The novelty at the Taba negotiations was to delink compensation from return, leaving Palestinian refugees with compensation as their only option.

And this option itself quickly disappeared with the collapse of the peace process that followed the Second Intifada and the election of Sharon as head of the Israeli government in Spring 2001. The short-lived revivals of the peace process in 2007 and 2008 could not bring the refugee question back to the negotiation table, let alone other forms of reparations.

This failure to grapple with the historical and ongoing injustice of the Nakba, from which the issue of refugees emerged, did not occur by accident but by design. The peace process was not meant to solve the refugee problem, but to dissolve it—that is, to undermine the framework that had made it a problem in the first place.[21] This occurred primarily by framing the refugees issue as a humanitarian one, a trend that goes back to 1948 when the entire question of Palestine was treated as a humanitarian question, rather than a question of justice and national self-determination. With the peace process, only parts of the West Bank and Gaza became subject to potential self-determination, further constraining the 1948 refugee issue to a humanitarian framework. For example, if one looks at the proceedings of the Refugee Working Group at the 1991 Madrid Multilateral conference, one notices a strong emphasis on humanitarian solutions. There, the multilateral negotiations were focused on discussing databases, family reunification, human resources development, public health, child welfare, job creation, and social infrastructure.[22] No doubt, these are important issues. However, when these become the *only* issues, they reduce the refugee question to a humanitarian problem. Israeli negotiators have systematically insisted on this humanitarian approach, which purposely sets aside issues of justice. Even when they accepted the return of a limited number of refugees at the Camp David Summit in 2000, they did so solely on humanitarian grounds (family reunification), not reparatory ones (historical injustice).[23]

The peace process also dissolved the refugee issue by imposing a new temporality to the conflict that blocked the Palestinian memory of 1948. By erecting the Green Line as a potential future border, the peace process delineated the field of territorial *and* historical negotiations. Only the land conquered in 1967 and the history that followed it were open to negotiations. What occurred before 1967 was placed off-limits and, therefore, off-memory.[24] "The Palestinian leadership knows that they have to forget Ramle and Lod and Jaffa," wrote the Israeli journalist Danny Rubinstein, referring to cities ethnically cleansed in 1948 and currently located in Israel. "If I was a Palestinian politician," he continued, "I would say that you don't have to remember. You have to forget."[25] Rubinstein's demand to forget is not coincidental but integral to the compromise signed in Oslo. Within the mindset of territorial partition, there is no place for a narrative of Palestinian ethnic cleansing, but only a narrative of Jewish rebirth; no Nakba (catastrophe), only *geula* (redemption).

Not only does partition erase the memory of the Nakba, it also displaces the issue of historical responsibility, deferring it to a future Palestinian state. "The basis for the creation of the state of Israel is that it was created for the Jewish people," Tzipi

Livni told Palestinian negotiators, and "your state will be the answer to all Palestinians including refugees."[26] According to Livni therefore, only a future Palestinian state, not Israel, will be responsible for the issue of Palestinian refugees. Such a state would offer them a country to "return" to, and in the process, wash Israel's hands clean of its past crimes. Surely, Livni was not alone in endorsing this position. At the negotiating table, she was representing a liberal Zionist consensus and negotiating with a Palestinian leadership that had accepted the principle of partition in 1988. Many within the Palestinian leadership hoped that partition would not entirely sacrifice justice for the refugees. This was naively optimistic, especially since Israel systematically denied its responsibility for the refugee problem. Even at the height of the process in the Taba negotiations in 2001, Israel rejected legal, historical, and moral responsibility. This is why Israeli negotiators insisted that monetary compensation payments for Palestinian refugees be *indirect*—that is, paid by an international fund and administered by an international commission.[27] The insistence is important, since direct compensations imply responsibility for the past (we are responsible, therefore we pay), while indirect ones do not (others pay, because we are not responsible).

THE PROMISE OF TRANSITIONAL JUSTICE

In light of these in-built problems and the inability of the Oslo peace process to deal with the past, many in the Palestinian camp have turned their attention to the issue of transitional justice. "As long as historical truth is denied or excluded," writes Nur Masalha, "there can be no peace, no reconciliation in the Middle East."[28] Palestinians and Israelis should therefore learn from countries such as Guatemala and South Africa that have relied on transitional justice mechanisms. As Masalha and a host of intellectuals, as well as NGOs such as the Israeli Zochrot and the Palestinian BADIL, have concluded, transitional justice is appealing for the following reasons.[29] First, it prescribes a wide range of legal and symbolic mechanisms to deal with the Nakba. Second, it supports integrative solutions to the conflict (variants of the one-state solution) that maintain the unity of all Palestinians. Finally, it allows for a swift transition away from the status quo. As I argue in the section that follows, however, transitional justice does not necessarily support these goals, for it depends on how its proponents are using it and for what political agenda or project.

Reparations for the Nakba

The primary appeal of applying transitional justice mechanisms to Palestine/Israel lies in their capacity to deal with historical and enduring injustices. To appreciate how this differs from the approach of the Oslo peace process, one could contrast the monetary compensation offered to the refugees at the Taba negotiations in 2001 to the reparations that transitional justice could potentially offer in the future.

Compensations are sometimes confused with reparations, but they are different since reparations cover a wider spectrum of remedies to past wrongs. According to the UN, reparations also include restituting original property to refugees, aiding their return, ending ongoing violations, holding perpetrators accountable, commemorating the victims, acknowledging wrongs, issuing a public apology, and implementing a variety of measures to prevent the reoccurrence of injustice.[30]

Israel and its allies have systematically rejected this wider understanding of reparations. When Palestinian negotiators brought up the issue of reparations they were met with disapproval and censure. The US Secretary of State Condoleezza Rice deemed Israeli reparations for Palestinian refugees "backward-looking" rather than "forward-looking,"—an attempt to halt the peace process rather than move it in the right direction.[31] Proponents of transitional justice disagree. The only way forward, they insist, is for Israel to reckon with its past through a host of transitional justice mechanisms. These include material remedies such as return, restitution, and compensation, as well as symbolic reparations like apologies. Had Israel issued an apology when it recognized the Palestine Liberation Organization (PLO), notes Meron Benvenisti, the peace process would have been placed on an entirely different footing.[32] "A sincere Israeli apology," writes George Bisharat, "would be a milestone toward reconciliation that no Palestinian could ignore."[33] Both recommend that Israel follow the example of other governments that have issued apologies for crimes of mass violence, such as ethnic cleansing, internment, slavery, and apartheid. Of course, apologies can be cheap. However, if they acknowledge responsibility, expresses remorse, and are supported by a host of legal and material remedies, they can be meaningful and consequential.[34]

Besides apologies, truth commissions are another way of acknowledging past crimes. For proponents of transitional justice in Palestine/Israel—especially NGOs such as Zochrot and BADIL—they figure high on the list of mechanisms to deal with the Nakba. Truth commissions can expose perpetrators of ethnic cleansing and provide a platform for its victims. This puts them at odds with a peace process that has protected the former and silenced the latter. Surely, Palestinian refugees were the objects of heated negotiations since 1991. They were debated, studied, quantified, and measured. However, they were never heard and were purposely cast aside from the peace process.[35] Truth commissions can potentially bring them back to the center, providing them and their descendants a space to voice their stories and demand acknowledgment. Putting theory into practice, the Israeli NGO Zochrot already set up its own truth commissions to expose Israeli crimes committed in the Negev between 1948 and 1960. It has also engaged in other transitional justice work such as commemorating the Nakba, obtaining testimonies from 1948 Jewish fighters, and educating the Israeli public on what happened in 1948. Israeli public officials have responded aggressively to the work of Zochrot and other Palestinian NGOs commemorating the Nakba, issuing a series of memory laws ("Nakba laws") that criminalizes their activism.[36]

It is worth noting that, in most case, proponents of transitional justice in Palestine/Israel emphasize restorative mechanisms such as reparations and truth commissions over retributive ones.[37] There could be many reasons for this, but the primary one is power. Criminal trials punishing Israeli perpetrators will most likely never see the day, because Israel is the stronger party. This is why restorative mechanisms are privileged, with the understanding that they can offer a relative kind of justice. "No one gets absolute justice," writes Edward Said, "but there are steps that must be taken, like the ones taken at the end of apartheid."[38]

These limits notwithstanding, transitional justice offers a discourse that allows many in the Palestinian camp to demand justice for the Nakba, and this is its primary appeal. This discourse is novel, and it differs from the Palestinian revolutionary discourse through which the Nakba was originally (and in some cases still is) narrated. The early revolutionary discourse promised a solution to the plight of refugees in a Palestine that was fully liberated from Zionist colonization. It sought absolute justice. Transitional justice, on the other hand, promises reconciliation between Jews and Arabs in living in historic Palestine. It seeks relative justice. The revolutionary discourse was pan-Arabist and excluded Israel. Transitional justice challenges the Arab-Jewish binary and calls for new forms of Jewish and Arab engagement; for example, by linking the memories of the Holocaust and the Nakba.[39] Finally, historical responsibility in the revolutionary discourse was framed in internal terms: How did we, Arabs, allow this tragedy to happen?[40] In the transitional justice discourse, historical responsibility is framed in external terms: How can Israelis take responsibility for the Nakba?

Integrative Solutions and Decolonization

Transitional justice is also appealing for critics of the Oslo peace process because, by returning to the Nakba, it reframes the entire land of historic Palestine as one political unit and Palestinians as one people.[41] This counters the fragmentation codified by the Oslo Accords, which divided Palestinians into separate entities: Palestinian citizens of Israel, refugees, members of the diaspora, East Jerusalemites, West Bankers, and Gazans. Transitional justice also supports integrative solutions to the Israeli-Palestinian conflict, such as a one-state democracy, because the paradigmatic cases of transitional justice, like South Africa, have all occurred within a single state. This does not mean, however, that transitional justice prescribes specific institutional arrangements, whether one or two states. In fact, the mechanisms of transitional justice can go either way. Restitution, for example, is premised on reversing the consequences of conflict and returning to the status quo ante. As such, it pushes against a two-state solution that formalizes the results of war and displacement.[42] Mechanisms such as apologies and compensation, on the other hand, could satisfy either a one-state or a two-state solution.[43]

Besides supporting integrative solutions to the conflict, transitional justice is appealing because it promises a uni-directional journey that is drastic, uniform, and absolute. As Fionnuala Ní Aoláin and Colm Campbell note, "there was a specific point at which the Berlin Wall came down, and at which the apartheid government and the Argentinean military relinquished power."[44] This is unlike the slow and incremental transition of the Oslo Accords where addressing the most contentious issues (sovereignty, refugees, borders, settlements, and Jerusalem) was constantly delayed, and interim arrangements halted and reversed.[45]

As a result of this promise of radical and absolute transitions—dealing with past injustices, supporting integrative solutions, and promising radical transitions—transitional justice in Palestine/Israel is sometimes associated with decolonization. Reconciliation, argues Nadim Rouhana, could be framed as decolonization, especially when it acknowledges the power asymmetry between colonized and colonizer and offers to overturn this asymmetry in a new, democratic political order.[46] The link between the two might come as a surprise, especially since decolonization is usually associated with armed resistance and the ousting of colonial power. This was the case with early Palestinian calls for decolonization, but not with recent ones. Increasingly, decolonization is discussed in nonviolent rather than violent terms, as a vehicle for civil equality rather than mutually exclusive self-determination and as grounded in universal human rights rather than particular national rights.[47] These new understandings bring decolonization and transitional justice closer, rather than further apart.

These new understandings of decolonization draw on the South African experience, which Palestinian academics and activists often point to when discussing alternatives to the Oslo peace process. "The ideological collapse of the two-state solution," writes Ali Abunimah, "leaves no alternative but to shift our discourse and practice toward democratic and decolonizing alternatives [such as] South Africa."[48] As in South Africa, transitional justice in Palestine/Israel would lead to one state and hinges on dealing with the crimes of the past. And as in South Africa, the transition would be a drastic shift towards a new democratic regime. This does not mean that South Africa was a success story in which transitional justice completely dismantled the apartheid system. It did not, especially not in the socioeconomic sphere. References to South Africa are meant to rethink the terms and conditions of a just peace in Palestine/Israel, rather than to idealize the South African experiment.

THE LIMITS OF TRANSITIONAL JUSTICE

Transitional justice has its promises, but it also its limits. While it can offer a viable way to decolonization, as Nadim Rouhana suggests, it can also pave roads similar to the Oslo peace process, or even paths that run against Palestinian demands for justice. Transitional justice can serve these divergent ends because it leaves open crucial questions, namely: What counts as a historical injustice? When does a historical justice begin and end? What are we transitioning to and from? And how do we transition?

What Historical Injustice? Whose Historical Injustice?

In current discussions on transitional justice in Palestine/Israel, the Nakba figures high on the list of past wrongs to be remedied. However, it is not the only one to be addressed. Ron Dudai, for example, argues that dealing with past injustices also means dealing with Palestinian acts of violence against Israeli citizens, some of which qualify as war crimes according to international law. It also means addressing intra-Palestinian violence such as the assassination of real or alleged collaborators, the violence committed between Palestinian factions in Gaza, and the human rights violations committed by the Palestinian Authority against its own people. This would be similar to the way the South African truth commissions addressed the issue of "black-on-black" violence between the Inkatha Freedom Party and the ANC. Applying transitional justice in Palestine/Israel would require a similar reckoning with intra-Palestinian violence, namely the split between Fatah and Hamas. Israelis, Dudai argues, would have to deal with "intra-Israeli violence," by which he means violence committed by the state of Israel against Palestinians with Israeli citizenship.[49] Details aside, the point is that transitional justice will be demanding on Israelis, but also on Palestinians. This, in itself, should not be surprising. Reconciliation is costly for both victim and perpetrator. The question, however, is how demanding and what demands can be made on Palestinians in the name of transitional justice? And for what purpose?

Because transitional justice can open the Pandora's box of historical injustices, it could potentially heighten competition over victimhood between Israelis and Palestinians, rather than pave the way to political reconciliation. This is already happening with the issue of Arab Jewish refugees and Palestinian refugees. For a long time, Israel has equated the exile of Arab Jews with the exile of Palestinians refugees, claiming that what happened in 1948 was not ethnic cleansing but population exchange, a practice that was legal in the beginning of the twentieth century. In this view, Palestinian Arabs were "moved" to neighboring Arab countries and Jews from these same countries were "moved" to Israel, much as Greeks and Turks were in 1923.[50] Today, Israel has upgraded this argument and turned it into public diplomacy campaign by using the discourse of transitional justice. The Israeli foreign ministry's website, for example, notes that "a true solution to the issues of refugees will only be possible when the Arab League will take *historic responsibility* for its role in creating the Jewish and Palestinian refugee problem."[51] Similarly, advocacy organizations such as Justice for Jews from Arab Countries demand that Arabs and Palestinians take historical responsibility, issue apologies, and offer reparations, in the name of a future reconciliation. Even the term Nakba, whose use is a long-standing taboo in Israeli society, is employed to highlight the exile of Arab Jews. "The Palestinian Nakba narrative must be seen in direct parallel to the Jewish Nakba," reads an editorial published by *The Jerusalem Post*. "The basic facts of the history of this conflict must become known so that the world recognizes that two peoples suffered and were uprooted."[52] The article also decries the Palestinian "refugee industry" in the Arab world, contrasting it with the successful assimilation of Jewish Arab refugees in Israel. Like the foreign ministry and advocacy organizations, it also holds Palestinians and Arabs directly responsible for causing the Palestinian and Jewish refugee problems.

Discursively, these public diplomacy campaigns are weaponizing the language of transitional justice against Palestinians. In the process, they are erasing the racism Sephardi Jews suffered at the hands of their Ashkenazi counterparts. In *The Human Right to Dominate*, Nicola Perugini and Neve Gordon show how Israeli settler groups mimic, invert, and co-opt the discourse of human rights to legitimize their colonization of Palestinian land.[53] A similar dynamic is happening with the discourse of transitional justice, which draws heavily on human rights. Pitting a "Jewish Nakba" against a Palestinian one is one example of such inversions. Rather than bridge the experience of Arab Jews and Palestinians, it creates competing claims with the sole purpose of adding more chips to the negotiating table.[54] If these strategies were to succeed, the Palestinian Authority and Arab states would be the ones apologizing for past wrongs, not Israel.

The Mechanisms and Temporal Scope of Historical Injustice

Even if the historical injustice of the Nakba eventually becomes the focus of transitional justice work in Palestine/Israel, there will still be contestation over its temporal scope—that is, when the Nakba began and when it ended. Disagreements over the temporal scope of historical injustices are common and can be found in other settler-colonial states. For example, in 2008, Canada employed transitional justice mechanisms to address the forced removal of First Nations, Métis, and Inuit children and their relocation to residential schools. Indigenous leaders and activists welcomed the government's decision to deal with a crime that affected more than 150,000 children in the nineteenth century. However, they disagreed with the government's understanding of when these injustices began and when they ended.

For the Canadian government, the injustice of the residential schools referred to a specific event in time, and employing mechanisms of transitional justice meant moving "to an even playing field in which the government can no longer be held accountable for past wrongs."[55] For indigenous peoples, however, transitional justice meant another thing. As Courtney Jung argues, the "interest in using apologies, compensation and truth commissions is to draw history into the present, and to draw connections between past policy, present policy and present injustices . . . . The 'transition' is to a relationship in which connections between pasts and present are firmly acknowledged, and in which the past guides present conceptions of obligation."[56] Indigenous leaders, writes Jung, wanted to use transitional justice as a bridge to connect past with present injustices, linking what was happening today to a larger history of settler-colonialism. The Canadian government, however, wanted to use it as a wall, separating historical injustices inflicted on indigenous people from current ones.

Similar disagreements will most likely arise should Israel employ transitional justice mechanisms. Israel, for example, can acknowledge the Nakba as a historical injustice that occurred between 1948 and 1949. This, however, would clash with the way Palestinians see the Nakba as a historical and ongoing injustice *(al Nakba al mustimirriah)*.[57] To paraphrase Patrick Wolfe, the Nakba is a structure, not a single event.[58] The expulsions of Tantura in 1948 and the assaults on Gaza in 2021 form a long chain of injustices that cannot be severed. A transitional justice approach, however, does not have to treat them as such. It can accommodate both interpretations, thus creating opportunities for contestation.

Disagreements on the temporal scope of historical injustices will influence another important issue, that of the mechanisms used to deal with the Nakba. Do we deploy the full breadth of legal and symbolic mechanisms, or do we take a more limited approach? Since Palestinians see the Nakba as a historical and ongoing injustice, they could demand compensation and restitution to provide refugees with material justice; apologies and truth commissions to provide them with symbolic justice; constitutional and institutional reforms to overturn a system designed to exclude them. Israel, on the other hand, could opt for much less. Delimiting the Nakba to a specific event in time, Israeli negotiators could acknowledge it, offer some compensations, and stop there. This acknowledgment would "act as a no-further-claims clause, vaccinating Israel against further Palestinian demands, foremost among them the right of return."[59] This targeted approach would do more to absolve the consciousness of Israelis than provide justice for Palestinians, but it would still be consistent with a transitional justice approach.

Transition to What? Which Transition?

Earlier, I argued that most advocates of transitional justice are also supporters of integrative solutions to the Israeli-Palestinian conflict.[60] Paradigmatic cases of transitional justices have all occurred within one state, not between states, thus lending support to their position. Transitional justice, however, can justify alternative positions. "In Israel/Palestine," writes Ron Dudai, "reconciliation would be between two states, not in a single society. It would thus entail not 'learning to live together' but 'learning to live side by side.' Perhaps a less ambitious task."[61] Dudai suggests a three-strand approach to transitional justice. The process would be Israeli-Palestinian, intra-Israeli, and intra-Palestinian. Reconciliation would take place primarily among Palestinians in the West Bank and Gaza, Israeli Jews, and Israeli Arabs, and later between the state of Israel and a future state of Palestine. And rather than a drastic transition away from the status quo, there would be an incremental transition that would not fully break with current institutional arrangements: "The potential for transitional justice programs lies in an incremental process of narrow mechanisms and small steps through a long process of transition, rather than in one high-profile and all-encompassing mechanism in the post-conflict state, as in the case of the South African Truth and Reconciliation

Commission."[62] Transitional justice, in this view, would work as a corrective to the Oslo peace process, not as an alternative. It would not change the incremental nature of the process, but only add extra steps to the process. Such a proposal maintains continuity with the status quo, rather than a break with the current regime. Edward Kaufman and Ibrahim Bisharat defend a similar position. While dealing with the past is typically undertaken by a new regime, they argue, in Israel/Palestine "there will be two sovereign governments, each representing more continuity than change and both with a history of involvement in individual, group and state terror."[63]

This is surely not what advocates of the one-state solution have in mind when advocating for transitional justice. And while the above-mentioned proposals are not paradigmatic, they are in line with the current broadening of transitional justice and its application to a wide array of contexts. In the case of Canada, mentioned above, for example, there was simply no transition. Mechanisms of transitional justice were employed in an ad hoc manner to address specific historical injustices. They did not move Canada towards a new regime but reinstated the moral legitimacy of the state and its basic structures. The larger point is this: transitional justice per se does not offer guidance on what we are transitioning to (one state or two states) nor how we transition (incrementally or drastically). Rather, it can support all these solutions.

CONCLUSION

This chapter defended two arguments. The first highlighted the promise of transitional justice in Palestine/Israel, the second, its limits. The promise of transitional justice, I argued, hinges on dealing with past injustices, offering reconciliation, and guaranteeing equality from the river to the sea. Its pitfalls, however, are the multiple meanings of "past injustices," "reconciliation," and "equality." While both arguments push against one another, they essentially boil down to one. In Palestine/Israel, transitional justice is an essentially contested concept, for while there is some broad agreement on what transitional justice means, there remain deep disagreements on whose historical injustice we should address, with what mechanisms, and towards what ends. As such, transitional justice can be used for divergent political projects and goals.

Should one draw a conclusion from this analysis, it is a cautionary one. Avoiding the pitfalls and harnessing the promises of transitional justice depends on a larger political project that sets clear goals and strategies. Absent such a political project, transitional justice is but a means, one that can be mobilized to serve a variety of ends. If the future after apartheid is reconciliation, we should learn from three decades of transitional justice and formulate a Palestinian approach to it. The task is demanding, but important. If we do not do it, someone else is bound to do it for us.

NOTES

1. I would like to thank Leila Farsakh as well as Hilde Restad, Mandy Turner, Bashir Bashir, and Brendan Browne for their careful reading and suggestions. This work was supported by the Globalizing Minority Rights project funded by the Norwegian Research Council (NFR 259017).

2. United Nations, "Guidance Note of the Secretary-General: United Nations Approach to Transitional Justice," 2010, https://www.un.org/ruleoflaw/files/TJ_Guidance_Note_March_2010FINAL.pdf.

3. While the distinction between retribution and restoration is central to debates on transitional justice, it is not absolute. In fact, proponents of transitional justice are increasingly arguing for a combination of both, rather than an either-or approach. The distinction is also problematic because some transitional justice mechanisms can be both punitive and restorative. Reparations, for example, were originally conceived as a punitive measure imposed on the losers of a war, as in the case of Germany after the Treaty of Versailles in 1919. After the Second World War, however, reparations took on a more restorative dimension. See Elazar Barkan, "Restitution and Amending Historical Injustices in International Morality," in *Politics and the Past: On Repairing Historical Injustices*, ed. John Torpey, 91–102 (Lanham: Rowman and Littlefield, 2003).

4. Pierre Hazen, *Judging War, Judging History: Behind Truth and Reconciliation* (Stanford, CA: Stanford University Press, 2010), 1.

5. Thabo Mbeki, *Africa: The Time Has Come: Selected Speeches* (Cape Town: Tafelberg Publishers, 1998), 29.

6. Priscilla B. Hayner, *Unspeakable Truths: Transitional Justice and the Challenge of Truth Commissions* (New York: Routledge, 2001).

7. Charles Villa-Vicencio and Erik Doxtader, *Pieces of the Puzzle: Keywords on Reconciliation and Transitional Justice* (Cape Town: Institute for Justice and Reconciliation, 2004), 33.

8. It is important to note that not all definitions of transitional justice include reconciliation. Opting for a definition that includes reconciliation is motivated by the way transitional justice is used in Palestine/Israel, where references to the South African Truth and Reconciliation Commission abound.

9. Nadim Rouhana, "Group Identity and Power Asymmetry in Reconciliation Processes: The Israeli-Palestinian Case," *Peace and Conflict: Journal of Peace Psychology* 10, no. 1 (2004): 33–52.

10. Rouhana, "Group Identity and Power Asymmetry," 35.

11. Rouhana, "Group Identity and Power Asymmetry," 35.

12. Erin Daly and Jeremy Sarkin, "Too Many Questions, Too Few Answers: Reconciliation in Transitional Societies," *Columbia Human Rights Law Review* 35, no. 3 (2004): 101–64.

13. Michael Humphrey, "From Victim to Victimhood: Truth Commissions and Trials as Rituals of Political Transition and Individual Healing," *Australian Journal of Anthropology* 14, no. 2 (2003): 171–87.

14. United Nations, "Guidance Note of the Secretary-General."

15. Sara Roy, "Why Peace Failed: An Oslo Autopsy," *Current History* 100, no. 651 (2002): 8–16; Edward Said, "The Morning After," *London Review of Books* 15, no. 20 (1993); Hilde Waage, "The 'Minnow' and the 'Whale': Norway and the United States in the Peace Process in the Middle East," *British Journal of Middle Eastern Studies* 34, no. 2 (2007): 157–76.

16. Ron Dudai, "A Model for Dealing with the Past in the Israeli-Palestinian Context," *International Journal of Transitional Justice* 1, no. 2 (2007): 249–67, 252.

17. Yitzhak Rabin, "Speech to the Knesset, April 18th, 1994," in *The Israel-Arab Reader*, eds. Walter Laquer and Barry Rubin (London: Penguin Books, 2008), 461.

18. Uri Savir, *The Process* (New York: Vintage Books, 1998), 15.

19. Ahmed Qurei, *From Oslo to Jerusalem: The Palestinian Story of the Secret Negotiations* (London: I.B. Tauris, 2006), 58.

20. Rex Brynen and Roula El-Rifai, "Introduction," in *Compensation to Palestinian Refugees and the Search for Palestinian-Israeli Peace*, eds. Rex Brynen and Roula El-Rifai, 1–18 (London: Pluto Press, 2013), 6.

21. Nadim Khoury, "National Narratives and the Oslo Peace Process: How Peacebuilding Paradigms Affect Conflicts over History," *Nations and Nationalism* 22, no. 3 (2016): 465–83; Nur Masalha, *The Politics of Denial: Israel and the Palestinian Refugee Problem* (London: Pluto Press, 2003); Rosemary Sayigh, "Dis/Solving the 'Refugee Problem'," *Middle East Report*, no. 207 (1998): 19–23.

22. Masalha, *Politics of Denial*; Shahira Samy, *Reparations to Palestinian Refugees: A Comparative Perspective* (Oxon: Routledge, 2010).

23. Rex Brynen and Jill Tansely, "The Refugee Working Group of the Middle East Multilateral Peace Negotiations," *Palestine-Israel Journal* 2, no. 4 (1995).

24. Khoury, "National Narratives and Oslo"; Ilan Pappe, "Historophobia or the Enslavement of History: The Role of the 1948 Ethnic Cleansing in the Contemporary Israeli-Palestinian Peace Process," in *Partisan Histories: The Past in Contemporary Global Politics*, eds. Max Friedman and Padraic Kenney, 127–44 (New York: Palgrave Macmillan, 2005); Yehouda Shenhav, *Beyond the Two State Solution: A Jewish Political Essay* (Cambridge: Polity, 2012).

25. Danny Rubinstein, quoted in Ian Black, "Remembering the Nakba: Israeli Groups Puts 1948 Palestine Back on the Map," *The Guardian*, May 2, 2014, https://www.theguardian.com/world/2014/may/02/nakba-israel-palestine-zochrot-history.

26. Tzipi Livni, quoted in Gregg Carlstrom, "Qurei to Livni: I'll Vote for You," *Al-Jazeera*, January 24, 2011, http://www.aljazeera.com/palestinepapers/2011/01/20111241517890936.

27. Brynen and El-Rifai, "Introduction," 6.

28. Nur Masalha, "Remembering the Palestinian Nakba: Commemoration, Oral History and Narratives of Memory," *Holy Land Studies* 7, no. 2 (2008): 123–56, 151.

29. Ali Abunimah, *The Battle for Justice in Palestine* (Chicago: Haymarket Books, 2014); Bashir Bashir, "The Strengths and Weaknesses of Integrative Solutions for the Israeli-Palestinian Conflict," *Middle East Journal* 70, no. 4 (2016): 560–78; Meron Benvenisti, *Sacred Landscape: The Buried History of the Holy Land since 1948*, trans. Maxine Kaufman-Lacusta (Berkeley: University of California Press, 2000); George Bisharat, "The Power of Apology," *Haaretz*, January 2, 2004; Rashid Khalidi, "Truth, Justice and Reconciliation: Elements of a Solution to the Palestinian Refugee Issue," in *The Palestinian Exodus 1948–1998*, eds. Ghada Karmi and Eugene Cotran, 221–41 (Reading, UK: Ithaca Press, 1999); Yoav Peled and Nadim Rouhana, "Transitional Justice and the Right of Return of the Palestinian Refugees," *Theoretical Inquiries in Law* 5, no. 2 (2004): 317–32; Pappe, "Historophobia or the Enslavement of History;" Munir Nuseibah, *Forced Displacement in the Palestinian-Israeli Conflict, International Law and Transitional Justice* (London: University of Westminster, 2013); Edward Said, "Truth and Reconciliation," *Al-Ahram Weekly*, January 14, 1999.

30. United Nations Office of the High Commissioner on Human Rights, "General Assembly Resolution 60/147: UN Basic Principles and Guidelines on the Right to Remedy and Reparation of Victims of Gross Violations on International Human Rights Law and Serious Violations of International Humanitarian Law, A/RES/60/147," December 16, 2005, https://www.un.org/ruleoflaw/files/BASICP~1.PDF.

31. "Palestine Papers," *Al Jazeera*, July 16, 2008, http://transparency.aljazeera.net/files/2942.PDF.

32. Benvenisti, *Sacred Landscape*, 330.

33. Bisharat, "Power of Apology."

34. Melissa Nobles, *The Politics of Official Apologies* (New York: Cambridge University Press, 2008), 3.

35. Sayigh, "Dis/Solving the 'Refugee Problem.'"

36. Yifat Gutman, *Memory Activism: Reimagining the Past for the Future in Israel-Palestine* (Nashville: Vanderbilt University Press, 2017).

37. Criminal courts have become an essential battleground between Israelis and Palestinians, especially since the Palestinian Authority joined the International Criminal Court in 2015. The proceedings the PA has issued against Israel in the ICC, however, only qualify as ad hoc transitional justice

measures. They are not part of a larger transition meant to move Palestinians and Israelis away from the conditions of colonial conflict. See Brendan Browne, "Transitional Justice: The Case of Palestine," in *The International Handbook on Transitional Justice*, eds. Cheryl Lawther, Luke Moffett, and Dov Jacobs, 488–507 (Cheltenham: Edward Elgar Publishing, 2017).

38. Edward Said, *Power, Politics and Culture* (New York: Vintage, 2001), 449–50.

39. Bashir Bashir and Amos Goldberg, "Deliberating the Holocaust and the Nakba: Disruptive Empathy and Binationalism in Israel/Palestine," *Journal of Genocide Research* 16, no. 1 (2014): 77–99; Ilan Gur-Ze'ev and Ilan Pappe, "Beyond the Destruction of the Other's Collective Memory: Blueprints for a Palestinian/Israeli Dialogue," *Theory, Culture and Society* 20, no. 1 (2003): 93–108; Nadim Khoury, "Postnational Memory: Narrating the Holocaust and the Nakba," *Philosophy and Social Criticism* 46, no. 1 (April 2019): 91–110; Edward Said, "Israel-Palestine: The Third Way," *Le Monde Diplomatique*, September 1998.

40. Anaheed Al-Hardan, "Al-Nakbah in Arab Thought: The Transformation of a Concept," *Comparative Studies of South Asia, Africa and the Middle East* 35, no. 3 (2015): 622–38.

41. Bashir, "Strengths and Weaknesses of Integrative Solutions;" Tom Hill, "1948 after Oslo: Truth and Reconciliation in Palestinian Discourse," *Mediterranean Politics* 13, no. 2 (2008): 151–70.

42. Leila Hilal, *Transitional Justice Responses to Palestinian Dispossession: Focus on Restitution* (New York: International Center for Transitional Justice, 2012).

43. Peled and Rouhana, "Transitional Justice and Right of Return."

44. Fionnuala Ní Aoláin and Colm Campbell, "The Paradox of Transition in Conflicted Democracies," *Human Rights Quarterly* 27, no. 1 (2005): 172–213, 181.

45. Waage, "The 'Minnow' and the 'Whale,'" 166.

46. Nadim Rouhana, "Decolonization as Reconciliation: Rethinking the National Conflict Paradigm in the Israeli-Palestinian Conflict," *Ethnic and Racial Studies* 41, no. 4 (2018): 643–62. Zochrot makes a similar link between decolonization and transitional justice.

47. Omar Barghouti, "Organizing for Self-Determination, Ethical Decolonization and Resisting Apartheid," *Contemporary Arab Affairs* 4, no. 4 (2009): 576–86. Hunaida Ghanim, "Between Two 'One-State' Solutions: The Dialectics of Liberation and Defeat in the Palestinian National Enterprise," *Constellations* 23, no. 3 (2016): 340–50. Bashir Bashir and Rachel Busbridge, "The Politics of Decolonisation and Bi-Nationalism in Israel/Palestine," *Political Studies* 67, no. 2 (2019): 388–405.

48. Abunimah, *Battle for Justice*, 47.

49. Dudai, "Model for Dealing with the Past." The problem with such arguments is that they risk equating the violence committed by Israel against "Israeli-Palestinians" and the violence committed among Palestinians themselves. They thus conflate the violence of the colonizer and the violence of the colonized. This reproduces the mindset of the existing peace process, which creates a false symmetry between the parties, rather than breaks away from it.

50. Masalha, *Politics of Denial*.

51. Raphael Ahren, "Changing Tack, Foreign Ministry to Bring 'Jewish Refugees' to Fore," *Times of Israel*, April 3, 2012, https://www.timesofisrael.com/foreign-ministry-promotes-the-jewish-refugee-problem/. My emphasis.

52. JPost Editorial, "The Jewish Nakba," *Jerusalem Post*, December 9, 2015, https://www.jpost.com/Opinion/The-Jewish-Nakba-436834.

53. In *The Human Right to Dominate*, Nicola Perugini and Neve Gordon explore how Israeli settler groups mimic, invert, and co-opt the discourse of human rights to legitimize their colonization of Palestinian land. Nicola Perugini and Neve Gordon, *The Human Right to Dominate* (New York: Oxford University Press, 2005).

54. Michael Fischbach, "Linking Palestinian Compensation Claims with Jewish Property Claims against Arab Countries," in *Compensation to Palestinian Refugees and the Search for Palestinian-Israeli Peace*, eds. Rex Brynen and Roula El-Rifai, 69–88 (London: Pluto Press, 2013).

55. Courtney Jung, "Transitional Justice for Indigenous People in a Non-Transitional Society," International Center for Transitional Justice, 2009, p. 2.

56. Jung, "Transitional Justice for Indigenous People," 3.

57. Yara Hawari, "Palestine Sine Tempore?" *Rethinking History* 22, no. 2 (2018): 165–83.

58. Patrick Wolfe, "Settler Colonialism and the Elimination of the Native," *Journal of Genocide Research* 8, no. 4 (2006): 387–409.

59. Hill, "1948 after Oslo," 163.

60. See also Cherine Hussein, *The Re-emergence of the Single State Solution in Palestine/Israel: Countering an Illusion* (Oxon: Routledge, 2015).

61. Dudai, "Model for Dealing with the Past," 254; see also Daphna Golan-Agnon, "Between Human Rights and Hope: What Israelis Might Learn from the Truth and Reconciliation Process in South Africa," *International Review of Victimology* 17, no. 1 (2010): 31–48.

62. Dudai, "Model for Dealing with the Past," 250.

63. Edward Kaufman and Ibrahim Bisharat, "Introducing Human Rights into Conflict Resolution: The Relevance for the Israel-Palestinian Peace Process," *Journal of Human Rights* 1, no. 1 (2002): 71–91, 84.

BIBLIOGRAPHY

Abunimah, Ali. *The Battle for Justice in Palestine*. Chicago: Haymarket Books, 2014.

Al-Hardan, Anaheed. "Al-Nakbah in Arab Thought: The Transformation of a Concept." *Comparative Studies of South Asia, Africa and the Middle East* 3, no. 3 (2015): 622–38.

Barghouti, Omar. "Organizing for Self-Determination, Ethical Decolonization and Resisting Apartheid." *Contemporary Arab Affairs* 2, no. 4 (2009): 576–86.

Barkan, Elazar. "Restitution and Amending Historical Injustices in International Morality." In *Politics and the Past: On Repairing Historical Injustices*, edited by John Torpey. Lanham: Rowman and Littlefield, 2003.

Bashir, Bashir. "The Strengths and Weaknesses of Integrative Solutions for the Israeli-Palestinian Conflict." *Middle East Journal* 70, no. 4 (2016): 560–78.

Bashir, Bashir, and Rachel Busbridge. "The Politics of Decolonisation and Bi-Nationalism in Israel/Palestine." *Political Studies* 67, no. 2 (2018): 388–405.

Bashir, Bashir, and Amos Goldberg. "Deliberating the Holocaust and the Nakba: Disruptive Empathy and Binationalism in Israel/Palestine." *Journal of Genocide Research* 16, no. 1 (2014): 77–99.

Benvenisti, Meron. *Sacred Landscape: The Buried History of the Holy Land since 1948*. Translated by Maxine Kaufman-Lacusta. Berkeley: University of California Press, 2000.

Browne, Brendan. "Transitional Justice: The Case of Palestine." In *The International Handbook on Transitional Justice*, edited by Cheryl Lawther, Luke Moffett, and Dov Jacobs, 488–507. Cheltenham: Edward Elgar Publishing, 2017.

Brynen, Rex, and Roula El-Rifai. *Compensation to Palestinian Refugees and the Search for Palestinian-Israeli Peace*. London: Pluto Press, 2013.

Brynen, Rex, and Jill Tansely. "The Refugee Working Group of the Middle East Multilateral Peace Negotiations." *Palestine-Israel Journal* 2, no. 4 (1995).

Daly, Erin, and Jeremy Sarkin, "Too Many Questions, Too Few Answers: Reconciliation in Transitional Societies." *Columbia Human Rights Law Review* 35, no. 3 (2004): 101–64.

Dudai, Roni. "A Model for Dealing with the Past in the Israeli-Palestinian Context." *International Journal of Transitional Justice* 1, no. 2 (2007): 249–67.

Fischbach, Michael. "Linking Palestinian Compensation Claims with Jewish Property Claims against Arab Countries." In *Compensation to Palestinian Refugees and the Search for Palestinian-Israeli Peace*, ed. Rex Brynen and Roula El-Rifai, 69–88. London: Pluto Press, 2013.

Ghanim, Huneida. "Between Two 'One-State' Solutions: The Dialectics of Liberation and Defeat in the Palestinian National Enterprise." *Constellations* 23, no. 3 (2016): 340–50.

Golan-Agnon, Daphna. "Between Human Rights and Hope: What Israelis Might Learn from the Truth and Reconciliation Process in South Africa." *International Review of Victimology* 17, no. 1 (2010): 31–48.

Gur-Ze'ev, Ilan, and Ilan Pappe. "Beyond the Destruction of the Other's Collective Memory: Blueprints for a Palestinian/Israeli Dialogue." *Theory, Culture and Society* 20, no. 1 (2003): 93–108.

Gutman, Yifat. *Memory Activism: Reimagining the Past for the Future in Israel-Palestine*. Nashville: Vanderbilt University Press, 2017.

Hayner, Priscella. *Unspeakable Truths: Transitional Justice and the Challenge of Truth Commissions*. New York: Routledge, 2001.

Hawari, Yara. "Palestine Sine Tempore?" *Rethinking History* 22, no. 2 (2018): 165–83.

Hazan, Pierre. *Judging War, Judging History: Behind Truth and Reconciliation*. Stanford, CA: Stanford University Press, 2010.

Hilal, Leila. *Transitional Justice Responses to Palestinian Dispossession: Focus on Restitution*. International Center for Transitional Justice, 2012. https://www.ictj.org/sites/default/files/ICTJ-Brookings-Displacement-Palestine-CaseStudy-2012-English.pdf.

Hill, Tom. "1948 after Oslo: Truth and Reconciliation in Palestinian Discourse." *Mediterranean Politics* 13, no. 2 (2008): 151–70.

Humphrey, Michael. "From Victim to Victimhood: Truth Commissions and Trials as Rituals of Political Transition and Individual Healing." *Australian Journal of Anthropology* 14, no. 2 (2003): 171–87.

Hussein, Cherine. *The Re-emergence of the Single State Solution in Palestine/Israel: Countering an Illusion*. Oxon: Routledge, 2015.

Jung, Courtney. "Transitional Justice for Indigenous People in a Non-Transitional Society." International Center for Transitional Justice, 2009. https://www.ictj.org/sites/default/files/ICTJ-Identities-NonTransitionalSocieties-ResearchBrief-2009-English.pdf.

Kaufman, Edward, and Ibrahim Bisharat. "Introducing Human Rights into Conflict Resolution: The Relevance for the Israel-Palestinian Peace Process." *Journal of Human Rights* 1, no. 2 (2002): 71–91.

Khalidi, Rashid. "Truth, Justice and Reconciliation: Elements of a Solution to the Palestinian Refugee Issue." In *The Palestinian Exodus 1948–1998*, edited by Ghada Karmi and Eugene Cotran, 221–41. Reading, UK: Ithaca Press, 1999.

Khoury, Nadim. "National Narratives and the Oslo Peace Process: How Peacebuilding Paradigms Affect Conflicts over History." *Nations and Nationalism* 22, no. 3 (2016): 465–83.

———. "Postnational Memory: Narrating the Holocaust and the Nakba." *Philosophy and Social Criticism* 46, no. 1 (April 2019): 91–110.

Masalha, Nur. *The Politics of Denial: Israel and the Palestinian Refugee Problem*. London: Pluto Press, 2003.

———. "Remembering the Palestinian Nakba: Commemoration, Oral History and Narratives of Memory." *Holy Land Studies* 7, no. 2 (2008): 123–56.

Massagee, Anne. "Beyond Compensation: Reparations, Transitional Justice, and the Palestinian Refugee Question." In *Compensation to Palestinian Refugees and the Search for Palestinian-Israeli Peace*, edited by R. Brynen and R. El-Rifai, 282–307. London: Pluto Press, 2013.

Mbeki, Thabo. *Africa: The Time Has Come: Selected Speeches*. Cape Town: Tafelberg Publishers, 1998.

Ní Aoláin, Fionnuala, and Colm Campbell. "The Paradox of Transition in Conflicted Democracies." *Human Rights Quarterly* 27, no. 1 (2005): 172–213.

Nobles, Melissa. *The Politics of Official Apologies*. New York: Cambridge University Press, 2008.

Nusseibeh, Munir. *Forced Displacement in the Palestinian-Israeli Conflict, International Law and Transitional Justice*. London: University of Westminster Press, 2013.

Pappe, Ilan. "Historophobia or the Enslavement of History: The Role of the 1948 Ethnic Cleansing in the Contemporary Israeli-Palestinian Peace Process." In *Partisan Histories: The Past in Contemporary Global Politics*, edited by Michael P. Friedman and Padraic Kenney, 127–44. New York: Palgrave Macmillan, 2005.

Peled, Yoav, and Nadim Rouhana. "Transitional Justice and the Right of Return of the Palestinian Refugees." *Theoretical Inquiries in Law* 5, no. 2 (2004): 317–32.

Perugini, Nicola, and Neve Gordon. *The Human Right to Dominate*. New York: Oxford University Press, 2005.

Qurei, Ahmed. *From Oslo to Jerusalem: The Palestinian Story of the Secret Negotiations*. London: I.B. Tauris, 2006.

Rabin, Yitzhak. "Speech to the Knesset, April 18th, 1994." In *The Israel-Arab Reader*, edited by Walter Laqueur and Barry, 461. Rubin. London: Penguin Books, 2008.

Rouhana, Nadeem. "Decolonization as Reconciliation: Rethinking the National Conflict Paradigm in the Israeli-Palestinian Conflict." *Ethnic and Racial Studies* 41, no. 4 (2018): 643–62.

———. "Group Identity and Power Asymmetry in Reconciliation Processes: The Israeli-Palestinian Case." *Peace and Conflict: Journal of Peace Psychology* 10, no. 1 (2004): 33–52.

Roy, Sara. "Why Peace Failed: An Oslo Autopsy." *Current History* 100, no. 651 (2002): 8–16.

Said, Edward. *Power, Politics and Culture*. New York: Vintage, 2001.

Samy, Shahira. *Reparations to Palestinian Refugees: A Comparative Perspective*. Oxon: Routledge, 2010.

Savir, Uri. *The Process*. New York: Vintage Books, 1998.

Sayigh, Rosemary. "Dis/Solving the 'Refugee Problem.'" *Middle East Report*, no. 207 (1998): 19–23.

Shenhav, Yehouda. *Beyond the Two State Solution: A Jewish Political Essay*. Cambridge: Polity, 2012.

United Nations. "Guidance Note of the Secretary-General: United Nations Approach to Transitional Justice." 2010. https://www.un.org/ruleoflaw/files/TJ_Guidance_Note_March _2010FINAL.pdf.

United Nations Office of the High Commissioner on Human Rights. "General Assembly Resolution 60/147: UN Basic Principles and Guidelines on the Right to Remedy and Reparation of Victims of Gross Violations on International Human Rights Law and

Serious Violations of International Humanitarian Law." December 16, 2005. United Nations Office of the High Commissioner on Human Rights. https://www.ohchr.org/en/professionalinterest/pages/remedyandreparation.aspx.

Villa-Vicencio, Charles, and Erik Doxtader. *Pieces of the Puzzle: Keywords on Reconciliation and Transitional Justice*. Cape Town: Institute for Justice and Reconciliation, 2004.

Waage, Hilde. "The 'Minnow' and the 'Whale': Norway and the United States in the Peace Process in the Middle East." *British Journal of Middle Eastern Studies* 34, no. 2 (2007): 157–76.

Wolfe, Patrick. "Settler Colonialism and the Elimination of the Native." *Journal of Genocide Research* 8, no. 4 (2006): 387–409.

7

Alternatives to Partition in Palestine

Rearticulating the State-Nation Nexus

Leila Farsakh

It might sound absurd to discuss alternatives to partition in Palestine when a Palestinian state in the West Bank and Gaza has been recognized by over 138 countries and was admitted as a nonmember state into the United Nations in 2012. Partition, defined as separating Palestinians from Israelis, has long been considered the only solution to the intractable Arab-Israeli conflict. It is enshrined in UN Resolution 181 of 1947, which called for the creation of two states in historic Palestine. Partition is also ingrained in the first peace agreement signed between the Palestinians and the Israelis, in 1993, which initiated what came to be known as the Oslo peace process. Even if it was never spelled out clearly, the aim of this process has been assumed to be the establishment of a Palestinian state living side by side with Israel in peace and security. In 2009 the Israeli government declared its acceptance of such a state in principle, so long as it met Israel's conditions.[1]

Despite all these recognitions, however, a Palestinian state is unable to materialize on the ground. Partition—in the form of over ninety-nine checkpoints separating Palestinians from Israelis, the 708-kilometer Separation Wall that Israel built to encompass its settler population in the West Bank and East Jerusalem, which doubled to over 643,000 in 2018, and the siege on the Gaza Strip—makes a contiguous Palestinian state impossible, and has led many academics and activists to call for a revival of the one-state solution as a political alternative.[2]

This chapter explores some of the key political questions that need to be answered in any rejection of partition as a political solution to the Israeli-Palestinian conflict. It focuses on two key historical documents that promoted one-state solutions in Palestine. These include *Palestine: A Bi-National State*, written by Martin Buber, Judas Magnus, and Moses Smilansky, published by Ihud in 1946 and "Towards a Democratic State in Palestine for Muslims, Christians and Jews," published by the Palestine Liberation Organization (PLO) in 1970, the latter of which formed the basis of the Palestinian National Council's call in 1971 for the establishment of a democratic state in all of Palestine. These two documents provide insights into how to rearticulate the relation between the nation and the state in a way that allows for competing national claims to the land to be accommodated without compromising individual political rights to equal citizenship and justice. The chapter also examines the reasons offered over the past two decades for reviving the one-state idea and the challenges still facing it.

ALTERNATIVES TO PARTITION: PREMISES AND PROMISES

The one-state solution to two national groups fighting over the same land is not new. It has been proposed by Jewish Zionists as well as Palestinians. It was also considered by the international community, which has always been a central actor in this ongoing conflict. Its appeal stems from its promise to protect citizen rights over what some consider chauvinist national claims, since it guarantees equal political rights to all those wishing to live in Palestine, be they Jewish, Christian, or Muslim, immigrant or native. Its problem has lain in how it can reconcile individual rights with national rights within a single polity; in other words, with how to protect citizens' individual political rights to representation and equality as well as their collective rights to speak their own languages, protect their cultures, and define themselves as national entities with the right to self-determination, that is, to rule themselves by themselves.

Proponents of the one-state idea have attempted to tackle this problem by proposing two main political structures for it: a singular democratic state or a binational state. The former prioritizes individual over collective rights, leaving it to specific constitutional arrangements to sort out the ways in which group rights can be protected. The latter envisages a federated or confederated state along the Belgium or Swiss model, one that protects Israeli and Palestinian cultural and political institutions while giving them local autonomy within a democratic, binational state. It acknowledges the right of each national group to have their own elected local government, levy local taxes, control their domestic police, and speak their language. Both groups would form a federal representative government, one that would have control over a common foreign and defense policy.

At the heart of any one-state solution is an attempt to redefine the relationships between sovereignty, nationhood, and statehood. Examining how proponents of a unitary solution in Palestine have historically articulated the link between these concepts can shed light on the political challenges, as well as the opportunities, involved in advocating today for a one-state solution to the Israeli-Palestinian conflict.

Historical Origins

The genesis of the one-state solution can be traced back to the British Mandate, specifically to the period between 1922 and 1928 when the colonial power treated the newly demarcated state of Palestine as a single political and administrative unit. Britain, while incorporating the Balfour Declaration in its mandate, drafted a constitution for Palestine in 1922 that included the different communities in a single polity. It issued a single Palestinian nationality, recognized Arabic, Hebrew, and English as official languages, and provided for the creation of a legislative body that would consult with the British high commissioner, who held the executive power of this new modern state. This legislative body was to represent the whole population and be the parliament of the single state. It was to be composed of twenty-three members, twelve of whom would be elected in proportion to the population size of the respective communities (eight Muslims, two Christians, and two Jews) with the other eleven chosen by the high commissioner.[3] The Zionist leaders at the time gave this idea a lukewarm reception but, according to Ilan Pappe, they were not really interested in it, since they sought separation from, not integration with, the Arab population of Palestine.[4] The Arab leadership opposed the plan, mainly because it opposed the mandate and the Balfour Declaration, but by 1928 many leading Palestinian notables were willing to endorse it.[5] The Western Wall riots of 1929, however, made the British Mandate abandon the idea of a single polity in Palestine. The Peel Commission recommendation in 1937, and later UN Resolution 181 in 1947, enshrined partition as an imperial and, later, the internationally sanctioned solution.

A Zionist Rationale for a Binational State

Historically, among the Jewish Zionist community, the most vocal supporters of a one-state solution in Palestine have been members of Brit-Shalom, formed in 1925, and of Ihud, formed in 1942. The latter included Jewish intellectuals such as Martin Buber and Judah Magnus, the first chancellor of Hebrew University of Jerusalem, as well as business leaders such Moses Smilansky among others.[6] Together, they sought to influence the Zionist leadership with their ideas and convince Arab notables to join their plan for a binational state in Palestine.

Ihud's members tended to view Zionism as a quest for a spiritual and cultural Jewish redemption, one that required the creation of a Jewish nation but not necessarily that of a separate Jewish state. Magnus argued that the Jewish people do not "need a Jewish state to maintain its very existence" and that the Jewish nation did not need to be conceptualized or guaranteed in territorial terms.[7] Martin Buber maintained that a Jewish home in Palestine could not be successful without addressing what he defined as the "Arab question," which he defined as the legitimate presence of Arabs living in Palestine.[8]

Ihud's document, entitled *Palestine: A Bi-National State*, written by Martin Buber, Judas Magnus, and Moses Smilansky in 1946, presents the clearest Zionist position in favor of a one-state solution in Palestine, one it clearly defines as a binational state. It is Zionist insofar as its writers define themselves as people committed to the right of the Jews to return to Palestine and establish a home there, who maintain that Jews form a national, not simply religious, entity. As Martin

Buber put it, "Jewish settlement in Palestine . . . was embarked upon in order to enable the Jewish people to survive as a national entity and which in its social, economic and cultural aspects constitutes an enterprise of universal significance."[9]

The Ihud document, presented to the Anglo-American Committee of Inquiry in 1946 and to the visiting United Nations Special Committee on Palestine (UNSCOP) in 1947, was committed to Jewish migration to Palestine. However, it called for " the union of Jews and Arabs in a bi-national Palestine based on parity of the two peoples; and for the union of the bi-national Palestine with neighboring countries."[10] It defines this binational country as one in which "the two nations [will] have equal freedom and independence, equal participation in government and equality of representation and one people shall not be stronger than the other . . . s. they must make the country into *a country of nationalities. This is altogether different from a nationalist country*."[11]

The Ihud document thus emphasizes three notions that are central to any alternative to partition in Palestine. The first is the notion of equality. This applies to equality in basic rights, such as freedom, as well as in political rights, such as representation and governance. The authors also acknowledge the "natural rights of the Arabs in Palestine," by virtue of having been the country's inhabitants and "tilled its soil," which they juxtapose with the "*historical* rights of Jews in Palestine" (emphasis added). They thus equate two kinds of entitlements, both related to the land, but one created through labor and actual presence, and the other through a historical connection, which has often been defined as mythical, albeit meaningful.[12] "We regard the historical rights of the Jews and the natural rights of the Arabs as, under all the circumstances, of equal validity, and it is the task of statesmanship to find ways of adjustment between these contending claims."[13] The equality of these claims is based on the comparability of rights rather than their sameness.

The second rationale for the binational state relates to the right to self-determination and self-government. Buber and Magnus were well aware of the Palestinian struggle for political independence, which they attributed to the rise in Palestinian "political maturity" in the wake of the anticolonial struggles worldwide at the end of WWII. However, they wanted to make the case that this right was compatible with the Jewish struggle for self-determination. They maintained that Jewish and Palestinian self-determination could be accommodated within a single political space by respecting the national claims of each party and detaching sovereignty from statehood. The authors use concepts of state and country interchangeably throughout the document, reflecting an interest in prioritizing the notion of national self-determination over notions of territorial sovereignty or statehood per se. National rights here mean collective political rights that can be fulfilled in various political configurations. Nationalism, in their view, need not be *nationalistic*, that is, chauvinistic or separatist, and can be accommodated within larger political entities—such as the European Union today. As the authors put it: "We contend that the sovereign independence of tiny Palestine, whether it be Jewish sovereignty or Arab sovereignty, is a questionable good in this post war period when even great states must relinquish something of their sovereignty and seek union, if the world is not to perish. We contend that for this Holy Land the ideal of a bi-national Palestine is at least as inspiring as that of an Arab sovereign Palestine or Jewish sovereign Palestine."[14]

The third rationale the authors make for the binational state lies in the fact that it prevents the domination of one group over another. The authors were concerned about the tyranny of majority rule over the minority, a likely outcome in 1947, given that Jews comprised approximately one third of the population in Palestine at that time. Moreover, Ihud was opposed to the creation of a Jewish state through violence, which Magnus rejected morally and politically since it would have led to domination, if not expulsion, of one group by the other.[15] In a binational state, the Ihud document insists, Jews should have a right to immigrate until demographic parity is reached, after which a board would be formed of Jews and Arabs to decide who was entitled to enter the new binational state. Ihud members drew on the example of Switzerland, considered to be a comparison "most relevant to Palestine" despite its differences in level of economic development. They argued that a "federal multi-national state, based on the parity of nationalities is a most hopeful way of enabling [the people] to retain their national identity and yet of coalescing in a larger political framework. It results in separate nationalities yet a single citizenship."[16]

This 1946 document laid the foundation for future calls, put forward most vocally by 'Azmi Bishara in the 1990s, for Israel to become a state of its citizens.[17] Its emphasis on equality and on separating the nation from the state reflects an understanding of the state as a juridical entity responsible for protecting its citizens' rights, both individual and collective, irrespective of their national identity. Sovereignty is understood to be tied to the people, not to the land. The state is a political structure responsible for law and order that can combine within its territorial boundaries various national groups who are represented and can exercise some political autonomy within the state. Ihud members envisaged this binational state as part of the Arab world, in a regional union that acknowledged Jewish historical attachment to Palestine. They envisaged a multicultural state that was not too common in the 1940s, but one that is relevant to the twenty-first century, given the effect of globalization and international migration in constraining the scope of state political power.

The Palestinian Vision of a One-State Solution

The Palestinian vision of the one-state solution is most clearly presented in the PLO's pamphlet "Towards a Democratic State in Palestine for Moslems, Christians and Jews," published in 1970. The ideas proposed in this pamphlet, written by a Fatah member under a pseudonym, were largely adopted by the PLO in 1971.[18]

They build on ideas expressed by the Democratic Front for the Liberation of Palestine and its leader, Nawaf Hawatmeh.[19]

The pamphlet, as well as the eighth Palestinian National Council (PNC) of the PLO in 1971, calls for the creation of a democratic, nonsectarian, state in Palestine inclusive of Muslims, Christians, and Jews. The PNC then declares that "the armed struggle of the Palestinian people is not a racial or religious struggle directed against the Jews. This is why the future state that will be set up in Palestine liberated from Zionist Imperialism will be a democratic state, all those who wish will be able to live in peace there with the same rights and same duties."[20] Although the PLO called for the destruction of Israel, which it defined as a colonial entity, its one-state position in 1971 provided the first official Palestinian attempt to accept Jewish presence in Palestine. It acknowledged their individual, if not their national, political rights.

The Palestinian version of the democratic single state remained the official PLO plan for resolving the conflict up until 1988. It represented the Palestinian interpretation of its right to self-determination, at a time when Israel and the international community, with UN Resolution 242, had not acknowledged the existence of the Palestinian people. The PLO 1971 state project thus was as much about proposing a solution to that conflict that would affirm Palestinian existence as a national, not humanitarian, entity, with a right to self-determination, as it was about being inclusive of Jews in a single polity.

The revolutionary element in the Fatah 1970 proposal, as far as the author put it in his pamphlet, lies in its acceptance of the Jews, both those living in this new state and those wishing to come to it. One could argue that the Fatah and PLO proposal seeks to repair the injustice that the creation of the state of Israel generated and that Ihud had predicted. It wants to eliminate the Zionist domination Magnes and Buber warned against. The democratic state the PLO is proposing, though, is neither binational nor clearly secular in the true sense of the term.[21] The constitutional shape of the state is not discussed, nor is the relation between state and religion, though the document recommends the teaching of Hebrew and Arabic in the public schools of the future democratic state.

The 1970 text, in fact, clearly rejects binationalism because it argues that "religious and ethnic lines clearly cross in Palestine so as to make the term bi-national and the Arab-Jewish dichotomy meaningless or at best quite dubious."[22] The document does not consider that Jews form a nation, and refuses to deal with them as a unified cultural group either. It considers them rather a diverse group of people, of different nationalities, never holding "a truly monolithic Jewish opinion"; all the while, though, it acknowledges the persecution they have suffered as a people.[23] It notes that "the majority of Jews in Palestine today are Arab Jews," who are thus assumed to have Arab nationalities.[24] The author thereby highlighted the notion of the Arab Jew, a concept completely absent from the Zionist document reviewed. As Ella Shohat has already demonstrated, Zionist thinking remains Orientalist in its mission to modernize oriental Jews and homogenize them into a newly created, Jewish-Askenazi defined Israeli identity.[25]

Central to the Palestinian vision of a one-state solution thus is the separation it clearly makes between Jews and Zionists. It is a vision that maintains that the democratic state cannot be Zionist or include Zionists, for Zionism is a settler-colonial project that seeks to eliminate the indigenous Palestinians. It does, however, include Jews, even Israelis born after 1948, so long as they give up Zionism. The document thus marks a shift in the PLO's 1964 position, which maintained that only Jews born before 1914 are entitled to be in Palestine. It states that "All Jews, Muslims and Christians living in Palestine or forcibly exiled from it will have the right to Palestinian citizenship . . . . Equally this means that all Jewish Palestinians—at the present Israelis—have the same right provided of course they *reject Zionist racist chauvinism and fully accept to live as Palestinian in the New Palestine.*"[26]

The nationality of the state is thus Arab Palestinian, as it "will be part of the Arab Homeland."[27] From Fatah's point of view, the democratic state provides the basis on which reconciliation with the Jewish people is possible. As the author of the document puts it: "The call for an open new tolerant Palestine for Jews and non-Jews is a dramatic change in the Palestinian struggle, but it is hardly a new idea . . . what is new, is the fact that the non-Jewish Arab exiles who have been deprived of their homes and displaced by the Jews in Palestine can still . . . call for a new country that combines the ex-aggressor and the persecutor."[28]

In this respect, the 1970 document refuses to separate the nation from the state. It is, however, in direct Palestinian dialogue with the Jewish presence in Palestine, albeit on its own terms. While its author acknowledges Jewish suffering, denounces the injustice done to them by Arab countries in the 1940s, and invites them to create a new polity, the Palestinian version of the one-state solution does not explain how the collective rights of citizens will be protected. The emphasis is on notions of reconciliation and recognition. Jewish rights are defined as individual, political rights of citizens of a state, a state that is fundamentally Arab, not binational. Self-determination is thus recognized for the Arabs only, since, in the author's view, the Jews cannot be a national group. If they were, they would become a racist colonial state, just as Israel, the author argues, has demonstrated itself to be.

THE TWO-STATE SOLUTION: WHAT WENT WRONG?

The Palestinian state project declared in 1971, though, was soon shelved in favor of the two-state solution. The Palestinian leadership was aware by the mid-1970s that a Palestinian state could not materialize on all of historic Palestine, given Zionist rejection of it and the international community's support for the two-state solution. In 1988 the PLO issued its Declaration of Independence, officially acknowledged Israel, and accepted UN Resolution 242 as the basis for peace negotiation. This paved the way for the signing of the Oslo Accords in 1993 and 1995.

The Oslo agreements indirectly acknowledged the Palestinian right to self-government in the West Bank and Gaza. They allowed the formation of Palestinian elected representative institutions and the creation of a whole infrastructure of security coordination between the Israeli military and the Palestinian Authority. Although the signed agreements never promised the independence of a Palestinian state in the Occupied Territories, the Palestinian leadership and the international community saw as the aim of the peace process the eventual establishment of a Palestinian state, as acknowledged by the Quartet Road Map for Peace in 2003. A Palestinian state on 22 percent of historic Palestine was considered better than no state. It was also an act of historical reconciliation with Israel, one that acknowledged Jewish individual and collective political rights to their own state on part of Palestine.

The developments of the past thirty years, though, reveal that a Palestinian state cannot materialize. The present revival of the one-state solution today is part of an attempt by activists and intellectuals to challenge the Oslo conceptualization of the conflict and the means to resolve it, stressing the way in which the peace process deepened, rather than repealed, Israel's colonial domination. These activists argue that the conflict was never a struggle between two equal competing national groups but rather as a struggle for ending colonialism and achieving political liberation.[29]

Three reasons explain the revived interest in a one-state solution in Palestine since 2000. The first argument lies in the fact that Zionism proved determined to destroy, rather than respect, Palestinian national self-determination. The bet that many Palestinians were willing to make in September 1993, when the first Oslo Accord was signed, that the end of the occupation would create a Palestinian state on 22 percent of Palestine that would protect their fundamental rights, was lost with the Camp David negotiations in 2000 and the Israeli military response to the Second Intifada.

Moreover, facts on the ground reveal that Israel instituted by a de facto apartheid structure of domination. Israel devised a segregated system of control by which Israeli citizens are governed by democratic rules while Palestinians are deprived of political rights. The US stance in 2020, in which the Trump administration accepted Israeli claims over East Jerusalem and the annexation of Palestinian land, confirmed Israeli colonial control and trivialized the scope of the Palestinian territorial and political jurisdiction.[30]

Secondly, the Palestinian quest for statehood under the Oslo peace process has compromised Palestinian collective and individual political rights. These rights include not only the end of Israeli occupation in the West Bank and Gaza, but also Palestinian sovereignty and access to East Jerusalem and a recognition of the right of return, which is protected by UN Resolution 194. The Oslo agreements, by prioritizing the Palestinian National Authority (PNA) over the all-encompassing PLO institutions, separated refugees from those living in the West Bank and the Gaza Strip, who were in turn separated from Palestinians living inside Israel and the Palestinian diaspora. It fragmented the Palestinian body politic by locking Palestinian national aspiration to the West Bank and Gaza. At the same time, the Palestinian Authority has forsaken the unity of the Palestinian people for a promise of independence that provided financial gains to a small stratum of the population. It proved uninterested in protecting citizens' rights. In the West Bank, the PNA tried to buy legitimacy and divert calls for political accountability by providing unsustainable economic opportunities.[31] In Gaza, the Hamas government sought political legitimacy by asserting the right to resistance, promising security, and fighting Israel, not by protecting freedom of expression and political representation.

Thirdly, the demographic reality on the ground threatens the political sustainability of the segregated political structure Israel has created. In 2020, 6.87 million Jews were living in Israel/Palestine, which is close to the number of Palestinians living in it (5.03 million in the West Bank and Gaza and 1.96 million living inside Israel). By 2025 Palestinians will be a majority in Israel/Palestine, given their higher population growth rate (2.7 percent compared with 1.8 percent in Israel), making the question of their lack of real political rights increasingly troublesome, both to the Israelis and the present Palestinian leadership.[32] For many Palestinians, inside and outside the West Bank and Gaza, the quest for separate statehood is void, if not altogether outdated.

POLITICAL FRAMEWORK AND PRINCIPLES

Turning the one-state apartheid reality that the Oslo years have institutionalized into a one-state solution, though, is not an easy task. It requires a political will to undo the colonial structure that Israel perpetuates as well as the ability to articulate the components of a viable democratic state that is inclusive of the individual and collective rights of Palestinians and Israelis. It is thus necessary for any political alternative to partition, whether a democratic binational state or a democratic federal state, to explain how the political visions introduced in the 1940s and 1970s can be reworked in view of the developments that have taken place over the past decades. In other words, it needs to rearticulate the relation between the nation and the state as well as explain how the colonial power relations that the partition paradigm consolidated can be dismantled.

The Right to Self-Determination: Decoupling the State from the Nation

The right to self-determination, ever since it was recognized by international law, has been tied to the notion of statehood. The definition of the state, and the political expression of the right to self-determination, however, have remained contested as much as historically determined. The state has been perceived in Western thought not only as the highest form of political union between free individuals, but also as a tool of domination, particularly in Marxist thinking. The twentieth-century Weberian definition of the state as a "human organization that has the legitimate monopoly over the use of force in a specific territory," has tied it to a Westphalian understanding of the world, that is, a world made of clearly demarcated states defined by specific borders. Although the state is never a neutral entity, as the Weberian definition leads one to believe, since it reflects, as much as articulates, different class interests within a given social formation, it has remained a core site of sovereignty and control.

Self-determination has also been more closely tied to the concept of the nation, which remains a far more nebulous term than statehood. The nation is understood today to be a "imagined community," a political entity that affirms the right of the people, however they define their collective sense of "we," to have collective, not just individual, rights, and to have the right to rule themselves by themselves.[33] People under colonial rule have used the notion of self-determination to claim their right to political independence, one that is associated with statehood. The demand for an independent state has been a central demand of most nationalist movements precisely because the state asserts sovereignty (since it has the monopoly over the use of violence) and confers international recognition of the nation's right to political agency, or self-determination.

There has always been an inherent tension, though, in the quest to exercise self-determination through the creation of an independent nation-state. This tension arises from the inherent incongruency between the state, which is a territorially bound political concept, and the nation, whose boundaries can transcend the territorial frontiers of a given state.[34] This tension also stems from the ambiguity surrounding the notion of sovereignty. Ever since the eighteenth century, sovereignty has been articulated as springing from the people, who create the polity called the state and are the source of its legitimacy. The state speaks for the people as much as represents them through its representative institutions, especially when it claims to be a democratic state. However, once established, the state becomes juridically sovereign in the sense that it has the ultimate power over the life and death of its citizens.

As Arendt has argued, a state is needed to affirm people's right to have rights, that is, to exist juridically as a political entity and have a political structure that protects its citizenship rights. However, as soon as the nation-state is established it inadvertently leads to the exclusion of others, those who do not belong to the nation, creating categories of minorities and of refugees, or stateless people deprived of their basic human rights.[35] While international law has tried resolve this tension through international human rights law, which protects individual human rights irrespective of political affiliation, it also admits that human rights are tied to citizenship rights, that is, to belonging to a state. International law ultimately leaves it to individual states to define their own juridical and constitutional structures to protect the collective and individual rights of their citizens.

Various scholars have sought to readdress the exclusionary nature of the nation-state and the problem of minorities it creates by calling on the state to be above the nation.[36] They privilege a definition of the state in civic, rather than in ethnic terms, confining it to the juridical role of executing the will of citizens living within its boundaries. The state thus becomes an instrument, or executor, of the law enacted by the people, who are sovereign. Such a definition of the state implies a commitment to a constitutional and deliberative democratic political order. While such a conceptualization of the state is liberal and does not address fundamental questions about the historical injustices and colonial foundation of the modern state, it does decouple the nation from the state while giving space for a civic engagement that alone can determine the means by which a state can be decolonized; in other words, one that is able to reconcile with its past while being inclusive of all those who live on the land as equal citizens irrespective of their ethnicity.

Reified versus Divisible Sovereignty

The political framework for any alternative to partition in Israel/Palestine must transcend people's obsession with the state as the only protector of people's rights. This is not easy given that the official political discourse of both Zionists and Palestinians remains staunchly attached to the nation-state. This discourse conceptualizes sovereignty as territorially bound, with one group of people entitled to it. The Palestinian obsession with statehood, as much as Zionism's, stems from a belief that only a state can protect national identity and existence. According to Israeli Prime Minister Benjamin Netanyahu, the Jewish state is the only means to protect the Jewish people worldwide, an assertion that continues to be contested by world Jewry but is central to mainstream Zionism.[37] It is a contention that inevitably leads to racist and exclusionary politics, as Israel's nationality law of 2018 proves. This law confers the right of self-determination only to Jewish people within the historic land of Palestine, denying the equal rights of Palestinian citizens of Israel as well as those living in the West Bank and Gaza Strip.

Palestinians, particularly those in the West Bank and Gaza, also remain keen on their own state, albeit one that would extend over just part of Palestine. In a survey conducted by the Birzeit University Center for Development Studies (CDS) in 2015 regarding Palestinian views on the present status quo and possible alternatives to it, over 80 percent of respondents supported the idea of a Palestinian state in the West Bank and Gaza.[38] They considered it a necessity, despite the fragmentation of Palestinian land and people, and the low possibility of its creation. Nearly half of respondents (47 percent) maintained that such a state is necessary because it would provide security; 22 percent who saw its role as protector of political and civil rights as the most important rationale for its existence. The majority of respondents associated state sovereignty with the ability to have a passport and to be able to move freely and be secure in their home.[39] While many were critical of the PNA and aware that the state-building project has benefited certain economic classes while usurping power in the name of national unity, the majority viewed political independence in a two-state solution as the only politically realistic option.

Most recently, some authors have proposed a parallel-states structure that would allow Palestinians and Israelis joint sovereignty of the whole land.[40] This proposal represents a reformulation of the binational ideal by acknowledging present government structures rather than seeking to dismantle them. A parallel-states structure would accept the presence of Israelis settlements as well as the rights of Palestinian refugees to return. It takes as given the national autonomy of Palestinians and Israelis, acknowledging the existence of what it calls "territorial heartlands" for each group, while allowing both Israelis and Palestinians to have joint sovereignty over Jerusalem. Its proposal is not different from the confederated or federated structure that binationalists have envisaged, wherein the autonomy each community is recognized under the umbrella of a common defense and foreign policy.

Without dismantling the colonial foundation of Israel, however, the parallel-state proposal will simply perpetuate Israel's colonial power and Palestinian dispossession. On a most rudimentary level, it is difficult to imagine how to get two groups of people who have been separated by 708 kilometer walls, over ninety-nine checkpoints and a siege on 2 million Palestinians in Gaza to talk, let alone to want to live together. The Israel government has shown no intention of treating the Palestinians as equal, let alone of relinquishing its control of land and resources. Some among the Israeli political right, meanwhile, are willing to give Palestinians political rights but no national rights in what it defines as greater Israel.[41] The majority of Israelis have no intention of living with Palestinians together in one state, as the 2021 Israeli war on Gaza and the Palestinians revealed.

Moreover, political elites both within Israel and among the PNA consider the one-state option a capitulation of their respective national projects, rather than a fulfillment of each party's right to self-determination. Judging from the 2015 CDS survey, the average Palestinian in the West Bank and Gaza also is not keen on the one-state idea. In the survey over 66 percent of respondents rejected the idea of a democratic state guaranteeing equal political rights to Palestinians and Israelis. Only Palestinian citizens of Israel accept political representation and voting rights for Palestinians and Israelis in a single state (over 80 percent of respondents compared to under 40 percent in the West Bank and Gaza).[42] While many Palestinians in the West Bank and Gaza lament the siege of Gaza, and the lack of independence of the West Bank, they demand the lift of the siege, not integration into Israel. By contrast, the advocates of a one-state solution are concentrated in the diaspora and among Palestinian citizens of Israel. Unless they form a political movement that can galvanize the population both in Israel and inside the Occupied Territories, it is difficult to see how the one-state model can become a viable political project rather than an expression of despair or a threat

Domination versus Equality

It would difficult to move forward with any alternative to partition without proposing a political and legal strategy for dismantling Israeli colonialism. Such a dismantlement would require rebalancing the power inequalities between Israelis and Palestinians, both militarily and economically. Israel has an economy that is over 20 times the size of the Palestinian economy, with developed industrial and buoyant trade sectors that will continue to dominate Palestinian economic growth.[43] This difference in comparative advantage between Israel and the West Bank and Gaza would allow Israeli capital to dominate in Palestinian sectors while Palestinian workers continued to serve as cheap labor. While liberal economic theory argues that such a division of labor is beneficial to everyone, free market forces can also lock each party into its own sphere of comparative advantage. Although in the long run consumers and producers will benefit from a more efficient allocation of resources across the Green Line, various vested interests will be harmed in any one-state configuration, especially in the short run, among them small Palestinian businesses and unionized Israeli labor.

A constitutional arrangement that guarantees the equality of all citizens before the law, dismantles Jewish privileges, and sets up compensation mechanisms to address the present economic and political inequalities, could help alleviate these worries. International law can also offer insight for moving forward. It has already offered various models for a federal state in Palestine, such as the minority report proposed by the UNSCOP in 1947, which proposed an economic union between Israelis and Palestinians. Creating appropriate institutional support systems (such as affirmative action) that can redress the present economic inequality and offer increased investment and openness could also help, as already seen in other cases where economies of different sizes integrate (European Union, South Africa, etc.).

Recognition and Reconciliation: The Rights of the "Other"

For any political alternative to partition to work, it will inevitably need to address the issues of historical reconciliation and recognition. The two-state model sought a historical reconciliation through territorial separation. It was premised on the merit of acknowledging the collective rights of Israelis and Palestinians in two separate political entities. It thus avoided addressing the fundamental injustices created in 1948 by focusing on the post-1967 reality. The very fact that Israel refused to abide even to this paradigm, by continuing building settlements and insisting on the Jewishness of the state, has shown that reconciliation cannot be achieved without addressing the core issues of the Israeli-Palestinian conflict. These include not simply right to the land, but also freedom of movement, return, and equality before the law for all.[44] Insofar as Israel is concerned, the challenge is how to acknowledge the collective rights of the Palestinians in a polity that does not ensure Jewish supremacy. Insofar as the Palestinians are concerned, they need to confront the reality of Jewish attachment to Palestine, as much as grapple with the question of what rights of Jews in Palestine are entitled to as a political community rather than as a religious group or as individuals.[45] This is a thorny question that requires addressing the right of the indigenous as much as the right of migrants, the refugee as much as the exiled.

No alternative to partition can materialize before each side recognize the rights of the "other" in Palestine. In this regard, the Palestinian national movement needs to address what can be defined as the Jewish question, namely Jews' attachment to Palestine and the Jewish claim to a home in Palestine. This does not mean that Palestinians should accept Zionism or give up on dismantling Israel's colonial structure. They need, though, to explain how to decolonize Israel without negating the Jewish Israeli culture it has created over the past seventy years: to accommodate the political rights of the Jews to live and prosper in Palestine, to continue to speak Hebrew, and to have political autonomy. The challenge for the Palestinians remains how to create a new polity that includes the Jews rather than seeks to reconvert them into Arabs. The PLO's 1971 appeal for of a single democratic state needs thus to be reworked to take into consideration the reality on the ground today. It needs to explain how the Jewish Israeli can be part of that state without necessarily becoming a rehabilitated Arab citizen or alternative, only a resident not entitled to full equal citizenship.

Israelis, for their part, need to address what Martin Buber has already called the "Arab question." They need to give up their privileges and acknowledge Palestinian collective and individual rights in all the land under Israel's control. This is not an easy matter for Israelis to face, for it would force them to admit the colonial dimension of their emancipatory project of nation-building, as well as give up their privileges. Just as challenging, facing the Arab question implies that Israelis have to confront the fact that they live in an Arab world, that over 50 percent of their Jewish population is of Arab descent, and that the future state will also be part of the Arab world, not Europe. At a fundamental level, it implies that Jews in Israel need to confront the Arab dimension of their Jewishness. Zionism cannot deal with such a reality, since it is fundamentally a Western civilizing enterprise that seeks to universalize Jews, including Arab Jews, and turn them into an enlightened, that is, Western Ashkenazi Jews who have their own home as all civilized nations do. Negation of the Arab Jew, already noted by Ella Shohat among others, is still profound in Israeli society.[46] Yet reviving as much as reconstructing the Arab Jew would be central to this new state: the Arab Jew partakes as much part in Jewish identity as in the Arab world. At present both are negated and in need of rehabilitation within their historical context. They also need to be rearticulated in today's reality as part of an attempt to create a new collective "we" for a post-partition, single democratic state (whether its constitutional shape were binational, federal, unitary, etc.; see chapter 9 in this book).

CONCLUSION

Partition as a solution to Palestine has failed, but the one-state solution as a clear and acceptable political project is still not born. Its birth will require a political movement that has been growing but still has work to do to reach mainstream discourse. Success will depend on the ability of its advocates to formulate a clear political agenda that protects the individual and collective rights of citizens irrespective of their ethnicity. The Palestinian citizens of Israel are the best placed to lead the movement, for they know well both sides of the conflict and can act as a bridge between both national movements. The historical juncture that the conflict is in puts them in the best place to push the one-state solution forward. Whether they can take on this role is still to be seen. What is clear is that they will work with the various Palestinian constituencies. They need to be reincorporated in the Palestinian national movement, the PLO, which today needs to be redefined and reinvigorated. International pressure on Israel will also be key in any attempt to force it to give up its privileges, uphold its international obligations, and renounce the ethno-racist definition of identity that Israel's 2018 nationality law enshrined.

NOTES

Parts of this chapter are drawn from Leila Farsakh, "Common State in Israel-Palestine: Historical Origins and Lingering Challenges," *Ethnopolitics* 15:, no. 4 (2016): 380–92.

1. Isabel Kershner, "Netanyahu Backs Palestinian State, with Caveats," *New York Times*, June 19, 2009, http://www.nytimes.com/2009/06/15/world/middleeast/15mideast.html?pagewanted=all&_r=0.

2. See, among others, Hani Faris, ed., *The Failure of the Two-State Solution: The Prospects of One State in the Israel-Palestine Conflict* (London: IB Tauris, 2013); Virginia Tilley, *The One-State Solution: A Breakthrough for Peace in the Israeli-Palestinian Deadlock* (Ann Arbor: University of Michigan Press, 2005); Ali Abunimeh, *One Country: A Bold Proposal to End the Israeli-Palestinian Impasse* (New York: Henry Holt, 2006). For checkpoints, see "List of Military Checkpoints in the West Bank and Gaza Strip," B'Tselem, last updated September 25, 2019, http://www.btselem.org/freedom_of_movement/checkpoints_and_forbidden_roads; for settlements, see "Statistics on Settlements and Settler Population," B'Tselem, last updated January 16, 2019, https://www.btselem.org/settlements/statistics.

3. Charles Smith, *Palestine and the Arab-Israeli Conflict* (Boston: Bedford/St. Martin's, 2010), 110.

4. Ilan Pappe, "The Birth, Demise and Future Prospective of One Palestine Complete," *Electronic Journal of Middle East Studies* 8 (Spring 2008): 151–64.

5. The Nashashibi faction privately favored the plan and by 1928 the Arab Executive, under Kazem al Husseini, was also willing to endorse it. Both Palestinian factions began talks with the High Commissioner over the proposed legislative council in January 1929. Smith, *Palestine and the Arab-Israeli Conflict*, 110–12.

6. Although mainstream Zionist parties such as Labor Zionists and Revisionists opposed the binational idea, Mapai and Hashomer Hatzair were inclined towards it. Susan Hitti, *The Bi-National Idea* (Jerusalem: Shikmona, 1979).

7. Judas Magnus, *Like All Nations* (Jerusalem: Weiss Press, 1930), 15.

8. Buber defined this problem as consisting "in the relation between Jewish settlement in Palestine and Arab life, or as it may be termed, the intra-national basis of Jewish settlement . . . one which starts out from the concrete relationships between neighboring and inter-dependent nations, when considering the given economic and political facts." Martin Buber, "The Bi-National Approach to Zionism," in *Towards a Union in Palestine*, edited by Martin Buber, Judas Magnus and Akibah Simon, 7–13 (Ihud: Jerusalem, 1947), 7.

9. Buber, "The Bi-National Approach," 7.

10. Martin Buber, Judas Magnus, and Moses Smilansky, *Palestine: A Bi-National State* (Jerusalem: Ihud, 1946), 7.

11. Buber, Magnus, and Smilansky, *Palestine*, 8–9. Emphasis added.

12. Chaim Ganz, *Just Zionism: On the Morality of the Jewish State* (Oxford: Oxford University Press, 2008), 7

13. Buber, Magnus, and Smilansky, *Palestine*, 11.

14. Buber, Magnus, and Smilansky, *Palestine*, 19.

15. Judas Magnus, "A Solution Through Force?" in *Towards a Union in Palestine*, edited by Martin Buber, Judas Magnus and Akibah Simon, 14–21 (Ihud: Jerusalem, 1947), 15–17.

16. Buber, Magnus, and Smilansky, *Palestine*, 20–21.

17. 'Azmi Bishara, *On the Democratic Option: Four Critical Studies* (Beirut: Center for Arab Unity Studies, 1993), in Arabic; 'Azmi Bishara, *Min yahudiyat al-dawla hata Sharon* [From the Jewishness of the state to Sharon] (Ramallah: Muwatin, 2005).

18. Mohammad Rasheed, *Towards a Democratic State in Palestine for Moslems, Christians and Jews* (Beirut: PLO Research Center, 1970), 38.

19. Alain Gresh, *The PLO: The Struggle Within* (London: Zed Books, 1988).

20. Quoted in Gresh, *PLO*, 48.

21. The word *secular* never appears in the document, unless we take the term "nonsectarian" to mean secular.

22. Rasheed, *Towards a Democratic State in Palestine*, 38.

23. Rasheed, *Towards a Democratic State in Palestine*, 29, 16, 29–31.

24. Rasheed, *Towards a Democratic State in Palestine*, 38.

25. Ella Shohat, "Sephardim in Israel: Zionism from the Standpoint of its Jewish Victims," *Social Text* 19/20 (Autumn 1988): 1–35.

26. Rasheed, *Towards a Democratic State in Palestine*," 35. Emphasis added.

27. Rasheed, *Towards a Democratic State in Palestine*, 34.

28. Rasheed, *Towards a Democratic State in Palestine*, 12–13.

29. See, among others, Faris, *Failure of the Two-State Solution*; Ali Abunimeh, *The Battle for Justice in Palestine* (New York: Haymarket, 2014); and Ghada Karmi, *Married to Another Man* (London: Pluto Press, 2007).

30. Leila Farsakh, "The Political Economy of Israeli Occupation: What Is Colonial about It?" *Electronic Journal of Middle East Studies* (Spring 2008): 41–58.

31. Raja Khalidi and Sobhi Samour, "Neoliberalism as Liberation: The Statehood Program and the Remaking of the Palestinian National Movement," *Journal of Palestine Studies* 158, no. 2 (2011): 6–25.

32. Israeli Central Bureau of Statistics, *Statistical Abstract of Israel* (Jerusalem: Israeli Central Bureau of Statistics, 2020), available at https://www.cbs.gov.il/en/mediarelease/Pages/2019/Population -of-Israel-on-the-Eve-of-2020.aspx; and Palestinian Central Bureau of Statistics, "On the Occasion of the International Population Day 11/07/2020," July 9, 2020, available at http://pcbs.gov.ps/site/512 /default.aspx?lang=en&ItemID=3774.

33. Benedict Anderson, *Imagined Communities: Reflections on the Origin and Spread of Nationalism* (Cambridge: Cambridge University Press, 1981).

34. Ernst Gellner, *Nation and Nationalism* (London: Blackwell Publishing, 1983).

35. Hannah Arendt, *The Origins of Totalitarianism* (New York: Harcourt, Brace, and Jovanich, 1968).

36. Arendt, *The Origins of Totalitarianism*; and Seyla Benhabib, *The Rights of Others: Aliens, Residents and Citizens* (Cambridge: Cambridge University Press, 2004).

37. Laurence Silberstein, ed., *Post Zionism: A Reader* (New Brunswick: Rutgers University Press, 2008). Lahav Harkov, "Netanyahu Announces Support for Jewish State Bill," *Jerusalem Post*, November 16, 2014, http://www.jpost.com/Israel-News/Politics-And-Diplomacy/Netanyahu-announces -support-for-Jewish-State-Bill-381926.

38. The survey included a sample of 1,060 respondents distributed between the West Bank, Gaza Strip, and Palestinian citizens of Israel. For more details, see Leila Farsakh, "The Legal and Political Limitation of the Oslo Agreements," policy paper, Center for Development Studies, Birzeit University, June 2016.

39. Farsakh, "Legal and Political Limitation of the Oslo Agreements," tables 1 and 2.

40. Mark LeVine and Mathias Mossberg, *One Land, Two States: Israel and Palestine as Parallel States* (Berkeley: University of California Press, 2014).

41. Leila Farsakh, "The One-State Solution and the Israeli-Palestinian Conflict: Palestinian Challenges and Prospects," *Middle East Journal* 64, no. 1 (2011): 20–45.

42. Farsakh, "Legal and Political Limitation of the Oslo Agreements," table 2.

43. Israeli GDP in 2019 was 394 billion dollars, compared with 16 billion dollars in the West Bank and Gaza. Per capita income in Israel in 2013 was $43,588 compared with $3,562- in the West Bank and Gaza. "GDP per capita (Current US$): Israel," World Bank, https://data.worldbank.org/indicator /NY.GDP.PCAP.CD?locations=IL&name_desc=true.

44. In this regard, see Bashir Bashir and Azar Dakwar, *Rethinking the Politics of Israel/Palestine: Partition and its Alternatives* (Vienna: Kreisky Forum, 2015).

45. Yehouda Shenhav, *Beyond the Two-State Solution: A Jewish Political Essay* (London: Polity Press, 2012).

46. See Ella Shohat, *On the Arab-Jew, Palestine and Other Displacements: Selected Writings* (London: Pluto 2017); and Yehouda Shenhav, *The Arab Jews: A Postcolonial Reading of Nationalism* (Stanford, CA: Stanford University Press, 2006).

BIBLIOGRAPHY

Abunimeh, Ali. *The Battle for Justice in Palestine*. New York: Haymarket, 2014.

———. *One Country: A Bold Proposal to End the Israeli-Palestinian Impasse*. New York: Metropolitan Books, 2006.

Anderson, Benedict. *Imagined Communities: Reflections on the Origin and Spread of Nationalism*. Cambridge: Cambridge University Press, 1981.

Arendt, Hannah. *The Origins of Totalitarianism*. New York: Harcourt, Brace, and Jovanich, 1968.

Azoulay, Ariella, and Adi Ophir. *The One-State Condition: Occupation and Democracy in Israel/Palestine*. Stanford, CA: Stanford University Press, 2012.

Bashir, Bashir, and Azar Dakwar. *Rethinking the Politics of Israel/Palestine: Partition and its Alternatives*. Vienna: Kreisky Forum, 2015.

Benhabib, Seyla. *The Rights of Others: Aliens, Residents and Citizens*. Cambridge: Cambridge University Press, 2004.

Bishara, 'Azmi. *Min yahudiyat al-dawla hata Sharon* [From the Jewishness of the state to Sharon]. Ramallah: Muwatin, 2005.

———. *On the Democratic Option: Four Critical Studies*. Beirut: Center for Arab Unity Studies, 1993. In Arabic.

Buber, Martin. "The Bi-National Approach to Zionism." In *Towards a Union in Palestine*, edited by Martin Buber, Judas Magnus, and Akibah Simon, 7–13. Jerusalem: Ihud, 1947.

Buber, Martin, Judas Magnus, and Moses Smilansky. *Palestine: A Bi-National State*. Jerusalem: Ihud, 1946.

Davis, Uri. *Apartheid Israel*. London: Zed Books, 2003.

Faris, Hani, ed. *The Failure of the Two-State Solution: The Prospects of One State in the Israel-Palestine Conflict*. London: I.B. Tauris, 2013.

———. "The Legal and Political Limitation of the Oslo Agreements." Policy paper, Center for Development Studies, Birzeit University, June 2016.

———. "The One-State Solution and the Israeli-Palestinian Conflict: Palestinian Challenges and Prospects." *Middle East Journal* 64, no. 1 (2011): 20–45.

———. *Palestinian Labor Flows to Israel: Land, Labor and Occupation*. London: Routledge, 2005.

———. "The Political Economy of Israeli Occupation: What Is Colonial about It?" *Electronic Journal of Middle East Studies* (Spring 2008): 41–58.

Ganz, Chaim. *Just Zionism: On the Morality of the Jewish State*. Oxford: Oxford University Press, 2008.

Gellner, Ernst. *Nation and Nationalism*. London: Blackwell Publishing, 1983.

Gresh, Alain. *The PLO: The Struggle Within*. London: Zed Books, 1988.

Hitti, Susan. *The Bi-National Idea*. Jerusalem: Shikmona, 1979.

Israeli Central Bureau of Statistics. *Statistical Abstract of Israel*. Jerusalem: Israeli Central Bureau of Statistics, 2019.

Karmi, Ghada. *Married to Another Man*. London: Pluto Press, 2007.

Khalidi, Raja, and Sobhi Samour. "Neoliberalism as Liberation: The Statehood Program and the Remaking of the Palestinian National Movement." *Journal of Palestine Studies* 158, no. 2 (2011): 6–25.

LeVine, Mark, and Mathias Mossberg. *One Land, Two States: Israel and Palestine as Parallel States*. Berkeley: University of California Press, 2014.

Magnus, Judas. *Like All Nations*. Jerusalem: Weiss Press, 1930.

———. "A Solution through Force?" in *Towards a Union in Palestine*, edited by Martin Buber, Judas Magnus and Akibah Simon, 14–21. Ihud: Jerusalem, 1947.

Makdisi, Sari. *Palestine Inside Out: An Everyday Occupation*. New York: W.W. Norton, 2007.

Pappe, Ilan. "The Birth, Demise and Future Prospective of One Palestine Complete." *Electronic Journal of Middle East Studies* 8 (Spring 2008): 151–64.

Rasheed, Mohammad. *Towards a Democratic State in Palestine for Moslems, Christians and Jews*. Beirut: PLO Research Center, 1970. In Arabic.

Shenhav, Yehouda. *The Arab Jews: A Postcolonial Reading of Nationalism*. Stanford, CA: Stanford University Press, 2006.

———. *Beyond the Two-State Solution: A Jewish Political Essay*. London: Polity Press, 2012.

Shohat, Ella. *On the Arab-Jew, Palestine and Other Displacements: Selected Writings*. London: Pluto, 2017.

———. "Sephardim in Israel: Zionism from the Standpoint of its Jewish Victims." *Social Text* 19/20 (Autumn 1988): 1–35.

Silberstein, Laurence, ed. *Post Zionism: A Reader*. New Brunswick, NJ: Rutgers University Press, 2008.
Smith, Charles. *Palestine and the Arab-Israeli Conflict*. Boston: Bedford/St. Martin's, 2010.
Tilley, Virginia. *The One-State Solution: A Breakthrough for Peace in the Israeli-Palestinian Deadlock*. Ann Arbor: University of Michigan Press, 2005.

8

Palestinian Nationality and "Jewish" Nationality

From the Lausanne Treaty to Today

Susan M. Akram

This chapter assesses the legal foundations of Zionist and Palestinian national claims over the land of Palestine since the British Mandate. It explores the legal basis and implications of the claim of Jewish nationality in Palestine and compares it with the claim of Palestinian nationality. The question of national rights, and who can claim them, is central to rethinking the statehood and residency rights of those living today in the area of historic Palestine. The law of nationality is at the core of the protections of peoples' right to self-determination, and understanding the principles underlying nationality law is essential to separating claims from rights in considering Palestinian and Jewish peoples' supposedly conflicting claims to residency and right of return.

The central premise in applying international nationality law to the conflict over territorial claims is that Palestinians possess a defined nationality that remains valid and legally cognizable today. Moreover, as a legal matter, Palestinian nationality is not negated by the claim of a Jewish state in Israel, or by an extraterritorial claim to Israel by Jews elsewhere in the world. In order to understand the difference between Israeli, Jewish, and Palestinian national statuses, it is critical to appreciate that the international law of nationality operates to protect a fundamental connection between peoples and their lands of origin: the territorial and direct "bloodline" connection, not a religious connection, determines national rights. This chapter will analyze the key norms of international nationality law, and apply them to the relevant legal instruments affecting the conflict over rights to territory in Palestine. It examines not only the application of the norms to this conflict, but also how (and whether) instruments such as the British Mandate, the Balfour Declaration, and the most relevant United Nations resolutions affected the claims of Jews and Palestinians to national status in the territory. In essence,

192

this short excursus into the legal and historical background of the conflicting claims of self-determination to and in Palestine illustrates how "getting the law right" paves the way for a different and more equitable shared future in the same land for Jews and Palestinians, both those now living there and those who have the right to return there.

INTERNATIONAL LEGAL DEFINITIONS OF NATIONALS AND CITIZENS

At the outset, it is important to define the meaning of the terms *citizen* and *national*. Although these terms are frequently used interchangeably, they have distinct legal meanings. *Nationality* has both a sociological meaning and a legal one; the sociological understanding is quite distinct from but more commonly understood than its legal definition. In sociological terms, nationality encompasses ethnonational identity, that is, self-identification with a particular group considered to have a common ethnic origin—for example, Bosnians, Serbs, Kurds, Tamils, or Armenians—regardless of the territory in which they are located. The legal meaning is quite different, however, and refers to a legal relationship between an individual and a particular state or territory. Under classical international law theory, nationality determines which state a person belongs to for purposes of disputes with other states. Since nationality is "the link between [international] law and the individual," it is critical to determine who is a "national" of a state or territory, and hence what rights in and to that state or territory the individual has as a matter of international law.[1] From the legal perspective, the ethnonational identity of a person is irrelevant, as it is the connection the person has to a particular state or territory—that is, their membership in it—which defines a person's legal nationality and political rights.[2]

Nationality as an international legal concept was defined as early as 1939 by the Permanent Court of International Justice as "the bond . . . between the State and the individual," and further interpreted by the successor International Court of Justice (ICJ) as the "genuine link" between an individual and a territory.[3] The core principle of which "genuine links" establish nationality was already incorporated in domestic laws and treaties by the late 1800s and included birth on the soil of the territory *(jus soli)*, birth to a parent with the national status of the territory *(jus sanguinis)*, and less frequently and with less certain rules, long-term residence on the territory *(jus domicilii)*.[4] By the early 1900s, nationality principles had solidified around these norms to exclude race, religion, language, or ethnic origin alone as the basis for national status. Birth on the territory, direct blood relationship through a parent holding the nationality, and/or long-term ("habitual") residence were the key "genuine links" for nationality status to be recognized under international law.[5] Equally important during the colonial era was the obligation to conform any nationality legislation to binding treaties regulating the status of inhabitants of territories, whether such inhabitants were part of independent states or under colonial rule.[6]

The term *citizen* is of significance as a matter of the domestic law of states; that is, a state can determine through its internal laws who among its residents has the preferred status of citizenship, with its particular privileges and benefits, as well as its concomitant responsibilities. A state's prerogative to define its citizens, however, has normative limitations, as it cannot define citizens in an arbitrary or discriminatory way that is prohibited by treaty or international custom. In other words, a state's ability to pass domestic law on citizenship is circumscribed by certain international legal rules.[7] The most important of these rules is the "genuine links" principle described above. Another key rule that was already recognized as customary international law by the time of the Harvard study on nationality laws in 1929 was that inhabitants of a territory undergoing a change of sovereignty automatically acquire nationality in the new state.[8]

A corollary to this principle, now codified in human rights treaties, is the principle that no state can denationalize an individual on an arbitrary basis—this prohibits, for example, denationalization or prevention of return to the territory of nationality for reasons of race, religion, or national or ethnic origin.[9] The rule requiring states to conform to these treaty requirements is as absolute today as it was during the colonial or mandate era.[10] Although in classical international law terms the nationality of a person is determined by international law and citizenship by domestic law, the distinction between the two has become less significant with the growing importance of human rights law. In the Palestinian case, and in most of the Arab world, however, the distinction between the two remains both relevant and critical, primarily because most of these states have not ratified the relevant treaties that would apply human rights law to nationality, citizenship, and related principles regarding stateless people and refugees.

One of the prime illustrations of the importance of distinguishing between the concepts of citizenship and nationality is with regard to the definition of statelessness. The international legal definition of a stateless person under the 1954 Stateless Persons Convention is one "who is not considered as a national by any State under the operation of its law," a definition clearly connected to domestic citizenship legislation.[11] However, if the relevant domestic citizenship law fails to conform to international principles, is the individual truly stateless? The 1961 Convention on the Reduction of Statelessness adopted a recommendation that persons who were effectively deprived of nationality should be treated as meeting the international definition of stateless persons *de jure*.[12] In the Palestinian case, it is the premise of this chapter that Palestinians remain nationals of Palestine today, but are effectively stateless because they have been wrongfully deprived of their nationality in violation of international law. Stateless nationals of Palestine number approximately twelve million persons worldwide today, all of whom are entitled to return to their original homes and lands, and obtain either Palestine nationality or the nationality of the successor state regardless of race, religion, or ethnic origin.[13]

THE LEGAL STATUS OF PALESTINIANS AND JEWS IN PALESTINE BEFORE 1948

Palestinian Nationality

The legal history of Palestinian nationality begins with the Ottoman Empire. The area of historic Palestine was settled continuously by a majority Arab population and was under Arab rule from the seventh century onwards, throughout the Crusader and Turkish (Ottoman) periods, until British rule.[14] During the Ottoman period, from 1516 to 1917, Palestinians obtained Ottoman citizenship under the Ottoman Nationality Law of 1869, which was largely based on *jus sanguinis* and *jus soli* principles discussed above, and not on religious or ethnic criteria.[15] The British occupation of Palestine began on December 9, 1917, by which time Palestinians had a recognized nationality through the Ottoman Nationality Law, and carried internationally recognized Ottoman passports. Following Britain's imposition of civil administration through the "Government of Palestine," it took steps to recognize Palestinian citizenship, including issuing passports and travel documents to Palestinian citizens.[16] Within the next ten years Palestinian nationality was attached to a territory with defined boundaries, distinct from its former Ottoman neighbors, which had attained statehood.[17]

The Palestine Mandate was adopted (and internationally "legalized") by the Council of the League of Nations on July 24, 1922 under the Covenant of the League of Nations.[18] The Palestine Mandate had a unique provision that obliged the (British) Palestine Administration to enact a nationality law that included provisions "to facilitate the acquisition of Palestinian citizenship by Jews who take up their permanent residence in Palestine."[19] This, of course, was the consequence of Zionist pressure, which also resulted in Britain's inclusion of the Balfour Declaration into the terms of the Palestine Mandate, as discussed below. Britain enacted various laws defining who were nationals and who were foreigners in Palestine, and regulated naturalization, entry, and egress from Palestine without passing formal nationality legislation until after the end of World War I.

The Treaty of Lausanne concluded World War I and was signed in Lausanne, Switzerland on July 24, 1923. It established the boundaries of modern Turkey and effectively ended the Ottoman Empire, as Turkey renounced all claims to territories outside the new boundaries. Article 30 of the Treaty of Lausanne specified: "Turkish subjects habitually resident in territory which in accordance with the provisions of the present Treaty is detached from Turkey will become *ipso facto*, in the conditions laid down by the local law, nationals of the State to which such territory is transferred."[20] Under the terms of the Lausanne Treaty, Ottoman citizens who resided in the territory of Palestine and were Turkish citizens (or Ottoman subjects) thus became Palestinian citizens on August 6, 1924, upon ratification of the treaty.[21] As a matter of international law, Palestinian nationality was formed on this date. The Lausanne Treaty also fixed borders and established separate nationalities for Transjordan, Egypt, Syria, and Lebanon. Following the Lausanne Treaty, each of these territories, including Palestine, had a citizenship law that codified its respective nationality status.[22]

One year after the Lausanne Treaty came into force, Palestinian citizenship was codified by British law in the Palestine Citizenship Order of 1925, which included the acquisition of Palestinian citizenship through birth in Palestine. Under the League of Nations mandate system, local people were not nationals of the mandate power that ruled their territory, although they could obtain diplomatic protection from the mandate country. Britain was under an obligation to conform its nationality law to the terms of the Lausanne Treaty. However, Britain sought to satisfy the demands of the Zionists, and to act consistently with provisions in the mandate, including a provision on nationality in Article 7: "The Administration of Palestine shall be responsible for enacting a nationality law. There shall be included in this law provisions framed so as to facilitate the acquisition of Palestinian citizenship by Jews who take up their permanent residence in Palestine." The Palestine Citizenship Order afforded Palestinian citizenship to all those who were Turkish subjects or citizens at the time of the Lausanne Treaty, and who were habitually resident in Palestine.[23] This included Muslims, Christians, and Jews living in Palestine at the time of the 1925 Citizenship Order without regard to religion. Palestinians could obtain passports, and over seventy thousand Palestinian passports were issued by the mandate authorities.[24] However, the 1925 order significantly narrowed the terms by which Palestinians living abroad could assert or retain their Palestinian citizenship, by limiting the time within which they could return and claim nationality. It also deprived descendants of Ottoman subjects of their right to claim nationality on the basis of *jus sanguinis* if they were born abroad, and restricted the right of Palestinians temporarily traveling abroad to return and claim Palestinian nationality.[25] In contrast, the citizenship order included naturalization provisions specifically intended to grant Palestinian citizenship to Jewish immigrants who were either foreign residents or illegal immigrants who would not have qualified for Palestinian citizenship under the terms of the Lausanne Treaty. By proclamation of September 1922, the British government had provided that "any person of other than Ottoman nationality, habitually resident in Palestine on that date, might apply for Palestinian Citizenship." Approximately thirty-eight thousand people were granted Palestinian citizenship under the proclamation, mostly Jews.[26]

Under the Lausanne Treaty, the recognition and codification of Palestinian nationality was consistent with international law: it attached to a majority population that was genuinely and intrinsically linked to a defined territory with specified borders, and was passed through blood, residence, or birth on the territory *(jus soli, jus domicilii* or *jus sanguinis).*[27] It was consistent with the customary law that inhabitants found on a territory when there is a change of sovereignty should automatically acquire the nationality of the successor state.[28] The Palestine Citizenship Order, however, varied key terms of the treaty and sought to incorporate terms of the Balfour Declaration that discriminated against native Palestinians and in favor of immigrant Jews. The total population meeting the criteria of the Palestine Citizenship Order numbered 847,000 people. This population included, however, the foreign residents—mostly immigrant Jews—who had immigrated to Palestine between 1920–22 and obtained citizenship under the 1922 British proclamation.[29]

The Balfour Declaration and the Claim of Jewish Nationality under British Mandate

As is well known, Britain incorporated the Balfour Declaration in its mandate on Palestine, an incorporation that the League of Nations de facto accepted. The mandate preamble essentially restated the Balfour Declaration, while Article 2 stated: "The Mandatory shall be responsible for placing the country under such political, administrative and economic conditions as will secure the establishment of the Jewish national home, as laid down in the preamble, and the development of self-governing institutions, and also for safeguarding the civil and religious rights of all the inhabitants of Palestine, irrespective of race and religion." The Balfour Declaration was incorporated into the mandate and set the stage for a two-tiered system of rights in Palestine, but it did not mention a Jewish state.[30] Setting aside the intentions of Zionists within the British government—whose views cannot "control" the plain language of the declaration—a discriminatory nationality system based on race and/or religion was manifestly illegal under international law even as it stood at the time.[31] In order to be consistent with international law, the Balfour Declaration must be interpreted as a proposal to provide for Jews a "home" in Palestine, but not a Jewish *homeland,* or Jewish *state.* This interpretation is affirmed by the language of the declaration itself and the history of its incorporation, Britain's preexisting obligations under the League of Nations Charter, the mandate's provision on minority treaties, and conformance with existing international law.[32] Moreover, Britain recognized repeatedly in government letters, statements, and actions that it intended to provide a sanctuary for Jews in Palestine without violating the rights of Palestinian Arabs or the rights of Jews in any other country in the world.[33]

Thus, despite the language of the Balfour Declaration and the inconsistent commitments of the British in exercising its the mandate, neither Balfour nor the terms of the Palestine Mandate itself disturbed the recognition of Palestine nationality as established in the Treaty of Lausanne. Nor did these instruments establish a Jewish nationality cognizable under international law.

THE UN AND THE QUESTION OF PALESTINIAN NATIONALITY

Resolution 181 (1947)

United Nations Resolution 181, passed on 29 November 1947, is often considered the key legal document that affirmed Zionist and Palestinian claims to statehood by calling for the creation of a Jewish and Arab state in Palestine. However, a careful reading of this resolution and its drafting history reveals that it does not affirm a claim to nationality status for the Jewish people.

To start with, it is important to note that Resolution 181 was a General Assembly (GA) resolution, not a Security Council resolution, and under the UN Charter, the GA merely makes recommendations to the parties but has no authority to divide territory or enforce any kind of obligation on states or peoples.[34] The UN Secretariat issued an interpretation stating that Resolution 181 "had no obligatory character whatsoever."[35]

Second, it is important to understand the actual provisions of UN Resolution 181. On the nationality question, it is true that the British, in incorporating the Balfour Declaration into the mandate, had given preference in permitting immigration and granting Palestinian citizenship to Jews who had entered and remained illegally during the mandate period. However, the Jews given citizenship under the Palestine Citizenship Order and the 1922 Proclamation were those actually *residing in Palestine*, not outside it. Resolution 181's recognition of a "Jewish" and an "Arab" state did refer to religious and racial criteria to identify territorial division, but referred to both peoples as the "two peoples of Palestine." The Partition Plan stated that "Palestinian citizens residing in Palestine . . . as well as Arabs and Jews who, not holding Palestinian citizenship, reside in Palestine . . . shall, upon the recognition of independence, become citizens of the State in which they are resident and enjoy full civil and political rights."[36] In other words, the Plan's principle was that regardless of religion, Palestinian citizens residing in the Arab state would become citizens of that Arab state, while Palestinian citizens residing in the Jewish state would become citizens of the Jewish state.[37] Finally, Resolution 181 required a one-year period of UN supervision prior to recognition of independence of either state, during which time both states had to incorporate constitutions that provided for *equal rights for all citizens* with no discrimination.[38] Thus, the Partition Plan, as detailed in Resolution 181, did not authorize either state to institutionalize superior rights for any religious or racial group.

In sum, up until 1948, the nationality law incorporated in the Lausanne Treaty, Palestinian citizenship (with the exception of naturalization provisions in the 1925 Palestine Citizenship Order), and Resolution 181 as applied to Jews and Palestinians living in Palestine largely conformed to the requirements of international law. Despite the preferential naturalization terms given to immigrant Jews during the British Mandate rule, the state of the law of nationality as applied to Palestine was that it granted equal nationality to all who lived in the territory and qualified for it on the basis of either prior recognized Palestinian national-ity or their residency in Palestine (or both), but not simply based on their ethnic or religious affiliation.

UN Resolution 194

The next critical instrument to consider on the question of nationality is UN General Assembly Resolution 194 of December 11, 1948.[39] Although Resolution 194 is commonly considered the main UN resolution on the rights of Palestin-ian refugees, its reference to refugees relates directly to the United Nation's view of Palestinian nationality as it stood by 1948. In passing Resolution 194, the GA framed the rights of Palestinian refugees in the context of their national claims; established the UN Conciliation Commission on Palestine (UNCCP) with a very broad mandate to resolve both the conflict and the massive refugee problem; defined the refugees "persons" for whom the UNCCP would provide "interna-tional protection"; and in paragraph 11, set out a legal formula for resolving the refugee problem.[40] Although there is no definition of "Palestine refugee" incor-porated in the language of Resolution 194, the drafting history and subsequent UN Secretariat interpretations clarify exactly which people were defined by the term. The UNCCP's authoritative analysis of Paragraph 11 of Resolution 194 states that "the term 'refugees' applies to all persons, Arabs, Jews and others who have been displaced from their homes in Palestine."[41] The UN legal advisor note to the UNCCP, issued on April 9, 1951, defined the categories of Palestinian refugees cov-ered by the terms of Resolution 194 as:

1. Persons of Arab origin who, after 19 November 1947, left territory at present under the control of the Israel authorities and who were Palestinian citizens at that date;

2. Stateless persons of Arab origin who after 29 November 1947 left the aforementioned territory, where they had been settled up to that date;

3. Persons of Arab origin who left the said territory after 6 August 1924 and before 29 November 1947 and who at that later date were Palestinian citizens; and

4. Persons of Arab origin who left the territory in question before 6 August 1924 and who, having opted for Palestinian citizenship, retained their citizenship up to 29 November 1947.[42]

In other words, the Resolution 194 definition of Palestine refugee as understood by the UN drafters meant the *entire group of persons who were covered by the Pal-estine nationality law of 1924*, emanating from the Lausanne Treaty. These were all habitual residents and citizens of Palestine defined as such by operation of these laws, as well as their descendants. Most important, this definition corrected the inconsistent changes made to the Lausanne Treaty provisions by the 1925 British Palestine Citizenship Order, which excluded Palestinians entitled to *jus sanguinis* or *jus soli* nationality who were either born abroad or residing abroad and unable to perfect their citizenship due to the discriminatory terms set in the Order. It covers all "persons" eligible for Palestinian nationality as determined by the Treaty of Lausanne.

1948: ISRAEL'S REDEFINITION OF NATIONALITY AND CITIZENSHIP IN PALESTINE

The Law of Return (1950) and the "Nationality Law" (1952)

Israel came into being on May 14, 1948 with a Declaration of Independence claiming that the new state would guarantee equal rights for all its citizens without discrimination.[43] However, shortly afterwards, Israel passed a series of laws that not only affected the rights and interests of the indigenous Palestinians to their property, but also permanently affected their legal connection to their homeland and purported to strip them of their nationality.[44] At the same time, the laws gave sweeping rights to Jews around the world who had neither the prior territorial connection or the "genuine link" to the country (*jus soli* or *jus sanguinis*) that international law recognizes as necessary for conferring nationality.[45] As noted earlier, a religious identity or ancient historical claim is not sufficient to grant nationality as an international legal matter.[46]

Concerning the status of those who would be citizens of the new state, Israel passed two separate laws on nationality/citizenship. The first was the 1950 Law of Return (passed on July 5, 1950 and subsequently amended several times), which provides that "every Jew has the right to come to this country [i.e., Israel] as an *oleh*" (i.e., as a Jewish immigrant moving to Israel).[47] Immigration to Israel under the Law of Return is exclusively reserved for Jews, and all Jews around the world can automatically become "Jewish nationals" and part of the Israeli state.[48] No connection to the territory is required under the Law of Return, only that the immigrant be Jewish.[49]

The second law is officially translated into English as the "Nationality Law" of 1952, but this is an erroneous translation as this law does not relate to nationality as legally understood, but to citizenship as determined exclusively on the basis of Jewish religious affiliation.[50] It was passed on July 14, 1952 and has remained central to Israel's definition of who is entitled to nationality. Two main provisions of this law are relevant to this discussion; the provisions on "acquisition of nationality" and "loss of nationality."

The Nationality Law specifies four methods for obtaining "Israel nationality": return (for Jews only, under the 1950 Law of Return, even for Jews who entered or were born in the country before the state's establishment); residence in Israel; birth; or naturalization.[51] Since the first method governed the acquisition of nationality by Jews only, non-Jews had to qualify under one of the other three methods. To qualify through residence, a person had to be an inhabitant of Israel and registered with Israeli authorities by March 1, 1952 under the Registration of

Inhabitants Ordinance of 1949; and they had to have remained as "inhabitant[s] of Israel" from the day Israel was established until the day the Nationality Law was passed, or they had to be able to demonstrate that they had entered legally during that time.[52] Not surprisingly, none of the 750,000 Palestinian refugees who were outside the country during the required residency period were able to satisfy these conditions.[53] Many of those Palestinians remaining in the country were also unable to satisfy the conditions since they had left the territory that became Israel at any time before the law was passed, or had been unable to meet the registration requirements. Another provision in the 1952 Nationality Law stated that only children born in the country of an Israeli national father or mother could become Israeli nationals.[54] Thus, the children of those Palestinians who remained but could not meet the registration requirement (and thus could not become "Israel nationals") were effectively denationalized and became stateless as a matter of common interpretation of the international legal definition.[55]

Israel's Nationality Law of 1952 also has an explicit denationalization provision. The law retroactively repealed the Palestinian citizenship that had been granted under the Palestine Citizenship Orders of 1925 to May 14, 1948, the date that Israel was declared a state. Under its "Loss of Nationality" section, the law states, "Any reference in any provision of law to Palestinian citizenship or Palestinian citizens shall henceforth be read as a reference to Israel nationality or Israel nationals."[56] Thus all Palestinians who could not meet the stringent requirements for obtaining "Israel nationality" became stateless under Israeli law, a conclusion affirmed by decisions of the Israeli courts.[57]

As a matter of international law, the Israeli law repealing the Palestine citizenship law and replacing it with one that denationalized the vast majority of Palestinians in 1952 was an illegal act. It violated two fundamental customary law principles: first, that all habitual residents of the territory of a state that succeeds another must be granted citizenship in the new state; and second, that no state can "arbitrarily" denationalize habitual residents of its state on the basis of protected grounds such as race, religion, ethnic, or national origin.[58]

"Israel" Nationality, Jewish "Nationality," and Two-tiered Israeli Citizenship

What is little understood about the so-called Israel Nationality Law is that it creates a legal fiction: in fact, there is no such thing as "Israel nationality," as even the Israeli High Court itself has confirmed.[59] Israeli law, official institutions, and records do not recognize an "Israel nationality" status. The Israeli Population Registry lists over one hundred nationalities; no "Israel nationality" is listed.[60] The only "nationality" to which the state's rights and privileges are attached is "Jewish nationality."[61] Jewish nationality is restricted to those qualifying under the 1950 Law of Return (i.e., the global community of Jews seeking to exercise *aliya*) and its specific amendments relating to *olim*, or Jews immigrating into Israel. Thus, the so-called "Nationality Law" of 1952 is in reality a *citizenship*, not a nationality law, as it defines who can obtain citizenship in Israel and how.[62]

The Law of Return and the Nationality Law thus set up a two-tiered system for acquiring Israeli citizenship: one for Jews anywhere in the world, who are deemed "nationals" of Israel and can automatically become citizens (through the Law of Return); and another for non-Jews, who can become citizens (through the other routes specified in the "Nationality Law"—residence, birth, or naturalization), but because they are not Jewish, can never achieve the superior rights available only to Jewish nationals.[63]

The superior rights that only Jewish nationals can enjoy include the exclusive rights to use, develop, reside on, and alienate the approximately 95 percent of the lands expropriated by Israel from Palestinians under a series of laws passed from 1948 onwards and codified in the Absentee Property Law.[64] These homes, lands, and public and agricultural areas were seized from Palestinians and converted into a land bank "owned" and operated by the Jewish National Fund and its affiliates as "Israel Lands" that remain exclusively for the use and enjoyment of Jews.[65] The discriminatory land laws and seizure of Palestinian land, the establishment of exclusive "Jewish-only" communities with superior housing rights, and Jewish settlements in the West Bank and Gaza have been legalized with the sanction of the Israeli Supreme Court.[66] The Absentee Property Law and its amendments are thus directly related to the distinction between "citizens" and "nationals" under Israeli law. However, Israel's granting of two-tiered "citizenship" under its "nationality" law violates customary rules on nationality that have become increasingly well settled since 1948.[67]

As an international legal matter, Israel could not define as its nationals persons who were nationals of other states with no connection to the territory, particularly if doing so did not require the specific consent of the individual foreign nationals and their states. The ICJ's decision in the Nottebohm case in 1955 simply restated and interpreted the well-established principle discussed earlier that from the perspective of international law, a state's granting of nationality must be based on some close connection between the state and the individual, and that decisions on nationality are not solely within the domestic purview of states.[68] In the Nottebohm case, contested between Guatemala and Lichtenstein, the ICJ established that a state cannot simply confer its nationality on persons of foreign nationality living in other states absent a close connection between the person and that state, even if the person accepts the nationality status.[69] Long before 1948, the question of who is a national was no longer within the sole discretion of states, and a conferred status of nationality could be denied international recognition if the requisite factors constituting a "genuine link" were missing.

This prohibition on granting nationality to those not resident in the country because of their religion or ethnicity is an ongoing, or "continuing" breach of international law since its consequences remain unredressed today. Continuing breaches require laws to be amended to conform to international criteria, in this case, by granting nationality status to Palestinians who have been deprived of nationality, and implementing the right of return to denationalized Palestinians who were expelled from their homes and lands.[70] Although there are limited mechanisms that could address and provide remedies for the denial of return, deprivation of nationality, and dispossession, understanding the law suggests both how Palestinian rights should be framed and which Palestinians must be part of any final peace agreement.

It is thus important to emphasize that, as a matter of international law, Jewish claims of nationality and self-determination must be clearly distinguished from the claims of Israeli Jews to nationality and self-determination.[71] Israel proclaimed her state on behalf of "the Jewish people," a definition that grants rights to and within the state on an extraterritorial basis to Jews living anywhere in the world. Israel enacted its citizenship law of 1950 to grant "nationality" to Jews only. However, the people entitled to national status in the "Jewish state" defined under GA Resolution 181 included both Jews and Palestinians already residing in the territory, all of whom were to be granted equal rights under a constitution that was to be in force in both new states prior to UN recognition.[72]

The United Nations, including its treaty bodies and the ICJ, has consistently called preferences for Jews under Israeli citizenship, property, and other laws a violation of the UN Charter and human rights treaties.[73] In other words, outside of Israel, there has been no international legal recognition of the "Jewish people" as a nationality concept that grants self-determination rights to Jews living outside of Israel. Nor is there legal support for the premise that Israel has a right to maintain a legal-preferencing system that grants superior rights to Jews as against other citizens of the Israeli state.[74]

In 2018, Israel passed a new law on nationality and citizenship, the Jewish Nation-State Basic Law, which clarifies in unambiguous terms the identity of Israel as a nation-state exclusively for and of the Jewish people.[75] It is important to understand that the Nation-State Law is different from the Nationality Law and the Law of Return, in that it is a "basic law," which in Israel is the equivalent of a constitutional provision.[76] The 2018 Jewish Nation-State Basic Law states: "The Land of Israel is the historical homeland of the Jewish people, in which the State of Israel was established . . . . the State of Israel is the nation-state of the Jewish people."[77] There are three main aspects to this law of significance to Palestinian national rights. First is the provision that self-determination in Israel belongs exclusively to the Jewish people. This provision formally entrenches state discrimination against non-Jews, and particularly Palestinians, who today comprise 20 percent of the population within Israel. It formalizes the legal status of Palestinians as second-class citizens, that is, citizens who are not entitled to equal civil and political rights in the state.

Second is the establishment of Hebrew as the official language of Israel and the commitment to promoting only Jewish symbols and Jewish culture both within

Israel and in Jewish communities worldwide.[78] This provision reverses the long-standing status of Arabic as an official language along with Hebrew.

Third is the explicit promotion of Jewish settlement as a "national value" that the state will "encourage and promote."[79] This provision legitimizes the Israeli settlement project in the Occupied Territories and East Jerusalem, which has independent international consequences from the issues of nationality. That is, aside from an act of formal annexation of occupied territory, which is uncontrovertibly illegal under international law, the extension of the Nation-State Law to the Occupied Territories formally entrenches an apartheid system.[80] The crime of apartheid involves policies and practices of "racial discrimination . . . based on race, colour, descent, or national or ethnic origin" for purposes of domination or systemic oppression by one group against another.[81] The Nation-State Law expressly declares the intent to discriminate against Palestinians in every field, establishing preferential rights for Jews and Jewish settlers, and another lesser set of "rights" for Palestinians and Arabs in Israel. The law legitimizes discrimination in citizenship, language, culture, land ownership and use, and every other sphere of public and private life.[82]

Israel "Nationality" and the Palestinian Right of Return

As explained above and as has been discussed by various scholars, Israel's law of nationality was as much directed at attracting the largest number of Jewish migrants into Israel as it was at preventing Palestinians from claiming their political rights to return to their home. Its passage in the Israeli Knesset in 1952 does not, from an international legal point of view, abrogate UN Resolution 194, the customary international law norms on which that resolution rests, nor the laws pertaining to the rights of refugees and forcibly displaced persons more generally.[83]

Since their forced departure and expatriation from their homeland by Israel, Palestinian refugees have continuously asserted that they have a legal right, popularly referred to as the "right of return." Israel has contested the legal basis for this right on a number of grounds, including that it did not forcibly expel Palestinians, and that as a sovereign state it has the right to define who is entitled to enter its borders and who can remain.[84] From an international legal point of view, Israel's position on each of its key arguments is either weak or simply without merit.[85] In general, the right of return represents a complex, interrelated set of rights grounded in distinct bodies of treaty and customary international law. For this discussion, however, the most important and relevant argument on right of return relates to the right of an individual to return to his place of origin or nationality.[86]

Two core human rights treaties ground the critical aspects of the right of return, and are at the heart of the contest over whether Palestinians have such a right: the International Covenant on Civil and Political Rights (ICCPR), and the Convention on the Elimination of Racial Discrimination (CERD). The ICCPR states in Article 12(4) that "no one shall be arbitrarily deprived of the right to enter his own country."[87] This language raises questions about the meaning of the phrase "his own country." Does it apply to someone who is a national of the country, someone who is a refugee, someone who was born outside "his" country, or to individuals in all these situations? The drafting history of this provision shows that the drafters rejected proposals to replace "his country" with "the country of which one is a national" because they wanted to include "those persons who under domestic law enjoy a right to 'return' or reside in a country even though they are not nationals of that country." The drafters also chose "enter" over "return" in order to ensure its application to those who were nationals or citizens of the country but had never lived there.[88]

The other ambiguous term in ICCPR 12(4) is "arbitrarily." The drafting history reflects that "arbitrary" was used with a specific meaning.[89] The UN Study of the Right of Everyone To Be Free from Arbitrary Arrest, Detention and Exile differentiated "arbitrary" under international law from "illegal"; that is, an act could be legal under domestic law but would be arbitrary if it were discriminatorily applied or were otherwise incompatible with international norms.[90] There is legal consensus that an act such as denationalization, even if it conforms to domestic law, is arbitrary and thus prohibited if it violates principles of international law.[91] "For international law purposes, states do not enjoy the freedom to denationalize their nationals in order to expel them as 'non-citizens.'"[92]

The CERD's provision on return is found in Article 5(d)(ii), which requires states to prohibit and eliminate racial discrimination "in all its forms," and requires them to "guarantee the right of everyone, without distinction as to race, colour, or national or ethnic origin, to equality before the law, notably in the enjoyment of . . . the right to leave any country, including one's own and to return to one's country." The CERD's provision on right of return also prohibits a state from establishing citizenship/nationality criteria that discriminate on these grounds. A state cannot prohibit someone from entering "his country" on the basis of race, nationality, or ethnic origin. The near-universal ratification of these instruments has now bound most states to the right as a matter of treaty.

In 1961, the UN Convention on the Reduction of Statelessness was adopted, which prohibits depriving anyone of nationality on the basis of race or ethnicity, religion, or political opinion.[93] In 1963, the UN Subcommission on Prevention of Discrimination and Protection of Minorities produced Draft Principles on the Right to Leave and Return. Section II of these principles states: "Everyone is entitled, without distinction of any kind, such as race, colour, sex, language, religion, political or other opinion, national or social origin, property, birth, marriage or other status, to return to his country; no one shall be arbitrarily deprived of his nationality or forced to renounce his nationality as a means of divesting him of the right to return to his country; no one shall be arbitrarily deprived of the right to enter his own country."[94] The Draft Principles informed the UN drafters and led to the adoption of the language in Article 12 of the ICCPR. One of the astonishing features about the highly fractious debate on the right of return is that it questions a right that was almost universally accepted as state practice, though not codified until the first international humanitarian law treaties were drafted in the first part of the twentieth century.[95] But lack of codification did not affect state practice on individual return or organized repatriation, both of which occurred in every part of the globe long before the first treaties incorporated the principles, and without serious question about the underlying right of the individual returnee.

When one carefully examines the nature of the challenge to the right of return, one can conclude that the only serious attack on it as a principle or practice is in its application to the Palestinian refugees. The international community has never legitimized any other states' denial of its nationals the right to return to their homes on the basis of race or religion, even though many states persecute their nationals such that the latter are unable or unwilling to return.[96] It is sufficient to conclude here that the right to return to one's country is expressly recognized in most international and regional human rights instruments, and UN bodies have, on numerous occasions, asserted such a right. This, along with recent state practice, has led to the formation of a norm of customary international law that assures that an individual outside their own country has the right to return to it.[97]

THE OSLO PEACE PROCESS AND PALESTINIAN NATIONALITY

With the occupation of the West Bank and Gaza Strip in the aftermath of the 1967 war, Israel created a separate set of laws, primarily through military orders, in the Occupied Territories to avoid bestowing citizenship rights on the Palestinian residents of these areas. While it was extending military occupation rules to Palestinians, Israel began its settlement project and extended Israeli domestic laws to the settlers in both the West Bank and Gaza. Palestinian residents in the West Bank and Jerusalem were allowed to retain the Jordanian nationality that Jordan had extended to Palestinians after the 1948 conflict, while those in Gaza were given Egyptian *laissez-passer*.[98] At the same time, Israel implemented various mechanisms for maximizing Israel's control over the land through settlement construction, land confiscation, and military control.

Three months after the 1967 conflict, in September 1967, Israel conducted a population census. The census counted the 954,898 Palestinians physically present in the West Bank and Gaza at the time, but did not include the at least 270,000 Palestinians who were absent, either because they had fled during the conflict or were abroad for other reasons.[99] Based on its census, Israel created a population registry and refused to recognize the right of those who were absent to return home. Palestinians registered on the census were granted resident status and the right to reside in the territory under military occupation, but Israel did not confer any political rights on them. Any Palestinian who was not registered in the population registry could acquire residency only through a prescribed family reunification procedure.[100] This process was complex, prolonged, and often unsuccessful—and has become even more so today. Applications languish in the system for years. Until 1995, residents who remained outside the territories for more than six consecutive years had their residency revoked by Israel.[101] Moreover, Palestinian residents of Jerusalem who travel abroad to study, work, or for other reasons are routinely stripped of their residency under a law that requires them to maintain their "center of life" in Jerusalem. The center of life law does not apply to Jews. About one hundred thousand Palestinians have lost their Jerusalem residency in this way.[102]

The Oslo Peace negotiation process seemed to signal the possibility that Palestinians would finally achieve at least a partial implementation of their right to return and some semblance of statehood. The signing of the Declaration of Principles between Israel and the Palestine Liberation Organization (PLO) in 1993 accompanied a formal recognition by the PLO of Israel as a state and a concomitant recognition of the PLO's legitimacy by Israel. Israel's official recognition of the PLO as the legitimate representative of the Palestinian people seemed to imply recognition of their right to self–determination. However, the Oslo process precluded any rights-based solution for the Palestinians, and had limited, if any, reference to Palestinian refugee rights.[103]

Although the past twenty-five years have not brought about an end to Israeli occupation, they have ushered in the establishment of a Palestinian Authority (PA) that in fits and starts has attempted to build the legal and economic basis of a Palestinian state in the West Bank and Gaza. The Oslo agreements gave the PA the authority to issue both identity cards and passports for Gazans and West Bankers, but only with the permission of Israel.[104] The PA was also able to grant permanent residence to persons residing in the West Bank and Gaza, as well as to limited categories of Palestinians returning from abroad, but again only with permission of Israel.[105] The Oslo agreements also defined who were West Bank and Gaza "citizens" for purposes of voting.[106]

In 1997, the Palestinian Legislative Council passed the Palestinian Basic Law, intended to provide a temporary constitution until an independent Palestinian state could be established with a permanent constitution. The Basic Law was ratified by President Yasser Arafat in 2002, and has been amended twice (in 2003 and 2005).[107] However, the Basic Law addresses Palestinian nationality or citizenship in very limited fashion in three articles: 1, 4 and 7. Article 1 defines Palestine as "part of the larger Arab world, and the Palestinian people are part of the Arab nation. Arab unity is an objective that the Palestinian people shall work to achieve." In other words it defines Palestinian identity as synonymous with "Arab" identity. Article 7 states that "Palestinian citizenship shall be regulated by law."[108] Presumably, the "nationals" entitled to become citizens of the Palestinian state would be those whose nationality was redefined under the Palestinian Basic Law, but that law makes no reference to Palestinian nationality as internationally defined. Absent such a reference, it is unclear whether the language of Article 1 of the Basic Law is intended to cover only those Palestinians residing within the 1967 borders of the West Bank and Gaza, or the global population of Palestinians entitled to Palestinian nationality as discussed earlier. Moreover, the PA has legitimacy to govern only approximately 30 percent of the global Palestinian population that voted for it—and even this is questionable, as it has long exceeded its term of office and has been replaced in Gaza by the Hamas government. Thus, the question of who is meant by the reference to the "Palestinian people" is ambiguous and highly contentious, both as a matter of politics and a matter of international law.

There have been two attempts at drafting a Palestinian citizenship law: one by the PA, and one on behalf of the PLO. In 1995, the Palestinian Ministry of the Interior drafted a citizenship law that was based on the 1925 Palestinian Citizenship Order and the 1954 Jordanian Citizenship Law. "In its twenty-five articles, the draft defined who is a Palestinian, fixed the modes of citizenship acquisition, naturalization, revocation and repatriation, covered issues such as the citizenship of spouses and children, and contained other provisions that normally exist in the citizenship legislation of independent States."[109] This bill was was not publicly disseminated and was never taken up for deliberation by the Palestinian Legislative Council.

In 2012, a citizenship law was also drafted for the PLO.[110] The draft law incorporated a sophisticated legal understanding of the international legal underpinnings of Palestinian nationality. It recognized the conferment of nationality on the basis of eligibility stemming from the Treaty of Lausanne provisions and the individual choice to acquire (or reacquire) Palestinian nationality. Its basic "rule" for nationality states: "Palestinian citizens are those persons who acquired or had the right to acquire Palestinian nationality as of 6 August 1924, the date on which the Treaty of Lausanne that was signed by Britain . . . and Turkey . . . came into force whereby Palestine ceased to be part of the Ottoman Empire. In addition, this Draft Law is based on factors that have emerged since the signing of the said treaty; such factors can be found in international law and comparative nationality law."[111] The draft law conferred citizenship on three general categories of people (while also breaking those into various subcategories): inhabitants of the West Bank and Gaza, refugees from Mandate Palestine, and Israeli inhabitants. The law was circulated among a few international experts for commentary and discussed internally within the PLO and certain members of the PA, but never tabled for debate by the Legislative Council. The effort to finalize and pass the citizenship law was stymied by the complex and fraught political and legal issues involved. The draft law, however, represented an initiative to conform a future Palestinian citizenship law with international legal standards and the international status of Palestinian nationality. A precise definition of Palestinian nationality remains as crucial under current conditions as ever, as it would identify the "nationals" to whom the right of return would apply.

RIGHT OF RETURN, ISRAEL'S NATIONALITY LAWS, AND PALESTINIAN NATIONALITY TODAY

So, from an international law point of view, what is the status of Palestinian nationality today, and what relevance does that have to the right of return? On the one hand, there is an argument that Palestinians continue to retain Palestinian nationality to the present. This is based on the historical and legal facts described in this chapter, including that Israel's revocation of Palestinian citizenship and denaturalization of Palestinians was illegal, and its denial of Palestinian return is also illegal. This argument rests on the claim that Israel's illegal acts and laws that violate international norms do not affect Palestinian nationality as a matter of international law, and that Palestinian nationality is unbroken today, despite the inability of the majority of Palestinians to return to their homes.

Israel is a party to the major treaties that ground the right of return: the Fourth Geneva Convention, the ICCPR and ICERD.[112] Israel's massive denationalization of Palestinian Arabs on the basis of their national/ethnic origin was a violation of law at the time it occurred, and Israel remains bound today, despite the long passage of time, to remedy the denationalization and expulsion by implementing the right of return. UN General Assembly and UN Security Council resolutions over decades affirm and reaffirm the right of return for refugees to their homes in every part of the world.[113] From state and international practice alone, it is evident that under international law, refugee return is the rule, and nonrecognition of Palestinian refugees' right to return is the aberration.[114]

On the other hand, there is the argument that Palestinians lost their nationality in 1948 and those unable to meet the criteria of Israel's Nationality Law became stateless.[115] My contention is that Palestinians are stateless *nationals*, and framing Palestinians as only refugees or stateless persons is the weaker argument, both legally and in terms of its consequences for Palestinians, in particular with regard to the right of return. The argument that Palestinians are stateless does have the advantage of triggering UN High Commissioner for Refugees (UNHCR) protection under the two conventions on stateless persons, but this is irrelevant in the Arab states, which are not parties to either of these treaties, and which explicitly prohibit UNHCR from providing protection to Palestinians through memoranda of understanding with state governments.[116] In the Western states, this is also only marginally helpful as UNHCR has not actually taken significant steps to advance the rights of Palestinians as stateless persons.[117]

From an international legal point of view, Palestinian nationality remains intact today, and their right of return is based squarely on their rights as *nationals* of Palestine, not only as refugees. Moreover, there is no parallel legal authority for a claim of Jewish nationality that negates Palestine national rights. Jews claim the right to return on the basis of historic religious claims to Palestine that are not cognizable under the international law of nationality, as religion and ancient "historic" claims are not "genuine links" for the purpose of nationality recognition. For Palestinians who have acquired a second citizenship, dual nationality is also no barrier to a right of return, as most Jews in Israel have Israeli and a second citizenship. The strongest claim for right of return is based on Palestinians as nationals, not as stateless persons and not just as refugees, and should be clearly framed around the language of and principles underlying the Lausanne Treaty provisions from which Palestinian nationality stems. Palestinian nationality is not undermined by any aspect of Resolution 181, Resolution 194, or Israel's Nationality Law.

Nevertheless, fashioning a nationality law for Palestinians remains a complicated proposition in the two-state scenario. The multiple categories of Palestinians that must be taken into account in order to craft an equitable and legally justified Palestinian nationality law make this an exceedingly daunting task. Just within a Palestinian state that would include the West Bank, Gaza, and East Jerusalem, there are multiple categories to consider: "the inhabitants of East Jerusalem, refugees who were expelled from the territory of Israel since 1948 and settled in the West Bank or Gaza, West Bankers or Gazans who lost their residence in these two areas at any point since 1925 and were prevented by Britain (1917–1948) or by Israel (since 1967) to return, and Jewish-Palestinian natives of the West Bank or Gaza who lost their residence therein since 1948."[118] The definition of nationality must also consider each category in the diaspora, including those with citizenship in Jordan and elsewhere who would be considered dual nationals, and refugees across the Arab world who are also Palestinian stateless nationals.

In the current climate, there is no serious prospect of implementing a citizenship law to codify Palestinian nationality for Palestinians outside Israel—whether in the West Bank, Gaza, the Arab world, or elsewhere in the diaspora. The PLO and PA have recognized, in the citizenship laws they have drafted and considered, that in the absence of independence accompanying statehood recognition, a Palestinian citizenship law remains aspirational. Although the right of return for Palestinians per se can be implemented in the absence of such a law, this is also unlikely under the current political conditions, particularly since passage of the Israeli Nation-State Law and the seeming official consensus that a two-state solution is still the only option. Ironically, Israel's passage of the Nation-State Law and its declaration that it intends to fully annex the West Bank make it evident that it has no intention to allow the establishment of any semblance of a Palestinian state. The right of return for all Palestinians no matter their location, and to their original homes and lands, is not acknowledged in the political discourse either.

If in a future changed political context it would be possible to contemplate a Palestinian nationality in a single state that would include equal citizenship with Jews in Israel, the "nationality" distinctions under current Israeli law would need to be repealed along with the denationalization provision of the 1950 Nationality Law and the Nation-State Law in its entirety. Palestinians in the West Bank and Gaza and all those in the diaspora could be included by applying the provisions of the Lausanne Treaty. In that sense, the general definition of who is a Palestinian is a simple one: all those who can claim nationality by *jus sanguinis* and/or *jus soli* as fixed on August 6, 1924 by the terms of the Lausanne Treaty, and all their descendants, are nationals of Palestine with the right to return to their homes and the right to obtain restitution and other compensation as recognized under international law.

NOTES

The author is grateful for the outstanding research assistance of Boston University law student Kristina Fried in the completion of this chapter.

1. Lassa Oppenheim, *International Law: A Treatise* (London: Longmans, Green, and Co., 1905), 1:345.

2. Asbjorn Eide, "Citizenship and International Human Rights Law: Status, Evolution, and Challenges," in *Citizenship and the State in the Middle East: Approaches and Applications*, edited by edited by Nils A. Butenschøn, Uri Davis, and Manuel Hassassian (Syracuse, NY: Syracuse University Press, 2000): 91–92.

3. See Panevezys-Saldutiskis Railway (Est. v. Lith.), Judgment, 1939 P.C.I.J. (ser. A/B/) No. 76, at 16 (Feb. 28). The International Court of Justice (ICJ) later referred to this as an established norm of international law and described the types of links between an individual and territory that conferred nationality: "Nationality is a legal bond having as its basis a social fact of attachment, a genuine connection of existence, interests and sentiments, together with the existence of reciprocal rights and duties." Nottebohm (Liech v. Guat.), Second Phase, 1955 ICJ Report 1955, at 23 (April 6).

4. The 1929 Harvard Research on Nationality Laws study compiled information regarding the basis of nationality legislation around the world. The study concluded that seventeen such laws were based on *jus sanguinis* alone, two on a combination of *jus sanguinis* and *jus soli*, twenty-five primarily on *jus sanguinis* but partially on *jus soli*, and twenty-six primarily on *jus soli* and partially on *jus sanguinis*. "The nationality law of no country is based solely upon *jus soli*. A combination of the two systems is found in the laws of most countries." See American Society of International Law, "The Law of Nationality" in "Draft Conventions and Comments on Nationality, Responsibility of States for Injuries to Aliens, and Territorial Waters, Prepared by the Research in International Law of the Harvard Law School," supplement, *American Journal of International Law* 61, S5 (1929): 21–79.

5. For an exhaustive review of sources for these contentions, see Mutaz M. Qafisheh, *The International Law Foundations of Palestinian Nationality: A Legal Examination of Nationality under Britain's Rule* (Leiden: Brill-Nijhoff, 2008).

6. Most critical for this discussion is that the post–World War I mandates were legally binding on the mandatory state, the populations in the mandate territories, and other states in their dealings with the mandate powers. This included the nationality/citizenship legislation passed by the mandate powers. See Mavrommatis Palestine Concessions (Greece v. Gr. Brit.), Objection to the Jurisdiction of the Court, 1924 P.C.I.J. (ser. A) No. 2 (Aug. 19); and International Status of South-West Africa, Advisory Opinion, 1950 ICJ Report 28 (July 11).

7. Oppenheim, *International Law*, 355; United Nations General Assembly, 1954 Convention Relating to the Status of Stateless Persons, September 28, 1954, Articles 12, 27, 28, 32, 360 United Nations Treaty Series 117.

8. "When a part of the territory of a state . . . becomes the territory of a new state, the nationals of the first state who continue their habitual residence in such territory lose the nationality of that state and become nationals of the successor state, in the absence of treaty provisions to the contrary"; American Society of International Law, "The Law of Nationality," 61. This provision was incorporated into Article 5 of the International Law Commission's Draft Articles on Nationality of Natural Persons in Relation to the Succession of States; International Law Commission, "Report on the Work of Its Fifty-First Session," UN Document A/54/10 (1999).

9. See International Convention on the Elimination of all Forms of Racial Discrimination, March 7, 1966, Articles 5(d)(ii), 5(d)(iii), 660 United Nations Treaty Series 195 (hereinafter CERD).

10. See Vienna Convention on the Law of Treaties arts. 26, 27, Jan. 27, 1980, 1155 United Nations Treaty Series 331 (hereinafter VCLT). Article 26 states that "Every treaty in force is binding upon the parties to it and must be performed by them in good faith" and Article 27 states that "A party may not invoke the provisions of its internal law as justification for its failure to perform a treaty." The VCLT codifies binding rules of treaty application and interpretation on all states, and most of the provisions of the VCLT have become customary international law and therefore binding even without state ratification.

11. United Nations General Assembly, 1954 Convention Relating to the Status of Stateless Persons, Article 1. The Article 1 definition has ripened into a binding rule of customary international law. See United Nations High Commissioner for Refugees, Guidelines on Statelessness, "No. 1: The Definition of 'Stateless Person' in Article 1(1) of the 1954 Convention relating to the Status of Stateless Persons," paragraph 2, UN Document HCR/GS/12/01 (2012).

12. Convention on the Reduction of Statelessness, Aug. 30, 1961, 989 United Nations Treaty Series 175; Final Act of the United Nations Conference on the Elimination or Reduction of Future Statelessness, August 29, 1961, UN Document A/CONF. 9/14. The United Nations High Commissioner for Refugees (UNHCR), the UN agency entrusted with protection of stateless persons, has interpreted the language "under the operation of its law" to include both law on the books and state policies that as a practical matter deny an individual his/her nationality. See UNHCR, "Handbook on Protection of Stateless Persons," UNHCR, 2014, 5, https://www.unhcr.org/dach/wp-content/uploads/sites/27/2017/04/CH-UNHCR_Handbook-on-Protection-of-Stateless-Persons.pdf. It advises that "persons outside the country of their nationality who are unable or, for valid reasons, are unwilling to avail themselves of the protection of that country" should be treated as de facto stateless.

13. The author is indebted to her partners at the Tibet Justice Center for the phrase "stateless nationals." See Tibet Justice Center, "Tibet's Stateless Nationals: Tibetan Refugees in Nepal," Tibet Justice Center, June 2002, http://www.tibetjustice.org/reports/nepal.pdf.

14. See John Quigley, *The Case for Palestine: An International Law Perspective* (Durham, NC: Duke University Press, 2005), 3–13.

15. "Ottoman Nationality Law Arts. 1–4, 9 (1869)," in *A Collection of Nationality Laws of Various Countries as Contained in Constitutions, Statutes and Treaties*, edited by Richard W. Flournoy and Manley O. Hudson, 568 (New York: Oxford University Press, 1929). Article 1 codified *jus sanguinis* nationality ("persons born to parents or a father of Ottoman nationality are Ottoman citizens"); Article 2 codified *jus soli* nationality ("any foreigner born in Ottoman territory may apply for Ottoman nationality within three years of attaining majority"); Article 9 codified *jus soli* and the presumption against statelessness principles ("every person residing in Ottoman territory shall be regarded as an Ottoman citizen unless foreign status is proved"). Under this provision, the presumption of citizenship applied to all children born in the territory with unknown or stateless parentage. Articles 3 and 4 codified *jus domicilii* principles ("any foreigner has the right to apply for Ottoman citizenship upon residing in Ottoman territory for at least five years" and "at its discretion the Ottoman government may waive the five year residence requirement and naturalize any foreigner"). Other provisions on expatriation are not on point here. Ottoman nationality was recognized abroad through the acceptance of Ottoman passports as well as identity documents. For a detailed examination of Palestinian nationality and the Ottoman Nationality Law, see Qafisheh, *International Law Foundations*, 25–44.

16. See the discussion of the Palestine Passports Regulations of 1920 in Qafisheh, *International Law Foundations*, 53–58. As an international legal matter, Britain was in belligerent occupation of Palestine, and under humanitarian law rules binding on Britain at the time, it could not change the laws in force prior to its occupation of the territory, nor could it implant settlers into occupied territory. See Hague Regulations Respecting the Laws and Customs of War on Land, July 22, 1899, Article 43, 32 Stat. 1803; see also Hague Regulations Concerning the Laws and Customs of Land Warfare,

Oct. 18, 1907, Article 43, 36 Stat. 2277. If Palestine was occupied territory, then Ottoman citizenship remained intact at least until 1925, despite the imposition first of British military law, then of civil (British) administration.

17. The borders of Egypt and Transjordan were drawn through bilateral agreement with Britain, and Egypt and Transjordan passed nationality legislation in 1926 and 1928, respectively. Syrian and Lebanese nationalities were codified in 1924. Mutaz M. Qafisheh, "Genesis of Citizenship in Palestine and Israel: Palestinian Nationality in the 1917–1925 Period," *Bulletin du Centre de recherche français à Jérusalem* 21 (December 2010), http://journals.openedition.org/bcrfj/6405.

18. See League of Nations, Mandate for Palestine, League of Nations Document C.529M.314 1922 VI (1922); and League of Nations Covenant, Article 22. Article 22 of the covenant established the mandates in order to supervise what was intended to be a transition to independence for the mandate territories.

19. League of Nations, Mandate for Palestine, Article 7.

20. League of Nations, Treaty of Lausanne, July 24, 1923, Article 30, 28 League of Nations Treaty Service 11.

21. Under the treaty, in order to obtain Palestinian citizenship an individual was required to be either a Turkish citizen or Ottoman subject (under the Ottoman Nationality Law) and a habitual resident of Palestine on August 6, 1924, the date of entry into force of the treaty. Palestinians outside of Palestine could opt for Palestinian citizenship based on the *jus sanguinis* principle under Article 34. The treaty language excluded foreigners who were not Ottoman or Turkish citizens residing in Palestine. League of Nations, Treaty of Lausanne, Article 34.

22. Transjordan's 1928 citizenship law retroactively extended Transjordanian nationality to all inhabitants who were Ottoman subjects residing in the area east of the Jordan river as of August 6, 1924. As noted above, Syria and Lebanon passed nationality regulations in August 1924, while Egypt passed its nationality law in 1926. Whether these populations were of indeterminate nationality during the Ottoman period or not, the Treaty of Lausanne definitely established separate and independent national identities, which were codified by the subsequent citizenship legislation of each country. See Qafisheh, "Genesis of Citizenship," 3, 4, 2.

23. Qafisheh, "Genesis of Citizenship," 15.

24. Qafisheh, *International Law Foundations*, 149.

25. Qafisheh, *International Law Foundations*, 87–103.

26. Mutaz M. Qafisheh, *Palestine Membership in the United Nations: Legal and Practical Implications* (Newcastle upon Tyne: Cambridge Scholars Publishing, 2013), 122.

27. See the principles established by the review of nationality laws in American Society of International Law, "The Law of Nationality."

28. Oppenheim, *International Law*, 355.

29. See Qafisheh, *International Law Foundations*, 66–67.

30. British policies created two de facto nationalities, as noted in a report by the League of Nations itself: "It was . . . found that a classification by 'race' (or nationality)—i.e., as Arabs, Jews or 'others'—had become a political necessity . . . the immigration and emigration statistics have been prepared on a racial basis. Of recent years, therefore, the population of Palestine has been classified according to the criteria both of religion and race." League of Nations, "The Mandate System: Origin—Principles—Application 78 (1945)," cited in Qafisheh, *International Law Foundations*, 255.

31. Since the Balfour Declaration is a legal instrument, interpreting its terms requires application of rules codified in the Vienna Convention on the Law of Treaties. Among the important aspects of these rules is which language "controls" or is determinative of the application of a treaty provision. Once a legal instrument has been signed, incorporated into law, or otherwise becomes operable, there is a hierarchy of interpretation to determine the "controlling" or "determinative" interpretation. The first hierarchy is that the ordinary legal interpretation of the language on its face is determinative ("controls") unless there is an ambiguity. In the case of the Balfour Declaration, the language speaks

for itself, and therefore any outside views are irrelevant and do not control its meaning.

32. Victor Kattan, *From Coexistence to Conquest: International Law and the Origin of the Arab-Israeli Conflict* (London: Pluto, 2009), 4 ("Article 22 of the Covenant of the League of Nations provided that the well-being and development of peoples placed under the mandatory system of administration 'form a sacred trust of civilization.'"); Kattan, *From Coexistence to Conquest*, 56, 57 (Under the mandate, "Britain was arguably vested with fiduciary duties in relation to the beneficiaries of this trust who were the indigenous peoples of Palestine. Inherent in the notion of a 'sacred trust' is the principle that the fiduciary must not profit from its position and must not allow personal interest to prevail over the duty owed to the principal (in this case, the League) . . . . In other words there was no principle of international law, provided in the mandates or in custom, which allowed a nation to expropriate the properties of another people on account of their colour, race or religion—for this would be tantamount to theft").

33. Qafisheh, *Palestine Membership in the United Nations*, 363 ("The mandate required the British to create a law for the acquisition of Palestinian nationality for the Jews. This nationality would give certain rights and obligations not only to the Jewish immigrants, but also to the majority Arab population since the mandate also stipulated that the Jewish national home policy could not prejudice the civil or religious rights of the existing majority population"); Kattan, *From Coexistence to Conquest*, 5 ("Even Lord Balfour, with his strong sympathies for Zionist aspirations, said that he never wanted the indigenous Palestinian Arab population to be dispossessed or oppressed"); Kattan, *From Coexistence to Conquest*, 7 ("In 1919, Lord Curzon warned Lord Balfour, rather prophetically, about the perils of the contradictory policy their government was pursuing in Palestine, creating a Jewish national home in a land that was almost entirely Arab: 'Personally, I am so convinced that Palestine will be a rankling thorn in the flesh of whoever is charged with its Mandate, that I would withdraw from this responsibility while we yet can.'").

34. UN Charter, Articles 10–17, October 24, 1945, 1 United Nations Treaty Series XVI. The resolution language itself begins with the words "The GA 'recommends.'"

35. UN Palestine Commission, "Relations between the UN Commission and the Security Council," working paper by the Secretariat, February 9, 1948, Section 3, Paragraph 4, UN Document A/AC.21/13.

36. GA Resolution 181 (II), Plan of Partition with Economic Union, Part I, Section C, Paragraph 1.

37. UN Special Committee on Palestine, "Report to the General Assembly," UN Document A/364 (1947); Ad Hoc Committee on the Palestinian Question; "Report of Sub-Committee 2," UN Document A/AC. 14/32, paragraph 64 (1947). Under the UNSCOP figures, the proposed Arab state would have comprised ten thousand Jews and almost one million Arabs, while the proposed Jewish state would have comprised 498,000 Jews and 407,000 Arabs. However, the UNSCOP figures were inaccurate, as they did not include the Bedouin population. British population data showed there were 509,780 Arabs and 499,020 Jews in the area of the Jewish state, which meant the Arabs would have remained a majority in both states; Kattan, *From Coexistence to Conquest*, 151–52.

38. GA Resolution 181 (II), paragraphs I(B)(10), I(C)(2)(2), I(C)(2)(3), I(C)(2)(8), I(C)(3)(1).

39. GA Resolution 194 (III), December 11, 1948.

40. GA Resolution 194, paragraphs 2, 11.

41. UN Conciliation Commission for Palestine, "Analysis of Paragraph 11 of the General Assembly's Resolution of 11 December 1948," UN Document W/45, May 15, 1950.

42. UN Conciliation Commission for Palestine, "Addendum to Definition of a 'Refugee' under Paragraph 11 of the General Assembly Resolution of 11 December 1948, Prepared by the Legal Advisor," UN Document W/61/Add.1, May 29, 1951.

43. "It will foster the development of the country for the benefit of all its inhabitants; it will be based on freedom, justice and peace as envisaged by the prophets of Israel; it will ensure complete equality of social and political rights to all its inhabitants irrespective of religion, race or sex; it will guarantee freedom of religion, conscience, language, education and culture; it will safeguard the Holy

Places of all religions; and it will be faithful to the principles of the Charter of the United Nations"; Declaration of the Establishment of the State of Israel (1948).

44. These laws are the Law of Return, the Nationality Law, and the Absentee Property Law, discussed further below.

45. Claims that the Jewish people are a nation or a race lack empirical support, and in any event cannot supersede normative nationality principles. See Shlomo Sand, *The Invention of the Jewish People* (London: Verso, 2008); Roselle Tekiner, "Race and the Issue of National Identity in Israel," *International Journal of Middle East Studies* 23, no. 1 (February 1991): 39–55.

46. Nottebohm (Liech. v. Guat.) ICJ Report 1955. A genuine link may be based on *jus soli* or *jus sanguinis*, as well as permanent residence acquired through legal migration. See Peter J. Spiro, "Citizenship Overreach," *Michigan Journal of International Law* 38, no. 2 (2017): 173–200, 173, 178, 181.

47. The translator's note in the official Israeli government translation states: "*Aliya* means immigration of Jews, and *oleh* (plural: *olim*) means a Jew immigrating, into Israel."

48. Laws of the State of Israel, vol. 4 (1950), 114.

49. Nancy C. Richmond, "Israel's Law of Return: Analysis of Its Evolution and Present Application," *Penn State International Law Review* 12, no. 1 (1993): 95–133, 99, 109. Although the Law of Return requires only that an *oleh* be Jewish, the definition of who is a Jew for the purposes of the Law of Return is narrow and has been subject to controversy over the last few decades. The law was amended in 1970 to define a Jew as "a person born of a Jewish mother or having converted to Judaism, not being a person affiliated to some other religion." At the same time, the law was extended to non-Jewish spouses and children. Current acceptable proof of being Jewish for the purposes of the Law of Return is listed on the website of the Israeli Ministry of the Interior. "Documents Needed for Aliyah—Guided Aliyah from within Israel," Nefesh B'Nefesh, https://www.nbn.org.il/aliyahpedia /aliyah-process/aliyah-processing-flight-logistics/documentation-requirements-aliyah-from-within -israel/, accessed March 2019. Acceptable proof includes a letter from a recognized rabbi if you are Jewish by birth, otherwise, other proof of conversion is required.

50. Nationality Law, 5712–1952, Official Gazette (Israel) 93, no. 11 (1952).

51. Nationality Law, 5712–1952, sections 2–8.

52. Registration of Inhabitants Ordinance, 5709–1949. Nationality Law, 5712–1952, section 3.

53. Victor Kattan, "The Nationality of Denationalized Palestinians," *Nordic Journal of International Law* 74, no. 1 (January 2005): 67–102. The condition "that the Arab must be an inhabitant of Israel on the day of the coming into force of this [1952] law . . . and the following provision, ensured no Arabs outside Israel . . . could claim its nationality. . . . Only the few remaining Palestinian Arab inhabitants of the newly created State of Israel who resided there *continuously* from 14 May 1948 until 14 July 1952 could become Israel nationals. All those who had left in the meantime or who were resident abroad could not become nationals. This included 750,000 Palestinian Arab refugees."

54. Anis Kassim, "The Palestinian: From Hyphenated Citizen to Integrated Citizen," in *Citizenship and the State in the Middle East: Approaches and Applications*, edited by Nils A. Butenschøn, Uri Davis, and Manuel Hassassian, 201–24 (Syracuse, NY: Syracuse University Press, 2000), 205–6. ("The second paragraph of Article 3 of the Nationality Law, subsection 3(b) . . . reads 'A person born after the establishment of the State who is an inhabitant of Israel on the day of the coming into force of this Law, and whose father or mother becomes an Israel national under subsection (a), shall become an Israel national with effect from the day of his birth.' . . . The exact outcome of the application of these two paragraphs was that . . . if a child is born to a Palestinian father or mother who was not a citizen of Israel, he or she will become stateless.")

55. BADIL Resource Center, "Palestinian Refugee Children: International Protection and Durable Solutions," BADIL Resource Center, January 2007, http://www.badil.org/phocadownloadpap/Badil _docs/publications/refugeechildren-en.pdf; "Israel's 1952 Citizenship Law effectively denationalized 1948 Palestinian refugees and their descendants by establishing eligibility criteria for Israel citizenship that those refugees could not possibly fulfill—i.e. presence in Israel on the day the law was adopted."

Susan M. Akram, "The Search for Protection for Stateless Refugees in the Middle East: Palestinians and Kurds in Lebanon and Jordan," *International Journal of Refugee Law* 30, no. 3 (October 2018): 407–43; "All Palestinians who could not meet the 'Israel nationality' criteria were denationalized en masse, and their children who were born in the territory also became stateless."

56. Nationality Law, 5712–1952, section 18.

57. See CA 8573/08 Ornan v. Ministry of the Interior (2013) (Isr.); CrimC (TA) Oseri v. Oseri; HCJ 174/52 Hussein v. Governor of Acre Prison 6 PD 897 [1952] (Isr.).

58. GA Resolution 55/153, annex, Nationality of Natural Persons in Relation to the Succession of States, January 30, 2001, Articles 5, 14, 15; CERD, Article 5(d)(ii); Oppenheim, *International Law*, 355 ("The inhabitants of the subjugated as well as of the ceded territory acquiring *ipso facto* by the subjugation or cession the nationality of the state which acquires the territory").

59. George Rafael Tamarin v. State of Israel (1970) 26 PD I 197 ("There is no Israeli nation separate from the Jewish nation . . . composed not only of those residing in Israel but also of Diaspora Jewry." According to High Court Chief Justice Agranat, recognizing an Israel nationality "would negate the very foundation upon which the State of Israel was formed." Don Handelman, "Contradictions between Citizenship and Nationality: Their Consequences for Ethnicity and Inequality in Israel," *International Journal of Politics, Culture and Sociology* 7, no. 3 (Spring 1994): 441–59; Joseph Schechla, "'Jewish Nationality,' 'National Institutions' and Institutionalized Dispossession," *Al Majdal*, no. 24 (December 2004): 32–36, https://www.academia.edu/6585340/_Jewish_Nationality_National_Institu tions_and_Institutionalized_Dispossession; Tekiner, "Race and Issue of National Identity."

60. CA 8573/08 Ornan v. Ministry of the Interior (2013) (Isr.); Jay Rudderman and Yedidia Z. Stern, "Is 'Israeli' a Nationality," *Israel Democracy Institute*, March 9, 2014, https://en.idi.org.il/articles /6516; Tia Goldenberg, "Supreme Court Rejects 'Israel' Nationality Status," *Times of Israel*, October 4, 2013, https://www.timesofisrael.com/supreme-court-rejects-israeli-nationality-status/.

61. "On . . . [official identity] cards, which are issued by the Population Registry of the Interior Ministry, neither Jews nor non-Jews may indicate their *nationality* as 'Israel.' The Interior Ministry consequently denied all requests to do so, the acceptable response being either 'Jew' or other, such as 'Arab' or 'Druse.' 'Israel' is an acceptable response only to identify one's *citizenship*"; Tekiner, "Race and Issue of National Identity."

62. "Authoritative books written by reputable legal scholars . . . translate this law into English as 'Law of Nationality' . . . [t]hese erroneous translations imply that 'nationality' and 'citizenship' are interchangeable in Hebrew . . . but they are not . . . . Because the Law of Citizenship refers to both Jews and non-Jews, translating it as the 'Law of Nationality' conveys the false impression that nationality status in Israel is open to all." Tekiner, "Race and Issue of National Identity," 49.

63. Tekiner, "Race and Issue of National Identity," 49–50.

64. The first such law is the Absentee Property Law of 1950, which defined as "absentees" all Palestinians who left their homes even for a short time to flee the violence during the conflict. Once declared an absentee, the Palestinian lost all claim of right to their property *in futuro*. Palestinian property thus confiscated was transferred into the bank of Israel Lands. The law also applies to "present absentees," that is, Palestinians (but not Jews) who remained on their land but whose absence was fictionalized in order to seize their property. See Absentee Property Law, 5710–1950, Official Gazette (Israel) 4, no. 68 (1950).

65. Under the 1960 Basic Law, the Jewish National Fund and the state Development Authority ensured that "Israel Lands" would be reserved for the sole use and enjoyment of Jewish nationals in perpetuity. Similar legislation was passed to confiscate Palestinian property in the West Bank through military orders. Basic Law: Israel Lands, 5720–1960, Laws of the State of Israel 14, no. 48 (1960). For exhaustive treatment of the dispossession of Palestinian lands, the discriminatory Israeli laws that enabled the dispossession, and calculations of the magnitude of Palestinian losses, see Geremy Forman and Alexandre Kedar, "From Arab Land to 'Israel Lands': The Legal Dispossession of the Palestinians Dispossessed by Israel in the Wake of 1948," *Environment and Planning D: Society and Space* 22, no.

6 (December 2004): 809–30; Usama Halabi, "Israel's Land Laws as a Legal-Political Tool: Confiscating and Appropriating Palestinian Arab Lands and Creating Physical and Legal Barriers in Order to Prevent Future Property Restitution," BADIL Resource Center, December 2004, http://www.badil.org /phocadownloadpap/Badil_docs/Working_Papers/WP-E-07.pdf; Sami Hadawi, *Palestinian Rights and Losses in 1948: A Comprehensive Study* (London: Saqi Books, 1988).

66. Souad R. Dajani, "Ruling Palestine: A History of the Legally Sanctioned Jewish-Israeli Seizure of Land and Housing in Palestine," Centre on Housing Rights and Evictions, BADIL Resource Center, 2005; Hussein Abu Hussein and Fiona McKay, *Access Denied: Palestinian Access to Land in Israel* (London: Zed Books, 2003).

67. For treaty and customary law support for these rules, see the Convention on Certain Questions Relating to the Conflict of Nationality Laws, April 13, 1930, 179 League of Nations Treaty Service 89; Protocol Relating to Military Obligations in Certain Cases of Double Nationality, April 12, 1930, 178 League of Nations Treaty Service 227; Protocol Relating to a Certain Case of Statelessness, April 12, 1930, 179 League of Nations Treaty Service 115; Special Protocol Concerning Statelessness, April 12, 1930; Convention on the Nationality of Married Women, January 29, 1957, 309 United Nations Treaty Series 65; Convention Relating to the Status of Stateless Persons; Convention on the Reduction of Statelessness; International Covenant on Civil and Political Rights, Article 12, December 16, 1966, 999 United Nations Treaty Series 171 (hereinafter ICCPR); CERD, Article 5; International Law Commission, Report on the Work of its Fifty-First Session. For authoritative treatises on nationality and international law by 1948 and today, see P. Weis, *Nationality and Statelessness in International Law*, (London: Stevens and Sons, 1956); Laura Van Waas, *Nationality Matters: Statelessness under International Law*, (Cambridge: Intersentia, 2008).

68. Nottebohm (Liech. v. Guat.), ICJ Report 1955.

69. Nottebohm (Liech. v. Guat.), ICJ Report 1955, 23–24.

70. International Law Commission, Report on the Work of its Fifty-Third Session, UN Document A/56/10, Article 27 (2001). International law requires reversing illegal legislation as well as compensating for any material losses caused by the wrongful acts.

71. Rebecca Kook, "Citizenship and its Discontents: Palestinians in Israel," in *Citizenship and the State in the Middle East: Approaches and Applications*, edited by Nils A. Butenschøn, Uri Davis, and Manuel Hassassian, 263–87 (Syracuse, NY: Syracuse University Press, 2000).

72. GA Resolution 181 (II), chapter 3, paragraph 1 ("Palestinian citizens residing in Palestine outside the City of Jerusalem, as well as Arabs and Jews who, not holding Palestinian citizenship, reside in Palestine outside the City of Jerusalem shall, upon the recognition of independence, become citizens of the State in which they are resident and enjoy full civil and political rights").

73. See, for example, Report of the Committee on the Elimination of Racial Discrimination, Ninety-Third Session, Ninety-Fourth Session, Ninety-Fifth Session, UN Document A/73/18, (August 6, 2018), 11–12, which urges Israel to take action regarding "persisting discriminatory practices against Palestinians by Israel"; Human Rights Council, Report of the Independent International Fact-Finding Mission to Investigate the Implications of the Israeli Settlements on the Civil, Political, Economic, Social, and Cultural Rights of Palestinian People throughout the Occupied Palestinian Territory, Including East Jerusalem, UN Document A/HRC/22/63, (February 7, 2013), 21–22, which describes extensive international law violations in Israel's West Bank settlements, and finds that the settlements are "established for the exclusive benefit of Israeli Jews"; International Court of Justice, "Legal Consequences of the Construction of a Wall in the Occupied Palestinian Territory, Advisory Opinions," International Court of Justice, July 9, 2004, https://www.icj-cij.org/public/files/case-related/131/131-20040709 -ADV-01-00-EN.pdf, which finds that the construction of a wall on Occupied Palestinian Territory reinforces "the Israeli settlements illegally established on the Occupied Palestinian Territory" and was "aimed at 'reducing and parceling out the territorial sphere over which the Palestinian people are entitled to exercise their right of self-determination'"; Committee on Economic, Social and Cultural Rights, "Concluding Observations of the Committee on Economic, Social and Cultural Rights: Israel,"

UN Document E/C.12/1/Add.27, paragraph 10 (1998), in which "the Committee expresses concern that excessive emphasis upon the State as a 'Jewish State' encourages discrimination and accords a second-class status to its non-Jewish citizens . . . apparent in the lower standard of living of Israeli Arabs as a result, inter alia, of lack of access to housing, water, electricity and health care and their lower level of education."

74. See, for example, reports from the UN human rights bodies and mechanisms: Committee on Economic, Social and Cultural Rights, "Concluding Observations, Israel," UN Document E/C.12/ISR/CO/3 (2012); UN Human Rights Committee, "Concluding Observations, Israel," UN Document CCPR/C/ISR/CO/4 (2014); Human Rights Council, "Ninth Special Session: The Grave Violation of Human Rights in the Occupied Palestinian Territory Including the Recent Aggression in the Occupied Gaza Strip," UN Document A/HRC/S-9/2 (2009;. Committee on the Elimination of Racial Discrimination, "Concluding Observations, Israel," UN Document CERD/C/ISR/CO/14–16 (2012).

75. English Translation of the Hebrew Original Text of the Basic Law of 26 July 2018 [1] (2018) Basic Law: Israel—The Nation State of the Jewish People (hereinafter Basic Law: Nation State of the Jewish People [English translation]); see also Miriam Berger, "Israel's Hugely Controversial "Nation-State" Law, Explained," *Vox*, July 31, 2018, https://www.vox.com/world/2018/7/31/17623978/israel-jewish-nation-state-law-bill-explained-apartheid-netanyahu-democracy, which notes that the vote passed by a 62–55 vote and that Israeli Arab members of parliament decried the law as "apartheid" following the vote.

76. Knesset, Basic Laws of the State of Israel, https://main.knesset.gov.il/en/activity/pages/basiclaws.aspx, accessed September 2020 ("Since the Constituent Assembly and the First Knesset were unable to put a constitution together, the Knesset started to legislate basic laws on various subjects. After all the basic laws will be enacted, they will constitute together, with an appropriate introduction and several general rulings, the constitution of the State of Israel").

77. Basic Law: Nation State of the Jewish People (English translation), 1(b).

78. The key provisions of the law state that: the land of Israel is the historic home of the Jewish people, and self-determination rests solely in the Jewish people (Article 1); the symbols of the state are exclusively Jewish (Article 2); the capitol of Israel is Jerusalem, including East Jerusalem (Article 3); the official language of the state is Hebrew (Article 4); automatic citizenship through immigration is exclusively reserved for Jews (Article 5); the state will promote ties between Israel and Jewish people around the world and preserve the cultural heritage of Jews in the diaspora (Article 6); Jewish settlement is a national value, and the state will promote and encourage it (Article 7); Basic Law: Nation State of the Jewish People. See also Adalah: The Legal Center for Arab Minority Rights in Israel, "The Basic Law: Israel—The Nation-State of the Jewish People," Adalah, November 2018, https://www.adalah.org/uploads/uploads/Final_2_pager_on_the_JNSL_27.11.2018%20.pdf.

79. Basic Law: Nation State of the Jewish People (English translation), Article 7.

80. The annexation of occupied territory, whether de facto or de jure, is illegal. *See* GA Resolution A/73/447, Situation of Human Rights in the Palestinian Territories Occupied Since 1967 (Oct. 22, 2018). Establishing civilian settlements of the population of the occupier in occupied territory is a war crime and grave breach of the Fourth Geneva Convention; Geneva Convention (IV), Relative to the Protection of Civilian Persons in Time of War, August 12, 1949, Article 49, 6 UST 3516, 75 United Nations Treaty Series 287; Protocol Additional to the Geneva Conventions of 12 August 1949, and Relating to the Protection of Victims of International Armed Conflicts, Article 85(4)(a), June 8, 1977, 1125 United Nations Treaty Series 3; Rome Statute of the International Criminal Court, Article 8(2)(b)(xiii), 2187 United Nations Treaty Series 3 (July 17, 1998). The International Court of Justice, in its Advisory Opinion on Legal Consequences of the Construction of a Wall, of July 9, 2004, found that Israel's construction of the Separation Wall on Occupied Palestinian Territory was a violation of self-determination and of the prohibition against annexation of and settlement construction in occupied territory.

81. International Convention on the Suppression and Punishment of the Crime of Apartheid, Articles 1, 2, November 30, 1973, 1015 United Nations Treaty Series 243.

82. See Richard Falk and Virginia Tilley, "Israeli Practices towards the Palestinian People and the Question of Apartheid," United Nations Economic and Social Commission for Western Asia, March 15, 2017, https://www.middleeastmonitor.com/wp-content/uploads/downloads/201703_UN_ESCWA -israeli-practices-palestinian-people-apartheid-occupation-english.pdf; Virginia Tilley, ed., "Occupation, Colonialism, Apartheid? A Re-assessment of Israel's Practices in the Occupied Palestinian Territories under International Law," Human Sciences Research Council, May 2009, http://www.hsrc .ac.za/en/research-data/view/4634.

83. Interestingly, Israel has contested the claim of Palestinian right of return based on GA Resolution 194, claiming that Resolution 194 is nonbinding because it is only a General Assembly and not a Security Council resolution. At the same time, Israel has claimed its right to establish its state on the basis of Resolution 181, also a General Assembly and not a Security Council resolution. In fact, Resolution 194 has a unique character under international law for two reasons: (1) it is customary international law and rests on already established customary international law norms (in other words the norms in it are independently obligatory as a matter of state practice that has become customary international law); and (2) unlike any other UN resolution it has been reaffirmed overwhelmingly by the General Assembly every year since its passage (indicating that it remains the authoritative statement of what international law requires). See Susan Akram and Terry Rempel, "Temporary Protection as an Instrument for Implementing the Right of Return for Palestinian Refugees," *Boston University International Law Journal* 22, no. 1 (2004): 1–162.

84. Generally, Israel claims that there is no legal basis in international human rights, humanitarian, or refugee treaty or customary law that applies specifically to Palestinian refugees, and that only persons who are nationals of a country have a right to return there. As for Resolution 194, Israel claims that it does not have the force of law under the UN Charter and that in any event Palestinians have not met the preconditions to return cited in Resolution 194. Ruth Lapidoth, "Do Palestinian Refugees Have a Right to Return to Israel?" Israeli Ministry of Foreign Affairs, January 15, 2001, https://mfa.gov .il/mfa/foreignpolicy/peace/guide/pages/do%20palestinian%20refugees%20have%20a%20right%20 to%20return%20to.aspx.

85. Among a very large body of literature on the right of return under international law, see, for example, W. Thomas Mallison and Sally V. Mallison, "An International Law Analysis of the Major United Nations Resolutions Concerning the Palestinian Question," UN Committee on the Exercise of the Inalienable Rights of the Palestinian People, 1979, https://www.un.org/unispal/document/auto -insert-196128/; Gail J. Boling, *The 1948 Palestinian Refugees and the Individual Right of Return: An International Law Analysis* (Bethlehem: BADIL Resource Center, 2007); Kathleen Lawand, "The Right to Return of Palestinians in International Law," *International Journal of Refugee Law* 8, no. 4 (October 1996): 532–68. John Quigley, "Mass Displacement and the Individual Right of Return," *British Yearbook of International Law* 68, no. 1 (1997): 65–125; see also Susan Akram and Terry Rempel, "Recommendations for Durable Solutions for Palestinian Refugees: A Challenge to the Oslo Framework," in *The Palestine Year Book of International Law Online*, edited by Ardi Imseis, vol. 11, xiii–71 (Leiden: Brill-Nijhoff, 2000), https://doi.org/10.1163/221161401X00020; Akram and Rempel, "Temporary Protection," 4; and GA Resolution 2535 (XXIV), UN Document A/RES/2535(XXIV)A-C (December 10, 1969, which notes Israel's refusals to implement prior resolutions to ensure the return of Palestinians.

86. A full discussion and analysis of all the arguments contesting the right of return for Palestinians is beyond the scope of this chapter. As I noted, the right of return as a legal matter rests on at least three different bodies or sources of law. In this piece I analyze in detail only one source of law on the right of return: the law of nationality and state succession. This analysis does not cover all of the law that supports the right of return in general or the right of return for Palestinians.

87. ICCPR, Article 12(4).

88. For the drafting history of these provisions, see Marc J. Bossuyt, *Guide to the Travaux Prepara-toires of the International Covenant on Civil and Political Rights* (Dordrecht: Martinus Nijhoff, 1987). For the authoritative interpretation by the Human Rights Committee itself of the broad reading of the "country" and "enter" phrases in the ICCPR, see UN Human Rights Committee, CCPR General Comment No. 27: Article 12 (Freedom of Movement), paragraphs 19–21, UN Document CCPR/C/21/Rev.1/Add.9 (November 2, 1999). See also Lawand, "The Right of Return," 548–58.

89. Quigley, "Mass Displacement," 202 ("Even though exile as a penal sanction would appear to be permitted under art. 12, it is questionable whether it is permitted in light of the human right to a nationality, at least if exile would render the person stateless. In addition, a state may, by exiling a person as a penal sanction, require another state to accept the person").

90. UN Commission on Human Rights, Committee on the Rights of Everyone to Be Free from Arbitrary Arrest, Detention, and Exile, Preliminary Report, UN Document E/CN.4/826 (1962); Hurst Hannum, *The Right to Leave and Return in International Law and Practice* (Boston and Dordrecht: Martinus Nijhoff, 1987), 156.

91. See Hannum, *Right to Leave and Return*, citing the Strasbourg Declaration on the Right to Leave and Return, Article 6 (b), (Nov. 26, 1986), which reads "No person shall be deprived of nationality or citizenship in order to exile or to prevent that person from exercising the right to enter his or her country."

92. Guy Goodwin-Gill, *The Refugee in International Law* (Oxford: Clarendon Press, 1996), 242.

93. Convention on the Reduction of Statelessness, Article 9.

94. The draft principles and accompanying study of state practice on the rights to leave and return were prepared by the UN Special Rapporteur of the Sub-Commission on Prevention of Discrimination, Jose Ingles. See Jose Ingles, *Study of Discrimination in Respect of the Right of Everyone to Leave Any Country, Including His Own, and to Return to His Country* (New York: United Nations, 1963). The study and draft principles led to the issuance of the Strasbourg Declaration on the Right to Leave and Return, which clarified the absolute nature of the rights and the expansive definition of "own country" and informed the interpretations by the Human Rights Committee. See Hannum, *Right to Leave and Return*.

95. Ingles, *Study of Discrimination*, 1–5.

96. Lawand, "The Right to Return," 539–41 (discussing the generally recognized right of return and the complexities in the case of Palestinian refugees); and UNHCR, "The State of the World's Refugees: In Search of Solidarity," UNHCR, 2012, 12, https://www.unhcr.org/publications/sowr/4fc5ceca9/state-worlds-refugees-2012-search-solidarity.html. Israel's objections to a Palestinian right of return cannot be claimed as a matter of "persistent objection" because Israel has claimed the same right for Jews in all aspects of the right of return. Israel has claimed, for example, that Jews have a right to return to the territory of Israel because of an ancient right as original "Israelites" (nationals of the territory); that they have a right to the land due to victory during the 1947–49 conflict; and that they were given the territory by GA Resolution 181 in fulfillment of Jewish self-determination.

97. Eric Rosand, "The Right to Return under International Law Following Mass Dislocation: The Bosnia Precedent?" *Michigan Journal of International Law* 19, no. 4 (1998): 1,094–1,138.

98. Kassim, "The Palestinian," 69–71.

99. Bill Van Esveld, *"Forget about Him, He's Not Here": Israel's Control of Palestinian Residency in the West Bank and Gaza* (New York: Human Rights Watch, 2012).

100. Van Esveld, *"Forget About Him."*

101. Human Rights Watch, "Israel: Jerusalem Palestinians Stripped of Status," Human Rights Watch, August 8, 2017, https://www.hrw.org/news/2017/08/08/israel-jerusalem-palestinians-stripped-status#.

102. Harriet Sherwood, "Israel Stripped 140,000 Palestinians of Residency Rights, Document Reveals," *The Guardian*, May 11, 2011, https://www.theguardian.com/world/2011/may/11/israel-palestinians-residency-rights.

103. Susan M. Akram, "The Legal Trajectory of the Palestinian Refugee Issue: From Exclusion to Ambiguity," in *Palestine and the Palestinians in the Twenty-First Century*, edited by Rochelle Davis

and Mimi Kirk, 121–41 (Bloomington: Indiana University Press, 2013), 120, 123–24. The Oslo Process resulted in the 1993 Declaration of Principles, which sought to recognize "mutual legitimate and political rights"; the 1994 Gaza-Jericho Agreement refers to "'internationally accepted norms and principles of human rights' as governing the 'powers and responsibilities' of the parties." However, none of these make any direct reference to internationally recognized legal rights and references to the core UN resolutions protecting individual Palestinian rights—particularly the right of return—are absent. The 1995 Interim Agreement between Israel and the PLO requires Palestinians to respect rights "concerning government and absentee property acquired by Israelis in the Occupied Territories," without reciprocity for Palestinian rights.

104. See Interim Agreement on the West Bank and the Gaza Strip, Article 28, paragraph 7, Isr.-oPt., September 28, 1995.

105. Interim Agreement on the West Bank and the Gaza Strip, Article 28, paragraph 7, Isr.-oPt., September 28, 1995.

106. Interim Agreement on the West Bank and the Gaza Strip, Annex II, Article II, paragraph 1(g).

107. 2003 Amended Basic Law, Palestinian Basic Law, https://www.palestinianbasiclaw.org/basic-law/2003-amended-basic-law.

108. 2003 Amended Basic Law.

109. Cited and discussed in Mutaz M. Qafisheh, "Who Has the Right to Become a Palestinian Citizen? An International Law Analysis," in *Yearbook of Islamic and Middle Eastern Law*, edited by Martin Lau, vol. 18, 112–49 (Leiden: Brill, 2017). This draft has not been made public.

110. The law was drafted by Mutaz Qafisheh for the PLO Negotiation Affairs Department in January 2012 but not published; the draft is on file with Qafisheh. Qafisheh, "Who Has the Right," 113n5.

111. Qafisheh, "Who Has the Right," citing PLO, Draft Palestinian Citizenship Law, January 2012; unpublished draft, on file with this author.

112. "UN Treaty Body Database: Ratification Status for Israel," UN Office of the High Commissioner on Refugees, https://tbinternet.ohchr.org/_layouts/15/TreatyBodyExternal/Treaty.aspx?CountryID=84&Lang=EN, accessed May 2019; "Treaties, States Parties, and Commentaries: Israel," International Committee of the Red Cross, https://ihl-databases.icrc.org/applic/ihl/ihl.nsf/vwTreatiesByCountrySelected.xsp?xp_countrySelected=IL, accessed May 2019.

113. See, for example, GA Resolution 72/150, paragraph 50 (January 17, 2018); GA Resolution 55/74, paragraph 17 (February 12, 2001); GA Resolution 48/116 (March 24, 1994); SC Resolution 2003, paragraph 18 (July 29, 2011); SC Resolution 1716, paragraphs 9–10 (October 13, 2006); SC Resolution 1120, paragraph 3 (July 14, 1997); UNHCR, "Handbook on Housing and Property Restitution for Refugees and Displaced Persons," Food and Agriculture Organization, March 2007, 27, http://www.fao.org/3/al131e/al131e01.pdf ("A variety of UN resolutions dating back to 1948 confer housing and property restitution rights on displaced Palestinian refugees").

114. Committee on Human Rights, Report on the Work of its Fifty-Fourth Session, Guiding Principles on Internal Displacement, section V, UN Document E/CN.4/1998/53/Add.2 (February 11, 1998); UNHCR, "Handbook: Voluntary Repatriation: International Protection," UNHCR, 1996, https://www.unhcr.org/bg/wp-content/uploads/sites/18/2016/12/Handbook_Voluntary-Repatriation_1996.pdf.

115. Abbas Shiblak, "Stateless Palestinians," *Forced Migration Review* 26 (August 2006): 8–9, https://www.fmreview.org/sites/fmr/files/FMRdownloads/en/palestine/shiblak.pdf ("Today more than half of the eight million or so Palestinians are considered to be *de jure* stateless persons").

116. Susan M. Akram, "Assessing the Impact of the Global Compacts on Refugees and Migration in the Middle East," *International Journal of Refugee Law* 30, no. 4 (December 2018): 691–95.

117. BADIL Resource Center, "Closing Protection Gaps: A Handbook on Protection of Palestinian Refugees in States Signatories to the 1951 Refugee Convention," BADIL Resource Center, August 2011, 11, 14–15, http://www.badil.org/phocadownload/Badil_docs/publications/handbook/update2011/country%20profile/handbook2010.pdf.

118. Qafisheh, "Who Has the Right," 149.

BIBLIOGRAPHY

Abu Hussein, Hussein, and Fiona McKay. *Access Denied: Palestinian Access to Land in Israel.* London: Zed Books, 2003.

Adalah: The Legal Center for Arab Minority Rights in Israel. "The Basic Law: Israel—The Nation-State of the Jewish People." Adalah, November 2018.

Akram, Susan. "Assessing the Impact of the Global Compacts on Refugees and Migration in the Middle East." *International Journal of Refugee Law* 30, no. 4 (December 2018): 691–95.

———. "The Legal Trajectory of the Palestinian Refugee Issue: From Exclusion to Ambiguity." In *Palestine and the Palestinians in the Twenty-first Century*, edited by Rochelle Davis and & Mimi Kirk, 121–41. Bloomington: Indiana University Press, 2013.

———. "The Search for Protection for Stateless Refugees in the Middle East: Palestinians and Kurds in Lebanon and Jordan." *International Journal of Refugee Law* 30, no. 3 (October 2018): 407–43.

Akram, Susan, and Terry Rempel. "Recommendations for Durable Solutions for Palestinian Refugees: A Challenge to the Oslo Framework." In *The Palestine Year Book of International Law Online*, edited by Ardi Imseis, vol. 11, xiii–71. Leiden: Brill-Nijhoff, 2000.

———. "Temporary Protection as an Instrument for Implementing the Right of Return for Palestinian Refugees." *Boston University International Law Journal* 22, no. 1 (2004): 1–162.

American Society of International Law. "Draft Conventions and Comments on Nationality, Responsibility of States for Injuries to Aliens, and Territorial Waters, Prepared by the Research in International Law of the Harvard Law School." Supplement, *American Journal of International Law* 61, S5 (1929).

BADIL Resource Center. "Closing Protection Gaps: A Handbook on Protection of Palestinian Refugees in States Signatories to the 1951 Refugee Convention." BADIL Resource Center, August 2011: 14–15.

———. "Palestinian Refugee Children: International Protection and Durable Solutions." BADIL Resource Center, January 2007.

Boling, Gail J. *The 1948 Palestinian Refugees and the Individual Right of Return: An International Law Analysis.* Bethlehem: BADIL Resource Center, 2007.

Bossuyt, Marc J. *Guide to the Travaux Preparatoires of the International Covenant on Civil and Political Rights.* Dordrecht: Martinus Nijhoff, 1987.

Dajani, Souad. "Ruling Palestine, A History of the Legally Sanctioned Jewish-Israeli Seizure of Land and Housing in Palestine." Centre on Housing Rights and Evictions, BADIL Resource Center, 2005.

Eide, Asbjorn. "Citizenship and International Human Rights Law: Status, Evolution, and Challenges." In *Citizenship and the State in the Middle East: Approaches and Applications*, edited by Nils August Butenschøn, Manuel Sarkis Hassassian, and Uri Davis, 88–122. Syracuse, NY: Syracuse University Press, 2000.

Falk, Richard, and Virginia Tilley. "Israeli Practices Towards the Palestinian People and the Question of Apartheid." United Nations Economic and Social Commission for Western Asia, March 15, 2017.

Flournoy, Richard, and Manley O. Hudson. *A Collection of Nationality Laws of Various Countries, as Contained in Constitutions, Statutes and Treaties.* New York: Oxford University Press, 1929.

Forman, Geremy, and Alexandre Kedar. "From Arab Land to 'Israel Lands': The Legal Dispossession of the Palestinians Dispossessed by Israel in the Wake of 1948." *Environment and Planning D: Society and Space* 22, no. 6 (December 2004): 809–30.

Goodwin-Gill, Guy. *The Refugee in International Law.* Oxford: Clarendon Press, 1996.

Hadawi, Sami. *Palestinian Rights and Losses in 1948: A Comprehensive Study.* London: Saqi Books, 1988.

Halabi, Usama. "Israel's Land Laws as a Legal-Political Tool: Confiscating and Appropriating Palestinian Arab Lands and Creating Physical and Legal Barriers in Order to Prevent Future Property Restitution." BADIL Resource Center, December 2004.

Handelman, Don. "Contradictions between Citizenship and Nationality: Their Consequences for Ethnicity and Inequality in Israel." *International Journal of Politics, Culture and Society* 7, no. 3 (Spring 1994): 441–59.

Hannum, Hurst. *The Right to Leave and Return in International Law and Practice.* Boston and Dordrecht: Martinus Nijhoff, 1987.

Human Rights Watch. "Israel: Jerusalem Palestinians Stripped of Status." Human Rights Watch, August 8, 2017.

Ingles, Jose D. *Study of Discrimination in Respect of the Right of Everyone to Leave Any Country, Including His Own, and to Return to His Country.* New York: United Nations, 1963.

Kassim, Anis F. "The Palestinian: From Hyphenated Citizen to Integrated Citizen." In *Citizenship and the State in the Middle East: Approaches and Applications,* edited by Nils A. Butenschøn, Uri Davis, and Manuel Hassassian, 201–24. Syracuse, NY: Syracuse University Press, 2000.

Kattan, Victor. *From Coexistence to Conquest: International Law and the Origin of the Arab-Israeli Conflict.* London: Pluto, 2009.

———. "The Nationality of Denationalized Palestinians." *Nordic Journal of International Law* 74, no. 1 (January 2005): 67–102.

Kook, Rebecca. "Citizenship and its Discontents: Palestinians in Israel." In *Citizenship and the State in the Middle East: Approaches and Applications,* edited by Nils A. Butenschøn, Uri Davis, and Manuel Hassassian, 263–87. Syracuse, NY: Syracuse University Press, 2000.

Lapidoth, Ruth. "Do Palestinian Refugees Have a Right to Return to Israel?" Israeli Ministry of Foreign Affairs, January 15, 2001.

Lawand, Kathleen. "The Right to Return of Palestinians in International Law." *International Journal of Refugee Law* 8, no. 4 (October 1996): 532–68.

Mallison, W. Thomas, and Sally V. Mallison, "An International Law Analysis of the Major United Nations Resolutions Concerning the Palestinian Question." UN Committee on the Exercise of the Inalienable Rights of the Palestinian People, 1979.

Oppenheim, Lassa. *International Law: A Treatise.* London: Longmans, Green, and Co., 1905.

Qafisheh, Mutaz M. "Genesis of Citizenship in Palestine and Israel: Palestinian Nationality in the 1917–1925 Period." *Bulletin du Centre de recherche français à Jérusalem* 21 (December 2010).

———. *The International Law Foundations of Palestinian Nationality: A Legal Examination of Nationality under Britain's Rule.* Leiden: Brill-Nijhoff, 2008.

———. *Palestine Membership in the United Nations: Legal and Practical Implications.* Newcastle upon Tyne: Cambridge Scholars Publishing, 2013.

———. "Who Has the Right to Become a Palestinian Citizen? An International Law Analysis." In *Yearbook of Islamic and Middle Eastern Law*, edited by Martin Lau, vol. 18, 112–49. Leiden: Brill, 2017.

Quigley, John. "Mass Displacement and the Individual Right of Return." *British Yearbook of International Law* 68, no. 1 (1997): 65–125.

Richmond, Nancy C. "Israel's Law of Return: Analysis of Its Evolution and Present Application." *Penn State International Law Review* 12, no.1 (1993): 95–133.

Rosand, Eric. "The Right to Return under International Law Following Mass Dislocation: The Bosnia Precedent?" *Michigan Journal of International Law* 19, no. 4 (1998): 1,094–138.

Sand, Shlomo. *The Invention of the Jewish People*. London: Verso, 2008.

Schechla, Joseph. "'Jewish Nationality,' 'National Institutions' and Institutionalized Dispossession." *Al Majdal*, no. 24 (December 2004): 32–36.

Shiblak, Abbas. "Stateless Palestinians." *Forced Migration Review* 26 (August 2006): 8–9.

Spiro, Peter J. "Citizenship Overreach." *Michigan Journal of International Law* 38, no. 2 (2017): 173–200.

Tekiner, Roselle. "Race and the Issue of National Identity in Israel." *International Journal of Middle East Studies* 23, no. 1 (February 1991): 39–55.

Tibet Justice Center. "Tibet's Stateless Nationals: Tibetan Refugees in Nepal." Tibet Justice Center, June 2002.

Tilley, Virginia, ed. "Occupation, Colonialism, Apartheid? A Re-assessment of Israel's Practices in the Occupied Palestinian Territories under International Law." Human Sciences Research Council, May 2009.

Van Esveld, Bill. *"Forget about Him, He's Not Here": Israel's Control of Palestinian Residency in the West Bank and Gaza*. New York: Human Rights Watch, 2012.

Van Waas, Laura. *Nationality Matters: Statelessness under International Law*. Cambridge: Intersentia, 2008.

Weis, P. *Nationality and Statelessness in International Law*. London: Stevens and Sons, 1956.

9

Constitutional Frameworks for a One-State Option in Palestine

An Assessment

Mazen Masri

Statehood is inherently intertwined with the law. The powers of the state and their limits, the different organs of the state and their relationships with each other, the relationship between the citizens and the state, and the rights of citizens—all these are governed by constitutional law. The constitutional model to be adopted, the internal ordering of the state, the relationship between the citizenry and the state, and how the constitution addresses matters of membership, belonging, and rights are all significant questions in any exercise related to thinking about possible constitutional frameworks. These are especially important in the context of exploring options for creating a single democratic state in the area of historic Palestine (Israel and the West Bank and Gaza Strip) as part of resolving the Israeli-Arab conflict.

Any such thinking about solving the conflict will have to address the many challenges that the conflict presents. It is a longstanding conflict that has its roots in the late nineteenth century between two conflicting national movements. One of the movements, Zionism, shares many characteristics with settler-colonial movements in its ideologies, narratives, and strategies. Indeed, that is how the Palestinians, the native population, experienced and still experience the policies and practices of the Zionist movement and later on the state of Israel. As in other settler-colonial situations, the current reality reflects conditions of severe inequality between the settler population and the native population. This inequality is built into the political system, the economy, and law, reflecting the privileges that the settler population enjoys in the settler state. In addition to pervasive inequality there are certain events in the history of the conflict that became important landmarks because of the intensity of their violence and the profoundness of their impact. Events such as the Nakba came to embody decades of historical injustice.

A solution that is based on a single state built on the principles of equality and democracy has to address these challenges of inequality as well as tackle the injustices of the past and foster a sense of security and partnership for the future.

What would the possible constitutional frameworks for a single state be? What are the merits and demerits of each model? Would these models be able to satisfy the rights and needs of citizens of the future state? To guide the discussion and the assessment of the various options, this chapter will first discuss a number of guiding principles against which the models will be assessed. These principles are designed to address the problems under the current conditions, the historical injustices, as well as the needs, claims, and aspirations of the people living in this region today. It then moves to discussion of the different unitary models available, particularly the liberal state, the binational model, and the multicultural model. The chapter will also examine the possible federal models, mainly purely territorial federalism, and a mix between federalism and consociationalism. Finally it discusses human rights arrangements, assessing the role of human rights in any future constitutional settlement.

GUIDING PRINCIPLES

Constitutional design is not an abstract exercise conducted on a blank slate. While in this case it signifies a new beginning, no beginning and no thinking about constitutional design can be separated from its context. Constitutional design means thinking about the issues, the problems, the questions, and the controversies that affect a certain country, and thinking of ways to articulate the principles on which the new constitutional order will be built. In our context, these principles are meant to address the problems and the injustice of the current situation, problems that the two-state solution is unlikely to solve, as well as potential problems that are likely to emerge in the context of a one-state arrangement. Setting clear principles is also necessary to guarantee fairness and justice and a measure of stability for the regime that is being designed.

Equal Citizenship

Lack of equality between Palestinians and Israelis is one of the core problems and injustices that affect that daily lives of people, and it reverberates throughout Israel's legal and political system. It stems from the colonial outlook and policies implemented by Israel that have their roots in the early (pre-state Zionist) thought. If one were to classify the inhabitants of the area between the Mediterranean and the river Jordan according to their rights as a *matter of law*, it would be clear that there are a number of hierarchical categories. On the top we can find the Jewish citizens of Israel. They enjoy the full spectrum of rights, and their rights and interests almost automatically trump the rights of all those in the categories ranked below them. The second category is the Palestinian citizens living in

Israel. While formal citizenship gives them a measure of civil rights, their nominal citizenship does not grant full equality, for according to Israeli law and Zionist thought they do not belong to the "nation" that alone exercises self-determination in Israel. The rights enjoyed by this group do not extend to the full spectrum of rights.[1] The third category is the Palestinians of East Jerusalem, who, according to Israeli law, have residency rights but not citizenship rights. Under Israeli law, residency is a status that can be easily revoked if the individual lives outside Israeli areas for an extended period of time. Fourth are the Palestinians in the West Bank, who live under Israeli occupation. Israel has ultimate control over this territory, with the Palestinian Authority acting as the local agent that runs the day-to-day affairs of the population. Fifth are Palestinians in the Gaza Strip, which is legally still under Israeli occupation and who live under the most severe situation: while the Hamas-controlled Palestinian Authority rules over the population, the state of Israeli siege, prohibition of movement of people and goods, and the periodic bouts of violence visited upon the population by Israel make the conditions drastically more serious than in the West Bank. Finally, the group that is most disenfranchised and lacks even minimum rights are the Palestinian refugees. Many of the Palestinian refugees (those displaced in 1948) live in refugee camps and towns in the West Bank and Gaza Strip, but a significant number are concentrated in Jordan, Syria, and Lebanon as well as other countries in the world. A sizable number of these refugees are stateless.

While the question of inequality is inherently political, these hierarchies were created and are maintained by law, mostly Israeli law. This is clear in Israel's constitutional definition as a Jewish state, which designates the Jewish collective as the dominant group of the state and the public sphere. It is also clear in a range of laws and policies that affect the rights of Palestinians, whether they are in Israel, the West Bank, the Gaza Strip, or in exile.[2] This legally sanctioned inequality was put on a more firm footing with the enactment in 2018 of *Basic Law: Israel: The Nation State of the Jewish People*. This law, which has a constitutional status, reasserts many of the principles that are associated with the definition of the state as a Jewish state. It highlights the notion of self-determination as reserved exclusively for Jews in Israel and reaffirms the connections between Israel and Jewish communities elsewhere, the supremacy of Hebrew as the official language, and the importance of Jewish immigration and Jewish settlement. All of these ideas are already constitutional values in Israel, as stated repeatedly by Israeli courts. But the fact that Israeli politicians decided to reassert their importance in the form of a basic law (legislation that has constitutional status higher than ordinary legislation in the normative hierarchy) indicates the level at which the regime is determined to entrench inequality in Israel.

Any solution for the conflict should be based on the idea of equal citizenship for all of these population categories. Equality in this context could be divided into legal and political equality on the one hand, and social equality on the other. Legal and political equality means that all members of the categories mentioned above should be entitled to citizenship as a matter of right, and that each citizen should be entitled to the same basic bundle of rights. Equality should also extend to cultural, linguistic, and religious rights, such that each cultural group will be able to enjoy and preserve its culture. It is important to highlight that legal and political equality cannot be achieved without social equality, especially in a situation where there are several categories of people with significant economic and social differences among them. As such, in order to achieve equality, future arrangements should contain significant schemes to tackle the sources of inequality. Resources should be allocated with the view of eliminating social gaps, an effort which should include affirmative action plans. Furthermore, transitional justice schemes are needed and these should include reparations, especially with regard to the losses of the Palestinian refugees. Reparations, which should include restitution of property, would help in addressing the current state of economic inequality between Palestinians and Israelis.

Immigration, Residency, and Citizenship Laws and Policies

Citizenship and immigration laws and policies are essential components of membership in the polity, for they control who can enter the polity and the status of individuals and sometimes groups within it. For Palestinians, the 1948 ethnic cleansing has been described as the Nakba (catastrophe) and it entailed the mass displacement of the majority of Palestinians and the loss of a homeland and all of the entitlements that are associated with it—citizenship, land, dwellings, et cetera. On the other hand, the policy of creating a Jewish state in Palestine relied on Jewish immigration (in addition to expulsion of the indigenous Palestinians) in order to establish a critical Jewish mass or a majority that would create its own state. Immigration (and demography) was, and still is, vital for the Zionist project. Negotiations, contestations, and campaigns to increase Jewish immigration and the absorption of the resulting immigrants in Palestine were central to Zionist activities both before 1948 and after the creation of Israel. For the Zionist leadership these immigrants, many of whom were refugees fleeing atrocities in Europe, were an essential part of the process of building a Jewish majority.[3]

The current immigration and citizenship laws and policies are more or less a translation of this approach, and are characterized by serious discrimination and racism.[4] The various categories discussed above are essentially the outcome of the operation of citizenship and residency laws and policies that allocate rights differentially. Any new constitutional model adopted must address the issues of citizenship and immigration with the view of eliminating the current legal sources of inequalities, and should also strive to provide an equitable immigration policy for the benefit of the citizenry of the future state as well.

Such a model should eliminate the current immigration regime, particularly the idea of exclusive Jewish immigration, known as "return" or *shvout*, which was recently emphasized in the 2018 *Basic Law: Israel: The Nation State of the Jewish People*. This idea is not just a matter of the technicalities of immigration legislation (for at some point during or right after the transformational change that would bring about the creation of a single state, *all* existing legislation would need to be revised and adapted to the new situation) but extends to the level of fundamental principles. Jewish immigration, or *aliya*, as former Chief Justice of the Supreme Court of Israel Aharon Barak explained, is not a technical term. It is regarded as a fundamental political principle, or as Barak puts it, "a social, value-laden, and national term."[5] Accordingly, the Law of Return of 1950, even though it is not officially a basic law, is seen as "one of the most important laws in Israel, if not the most important." Its importance stems from the notion that it "is the key to entering the State of Israel, which constitutes a central reflection of the fact that Israel is not merely a democratic state, but also a Jewish state; it constitutes 'the constitutional cornerstone of the character of the State of Israel as the state of the Jewish people.'"[6]

The Law of Return therefore is not merely a matter of immigration: it is the main category of distinction between Jews and non-Jews (mainly Palestinians); a distinction between those who, according to Israeli law, have the right to self-determination and the right to a homeland in Israel with all of the associated national and collective rights, and those whose presence in the country is based on individual rights or status. This distinction is carried from this foundational point throughout the legal system and is used to justify discrimination against non-Jews.

On the other hand, the concept of Jewish "return" should not be confused with the right of return of the Palestinian refugees. While the former is based on a political ideology that was codified into law and has no equivalent anywhere else in the world, the latter is a well-established human right that refugees (and others who are arbitrarily denied the right to access their countries) are entitled to under international law.[7] The right of return of the Palestinian refugees is essential in equalizing rights and eliminating the current discriminatory hierarchy.

Group Rights

The population between the river Jordan and the Mediterranean belongs to two main groups: Jewish Israelis and Palestinians. While both groups are diverse in their composition (for example, Palestinians include Muslims and Christians but almost all are Arabic speakers; Jews include a number of subgroups, some of whom speak other languages such as Russian and Amharic; and some subgroups are not "legally" Jewish but speak Hebrew and embrace Jewish Israeli culture), the affiliation as Jewish or Palestinian/Arab is the cardinal division. This division is the main point of distinction that determines which people have rights under the current regime, and is the most pronounced in terms of defining the identity of the various populations living under Israeli rule. It also overlaps with the distinction (discussed below) of settler or indigenous.

These two groups (and in some cases the subgroups) each have their own distinctive language, culture, heritage, and religion. These markers are important markers of identity. Today, these two groups live more or less separately, even though they inhabit the same land. This separation is not between equals. The Jewish-Israeli collective is the dominant group in almost all aspects—politically, economically and linguistically, The Jewish group is the one that elects the government, it is the one that controls the economy, and Hebrew is the dominant language of governance and trade.[8] Palestinians, however, enjoy some cultural/religious autonomy in the areas of the Palestinian Authority. Palestinians who live in Israel seemingly enjoy some cultural autonomy in the form of separate religious institutions and courts and a separate education system, however these institutions are tightly controlled by the Israeli government and are designed to benefit the state rather than the members of these religious groups.

Accounting for the diversity of the population is crucial for a stable and just settlement of conflicts in countries with deep national, ethnic, or religious divisions. The constitutional principles and state institutions should acknowledge the fact that there are at present two main groups, and these groups have different identities that should be accommodated. This recognition and accommodation does not and should not mean dominance of one group over the other, or special rights or privileges for one group, as is the situation today. The principle of equality should be observed in the design and administration of group rights, both on the level of the group and that of the individuals belonging to each group. At the same time, special attention should be given in order to guard against a situation where belonging to a certain group, rather than citizenship or membership in the broader polity, becomes the most significant source of rights.

Historical Redress, Transitional Justice, and Transformative Constitutionalism

Constitutional change in a postconflict context cannot be a tool to preserve the past. At the same time, we cannot imagine a constitution that is totally separated from the conflict, its history, its injustices, and its underlying causes. The constitution should play a dual role: to anchor and facilitate transitional justice measures such as truth-telling, reparation, and prosecution.[9] The second role for the constitution is mainly forward-looking: to transform the present into an equal reality. It should mark a break with the past and its injustices and inequities, and signal the beginning of a new constitutional order that aims at transforming the state and society based on a new, just vision. Transformational constitutionalism, Karl Klare explains, is

> a long-term project of constitutional enactment, interpretation, and enforcement committed (not in isolation, of course, but in a historical context of conducive political developments) to transforming a country's political and social institutions and power relationships in a democratic, participatory, and egalitarian direction. Transformative constitutionalism connotes an enterprise of inducing large-scale social

change through nonviolent political processes grounded in law. I have in mind a transformation vast enough to be inadequately captured by the phrase "reform," but something short of or different from "revolution" in any traditional sense of the word. In the background is an idea of a highly egalitarian, caring, multicultural community, governed through participatory, democratic processes in both the polity and large portions of what we now call the "private sphere."[10]

Transformation cannot be an initiative that is undertaken solely by the legal system. It is essentially a political process with many actors and in which the legal system can play an important role. This role was articulated in the postapartheid jurisprudence of the South African Constitutional Court, which emphasized that the postapartheid interim Constitution of South Africa,

> is not simply some kind of statutory codification of an acceptable or legitimate past. It retains from the past only what is defensible and represents a radical and decisive break from that part of the past which is unacceptable. It constitutes a decisive break from a culture of Apartheid and racism to a constitutionally protected culture of openness and democracy and universal human rights for South Africans of all ages, classes and colours. There is a stark and dramatic contrast between the past in which South Africans were trapped and the future on which the Constitution is premised. . . . The relevant provisions of the Constitution must therefore be interpreted so as to give effect to the purposes sought to be advanced by their enactment. (*Shabalala and Others v Attorney-General of the Transvaal and Another*, 1995)

This vision helped transform South Africa, and made its Constitutional Court a leading actor especially with regards to social and economic rights, even if this transformation did not go far enough in some areas.[11] This kind of transformative thinking about the constitution is indispensable for a one-state model to work effectively, regardless of the model adopted. In our context it means a major change in the doctrines, principles, mindsets, and practices that have informed existing constitutional and legal thinking and have established and entrenched the current apartheid realities. It means that constitutional practice should be guided by the principles that ensure a viable and democratic single state, such as the principles discussed below.

Decolonization

Colonialism, and more specifically settler-colonialism, lies at the heart of the conflict between Palestinians and Jewish Israelis. The division is not just ethnic/national in its nature, but also a division between a settler society that has almost full control over the state, and an indigenous society that is resisting the status quo. As in other colonial situations, the colonization process was accompanied by widespread processes of elimination of the indigenous population. The uniqueness in the case of Israel is that Israel as a state was formed as a settler-colonial state, and at the same time acts as a colonial power in the West Bank under the guise of occupation.

Patrick Wolfe, a prominent theorist of settler-colonialism, identifies its essential feature as "the logic of elimination, a sustained institutional tendency to supplant the indigenous population which reconciles a range of historical practices that might otherwise seem distinct."[12] This colonial process applies to Israel. However, the characterization of Israel and the Zionist movement as settler-colonial is not accepted by many Israelis who think of Israel as the culmination of a historical and natural right to establish a Jewish state.[13] Many writers on the other hand see the Zionist project and the formation of the state of Israel as a form of settler-colonialism.[14] They highlight the intensive immigration from Europe with the intention of building a state exclusively for the benefit of the settler society. This approach is also accepted by a number of Israeli academics who agree that Israel and the Zionist project have a strong settler-colonial element, or who, like Baruch Kimmerling, have adopted the settler/native distinction without using the term settler-colonialism.[15] Some, like Wolfe, even observe that the Zionist logic of elimination is more exclusive than such logics in Australia or the United States.[16]

Since colonialism is one of the significant issues at the heart of the conflict, decolonization should be at the center of any solution. The concept of decolonization can have several meanings depending on context, location, and epoch, such as the decolonization in Asia and Africa in the 1950s–1970s and the creation of independent states. In our context we need to adopt an approach to decolonization that takes into account the particularities of the present Israeli-Palestinian situation. It does not mean the departure of members of the settler society, but rather a political process that addresses the main structures and manifestations of colonialism, and the distinctions, inequities, and injustices it has produced over the past one hundred years, with the view of transforming the relationships between the two major groups into ones that are built on equality. It entails, on the part of the settler society, the willingness to abandon colonial privileges and recognition of past injustices, and for the indigenous society, the willingness to accept that the settler society, having abandoned its colonial privileges, has the legitimate right to exist as an equal partner in the new state. The same way colonialism affects all aspects of life, decolonization should also address those aspects, and should be a central theme in the constitutional design. Decolonization is at the heart of the four principles discussed earlier (equal citizenship, immigration, group rights, and transitional justice and transformative constitutionalism). In some sense, it is the means to ensure that these four principles guarantee equality and justice.

CONSTITUTIONAL DESIGN I: A UNITARY STATE

A unitary state is one in which state power is centralized—that is, there are no competing sources of state power, and the different branches of the state control exercise the same level of power in the whole territory of the state. Autonomous regions are possible, but they are not seen as constituent components of the state. A unitary state could have a number of possible constitutional frameworks.

A Liberal, Difference-Blind State

A neutral state is one that does not adopt any preference regarding its citizens' values, preferences, or principles. It views the citizen first and foremost as an individual, and provides all citizens with the full range of liberal rights regardless of their belonging. It adopts a policy of difference-blindness when it comes to citizens' identities, whether they are cultural, linguistic, ethnic, or national. Such a state does not exist in reality. While there are states that adopt a policy of neutrality in certain areas such as religion, a state cannot be neutral in areas such as language for practical reasons. Rather, what exists in reality are states that try to promote what Charles Taylor calls "the politics of universalism," that is, the promotion of equality of all citizens and the avoidance of stratification of citizens into classes or ethnic identities.[17] This could be seen as the nation-building model: the state encourages a certain identity, culture, language, and political culture.[18] This approach applies to areas that are seen as "official" or public. The state on the other hand gives the citizens belonging to minority ethnocultural groups the liberty of using their languages or practicing their cultures in the private sphere.

It should be noted that what is seen as "universal equality" is in reality not universal, as it maintains a preference for particular cultures. It does promote a hegemonic culture; as Charles Taylor puts it, it is "a particularism masquerading as the universal."[19] France is generally adopted as the archetype for this model, with its emphasis on French republican values, French culture, and French language. These are seen as "universal" even if they are particular to France.

Adopting such a model for a new state in Israel/Palestine would raise many difficulties. Under the current situation, there is no one hegemonic culture that a clear and substantive majority would support. This obstacle, however, could be surmounted by leaving the question of hegemonic culture open and where absolutely necessary, adopting cultural elements of both groups, such as officially recognizing their respective languages as official languages. While this would be transformational in the sense that it would present a break with the current situation, in which Jewish Israelis dominate the state, this transformation would be of a limited scope because of the model's narrow conception of equality. For even though it is based on equality, and there is much to admire in the emphasis on "universal equality" among citizens, this kind of equality assumes uniformity, and is contrary to the realities of most societies. This concept understands equality in its narrow sense only. It is based on respect for individual equality and does not take into account individual and collective diversity. This indifference to diversity means that eventually one culture or group, whether through numeric preponderance, political power, or economic advantage, will eventually become hegemonic.

The emphasis on equality as uniformity and difference-blindness also creates problems when it comes to group rights, especially if those rights require some form of recognition of these groups and adjustment to their special interests or needs. Similarly, this model will hinder transitional justice, for transitional justice in the context of the Israeli-Arab conflict requires acknowledging group differences and identities. Under this model, there is no means to talk about settler society and indigenous society, but only individual citizens. The same problems arise regarding decolonization: for decolonization to work, one should first identify the colonial process and the privileges it created, which would be hard to achieve in a model based on uniformity.

The Binational Model

A binational state is one that acknowledges the political presence and rights of two national groups. Those who belong to the relevant national groups are able to enjoy individual and national rights, and their right to be represented in state institutions is constitutionally protected.[20] The origins of this approach in Palestine/Israel can be traced back to the Brit Shalom group, which was later recreated as Ihud and was active among the Jewish immigrants in Palestine in the 1920s–1940s. The impetus behind this group, which was small and politically marginal, was their understanding that the Palestinians would never agree to a Jewish state in their land since that would mean that they would not be able to exercise their right to self-determination. The group believed that Jews had "historical" rights over Palestine while the Palestinian Arabs had "natural rights." To reconcile those rights they proposed binationalism: the state would be composed of two nationalities (or nations), Jews and Arabs, and both groups would have equal political rights regardless of majority or minority status.[21]

But binationalism is to a large extent an abstract and vague concept that can mean a number of political configurations. It is possible to identify four levels or types of binationalism, as explained here.

Binationalism as Declarative.   Binationalism could be expressed on a declarative level as recognition by the state, through its constitution or other legal instruments, of the fact the majority of the citizens belong to two national or ethnic groups. If such a clause is kept at the declarative level and not given normative weight, then it has the potential to satisfy the aspirations of both groups. It provides recognition without providing special rights or privileges to any group. Such a clause would be compatible with the principle of equal citizenship and would not necessarily have implications for immigration policy. It may be be vague with regards to the issue of group rights, since it would depend on how these rights would be defined and on the level of involvement of the state in protecting them. If issues such as religion, language, and culture are seen as a matter of private preference only, the state would not promote any aspect of those, but at the same time would not interfere in regulating them.

Binationalism as Cultural Autonomy and Official Adoption of Symbols.   This level complements the declarative level with active measures that give expression to group preferences. The recognition of the two groups would extend to granting some form of cultural autonomy in areas such as religion, cultural institutions, and recognition of the equal status of both languages. Additionally, the recognition would extend to state symbols (flag, anthem, emblem), which would combine elements representing both groups.

Recognition and cultural autonomy could take different forms, and those would determine its compatibility with the principles set out in the earlier section. If both groups are given *exclusive* jurisdiction on their cultural affairs, then a number of problems might arise. First, this arrangement would mean that *all* citizens have to belong to one of the groups. This raises difficulties regarding those who do not belong, or do not want to belong, to either group. Second, this emphasis on strict group differentiation might be manipulated to provide rights or services in a discriminatory manner to different groups, as is the situation today in religious services in Israel. A third problem that would arise is the problem of accountability and state control: To whom will those autonomous institutions be accountable? What is the role of the state in their regulation?

Binationalism and Immigration.   The shape of the binational state is also going to be impacted by the way it deals with the issue of immigration and citizenship policy. Since it was enacted in 1950, the Law of Return has been justified and rationalized based on the right to self-determination, namely that a state in which a specific group exercises self-determination should allow members of that group the right to immigrate to it and become citizens. As such, Jews, as a national group, should be allowed to immigrate and join their conationalists in their national home.[22] If this logic is applied to binationalism then the binational state has to allow the immigration of members of both groups, or at least facilitate it significantly. This means the preservation of the Law of Return, or some variation of it. This component of binationalism was at the heart of the binational view promoted by Brit Shalom/Ihud. The group believed that there should be numerical parity between Palestinians and Jews in Palestine, and part of their plan was to allow unlimited Jewish immigration until this numerical parity was achieved.[23] This requirement might prove to be problematic on a number of levels.

Binationalism and Governance: Conscociationalism.   The principle of consociational democracy proposed by Arendt Lijphart is the most relevant model of sharing power between multiple ethnic groups within any given state. Lijphart's model aims to share, decentralize, and limit state power. The model has a number of elements. First, it institutes power-sharing on the executive level. Second, Lijphart advocates for proportional representation of the groups in parliament and in the main institutions of the state such as the civil services, judiciary, police force, and army. Third, this model allows each group to have mutual veto power on matters of vital interest. This is especially important for minorities whose representation is not always strong. Fourth, consociational democracy ensures segmental autonomy, in the form either of federalism or of group autonomy in areas linked closely to ethnic identity.[24]

Binationalism at the level of governance is indeed a form of consociationalism where the power is shared between the two groups. There is no one model to implement this system, but the principles listed above could be implemented in a number of ways. In the Israeli/Palestinian context, binationalism could entail a bicameral parliament, a cabinet composed of equal number of individuals belonging to both groups, quota systems in public service and other state offices, and veto rights on vital interests. This seems to be the thrust of the binational state proposed by Brit Shalom/Ihud in 1946. One of the main components of their proposal was the creation of a constituent assembly which would draw up a constitution and a legislative assembly which would include equal number of Palestinians and Jews.[25] This was at a time when Palestinians out-numbered Jews two to one, though the plan included massive Jewish immigration to bring about numerical parity. Parity would also be maintained at the level of the executive through the creation of an executive council. The proposal also spoke of a Jewish Council and a corresponding Arab Council which would be responsible for the cultural affairs of each community, such as issues related to education.

Binationalism: Pitfalls and Potential.   The first problem of binationalism as a state model to resolve the Israeli-Palestinian conflict lies in defining the identity of the two nations creating this new state. Two questions arise here: Who are the two nations? And who is included in each group and who is going to decide on that? As for the first question, it is not clear whether the non-Palestinian group is Jewish (that is, composed of anyone who is religiously or culturally Jewish) or Israeli. While there is overlap between the two categories, there is definitely a big difference between them. Even though sociologically one can identify an Israeli collective that has emerged in the past seventy years, one that has features that distinguish Israelis from Jews elsewhere, Israel has refused to acknowledge this fact. Officially and legally, there is no such thing as an Israeli nation, and the only nation in Israel is the Jewish nation (*Tamarin v. The State of Israel*, 1972). On the conceptual level, stating that all Jews have a right to self-determination and a stake in the state flies in the face of contemporary practices that emphasize citizenship, and not religious or ethnic belonging, as the main criteria for being member of the state. On a practical level, especially if this arrangement is accompanied with immigration rights similar to the ones adopted today, it means that millions of Jews whose only link to Palestine is religious will be able to immigrate to it and settle in it.

Equally problematic is the issue of who would be included in each group, or who is a Jew/Israeli, and who is a Palestinian. The question of "who is a Jew" has been a serious constitutional and political question in Israel. The question of who is Palestinian may prove to be easier to answer: anybody who originates from the area of Mandate Palestine is Palestinian. Yet there are some who could not be included in this category, yet could be seen as Palestinian by association, such as political figures who played important roles in Palestinian politics. Adopting a binational model means that these two categories need to be *legally* defined, since eligibility to participate in politics and access to some services will rest on the whether an individual belongs to one group or the other.

Similarly, this emphasis on group belonging in the power-sharing mechanisms assumes that all citizens belong to these two groups. But what about those who do not fit the definition? This emphasis might lead to absurd outcomes that undermine the principles of equality and citizenship. A case in point here is Bosnia Herzegovina and the decision of the European Court of Human Rights in the *Sejdić and Finci* case. As part of the Dayton Agreement, the preamble to the Constitution of Bosnia Herzegovina describes Bosnians, Croats, and Serbs as "constituent peoples." The presidency and all legislatures (on the federal level and state level) are shared with representatives from each group. In this case, Sejdić, who is of Roma origin, and Finci, who is of Jewish origin, wanted to stand for elections, but since they did not fit any of the three "constituent peoples," they were ineligible. The court ruled that this was a violation to their right to participate in free elections and their right to be protected from discrimination (*Sejdić and Finci v. Bosnia Herzegovina*, 2009). The other side of the coin here is the problem of compelled association: those who do not want to be part of any group, in order to participate in politics, would be compelled to associate with one of the two groups.[26]

The second problem that binationalism can give rise to relates to its emphasis on national/ethnic belonging as the main political criteria for belonging to the polity. It thus could be more conducive to highlighting what divides a polity rather than what unites it. Political power channeled through the ethnic/national affiliation makes membership in the communal group, rather than citizenship and membership in the state, the source of political power and rights. This might lead to both groups adopting initiatives to develop and highlight their particular identity in a manner not necessarily constructive for creating a new collective sense of "we," or a new common state identity.

In addition to these particular concerns, the academic literature points out other salient critiques of the consociational model. Critics argue that consociationalism tends to strengthen the elites of the national or ethnic groups, because its success relies on the elites' ability to demonstrate that they can enforce the consociational arrangements within their respective groups. Critics also observe that consociationalism limits competition among elites over issues of public concern and policy questions, which in turns produces weak and undemocratic government. Moreover, consociationalism hinders politics of economic distribution, especially because it focuses on cultural/ethnic recognition and ignores social class. Questions of allocation of resources can easily escalate into disputes between the two groups, especially in situations of economic disparity as in our case. Additionally, since consociationalism requires many actors and political parties to be in power in order to form of a broad ruling coalition, the official opposition tends to be small and very weak. Consociationalism effectively eliminates or significantly weakens official opposition, which is essential for the functioning of a democracy. This, according to critics of consociationalism, weakens democracy.[27]

Consociationalism is also likely to violate some of the principles mentioned above. Most significantly, it could potentially violate the principle of equal citizenship especially if the equally divided legislature advocated by Ihud were to be implemented. While the numerical composition of the population of a binational state is hard to assess at this point, and may well be close to parity, it is hard to guarantee that it will stay the same, and if this happens, an equally divided legislature will give more power to the group that is a minority. This could be dangerous in situations where, for example, the ethnic/national divide also overlaps with a socioeconomic divide. Similarly, because of the general weakness and instability of the state under this model, it would be hard to implement transitional justice initiatives and changes that are conducive to decolonization.

Despite these critiques and potential problems, some of the ideas that consociationalism promotes could be employed without emphasizing their ethnic/national dimension. The adoption of a parliamentary system, proportionate representation (of parties) in parliament, recognition of ethnic/national groups, language rights, and some form of cultural autonomy are all ideas that could be used and implemented without necessarily adopting some of the problematic aspects of consociationalism. This way, power is shared and diffused without necessarily strengthening sectarianism.

A Multicultural State

Principles.   A multicultural state is one that could potentially combine many of the benefits of a binational model and at the same time avoid the potential risks. There is no one universally agreed upon definition of multiculturalism, for it can take a number of different shapes or models.[28] The definition that Will Kymilcka, one of the leading theorists of multiculturalism, adopts could help clarify the concept. Kymlicka sees multiculturalism as "the view that states should not only uphold the familiar set of common civil, political, and social rights of citizenship that are protected in all constitutional liberal democracies, but also adopt various group-specific rights or policies that are intended to recognize and accommodate the distinctive identities and aspirations of ethnocultural groups."[29] Kymlicka identifies three principles useful in struggles to achieve multiculturalism.[30] The first is the idea that the state belongs to all citizens equally. The second principle involves the state according "recognition and accommodation to the history, language, and culture of non-dominant groups, as it does to dominant groups." The third principle directly addresses the issue of past injustices: "a multicultural state acknowledges the historic injustice that was done to minority/non-dominant groups by these policies of assimilation and exclusion, and manifests a willingness to offer some sort of remedy or rectification for them."[31] These three principles could help in devising a state model that maintains group recognition without entrenching group privileges and making them the main marker of politics.

Equality and Cultural Autonomy.   The starting point of such a model is equality. In our context, the state should recognize that nearly all citizens belong to one of two groups, Palestinians and Jewish Israelis, with different languages, culture, and history, and should give these groups a measure of cultural autonomy. This recognition includes recognition of Arabic and Hebrew as official languages of equal status, and recognition of the right of citizens to receive services from and communicate with the state in both languages. Also, special arrangements should be adopted to allow for the use of either language in government offices (both central and local), parliament, and the courts. Similarly, the state should adopt a policy of bilingualism and encourage (and in cases of critical services or monopolistic companies, mandate) the use of both languages. Both languages should be taught in all schools, whether public or private.

Cultural autonomy is commonly understood as allowing members of a distinct group to manage matters that are related to cultural affiliation, such as language, education, cultural and artistic production, and religious institutions. The state is a major player in these areas, and its policies should, as much as possible, leave the decisions on these cultural issues in the hands of the group as recognition of cultural distinctiveness. At the same time, policies encouraging cultural autonomy should be designed in a manner that highlights equality, diversity, and openness, and not adversity and difference.

A number of guiding principles could be adopted to achieve these goals. A major principle is related to group definition and membership. In our context, where the question of who is Jewish Israeli and who is Palestinian seems to be complicated and could potentially lead to disagreements, the best marker to define a group could be language. This way we can avoid the thorny question of group definition and membership and still maintain group recognition in a manner that is significant for the groups involved. As such, in all areas and institutions of cultural autonomy—except for religion—the autonomous institutions should first and foremost be based on language. In this way, membership in each group will be based on self-identification and preference and not, as it is today in Israel, based on religious criteria or compelled identification.

Other principles could be adopted to guarantee equality and openness, such as accountability. Government departments that provide cultural services should be accountable to the public as a whole, and not just to the particular community they serve. They should be committed to the principles of equality and diversity. They should not discriminate against individuals in the provision of service even if those individuals are deemed not to belong to the linguistic group they are intended to serve. Similarly, other administrative law norms that guarantee fairness and accountability should apply.

It should be highlighted that equality in the context of a multicultural state in historic Palestine cannot be abstract. Policies aimed at equality should be informed by decolonization such that the new constitutional framework is a way to decolonize the state apparatus and address the wrongs of the past. They should make clear that this conception of equality aims to remove the privileges of the settler society rather than recreate them or rename them. They should also support and facilitate measures of transitional justice, as equality cannot be achieved without addressing the injustices of the past.

Multiculturalism and Democratic Governance.   Multiculturalism does not offer specific guidelines about constitutional arrangements beyond the main principles discussed above. However one can use these principles, and borrow from some of the ideas discussed under consociationalism, to provide a framework that will help reflect the diversity of the population in the governing bodies and guarantee that no one group can abuse power in a manner that affects the rights of the other group, all while maintaining equal citizenship as the founding principle of the constitutional order.

The starting point should be constitutional entrenchment of the principles that are at the heart of multiculturalism such as equality, bilingualism, recognition of group rights, commitment to diversity, and acknowledgment of historical injustice. Constitutional amendments changing such principles should be possible with a large majority vote only. The Constitution of South Africa for example, provides that the principles of democracy, human dignity, nonracialism, and nonsexism may be amended only with the support of 75 percent of members of Parliament and the support of six out of nine provinces. These principles should be not just declarative in nature but also constitutional principles that legislation should observe and be compatible with.

Similarly, the system of governance could be designed in a manner in line with the general principles of multiculturalism. A parliamentary system is preferable to a presidential system because of its more collaborative nature. While a "first past the post" voting system (where the country is divided into regions, and the candidate with the highest number of votes wins) would potentially provide a result representative of the population because of the current state of segregation, it is not the most desirable one. A mix between a proportionate representation voting system where the whole country is seen as one electoral district, and a number of relatively large electoral districts would probably be a better way to guarantee adequate representation and at the same time provide candidates from different backgrounds with incentives to cooperate with each other. Such arrangements can guarantee that parliament is representative of the general population, and that the cabinet will also have significant representation of both groups without having to specify quotas in the constitution.

A multicultural system seems to be the one that is most compatible with principles outlined above. It guarantees equality both for individuals and groups, provides a significant measure of recognition of group identity, allows significant cultural autonomy, but at the same time maintains an emphasis on the idea that the main relationship between the individual and the state is that of citizenship and not ethnic/religious background. The ideas of transitional justice and decolonization could fit into this model given its emphasis on acknowledging historical injustice.

While multiculturalism seems to be a satisfactory model that could address many of the challenges in our context, it is important to be aware of the critiques leveled against it. Two critiques are especially important. First, critics argue that the emphasis on culture and identity diverts attention from social and economic justice and undermines class solidarity.[32] Second is the question of vulnerable internal minorities, or minorities within minorities. The emphasis on the protection of equality of group identity might worsen existing inequalities within each group.[33] Subgroups such as women, sexual minorities, and religious dissidents might be adversely affected by members of their own group. These critiques are indeed significant, but they could also be addressed using other tools.

CONSTITUTIONAL DESIGN II: A FEDERAL STATE

Federalism: Principles and Rationale

While there is no one universally agreed upon definition of federalism, a useful definition that captures the essence of many federal arrangements is William Riker's. Riker sees a constitution as federal "if (1) two levels of government rule the same land and people, (2) each level has at least one area of action in which it is autonomous, and (3) there is some guarantee (even though merely a statement in the constitution) of the autonomy of each government in its own sphere."[34] Essentially, the powers of the state are divided between the central or federal government and the regional or state government. The division of powers varies from one country to another depending on the history and the needs of each state. Some, like Switzerland, are very highly decentralized, and the cantons (the regional unit in Switzerland) enjoy a wide range of powers, many of them are exclusive. The cantons hold so much power that the preamble of the Federal Constitution of the Swiss Confederation names the cantons, in addition to the people, as the "authors" of the constitution. Other countries, such as Germany, are more centralized even within a federal framework.

Supporters of federalism argue that it bolsters democracy, as it gives the local population more voice in public affairs through the tiered government system. It also allows more political participation, especially that of small communities. Similarly, the proximity between citizens and local decision-makers means more responsive government. Supporters also argue that the division of state power between two levels of government limits this power and contributes to protecting liberties. Some theorists highlight the freedom of movement and choice of residence offered by a federal state, which makes it easier for people to move to like-minded communities.[35]

Federalism Implemented: Possible Scenarios

The overwhelming majority of federal states use territory as the basis of federalism. The exceptions, mainly Belgium and Bosnia and Herzegovina, combine the territorial dimension with a communal (ethnic/national) dimension. Territorial federalism is based on territory, and the region, state, or province has powers that are distinct and independent from the power of the federal government. The division of power is usually done through the constitution. In situations where the constituent states are not preexisting political units with defined borders, the most important question is the question of internal borders. In postconflict federalism the territorial units are designed in a manner to give national minorities a majority in their own regions.[36] This, it is thought, will dampen the secessionist sentiments of minorities, will provide a measure of control and participation at least on the local level, will provide regional jurisdiction over education, language, and other cultural aspects, and will address some of the demands of the national groups.

In our case, one approach would be to adopt the 1967 line, creating two territories where each group—Palestinians and Israeli Jews—will form a clear majority in one of the two. It would also be possible to make some amendments to the line to account for major population centers that belong to the other group. Another option would be to adopt a larger number of units with significantly smaller territories. This would allow for a significant measure of self-rule for the residents of the units; given the existing state of segregation, those units would likely be homogenous, with the exception of some highly mixed areas such as parts of Haifa, Yaffa, and Jerusalem.

Another important question concerns the powers of the territorial units in a federal state. In postconflict federalism, regional powers are usually given control on matters related to language, religious services, education, and other cultural aspects as a way to satisfy the aspirations of the particular group living in that area. The scope of regional power can be more challenging or contested in situations where questions of the distribution of natural resources (such as oil, gas, minerals) and their division arise. In the Israeli-Palestinian context though, this is not a major concern and the cultural aspects remain the most important domain for asserting regional autonomy. All other state functions and powers would be controlled by the federal state.

The other model of federalism is one that combines territorialism with consociationalism based on national/ethnic or linguistic dimensions. Belgium and Bosnia Herzegovina are the prime examples. Bosnia and Herzegovina is divided into two federal "entities": Republika Sparska and the Federation of Bosnia and Herzegovina. The federal legislature is composed of two chambers with quotas for the constituent peoples (Bosnians, Serbs, and Croats). The federal presidency is a joint presidency with the three peoples represented. The federal government has powers in limited areas related to international relations, trade, customs, immigration, and monetary policy. All other functions and powers are retained by the "entities."

The Belgian model is equally complicated. Belgium, as Article 1 of its constitution states, "is composed of Communities and Regions." There are three regions: Flanders (mostly Dutch-speaking), Wallonia (mostly French-speaking), and the mixed district of Brussels. There are three recognized communities, the French, Flemish, and the German-speaking community. The communities have powers in functional areas that are of cultural concern for the different linguistic groups, and in what is known as "person-related matters," which include certain aspects of healthcare, family policy, and education. The jurisdiction of the communities, however, is territorially defined, and each territorially defined region has power in economic areas and has its own elected parliament. In Brussels, for example, each community has authority with regards to members of its linguistic group. On the federal level, Belgium has a bicameral parliament. The constitution provides more seats for the Dutch-speaking population than for the French-speaking population, although linguistic parity is maintained in the federal Council of Ministers. For changing any current arrangement, the constitution requires a two-thirds majority as well as a majority of each linguistic group.[37]

A federal system that combined territorialism with communal belonging would be something along the lines of Belgium or Bosnia Herzegovina: it would add a layer of consociationalism to the federal structure. The particular powers given to the states or regions would be a matter to be decided, and a number of approaches could be taken. But since our concern here is with the cultural rights of national and linguistic groups, the states or the regions would have control over rights and services related to culture. Cultural autonomy (education, religion, language, et cetera) therefore would be overseen on the regional level. The region or the state would adopt policies and administer the cultural institutions. In addition, other powers could be given to the regions or states in service areas such as health, social security, housing, and other fields that deal with the particular needs of the local population.

On the federal level, a number of options could be adopted. In the 1940s, Ihud proposed a federal structure with a federal parliament and federal executive based on parity.[38] They also proposed an Arab Council and Jewish Council for cultural affairs, and smaller administrative units (counties). In some sense, the proposal by Ihud resembles the Belgian model in that it combines federalism with consociationalism.

Federalism: Promises and Risks

Many critics argue that the promises of postconflict federalism are exaggerated. Some even suggest that federalism in this context is likely to exacerbate conflict and not solve it. They contend that the model is unstable and likely to reinforce conflict between identity groups. Simple policy questions, they argue, will be recast as conflicts or tensions between national groups. Additionally, the fact that the different groups would be in control of different regions—even if only partially and within the confines of federalism—means that they could use resources and institutional tools in order to push for greater autonomy.[39] Another problem related to instability is posed by the borders between the states or regions. On the one hand, drawing borders in order to create regions that represent national or ethnic minorities is one of the rationales for adopting a federal model. On the other hand, studies show that borders that are designed to create homogenous populations are unstable.[40] Some suggest that creating heterogeneous territorial units is more likely to force the different groups to cooperate. Economic equality is another major issue that should be flagged. Several studies show that there is a correlation between income inequality and federalism.[41] Federalism, and decentralization in general, tend to preserve the economic status quo.[42]

All of these critiques are relevant if a federal model is adopted. It is possible to imagine states or provinces using resources in a manner that disproportionately benefits the national majority in their areas, or in a manner that is designed to achieve goals that are contrary to the goals of the federal state or the spirit of the political settlement. For example, states could act to strengthen the bond between individuals and their local state at the expense of the bond with the federal state. Similarly, the question of economic redistribution would be a thorny one, especially since the Palestinian-majority states/regions will be economically weaker given the current economic realities. For a federal model to work in our context, the federal state should have ultimate say in economic matters including the ability to overturn the policies and legislation of the states. Other risks include the fact that it will be impossible to create regions that are homogenous: there will always be a minority. Similarly, language presents a serious challenge: Would the regions be allowed to choose just one language for administration and service provision? In addition to these particular challenges that federalism would present, almost all of the challenges and risks discussed under binationalism are relevant when we consider federalism.

Given the nature of federalism and the risks in this model, there are important questions related to the compatibility of the model with the principles discussed above. While in theory the model could be accompanied by assurances regarding equality, comparative studies show its weakness when it comes to redistribution and inequality. Similarly, even though it satisfies the requirements related to group rights, it runs the risk of putting too much emphasis on group identity and group political power in a manner that might intensify tensions. The tendency to preserve the status quo that comparative studies associate with federalism could also cast some doubt about the ability of the state to implement transitional justice schemes or make changes in the context of decolonization.

HUMAN RIGHTS

The protection of human rights through an enforceable constitutional bill of rights has become an important feature of peaceful settlement of protracted ethnic/national conflict since the 1990s.[43] The Constitution of the Republic of South Africa is a good example. The Constitution of Bosnia and Herzegovina, which was adopted as an annex to the Dayton Agreement, integrated the European Convention on Human Rights and its protocols. The European Convention on Human Rights also played a role in the Good Friday Agreements in Northern Ireland.

One of the main debates in constitutional law and constitutional theory concerns judicially enforceable bills of rights, which give the judiciary the power to review legislation. Judicial review of legislation raises a number of problems. The rationale behind judicial review is that the legislature, as an organ of the state created and bound by the constitution, acts within its powers only when its actions do not violate the principles of the constitution, including the bill of rights. The problem arises when the legislative body is democratically elected. Here the conflict is between democracy, represented by the democratically elected parliament, and the idea of constitutionalism—the idea that powers of the state are limited by the constitution.

This debate has been one of the central debates in constitutional law, especially Anglo-American constitutional thought.[44] While cogent arguments are presented by both sides, the main question that concerns us here is the possible role that a bill of rights could play in the one-state model, and the desirability of such an approach. Some of the arguments in the debate on judicial review could be helpful. One of the most spirited opponents of judicial review is the constitutional theorist Jeremy Waldron. Waldron argues that judicial review is illegitimate from a democratic point of view, and that democratically elected legislatures are better suited to protect rights. His argument, however, is qualified: it is conditional upon satisfying a number of assumptions. Waldron's assumptions are

(1) democratic institutions in reasonably good working order, including a representative legislature elected on the basis of universal adult suffrage; (2) a set of judicial institutions, again in reasonably good order, set up on a nonrepresentative basis to hear individual lawsuits, settle disputes, and uphold the rule of law; (3) a commitment on the part of most members of the society and most of its officials to the idea of individual and minority rights; and (4) persisting, substantial, and good faith disagreement about rights (i.e., about what the commitment to rights actually amounts to and what its implications are) among the member of the society who are committed to the idea of rights.[45]

While the aspiration is to satisfy all these criteria, it is hard to anticipate whether this would be achieved in our case, especially in the transitional period. If they were not achieved, even according to the strongest arguments against judicial review, a bill of rights would be necessary.

Tom Ginsburg advances the theory that bills of rights serve as a form of political insurance in the context of transitions to democracy.[46] Hegemonic groups or parties who anticipate losing their control over the political system as a result of the democratic redistribution of political power are interested in being able to access a forum where they can challenge the legislature. In our context, where we have two large groups, and where it is not entirely clear which group will constitute a majority in the electoral sense (although it is expected that the number of Palestinians will increase if a significant number of refugees decide to return), this insurance model of judicial review could be helpful for both parties. In constitutional negotiations between the groups, each group would highlight and insist on constitutional protection of the issues that are of utmost interest for them.

One principle that should be given prominent status in the bill of rights is equality. Equality is the main guiding principle for any settlement based on a single state (regardless of the model adopted). In this context, the South African constitution provides a good example to follow: equality is mentioned in the preamble and in section 1, which can be amended only with a three-quarters majority of members of Parliament, and is also protected as part of the bill of rights. Equality should also be understood in the context of the conflict. The approach to equality should be one that is informed by decolonization and one that would allow for and even promote transitional justice and affirmative action. It should, for example, allow and facilitate measures such as land restitution and reparations.

Constitutional protection should not be limited to civil and political rights only. Social and economic rights should also be protected constitutionally. In a reality of deep social and economic inequality, the protection of social and economic rights is especially important in order to guarantee equality as well as the ability to participate in redistributive projects that can help redress economic inequalities. Beyond these fundamental ideas about the importance of social and economic rights, pragmatic factors also militate in favor of providing protection for such rights: the weaker (and more numerous) citizens will have an interest in the success of such a settlement.

EPILOGUE

The different models examined in this chapter show that the one-state solution is not necessarily one concrete idea. A variety of models could fit under this category, and each model's efficacy, potential, risks, and pitfalls depend to a very large extent on the details of its structure and implementation. As we saw, some models are more desirable and more amenable to addressing the important challenges, while others may end up recreating similar problems and even introducing new ones. The primary conclusion is that a number of models exist that could be described as democratic, and each model has its promises and risks. The hard task here is deciding which option to adopt. It is therefore very important, as a starting point for thinking about constitutional design, to have a clear understanding of the problems and challenges that need to be addressed, as well as a clear vision of future objectives to be achieved by the constitution. While some of these challenges and objectives were discussed in the first part of this chapter, these are inevitably intertwined with the social, political, historical, and economic questions discussed elsewhere in this book. The constitutional model should not be seen as an end, but rather a means to address challenges and achieve social and political ends.

The harder questions, therefore, are not the questions about what is legally desirable or what are the best practices in relation to constitutional design, but rather questions that go to the core of the political project that is being sought, namely decolonization, equality, and/or justice. The nature of the political project sought will dictate whether the constitution facilitates the political goals or hinders them. A constitution may include many clauses dealing with democracy, human dignity, diversity, and human rights and other concepts which sound very desirable when put on paper and discussed by jurists. But these ideas and concepts should go beyond debates among lawyers and elites and should also become the local currency of the population, as this is the ultimate test for the success of any postpartition constitutional design in Israel-Palestine. For this to happen the population should be able to see that the constitution is addressing its concerns and facilitating its political project of decolonization and guaranteed equality for all.

NOTES

1. Shourideh Molavi, *Stateless Citizenship: The Palestinian-Arab Citizens of Israel* (Leiden: Brill, 2013); Mazen Masri, *The Dynamics of Exclusionary Constitutionalism: Israel as a Jewish and Democratic State* (Oxford: Hart Publishing, 2017); Nadim Rouhana and Sahar Huneidi, *Israel and its Palestinian Citizens: Ethnic Privileges in the Jewish State* (Cambridge: Cambridge University Press, 2017).

2. Masri, *Dynamics of Exclusionary Constitutionalism.*

3. Masri, *Dynamics of Exclusionary Constitutionalism*, 101–25.

4. Raef Zreik, "Notes on the Value of Theory: Readings in the Law of Return—A Polemic," *Law and Ethics of Human Rights* 2, no. 1 (2008): 1–44; Hassan Jabareen, "Hobbesian Citizenship: How the Palestinians Became a Minority in Israel," in *Multiculturalism and Minority Rights in the Arab World*, edited by Will Kymlicka (Oxford: Oxford University Press, 2014); Masri, *Dynamics of Exclusionary Constitutionalism.*

5. *Toshbeim v. Minister of Interior*, 2004, para. 23.

6. *Toshbeim v. Minister of Interior*, 733.

7. The sources and literature on the issue of the right of return are immense. One of the main sources is UN General Assembly Resolution 194 (III), which resolved "that the refugees wishing to return to their homes and live at peace with their neighbours should be permitted to do so at the earliest practicable date." For a review of the literature, see Mazen Masri, "The Implications of the Acquisition of a New Nationality for the Right of Return of Palestinian Refugees," *Asian Journal of International Law* 5, no. 2 (2015): 356–86.

8. While Palestinians who are citizens of Israel are entitled to vote in the parliamentary elections, their participation does not influence legislation or policy.

9. Juan Méndez, "Constitutionalism and Transitional Justice," in *The Oxford Handbook of Comparative Constitutional Law*, edited by Michel Rosenfeld and András Sajó, 1,270–86 (Oxford: Oxford University Press, 2012).

10. Karl Klare, "Legal and Culture Transformative Constitutionalism," *South African Journal on Human Rights* 14, no. 1 (1998): 146–88, 146.

11. Dennis Davis and Karl Klare, "Transformative Constitutionalism and the Common and Customary Law," *South African Journal on Human Rights* 26, no. 3 (2010): 403–509, 403.

12. Patrick Wolfe, "Nation and MiscegeNation: Discursive Continuity in the Post-Mabo Era," *Social Analysis* 36 (1994): 93–152, 96.

13. Alan Dershowitz, *The Case for Israel* (Hoboken: John Wiley and Sons, 2003); Amnon Rubenstein and Alexander Yakoboson, *Israel and Family of Nations* (New York: Routledge, 2009).

14. Fayez Sayegh, *Zionist Colonialism in Palestine* (Beirut: Research Center–Palestine Liberation Organization, 1965); Maxime Rodinson, *Israel: A Colonial Settler State?* (New York: Monad Press, 1973); Edward Said, *The Question of Palestine* (New York: Times Books, 1979); Nahla Abdo and Nira Yuval-Davis, "Palestine, Israel and the Zionist Settler Project," in *Unsettling Settler Societies*, edited by Daiva Stasiulis and Nira Yuvl-Davis, 291–322 (London: Sage Publications, 1995).

15. Gershon Shafir, *Land, Labor and the Origins of the Israeli-Palestinian Conflict, 1882—1914* (Berkeley: University of California Press, 1989); Gershon Shafir and Yoav Peled, *Being Israeli: The Dynamics of Multiple Citizenship* (Cambridge: Cambridge University Press, 2004). Baruch Kimmerling, *Clash of Identities: Explorations in Israel and Palestinian Societies* (New York: Columbia University Press, 2008).

16. Patrick Wolfe, "Purchase by Other Means: The Palestinian Nakba and Zionism's Conquest of Economics," *Settler Colonial Studies* 2, no. 1 (2012): 133–71, 133.

17. Charles Taylor, "The Politics of Recognition," in *Multiculturalism*, edited by Amy Gutmann, 25–74 (Princeton, NJ: Princeton University Press, 1994).

18. Alan Patten, "Beyond the Dichotomy of Universalism and Difference: Four Responses to Cultural Diversity," in *Constitutional Design for Divided Societies: Integration or Accommodation?* edited by Sujit Choudhry, 91–110 (Oxford: Oxford University Press, 2008).

19. Taylor, "Politics of Recognition," 44.

20. Bashir Bashir, "The Strengths and Weaknesses of Integrative Solutions for the Israeli-Palestinian Conflict," *Middle East Journal* 70, no. 4 (2016): 560–78.

21. Martin Buber, Judah Leon Magnes, and Moshe Smilanksy, *Palestine: A Bi-National State*, (Jerusalem: Ihud Association of Palestine, 1946); Leila Farsakh, "A Common State in Israel–Palestine: Historical Origins and Lingering Challenges," *Ethnopolitics* 15, no. 4 (2016): 380–92.

22. Ruth Gavison, "The Jewish State: The Principle Justification and the Desirable Character," *Tkhelet* 13 (2002): 50 [Hebrew]; Aharon Barak, *A Judge in a Democratic Society* (Jerusalem: Nevo, 2004).

23. Buber, Magnes, and Smilansky, *Palestine*; Farsakh, "A Common State in Israel–Palestine."

24. Arendt Lijphart, *Democracy in Plural Societies: A Comparative Exploration* (New Haven, CT: Yale University Press, 1977); Arendt Lijphart, "Constitutional Design for Divided Societies," *Journal of Democracy* 15, no. 2 (2004): 96–109, 96.

25. Buber, Magnes, and Smilansky, *Palestine.*

26. Sujit Choudhry, "Group Rights in Comparative Constitutional Law: Culture, Economics, or Political Power?" in *The Oxford Handbook of Comparative Constitutional Law*, edited Michel Rosenfeld and András Sajó, 1,099–123 (Oxford: Oxford University Press, 2012).

27. Courtney Jung and Ian Shapiro, "South Africa's Negotiated Transition: Democracy, Opposition, and the New Constitutional Order," *Politics and Society* 23, no. 3 (1995): 269–308, 273; Rudey Andeweg, "Consociational Democracy," *Annual Review of Political Science* 3 (2000): 509–36, 509; Donald Rothschild and Philip Roeder, "Power Sharing as an Impediment to Peace and Democracy," in *Sustainable Peace: Power and Democracy after Civil Wars*, edited by Donald Rothschild and Philip Roeder, 29–50 (Ithaca, NY: Cornell University, 2005); John Nagel and Mary Clancy, *Shared Society or Benign Apartheid? Understanding Peace-Building in Divided Societies* (London: Palgrave, 2010).

28. Will Kymlicka, *Multicultural Odysseys: Navigating the New International Politics of Diversity* (Oxford: Oxford University Press, 2007).

29. Kymlicka, *Multicultural Odysseys*, 61.

30. Kymlicka, *Multicultural Odysseys*, 66.

31. Kymlicka, *Multicultural Odysseys*, 66.

32. Brian Barry, *Culture and Equality: An Egalitarian Critique of Multiculturalism* (Cambridge: Harvard University Press, 2001).

33. Leslie Green, "Internal Minorities and Their Rights," in *Group Rights*, edited by Judith Baker, 101–17 (Toronto: University of Toronto Press, 1994); Ayelet Shachar, *Multicultural Jurisdictions: Cultural Differences and Women's Rights* (Cambridge: Cambridge University Press, 2001).

34. William Riker, *Federalism: Origin, Operation, Significance* (Boston: Little, Brown and Company, 1964), 11.

35. Sujit Choudhry and Nathan Hume, "Federalism, Devolution and Secession: From Classical to Post-conflict Federalism," in *Comparative Constitutional Law*, edited by Tom Ginsburg and Rosalind Dixon, 356–86 (Cheltenham: Edward Elgar, 2011); Daniel Halberstam, "Federalism: Theory, Policy, Law," in *The Oxford Handbook of Comparative Constitutional Law*, edited by Michel Rosenfeld and András Sajó, 576–608 (Oxford: Oxford University Press, 2012).

36. Choudhry and Hume, "Federalism, Devolution and Secession."

37. Maurice Adams, "Disabling Constitutionalism. Can the Politics of the Belgian Constitution Be Explained?" *International Journal of Constitutional Law* 12, no. 2 (2014): 279–302, 279.

38. Buber, Magnes, and Smilansky, *Palestine.*

39. Philip Roeder, "Ethnofederalism and the Mismanagement of Conflicting Nationalisms," *Regional and Federal Studies* 19, no 2 (2009): 203–219, 203; Dawn Brancati, "Decentralization: Fueling or Dampening the Flames of Ethnic Conflict and Secessionism," *International Organizations* 60, no. 3 (2006): 651–85, 651.

40. Donald Horowitz, *Ethnic Groups in Conflict*, 2nd ed. (Berkeley: University of California Press, 2000); Henry Hale, "Divided We Stand: Institutional Sources of Ethnofederal State Survival and Collapse," *World Politics* 56 (January 2004): 165–93, 165.

41. Vicki Birchfield and Markus Crepaz, "The Impact of Constitutional Structures and Collective and Competitive Veto Points on Income Inequality in Industrialized Democracies," *European Journal of Political Research* 34 (1998): 175–200, 175.

42. Barry Weingast, "The Economic Role of Political Institutions: Market Preserving Federalism and Economic Development," *Journal of Law, Economics, and Organization* 11 (1995): 1–31, 1; Pablo Beramendi, "Inequality and the Territorial Fragmentation of Solidarity," *International Organization* 61 (2007): 783–820, 783.

43. Sujit Choudhry, "After the Rights Revolution: Bills of Rights in the Postconflict State," *Annual Review of Law and Social Science* 6 (2010): 301–22, 301.

44. For a good summary, see Nimer Sultany, "The State of Progressive Constitutional Theory: The Paradox of Constitutional Democracy and the Project of Political Justification," *Harvard Civil Rights-Civil Liberties Law Review* 47 (2012): 371–455, 371.

45. Jeremy Waldron, "The Core of the Case against Judicial Review," *Yale Law Journal* 115 (2006): 1,346–1,406, 1,360.

46. Tom Ginsburg, *Judicial Review in New Democracies: Constitutional Courts in Asian Cases* (Cambridge: Cambridge University Press, 2003).

BIBLIOGRAPHY

Abdo, Nahla, and Nira Yuval-Davi. "Palestine, Israel and the Zionist Settler Project," In *Unsettling Settler Societies*, edited by Daiva Stasiulis and Nira Yuvl-Davis, 291–322. London: Sage Publications, 1995.

Adams, Maurice. "Disabling Constitutionalism: Can the Politics of the Belgian Constitution Be Explained?" *International Journal of Constitutional Law* 12, no. 2 (2014): 279–302.

Andeweg, Rudey. "Consociational Democracy." *Annual Review of Political Science* 3 (2000): 29–50.

Barak, Aharon. *A Judge in a Democratic Society*. Jerusalem: Nevo, 2004. Hebrew.

Barry, Brian. *Culture and Equality: An Egalitarian Critique of Multiculturalism*. Cambridge, MA: Harvard University Press, 2001.

Bashir, Bashir. "The Strengths and Weaknesses of Integrative Solutions for the Israeli-Palestinian Conflict." *Middle East Journal* 70, no. 4 (2016): 560–78.

Beramendi, Pablo. "Inequality and the Territorial Fragmentation of Solidarity." *International Organization* 61 (January 2007): 165–93.

Birchfield, Vicki, and Markus Crepaz, "The Impact of Constitutional Structures and Collective and Competitive Veto Points on Income Inequality in Industrialized Democracies." *European Journal of Political Research* 34 (1998): 175–200.

Brancati, Dawn. "Decentralization: Fueling or Dampening the Flames of Ethnic Conflict and Secessionism." *International Organizations* 60, no. 3 (2006): 651–85.

Buber, Martin, Judah Leon Magnes, and Moshe Smilansky. *Palestine: A Bi-National State*. Jerusalem: Ihud Association of Palestine, 1946.

Choudhry, Sujit. "After the Rights Revolution: Bills of Rights in the Postconflict State." *Annual Review of Law and Social Science* 6 (2010): 301–22.

———. "Group Rights in Comparative Constitutional Law: Culture, Economics, or Political Power?" In *The Oxford Handbook of Comparative Constitutional Law*, edited by Michel Rosenfeld and András Sajó, 1,099–1,123. Oxford: Oxford University Press, 2012.

Choudhry, Sujit, and Nathan Hume. "Federalism, Devolution and Secession: From Classical to Post-conflict Federalism." In *Comparative Constitutional Law*, edited by Tom Ginsburg and Rosalind Dixon, 356–86. Cheltenham: Edward Elgar, 2011.

Davis, Dennis, and Karl Klare, "Transformative Constitutionalism and the Common and Customary Law." *South African Journal on Human Rights* 26, no. 3 (2010): 403–509.

Dershowitz, Alan. *The Case for Israel*. Hoboken, NJ: John Wiley and Sons, 2003.

Farsakh, Leila. "A Common State in Israel–Palestine: Historical Origins and Lingering Challenges." *Ethnopolitics* 15, no. 4 (2016): 380–92.

Gavison, Ruth. "The Jewish State: The Principle Justification and the Desirable Character." *Tkhelet* 13 (2002). [Hebrew.]

Ginsburg, Tom. *Judicial Review in New Democracies: Constitutional Courts in Asian Cases*. Cambridge: Cambridge University Press, 2003.

Green, Leslie. "Internal Minorities and Their Rights." In *Group Rights*, edited by Judith Baker, 101–17. Toronto: University of Toronto Press, 1994.

Halberstam, Daniel. "Federalism: Theory, Policy, Law." In *The Oxford Handbook of Comparative Constitutional Law*, edited by Michel Rosenfeld and András Sajó, 576–608. Oxford: Oxford University Press, 2012.

Hale, Henry. "Divided We Stand: Institutional Sources of Ethnofederal State Survival and Collapse." *World Politics* 56 (2004): 165–93.

Horowitz, Donald. *Ethnic Groups in Conflict.* 2nd ed. Berkeley: University of California Press, 2000.

Jabareen, Hassan. "Hobbesian Citizenship: How the Palestinians Became a Minority in Israel." In *Multiculturalism and Minority Rights in the Arab World*, edited by Will Kymlicka, 189–218. Oxford: Oxford University Press, 2014.

Jung, Courtney, and Ian Shapiro, "South Africa's Negotiated Transition: Democracy, Opposition, and the New Constitutional Order," *Politics and Society* 23, no. 3 (1995): 269–308.

Kimmerling, Baruch. *Clash of Identities: Explorations in Israel and Palestinian Societies.* New York: Columbia University Press, 2008.

Klare, Karl. "Legal and Culture Transformative Constitutionalism." *South African Journal on Human Rights* 14, no. 1 (1998): 146–88.

Kymlicka, Will. *Multicultural Odysseys: Navigating the New International Politics of Diversity.* Oxford: Oxford University Press, 2007.

Lijphart, Arend. "Constitutional Design for Divided Societies." *Journal of Democracy* 15, no. 2 (2004): 96–109.

———. *Democracy in Plural Societies: A Comparative Exploration.* New Haven, CT: Yale University Press, 1977.

Masri, Mazen. *The Dynamics of Exclusionary Constitutionalism: Israel as a Jewish and Democratic State.* Oxford: Hart Publishing, 2017.

———. "The Implications of the Acquisition of a New Nationality for the Right of Return of Palestinian Refugees." *Asian Journal of International Law* 5, no. 2 (2015): 356–86.

Méndez, Juan E. "Constitutionalism and Transitional Justice." In *The Oxford Handbook of Comparative Constitutional Law*, edited by Michel Rosenfeld and András Sajó, 1,270–86. Oxford: Oxford University Press, 2012.

Molavi, Shourideh. *Stateless Citizenship: The Palestinian-Arab Citizens of Israel.* Leiden: Brill, 2013.

Nagel, John, and Mary Alice Clancy. *Shared Society or Benign Apartheid? Understanding Peace-Building in Divided Societies.* London: Palgrave, 2010.

Patten, Alan. "Beyond the Dichotomy of Universalism and Difference: Four Responses to Cultural Diversity." In *Constitutional Design for Divided Societies: Integration or Accommodation?* edited by Sujit Choudhry, 91–110. Oxford: Oxford University Press, 2008.

Riker, William. *Federalism: Origin, Operation, Significance.* Boston: Little, Brown and Company, 1964.

Rodinson, Maxime. *Israel: A Colonial Settler State?* New York: Monad Press, 1973.

Roeder, Philip. "Ethnofederalism and the Mismanagement of Conflicting Nationalisms." *Regional and Federal Studies* 19, no 2 (2009): 203–19.

Rothschild, Donald, and Philip Roeder. "Power Sharing as an Impediment to Peace and Democracy." In *Sustainable Peace: Power and Democracy after Civil Wars*, edited by Donald Rothschild and Philip Roeder, 29–50. Ithaca, NY: Cornell University Press, 2005.

Rouhana, Nadim, and Sahar Huneidi. *Israel and its Palestinian Citizens: Ethnic Privileges in the Jewish State.* Cambridge: Cambridge University Press, 2017.

Rubenstein, Amnon, and Alexander Yakobson. *Israel and Family of Nations.* New York: Routledge, 2009.

Said, Edward. *The Question of Palestine.* New York: Times Books, 1979.

Sayegh, Fayez. *Zionist Colonialism in Palestine.* Beirut: Research Center–Palestine Liberation Organization, 1965.

Shachar, Ayelet. *Multicultural Jurisdictions: Cultural Differences and Women's Rights.* Cambridge: Cambridge University Press, 2001.

Shafir, Gershon. *Land, Labor and the Origins of the Israeli-Palestinian Conflict, 1882–1914.* Berkeley: University of California Press, 1989.

Shafir, Gershon, and Yoav Peled, *Being Israeli: The Dynamics of Multiple Citizenship.* Cambridge: Cambridge University Press, 2004.

Sultany, Nimer. "The State of Progressive Constitutional Theory: The Paradox of Constitutional Democracy and the Project of Political Justification." *Harvard Civil Rights-Civil Liberties Law Review* 47 (2012): 371–455.

Taylor, Charles. "The Politics of Recognition." In *Multiculturalism,* edited by Amy Gutmann, 25–74. Princeton, NJ: Princeton University Press, 1994.

Waldron, Jeremy. "The Core of the Case against Judicial Review." *The Yale Law Journal* 115 (2006): 1,346–406.

Weingast, Barry. "The Economic Role of Political Institutions: Market Preserving Federalism and Economic Development." *Journal of Law, Economics, and Organization* 11 (1995): 1–31.

Wolfe, Patrick. "Nation and MiscegeNation: Discursive Continuity in the Post-Mabo Era." *Social Analysis* 36 (1994): 93–152.

———. "Purchase by Other Means: The Palestinian Nakba and Zionism's Conquest of Economics." *Settler Colonial Studies* 2, no. 1 (2012): 133–71.

Zreik, Raef. "Notes on the Value of Theory: Readings in the Law of Return—A Polemic." *Law and Ethics of Human Rights* 2, no. 1 (2008): 1–44.

CASES CITED

Israel

CA 630/70 *Tamarin v. The State of Israel* (1972), IsrSC 26(1).

CA 8573/08 *Ornan v. Ministry of Interior* (2013), IsrSC.

HCJ 2597/99 *Toshbeim v. Minister of Interior* (2005), IsrSC 59(3) 721.

South Africa

Shabalala and Others v. Attorney-General of the Transvaal and Another (CCT23/94) [1995] ZACC 12.

European Court of Human Rights

Sejdić and Finci v. Bosnia Herzegovina (Applications nos. 27996/06 and 34836/06) 22.12.2009.

10

Between Two States and One

Palestinian Citizens of Israel

Maha Nassar

While numerous studies have examined the impact that the Oslo Accords and subsequent Israeli-Palestinian talks have had on Palestinians in the Occupied Territories, less attention has been paid to how the Oslo process affected the lives and political horizons of Palestinian citizens of Israel (also known as '48 Palestinians and Palestinians inside the Green Line). In large part this is because the Oslo Accords—and before that, the declaration of Palestinian statehood in 1988—excluded this group from the Palestinian national agenda. As a result, during the 1990s many Palestinian citizens sought to assimilate into Israeli society, assuming that the Oslo talks would solve the conflict in the form of a two-state solution and that their future lay within the Israeli state. But the outbreak of the Al-Aqsa Intifada in 2000, along with the steady rightward shift of the Israeli political landscape, forced Palestinians inside the Green Line to revisit many of their previously held beliefs about possible solutions to the conflict.

While recent polls of '48 Palestinians show that a majority still believe a two-state solution is the best proposal for solving the Palestinian-Israeli conflict, a growing number of Palestinian intellectuals and activists inside the Green Line are calling into question the fundamental premises of the two-state solution.[1] The development of these positions should be understood within a broader historical context of political debates among '48 Palestinians that goes back to the founding of the Israeli state. Despite living under restrictive military rule until 1966 and facing isolation from the Arab world, Palestinian political activists and intellectuals inside the Green Line have engaged in rich political discussions about their position within the Israeli-Palestinian conflict, and especially their relationship to their fellow Palestinians beyond the Green Line. While decolonization was a common thread in these discussions, the two dominant Palestinian political formations in Israel—the communist camp and the nationalist camp—had differing notions of how decolonization should be understood in the Israeli context. In this chapter, I argue that these historical discussions shape the political landscape today, especially with regard to the debates over one- and two-state solutions. I also show how Israel's shift since the 1990s toward emphasizing its Jewish character has led many Palestinians in Israel to adjust their earlier, more optimistic views of Oslo. Finally, I lay out some of the alternatives to the two-state solution that are being proposed among Palestinians in Israel, along with the challenges they face.

PALESTINIAN POLITICS UNTIL 1967: THE COMMUNIST AND NATIONALIST CAMPS

Since 1948, the main oppositional Palestinian forces in Israel largely have largely fallen into two dominant camps: a communist camp and a nationalist camp. The communist camp was represented by the Israeli Communist Party (ICP), which has consistently emphasized Jewish-Arab class solidarity and cooperation and, until 1991, hewed closely to the Soviet Union's official positions on all matters foreign and domestic. The ICP was known by its Hebrew acronym, Maki, until 1965, when it split along national lines into a predominantly Jewish Maki party and a new, predominantly Arab party that took the Hebrew acronym Rakah.

During the first several decades of the state, the ICP was the only legal, non-Zionist party in Israel that allowed Arabs and Jews to be equals. Members of the communist camp adopted broad concepts of decolonization that emphasized the need for everyone to live in peace and equality.[2] They further argued that the Zionist underpinnings of the state led Israel into the lap of imperialist powers, and they denounced the numerous discriminatory policies against the Palestinians who remained within the Green Line, arguing that they were not in keeping with Israel's democratic claims.[3] But it was not an anti-Zionist party: in keeping with Soviet ideology, the ICP recognized the state of Israel and did not question the fundamental legitimacy of Israel's founding. And although it earned the ire of Israeli leaders, as a legal political party it was allowed to operate. That included participating in Knesset elections, where the ICP ran lists with alternating Jewish and Arab names. While the party only held one to three seats in any given Knesset, it served as a venue in which MKs such as Emile Habibi and Tawfiq Tubi could raise uncomfortable issues about Israel's mistreatment of Palestinians from the dais.[4]

In contrast to the communists' general calls for decolonization around the world, members of the Arab nationalist camp adopted decolonization discourses that were more vociferously anti-Zionist than those of their communist counterparts. They questioned whether Israel could ever truly be both Jewish and democratic, thus sowing doubt about the legitimacy of the state. They identified more openly with Arab decolonization movements, especially the pan-Arab (*qawmi*) nationalist expressions of Egyptian leader Gamal Abdel Nasser, and they argued that for Palestinians inside the Green Line to be truly free, they needed to be part of a pan-Arab, Nasser-led, unified formation.[5]

Given the Israeli leadership's fears of Arab nationalism, Palestinian activists in Israel who expressed such viewpoints had much less political room in which to maneuver. Israeli government and establishment figures claimed that by openly siding with Israel's enemies, those activists posed an existential threat to the state. Moreover, with the vast majority of pre-1948 Palestinian national figures and institutions uprooted, and with the communist leadership taking a dim view of their positions, nationalist-minded Palestinians had very few venues in which they could express their ideas publicly. Yet Arab nationalist views had wide appeal, as evidenced during the brief appearance of the Ard (Land) group in 1959–60. Leaders of the Ard group were unabashedly Nasserist and pan-Arab nationalist, as demonstrated in their series of wildly popular single-issue papers, issued between October 1959 and January 1960, that lauded Egyptian president Gamal Abdel Nasser and stressed their desire for pan-Arab unity.[6] The communists opposed both these positions, arguing that the best way forward was to bring Jewish Israelis around to the belief that they could abandon certain elements of Jewish privilege while maintaining Israel as a Jewish state. The communists did not attack the nationalists directly, given the strong popular support they enjoyed, but the ICP leadership quietly seethed at the nationalists, believing that they undermined the communists' attempts to reassure Jewish Israelis that allowing for equality with Palestinians would not pose an existential threat to the state.[7]

As the Palestinian national movement began to gain traction in the mid-1960s, Arab nationalists in Israel who affirmed their connection to the Palestinian people ran further afoul of the government. In 1964 Ard leaders applied for formal state recognition as an association—a request that inherently signaled their recognition of the Israeli state. But their proposed articles of association stated in part that their group was aimed at "finding a just solution for the Palestinian problem, through its consideration as an indivisible unit—in accordance with the wish of the Palestinian Arab people."[8] The language of the clause bore a striking resemblance to Articles 3 and 4 of the PLO's Palestinian National Charter, signaling that there were Palestinians in Israel who were not reconciled to their perpetual minoritization within the Jewish state. The Israeli government denied the group's petition—a denial that the Israeli High Court ultimately upheld.[9] The fall of the Ard movement demonstrated that the Israeli authorities would not tolerate discursive framings that tied Palestinians in Israel to the Palestinian people as a whole, even if those framings were carefully worded in a way that accepted the Israeli state as a fait accompli. That experience would shape the work of subsequent intellectuals and activists, especially as the political landscape gradually opened up after the 1967 war.

This brief examination of the Palestinian political landscape in Israel prior to 1967 shows the spaces—and limits—of oppositional political discourse in Israel. While the communists adopted a language of decolonization that denounced, often vehemently, Israeli policies that discriminated against Palestinians and put Israel in league with imperialist forces, they did not question the legitimacy of the state itself. As a result, although they faced restrictions and attacks from the Israeli authorities, they nonetheless continued to operate as a sanctioned political party.

In contrast, the Palestinian Arab nationalists—especially those organized around the Ard movement—adopted a language of decolonization that criticized Israel at a more fundamental level, denouncing Israel's Zionist underpinnings as inherently discriminatory. While these activists offered de facto recognition of the state, Israeli authorities saw their calls for pan-Arab unity and Palestinian self-determination as too close to Palestinian nationalist rhetoric. As a result, Arab nationalists faced more severe punishment from the Israeli state and were not allowed to maneuver as freely as were the communists. The 1967 war and the rise of the Palestinian nationalist movement further enhanced these differences.

1967–1987: THE TWO-STATE DEBATE

The June 1967 war and the rise of the Palestinian resistance movement dramatically altered the political landscape of Palestinians inside the Green Line. Israeli officials grew alarmed at the rise in apprehensions of young men seeking to join the resistance, especially after the PLO's famous stance at Karamah in March 1968.[10] Ard leaders Sabri Jiryis and Habib Qahwaji also went into exile in 1969 and 1970, respectively, further signaling the perceived threat that Palestinian Arab nationalism posed to the state.[11]

For the Palestinian communist Rakah party, the crackdowns on the nationalists and the positions of the Soviet Union led them to emphasize the so-called '67 issues, of occupation and settlements in the West Bank, Gaza Strip, and East Jerusalem, rather than the so-called '48 issues, of Israeli colonization of historic Palestine and the return of refugees. The party strongly denounced Israel's land grab during and after the June 1967 war as illegal. After UN Security Council Resolution 242 was passed in November 1967, calling on Israel to withdraw from territories it had occupied in the war, Rakah leaders frequently invoked this resolution as a basis for solving the conflict. Party leaders also strongly denounced the treatment of Palestinians in the Occupied Territories, reporting regularly on violations of human rights and international law.[12] For Rakah, these positions were in keeping with the language of decolonization that it had advocated in earlier years.

But Rakah's focus on decolonizing the lands occupied in 1967 was at odds with the Palestinian national movement in exile, which stressed the need to decolonize all of historic Palestine. Thus, Rakah was critical of the Palestinian resistance movement, as well as the broader Palestinian consensus that armed struggle was necessary for the goal of liberating all of Palestine. By recognizing that the Israeli people had national rights to a homeland within the Green Line, by focusing only on territorial disputes in the 1967 territories, and by refusing to unequivocally call for the right of return of Palestinian refugees, Rakah adopted positions that diverged sharply from the Palestinian consensus at the time.[13]

Yet even these positions carried a heavy political cost inside Israel. Several of Rakah's political and cultural leaders were placed under house arrest for years following the 1967 war, while others were subjected to a sunset-to-sunrise curfew.[14] Such measures were aimed at limiting the reach of Palestinian activists in Israel who were critical of the state's policies in the Occupied Territories and its repression of Palestinian activists within the Green Line. Despite these oppressive measures, Rakah's history of political organizing and institution-building, coupled with a political maneuverability that the nationalists did not enjoy, allowed the party to gain steady support over the following years. But a new nationalist challenge would soon emerge.

During the early 1970s, a new awakening of nationalist thought emerged among younger Palestinian intellectuals living inside the Green Line. They had grown up under Israeli rule and were frustrated by the rampant discrimination and inequality they faced. But they were also increasingly aware of Palestinian decolonization discourses that were more uncompromising than before and that took into account what had happened to the Palestinians in 1948. For many, this nationalist rhetoric was more attractive than Rakah's calls for joint Arab-Jewish cooperation and its refusal to endorse armed struggle. Additional social and economic factors, such as greater employment opportunities in Israel's flourishing economy and a rise in the number of students who were finishing high school and attending college, led many younger intellectuals to feel a greater sense of independence.[15]

Some of these younger, bolder nationalists also grew more vocal in their criticism of Rakah, arguing that its refusal to examine critically the foundations of the Israeli state and its emphasis on Arab-Jewish cooperation "enabled the assimilation, as Israelis, of Arabs in the state."[16] In response to this growing desire to emphasize their identity as Palestinians, in 1972 several activists based in the central triangle town of Um al-Fahm formally declared the establishment of the Abna' al-Balad (Sons of the Village) movement. With a mix of Arab nationalists and former communists of various strains, members of Abna' al-Balad had many different ideological orientations, but they came together around a dual platform of "affirmation of the Palestinian identity among the Arab people in Israel" and "opposition to the communist party."[17]

Since Abna' al-Balad's members opposed participating in Knesset elections, they did not pose a direct electoral threat to Rakah. But they constituted a fundamental challenge to key Rakah ideological positions. Since 1967 Rakah had emphasized that Israeli withdrawal from the Occupied Territories was the first and most necessary step towards the establishment of a Palestinian state in the West Bank and Gaza Strip. At the same time, they demanded collective and individual equal rights as Palestinian *Israeli* citizens. Therefore, while Rakah endorsed the Palestine Liberation Organization (PLO) as the legitimate representative of the Palestinian people, the party did not agree that the PLO represented Palestinians in Israel. In contrast, Abna' al-Balad rejected the idea of a Palestinian state in the

West Bank and Gaza Strip as defeatist. They also argued that "the PLO is the sole legitimate representative of the Palestinian Arab people . . . which constitutes a single entity, wherever it may be." Thus, "any settlement of the Palestinian question must include an official recognition and international guarantees of the national rights of the Palestinians who live . . . in Israel as well."[18] In short, Abna' al-Balad saw itself "as part of the Palestinian national enterprise, which [strove] to establish one Palestinian state on all the Palestinian lands."[19]

Yet even Rakah's emphasis on ending the occupation and withdrawing from Palestinian lands was met with fear in many Israeli circles. By 1975 some on the Israeli right were calling for Rakah and its activities to be outlawed. More liberal Israelis warned that this would be a mistake, arguing that Rakah represented "a relatively moderate Arab nationalism" and was "a safety valve for Arabs in Israel, protecting them from slipping into extremist nationalism."[20] These Israeli fears had a direct bearing on the political calculations of Palestinian activists in the country, who worried constantly that if they crossed a discursive red line, they would be banned, as the Ard movement had been a decade earlier.

There were also more urgent pressures at home, including systematic discrimination against Palestinian citizens and the confiscation of their land. In response to these pressures, Rakah and Abna' al-Balad joined forces in March 1976 to organize a general strike and coordinate a series of large demonstrations that collectively became known as Land Day. The massive turnout, coupled with widespread outrage over the police killings of six unarmed protesters, led to greater politicization among Palestinians inside the Green Line.[21] At the same time, this increased political awareness among Palestinian citizens made the ongoing debates between the communists and nationalists all the more visible.

These tensions were especially palpable among youth groups and university students, who were debating with each other the possible solutions to the Palestinian-Israeli conflict and the fate of the '48 Palestinians. In fall 1976, Fouzi El-Asmar, a '48 Palestinian poet and former Ard member who returned for a time to his homeland after spending several years in the United States, captured the two sides of this debate:

> I heard from a number of people with whom I talked during my stay in the country that Communist political education of Arab youth encourages them to accept the status of an Arab minority in Israel with Israeli identities. A leader of the [Rakah] party explained this logic as follows: "When the Palestinian state is established alongside its sister Israeli state, we shall remain an Arab minority in Israel. Changing this situation will take generations and it may never change. The best thing is to raise our new generation with this perspective, for in the future it will help them in keeping their identity intact."[22]

But El-Asmar also observed that not everyone shared the assumption that a Palestinian state would (or should) be established. He cited one student journalist who wrote,

If we suppose that a Palestinian state is established in the West Bank and the Gaza Strip, then the Palestinians living inside Israel proper will remain as a persecuted minority. On the other hand, all those Palestinians who were kicked out of their homes in 1948 will move from their current refugee camps to other camps set up for them on the West Bank and Gaza. Subsequently their status will change but little. If such a solution is carried out it will solve the problem of only one segment of the Palestinians, namely the ones who have lived for generations on the West Bank and Gaza Strip. The solution to the Palestinian issue will come about only with the establishment of a state after the return of all the Palestinian refugees to their homes. The new state should be a state concerned with individual welfare, emphasizing collective humanity and not racial distinctions.[23]

Thus, while Rakah leaders defended their support for a Palestinian state in terms of pragmatism, their nationalist critics argued that a two-state solution—even if it were to come to fruition—would not address the ongoing oppression of the Palestinians living as a minority in Israel. For these nationalists, the best solution was a single democratic state that would be free of ethnonational preferences.

Throughout the mid-to-late 1970s the nationalists' position was more popular among university students, as evidenced by the consistent victories of Abna' al-Balad's student arm, the National Progressive Movement, in student government elections.[24] But Abna' al-Balad's firm position against participating in Knesset elections, coupled with restrictions it faced from the Israeli authorities, ultimately limited the impact it could have in the larger political sphere. In its absence, communist and other progressive parties that favored a two-state solution soon dominated the national political arena. The largest was the Democratic Front of Peace and Equality (DFPE—also known by its Hebrew acronym, Hadash, and its Arabic shorthand, Jabha). Comprised of Rakah members and noncommunist activists, it won 50 percent of the Palestinian vote when it first ran in the 1977 Knesset elections. In 1983 it was joined by the Progressive List for Peace (PLP), led by attorney and former Rakah activist Muhammad Mi'ari, which included radical Jewish leftists and former Abna' al-Balad members who disagreed with the leadership's refusal to participate in Knesset elections.[25] The DFPE and the PLP were bitter rivals and campaigned harshly against each other in the 1984 Knesset elections. But when it came to their positions on the Palestinian-Israeli conflict, their positions were virtually identical. Both supported the establishment of a Palestinian state in the West Bank and Gaza Strip alongside Israel, and both called for mutual recognition by Israel and the PLO of each other's right to self-determination, which was to be achieved through direct negotiations between Israel and the PLO.[26] In the 1984 elections the PLP received 18 percent of the Arab vote while the DFPE received 33 percent, totaling 51 percent of the Arab vote.[27] Abna' al-Balad continued to support a single democratic state in all of historic Palestine, but by the late-1980s the emergence of a Palestinian and regional consensus around two states pushed it to the margins, leading it to recede from the political scene.[28]

By the eve of the First Intifada, the political consensus among the dominant Palestinian political parties in Israel rested on the following pillars: "(1) support for a Palestinian state in the West Bank and Gaza Strip under PLO leadership; (2) full equality for Palestinian citizens of Israel; (3) that all political acts would be within the constraints of Israeli law."[29] But the political consensus of '48 Palestinians as a whole was not as clear-cut. In a nationally representative poll of the Palestinian minority taken by Israeli pollsters in December 1987, only 28 percent of respondents preferred the establishment of a Palestinian state alongside Israel, while 33 percent opted for a binational state, and 10 percent wished to see a Palestinian state in all of historic Palestine.[30] But in the same survey, when asked to rank their options for "*realistic* expectations," 78 percent of respondents favored "the establishment of a Palestinian state in the Occupied Territories with no modifications to the 1967 borders."[31]

In short, the transformation of the PLO's position towards an acceptance of the two-state solution shifted the balance of power among Palestinian factions inside the Green Line, lending greater weight to those who argued in favor of establishing a Palestinian state alongside Israel. The transformations brought about by the First Intifada and the Palestinian Declaration of Independence would soon solidify the political consensus around the two-state solution.

1988–2000: THE TWO-STATE CONSENSUS

The First Intifada, which broke out in December 1987, brought renewed international attention to the plight of the Palestinians living under Israeli occupation in the West Bank and Gaza Strip. It also gave new urgency to their demand for statehood in the Occupied Territories. That urgency, coupled with the PLO's desire to stay relevant in a rapidly changing international environment, led it to formalize what had been its de facto stance for several years.

In November 1988, the Palestine National Council (the PLO's highest decision-making body) adopted a series of resolutions, including a Palestinian Declaration of Independence that formalized its vision of a comprehensive two-state solution of the Palestinian-Israeli conflict.[32] While the Declaration of Independence did not specify the borders of the Palestinian state, the follow-up political communiqué called for "the withdrawal of Israel from all the Palestinian and Arab territories it occupied in 1967, including Arab Jerusalem," and "the annulment of all measures of annexation and appropriation and the removal of settlements established by Israel in the Palestinian and Arab territories since 1967."[33] No mention was made in either the Declaration of Independence or in the follow-up political communiqué of the Palestinians inside the Green Line.

By formally adopting a two-state formulation, the PLO's new policy prioritized the aspirations of Palestinians living in the West Bank and Gaza Strip, effectively excising the '48 Palestinians from the Palestinian national project.

As a result, the Intifada and the PNC resolutions "resurrected the Green Line in the consciousness of both Palestinian communities."[34] For Palestinians inside the Green Line, the PLO's Declaration of Independence and recognition of Israel sent a clear message that their political path would necessitate adopting a program that differed significantly from that of Palestinians under occupation.

As a result, many Palestinians concluded that their future lay within the Israeli state, and that integrating into the Israeli state would not harm the Palestinian cause.[35] In the 1992 Knesset elections, for the first time in nearly twenty years, a majority of Palestinian voters (53%) voted for Zionist parties, and five Arab Knesset members joined the Labor and Meretz parties to form a coalition government. But while the Rabin government loosened some of the laws restricting freedom of expression and accepted the establishment of some Palestinian social organizations in Israel, it made no meaningful concessions to the Palestinians citizens' more substantive demands regarding political and economic equality. In other words, a large number of Palestinian leaders in Israel were co-opted by the Israeli government without achieving material improvements in the conditions of their communities.[36]

Therefore, by the time the Declaration of Principles was signed in September 1993, Palestinian citizens of Israel had already been conditioned to believe that a two-state arrangement was the best solution to the Palestinian-Israeli conflict, and that they needed to stake their political claims within the Israeli state. Rather than marking a watershed moment, the Oslo Accords in many ways marked a return to earlier calls to integrate '48 Palestinians into the Israeli body politic, albeit in ways that severed them from Palestinians across the Green Line. The early- to mid-1990s saw Israeli government policies that allowed greater freedom of movement and expression, while Zionist parties (especially Labor and Meretz) sought to expand their "Arab sectors." In response, many Palestinian citizens became convinced that waiting for a comprehensive solution to the Palestine issue was futile and began undertaking acts that were once deemed unthinkable, such as joining Israeli military service, celebrating Israeli Independence Day (including raising the Israeli flag), and appearing with Israeli Jewish symbols in art, sport, cultural, and political venues.[37] Palestinian citizens who participated in these activities argued that with the PLO engaged in direct talks with Israel, it was only a matter of time before an independent Palestinian state would be established in the West Bank and Gaza Strip, Israel's security concerns would be alleviated, and they would therefore be able to enjoy full integration and equality within the Israeli state. They would soon be disappointed.

The PLO's recognition of Israel effectively took off the table the question of Israel's right to exist, at least within the Green Line. With that matter settled, a discursive shift took place within Israeli society, whereby Jewish Israelis began to emphasize the state's Jewish character more clearly than before. While the Israeli right had stressed Israel's Jewishness for decades, the formulation of Israel as a Jewish state was now articulated increasingly by the Zionist left, which had previously sidestepped questions about Israel's ethnic character. In other words, "the Oslo political climate legitimized ethnic conceptions of the state . . . allowing the Left to be vocal about its stance on Israel's Jewish essence."[38] The Zionist left's growing emphasis on Israel's Jewish character, even as it was trying to recruit Palestinian citizens into the Israeli body politic, highlighted the limits of assimilationism for Palestinians living inside the Green Line.

This discursive shift also led some Palestinian activists to conclude that the communist-led DFPE and other existing Arab parties were insufficiently prepared to address these changing political conditions. The notion that Palestinian citizens could be assimilated into Israel as full and equal citizens by working with the Zionist left (a key stance of the DFPE and its supporters) did not accord with the Zionist left's own shift towards privileging Israel's character as a Jewish state. Concerned by the growing push towards assimilating Palestinian citizens in ways that stripped them of their Palestinian identity, several former Abna' al-Balad activists decided to create a movement that would affirm their people's indivisibility from the Palestinian people, while simultaneously utilizing the political tools available to them as Israeli citizens. As former Abna' al-Balad leader Awad Abdel Fattah explained, "For the first time we [as a group] decided to take our citizenship seriously, but in combination with our nationalist identity. Because even if you call for equality, without focusing on adhering to the nationalist identity and aspirations, I think you'll get nowhere. You'll get civil rights, but you won't get national rights."[39]

In 1995 Abdel Fattah and several Palestinian nationalists and former communists established the National Democratic Assembly (NDA) party (also known by its Arabic name, Hizb al-Tajammu' al-Watani, and its Hebrew acronym, Balad). According to NDA leader 'Azmi Bishara, one of their key concerns was what they called the accelerating "process of Israelization," by which they meant "the marginalization of Palestinians in Israeli society and a gradual joining of Zionist parties."[40] Having accepted the two-state solution as the international and local consensus at the time, the NDA demanded equal rights for Palestinians within Israel at both the civic and—more importantly—national levels. In doing so, the party challenged the trend toward characterizing Israel as a Jewish state, adopting instead a platform that called for Israel to be "a state of all its citizens."[41]

The NDA's debut onto the political scene came at a time when hopes that the Oslo process would bring about both a truly independent Palestinian state on the 1967 lines and a collective improvement to the lives of Palestinians in Israel were already starting to dim. In October 1995, one month before his assassination, Prime Minister Yitzhak Rabin reassured fellow Knesset members that the Palestinians' hoped-for state would be "an entity which is less than a state," while the permanent borders of Israel would be "beyond the lines which existed before the Six Day War," and would encompass a "united Jerusalem, which will include both Ma'ale Adumim and Givat Ze'ev [settlements], as the capital of Israel, under Israeli sovereignty."[42] Not only did a truly sovereign Palestinian state seem further away than ever, but most of the economic improvements and legal changes that would have put Palestinian citizens of Israel on equal footing with Jewish Israelis did not come to fruition.[43]

Seeking to highlight these concerns, the NDP ran in the 1996 Knesset elections for the first time, joining with DFPE in order to meet the threshold of votes. These elections also saw the debut of the United Arab List (UAL, or al-Qa'ima al-'arabiyya al-muwahhada, also known by its Hebrew acronym, Ra'am), which was comprised of members of the southern branch of the Islamic movement and ran on a joint list with the Arab Democratic Party (ADP, or al-Hizb al-'arabi al-dimuqrati). Both the NDP-Hadash and the UAL-ADP lists called for the establishment of an independent Palestinian state on the 1967 lines and stressed equality for Palestinian citizens of Israel; they gained three and four Knesset seats, respectively. But their demands received little attention in the Knesset, especially as newly elected Likud Prime Minister Benjamin Netanyahu formed coalitions with far-right and religious Zionist parties whose leaders had loudly denounced both the Oslo talks and the integration of Palestinian citizens into Israel. Palestinian citizens in turn became increasingly skeptical that assimilation into Israel, even on Israeli terms, would lead to greater equality.

Building on that skepticism, the NDA began floating the idea of a binational state. In 1997, NDA leader and Knesset member 'Azmi Bishara predicted that "when it becomes apparent that an independent and democratic state occupying every inch of the West Bank and Gaza Strip free of Israeli settlements is not realizable either in this generation or the next, it will be time for the Palestinians to reexamine their entire strategy. We then will begin to discuss a binational state solution that will do away with the system of ethnic discrimination that is in place now." Pressed further, Bishara elaborated:

> It means that the Palestinians in the territories and the Palestinians in Israel will form a single political unit within a binational state. There will be a Jewish political unit and a Palestinian-Arab political unit, which together will constitute a Jewish-Arab polity with two separate legislative chambers as well as a common parliament. I believe this must become our demand in the future. I am not referring to a democratic secular state but to a binational state, a federal or confederal system comprising two ethnonational communities. Only in such a context will it be possible to resolve such problems as the refugees and the settlements. Settlements no longer will pose an insurmountable obstacle within the context of a single binational state: If the Israelis should choose to settle in the West Bank, then so be it; we, too, will have the right to set up residence in Jaffa, for instance.[44]

Bishara's early forays into discussions of binationalism came at a time when the Palestinian political consensus in Israel still stressed the need to work within the existing political parameters. In order to highlight the limits of those parameters, during the 1999 election campaign Bishara nominated himself for the position of Israeli prime minister, knowing that he did not have a chance of winning. The move garnered much media attention and offered Bishara a platform to highlight the fundamental lack of equality in Israel and to call for a shift to a binational state. In an interview Bishara stressed that it was still an academic discussion at that point, since no political momentum was mobilizing behind the idea, but he emphasized that this discussion was the first step toward a larger movement.[45] Bishara withdrew his nomination shortly before the election in the face of large-scale Palestinian mobilization to ensure that Netanyahu would be defeated by Labor candidate Ehud Barak. Barak campaigned on a slogan of "a state for all," receiving 95 percent of the Palestinian vote as a result.[46] But Barak's refusal to take seriously any of the demands of Palestinian citizens led growing numbers of Palestinians inside the Green Line to wonder if the political calculations they had made during the 1990s were accurate.

Largely absent during this period of the "two-state consensus" were formulations of Palestinian liberation that invoked the conceptual framework of decolonization. The PLO leadership framed national liberation as the establishment of a Palestinian state in the 1967 territories, while the Palestinian political leadership inside the Green Line framed liberation as achieving true equality within the Israeli state. The question of what liberation meant for Palestinians in exile remained unaddressed beyond vague references to the right of return. But the violence and trauma of the next several years would lead Palestinian activists on both sides of the Green Line to reassess this absence in their political thinking and would lead some to reintroduce decolonization as a guiding conceptual framework.

THE SECOND INTIFADA AND A RETURN TO DECOLONIZING DISCOURSES

In the months before the Second Intifada broke out in September 2000, Palestinian citizens of Israel continued to receive mixed messages as to whether they would be integrated into Israel as equals. In March, after a five-year legal ordeal, the Israeli High Court ruled that the Qa'dan family could not be prevented from moving into the predominantly Jewish Katzir community just because they were Palestinian citizens. Even though the court's ruling left plenty of room for the Katzir Community Cooperative to maneuver its way out of implementation, it nonetheless drew an outcry among Knesset members on the right who declared that the ruling marked "a black day for the Jewish people."[47]

At the same time, '48 Palestinians felt increasingly abandoned by the Labor Party. Prime Minister Barak refused to include any Arab parties as part of his coalition or to meet with the High Follow-Up Committee (the foremost representative body of Palestinians in Israel) during his first several months in office. The collapse of the Israeli-Palestinian talks at Camp David II that summer, which Barak blamed solely on the Palestinians, furthered their disillusionment.

By early September, tensions were already rising, not only between Palestinian citizens and the Israeli state, but also between Palestinians under occupation and the Israeli military. Thus, when Likud Knesset member Ariel Sharon walked onto al-Haram al-Sharif (the Temple Mount) surrounded by a bevy of armed Israeli guards on September 28, the provocative move triggered Palestinian protests that erupted into the Second (Al-Aqsa) Intifada. Dozens of Palestinians were killed in the first days of the new uprising, including twelve-year-old Muhammad al-Durrah, whose televised screams sparked international outcry. To protest the killings and signal support for their people on the other side of the Green Line, '48 Palestinians declared a general strike on October 1. During the protests that ensued over the following week, Israeli security forces killed thirteen unarmed Palestinians (twelve citizens of Israel and one from the West Bank). The killings were a major blow to those Palestinians who believed that their Israeli citizenship protected them from lethal force. They were also a severe blow to the argument that the future for Palestinians inside the Green Line lay in greater assimilation within Israel.

Following the killings, the Israeli government established the Orr Commission to examine the conditions of the Palestinian citizens of Israel. The commission's final report, issued in September 2003, marked the first time that an official Israeli body acknowledged that the creation of Israel as a Jewish state had inherently led to the unequal treatment of Palestinian citizens. The report's introduction framed the '48 Palestinians as an "indigenous minority" whose feelings of injustice were "fed by the obvious existence of collective rights for the Jewish [people]."[48] Yet despite this unprecedented acknowledgement by an official Israeli body, the report's conclusion offered only vague recommendations.

As a result, the Orr Commission's report did little to improve the conditions of Palestinians within the Green Line. Instead, the Israeli government, led by a series of far-right and center-right parties, passed laws that were even more discriminatory against Palestinian citizens than in the past. In 2003, the Knesset passed an amendment to the Citizenship Law that prevented Palestinian citizens of Israel from bringing in their Palestinian spouses from the West Bank and Gaza Strip. In 2007, the law was expanded to apply to spouses from the "enemy states" of Lebanon, Syria, Iraq, and Iran.[49]

In part these laws were promulgated to try to counteract the rise of a new generation of more assertive Palestinian citizens who were emerging onto the political scene. Born during the last quarter of the twentieth century, they came of age during the tumultuous years of the Second Intifada and had become "disillusioned with the prospect of ever becoming equal citizens in Israel."[50] Rather, they became increasingly vocal in asserting their identity as Palestinians, including spearheading collective actions that commemorated events significant to the Palestinian people as a whole, including Nakba Day and Land Day.[51] In doing so, they were part of a larger shift in Palestinian discourse and strategic thinking, one that sought to reframe Israeli-Palestinian relations in terms of colonialism—and more specifically settler-colonialism—and that had longer lineages and wider implications than the "two-state solution" discourses.[52]

This renewed attention to the colonial paradigm emerged in three documents issued by Palestinian NGOs in Israel in 2006 and 2007 that laid out a vision of what the relationship between Palestinian citizens and the Israeli state should be. Two of the documents explicitly framed the issue in terms of colonialism: the Haifa Declaration described the Zionist movement as having initiated a "settler-colonial project in Palestine," while the Future Vision document described Israel as "executing internal colonial policies against its Palestinian Arab citizens."[53] Though they differed slightly from one another in terms of the specific political entity they wished to see established, they stressed that "Israel should be a democratic binational state that guarantees full equality between Arabs and Jews within the Green Line."[54]

Although the Vision Documents (as they were collectively known) formally recognized the state of Israel within the Green Line, they were nonetheless met with widespread hostility by Jewish Israelis, who could not countenance a narrative of Israel's foundation that differed so wildly from their own.[55] Especially galling for many Israelis was the explicit positioning of the Palestinian citizens of Israel—along with the Palestinian people—as victims of Zionist and Israeli colonialism. Moreover, the documents were issued at a time in which more wide-scale and organized commemoration of the Nakba by Palestinian groups within the Green Line, such as the Association for the Defense of Rights of Internally Displaced Persons, were taking place. In response, in 2011 the Knesset passed a "Nakba Law" that criminalized active commemorations of Palestinians' displacement by Israel in 1948, thereby indicating that the Israeli authorities, too, saw a link between commemorations of the Nakba and the shift towards a centering of decolonizing discourses.[56]

But the law had a limited effect in counteracting the rise of these decolonizing discourses. A year after it was passed, Palestinian citizens marked the Nakba with a general strike, symbolizing the growing salience of the Nakba as central to the "collective consciousness" of '48 Palestinians.[57] In short, the Nakba has emerged as one of the primary markers of the shift back to decolonizing discourses and along with it, a return to the idea that all of historic Palestine needs to be liberated from the Zionist project. While this view continued to gain traction over the following decade, not everyone agrees that it is the best way forward.

TWO STATES OR ONE?

Bishara's 1997 prediction that Palestinians would start to call for a binational state once the two-state solution no longer seemed viable is gaining traction in some circles. With widespread decrees that the two-state solution is dead, some members of the nationalist camp are thinking once again of alternative ways in which

Jews and Palestinians can live together equally in the area between the Jordan River and the Mediterranean Sea. In 2008, for example, Abna' al-Balad introduced a revised political platform that has consistently reaffirmed its call for the establishment a single democratic state on all of Palestine.[58]

New initiatives are also emerging, such as the Popular Movement for One Democratic State on Historic Palestine, which was established in May 2013. Most of the group's fifty-some members hail from the West Bank and Gaza Strip, but it also includes leaders from Nazareth, along with Palestinians and Israelis living abroad. The Popular Movement argues that since there is already a one-state reality characterized by Jewish Israeli supremacy, "establishing one democratic state on the land of historical (mandatory) Palestine, a democratic state for all its inhabitants, based on a democratic constitution, the values of the Universal Declaration of Human Rights, which guarantee freedom, democracy and equality of rights without discrimination based on race, religion, gender, colour, language or political or non-political opinion, national or social origin, wealth, place of birth or any other status—establishing this state is, indeed, a just and feasible solution for the Palestinian-Israeli conflict."[59]

In response to these growing calls for a one-state solution, proponents of the two-state solution argue that it is not wise to abandon the goal of an independent Palestinian state, especially after so much Palestinian political capital has been expended to gain international support for it. As DFPE leader Ayman Odeh explained in 2015:

> I still believe that the most realistic and possible solution in the foreseeable future is the establishment of a Palestinian state in 1967, and I think it is a grave mistake to abandon this cause and go to the idea of a single state, because in practice we succeeded in persuading the whole world, as well as a slice within Israeli society, of the two-state solution. We cannot abandon it now and move on to talking about Haifa, Acre and Jaffa. We don't have the constituency for that. I personally cannot say to my people who suffer from the occupation on a daily basis, "Wait for the one-state solution."[60]

Odeh's argument bears a striking resemblance to those of previous Palestinian communists regarding pragmatism and the expeditiousness of the two-state solution. But there is a key difference: by speaking of "my people" who suffer under occupation, he demonstrates a discursive shift in which there is no longer a distinction being made between Palestinians in Israel and Palestinians in the Occupied Territories. According to Odeh, they are all one people whose futures are intertwined. This shift is important because it signals the success of the decolonial paradigm in positioning the Palestinians inside the Green Line as part of the Palestinian people as a whole, with a shared future, despite the call for two states.

Odeh's comments also indicate that while there is broad agreement that Palestinians on both sides of the Green Line share a future together, there is little agreement on how to operationalize that sentiment through existing political structures. In a poll conducted in 2015, 56 percent of '48 Palestinians and 55 percent of '67 Palestinians wanted to see Palestinians inside the Green Line play a greater role in the Palestinian national movement.[61] But when given several options for implementing this idea, there was no consensus. For example, while 73 percent of '67 Palestinians saw a need for Palestinian citizens of Israel to have real representation in Palestinian national political institutions, only 41 percent of Palestinians inside the Green Line saw such a need.[62]

Part of the reluctance among some '48 Palestinians to participate more robustly in Palestinian institutions is likely due to fears of Israeli punitive measures, given the state's long history and ongoing rhetoric accusing Palestinians in Israel of being a fifth column. It is also likely related to their experiences fighting for representation in Israeli institutions, which they would not want to give up. But we cannot overlook the role of the Palestinian national leadership's own disarray and lack of engagement with the Palestinians inside the Green Line. While there have been some meetings between Palestinian MKs and various PLO and PA leaders over the last few decades, there has yet to emerge a clear articulation of how Palestinians inside the Green Line fit into a broader, representative Palestinian national vision of the future. Nor has there been an accounting of how and why Palestinian citizens of Israel were excluded from the Oslo process in the first place.

This lack of accounting is also evident among the Palestinian leadership in Israel. In 2017, NDA Secretary General Mtanes Shehadeh called for a more critical appraisal of how the Palestinians' initial support of the Oslo framework undermined their project for greater equality in Israel while simultaneously marginalizing them from the Palestinian people as a whole. More important, he argued, was the need for Palestinians inside the Green Line to reassess the wisdom of trying to gain Palestinian liberation by working with the Zionist left: "Can a Zionist left that is part of a colonial project offer a solution that accords with the Palestinians' natural rights? Do we support and stand by the Zionist left in accordance with the political ceiling that it poses? [These are especially important questions] since we are aware today that the Zionist left does not propose a project that is fundamentally different from the Zionist right-wing project, but may differ to some extent from the religious-right settlement project."[63] Shehadeh's placement of the Israeli left within the Israeli colonial structures that have impacted Palestinians on both sides of the Green Line further indicates a more assertive discourse of decolonization among some '48 Palestinians. His questions also draw attention to the changes that took place in the Israeli political landscape during the 1990s, after the PLO officially recognized Israel, in which the Israeli demand shifted to recognizing Israel as a Jewish state. As noted above, members of the Zionist left advocated for a two-state solution on the basis that it would preserve the Jewish and democratic character of the Israeli state. For Shehadeh, this solution is unacceptable because it amounts to a continuation of the Zionist colonial project in which Palestinian citizens of Israel are relegated to permanent second-class status.

This more robust decolonizing rhetoric came at a time when Israel moved towards embracing its settler-colonialism even more clearly than before. Perhaps the clearest manifestation of this was the passage of the Jewish Nation-State Basic Law in July 2018. The law describes Israel as "the historic national home of the Jewish people," a people that alone "exercises its natural, cultural, and historic right to self-determination." Moreover, according to the law, "the state views the development of Jewish settlement as a national value and will act to encourage it and to promote and to consolidate its establishment."[64] The law makes no mention of Palestinian citizens' historic rights or connections to the land, thereby undermining claims that it is a democratic state. In addition, by refusing to define Israel's borders yet encouraging Jewish settlement in "the Land of Israel," the law provides legal cover for Israeli settlements in the Occupied Territories, making the establishment of a viable, sovereign, contiguous Palestinian state impossible. Together, these two aspects of the Jewish Nation-State Basic Law have demonstrated to many Palestinian citizens that they will not be able to attain full equality in a Zionist state of Israel, even if a Palestinian mini-state were to be established in parts of the Occupied Palestinian Territories.

In this climate of settler-colonial expansion, several proposals challenging the Oslo-based two-state consensus have been gaining ground. In addition to the Popular Movement for One Democratic State, which was launched in 2013, the One Democratic State Campaign (ODSC) has been holding planning meetings and plenary sessions since January 2018. Unlike its one-state predecessor, OSDC's core members are primarily Palestinians and Jews based inside the Green Line, and one of its leaders, Awad Abdel Fattah, has a long history of nationalist organizing as a former member of Abna' al-Balad and the former NDA secretary general. The OSDC envisions a future in which, "within a constitutional democracy in which all citizens enjoy a common citizenship, one common parliament and thoroughly equal civil rights, constitutional protection would also be granted to national, ethnic or religious collectivities desiring to retain their various identities and cultural lives if they so choose." Such a structure "allows people to move out of rigidly bounded ethnonational blocs into a more integrated, fluid and shared form of civil society."[65] These civil society groups are continuing to articulate their views, and while their advocates are heartened by the support they have received from Palestinians and Jewish Israelis, they readily acknowledge that these positions are still in the minority, at least among Israeli Jews.

The greatest willingness to accept such proposals can be found among the Palestinians inside the Green Line. A December 2017 survey found support for a number of possible outcomes. While support for the traditional two-state solution was strongest, at 83 percent, majorities also supported the idea of a one-state solution (59 percent) as well as a confederation arrangement with

Israel (70 percent).[66] The results indicate a desire among '48 Palestinians as a whole for a solution that would guarantee their political rights and those of their fellow Palestinians.

What is lacking is a consensus among the Palestinian leadership on both sides of the Green Line on how to move forward. As of this writing, Palestinian factionalism between Fatah and Hamas continues, with neither party able to overcome the structural impediments imposed by the Israeli occupation. As for the leadership inside the Green Line, there was considerable optimism when the Joint List was formed in 2015 to run in Knesset elections, bringing together the DFPE, NDA, and other smaller parties. However, with the continued dominance of Likud and other right-wing parties in the Knesset, and in the absence of a deeper conversation about how best to move forward, the Joint List has not been able to do much in terms of moving toward a clear political vision. At the same time, some younger Palestinian activists and intellectuals are questioning the wisdom for directing so much energy toward seeking inclusion in the Israeli body politic. They argue (in language strikingly similar to that of Abna' al-Balad in the 1970s) that focusing on electoral politics grants unwarranted legitimacy to the Israeli state and limits the political horizons of Palestinian citizens at a time when integration into Israel as equal is becoming evermore elusive.[67]

Even more elusive are the prospects for a viable Palestinian state, as Israel and the United States actively work to undermine any momentum toward full Palestinian sovereignty. In October 2018 the Institute for National Security Studies (INSS) at Tel Aviv University published a "Political-Security Framework for the Israeli-Palestinian Arena" that envisioned a Palestinian "state" in a mere 65 percent of the West Bank, excluding the Gaza Strip and East Jerusalem. Israel would "continue construction within the existing settlement blocs," and no settlers would be forcibly removed.[68] In January 2020 the Trump administration proposed a Palestinian "state" that would have neither contiguity nor sovereignty. Moreover, it floated the idea that borders could be redrawn such that the triangle communities in Israel would be transferred to the Palestinian state.[69] This move, which would potentially strip some 250,000 Palestinians of their Israeli citizenship, was the clearest indication yet that the "two-state solution" as envisioned by right-wing Israeli and American administrations would not result in the integration of '48 Palestinian citizens into Israel as equal citizens.

CONCLUSION

Since 1948, champions of Palestinian rights in Israel have largely fallen into two camps: the communist camp and the nationalist camp. While the communist camp has focused on decolonizing the Palestinian territories occupied by Israel in 1967, the nationalist camp has expanded its decolonizing discourses to include all of historic Palestine. Beginning in the early 1970s, the two-state solution championed by the communist camp became the dominant position among '48 Palestinians, but not all Palestinian intellectuals and activists supported the idea of two states. Nationalists associated with the group Abna' al-Balad provided the most clear-eyed advocacy of a single democratic state in Palestine, but their reach was largely limited to university campuses. Shifts in the PLO's official position towards endorsement of the two-state solution gave more weight to advocates of a Palestinian state.

The 1988 Palestinian Declaration of Independence, the 1993 Oslo Accords, and subsequent negotiations between Israel and the PLO seemingly took the binational-state option off the table. However, numerous political and cultural developments since 2000 have allowed for the gradual re-emergence and development of alternative proposals to the two-state solution, particularly the idea of a single democratic state. This has corresponded with a broader identification of '48 Palestinians as an inextricable part of the Palestinian people, as well as a growing salience of decolonization as a conceptual framework among Palestinians as a whole in order to counteract numerous forms of Zionist and Israeli settler-colonialism on both sides of the Green Line. However, in the absence of a clear Palestinian national political program or decision-making body that incorporates Palestinians in the '48 lands, there is no clear way to translate these sentiments into political agency.

NOTES

I wish to thank Lana Tatour for her comments on an earlier draft of this chapter.

1. Mtanes Shehadeh and 'Amid Sa'abnah, "The Role of '48 Palestinians and Their Place in the Palestinian National Project," *Majallat al-Dirasat al-Filastiniyah* 105 (Winter 2016): 56–60; Palestinian Center for Policy and Survey Research, "Palestinian-Israeli Pulse: A Joint Poll," Palestinian Center for Policy and Survey Research, December 2017, http://www.pcpsr.org/sites/default/files/Table%20of%20 Findings_English%20Joint%20Poll%204%20dec2017.pdf.

2. Maha Nassar, *Brothers Apart: Palestinian Citizens of Israel and the Arab World* (Stanford, CA: Stanford University Press, 2017).

3. Shira Robinson, *Citizen Strangers: Palestinians and the Birth of Israel's Liberal Settler State* (Stanford, CA: Stanford University Press, 2013).

4. Robinson, *Citizen Strangers*.

5. Nassar, *Brothers Apart*; Leena Dallasheh, "The Al-Ard Movement," in *The Palestinians in Israel: Readings in History, Politics and Society*, edited by Nadim N. Rouhana and Areej Sabbagh-Khoury, 139–48 (Haifa: Mada al-Carmel, 2018).

6. Nassar, *Brothers Apart*, 99–105; Dallasheh, "Al-Ard Movement," 142.

7. Nassar, *Brothers Apart*, 102–3.

8. Jacob Landau, *The Arabs in Israel: A Political Study* (London: Oxford University Press, 1969), 102.

9. Nassar, *Brothers Apart*, 135.

10. Don Peretz, "Arab Palestine: Phoenix or Phantom?" *Foreign Affairs* 48, no. 2 (January 1970): 322–33, 330.

11. Nassar, *Brothers Apart*.

12. Nassar, *Brothers Apart*.

13. Mahmud Khalid, *The Israeli Left Camp* (Amman: Manshurat Dar al-Karmal, 1986), 77–78.

14. Nassar, *Brothers Apart*.

15. 'Aziz Haider, *The Palestinians in Israel in the Shadow of the Oslo Accord* (Beirut: Mu'assasat al-dirasat al-filastiniya, 1997), 81–83.

16. Mohaned Mustafa, "Sons of the Village Movement," in *The Palestinians in Israel: Readings in History, Politics and Society*, edited by Nadim N. Rouhana and Areej Sabbagh-Khoury, 149–59 (Haifa: Mada al-Carmel, 2018), 150.

17. 'Aziz Haider, *The National Progressive Movement: Abna' al-Balad* (Beir Zeit: Markaz dirasat wa-tawthiq al-mujtama' al-filastini, 1989), 87.

18. Sabri Jiryis, "The Arabs in Israel, 1973–1979," *Journal of Palestine Studies* 8, no. 4 (Summer 1979): 40.

19. Mustafa, "Sons of the Village," 150.

20. Jiryis, "Arabs in Israel," 37.

21. Tamir Sorek, *Palestinian Commemoration in Israel: Calendars, Monuments and Martyrs* (Stanford, CA: Stanford University Press, 2015), 49–52.

22. Fouzi El-Asmar, "Israel Revisited, 1976," *Journal of Palestine Studies* 6, no. 3 (Spring 1977): 53–54.

23. El-Asmar, "Israel Revisited."

24. Elie Rekhess, "The Arab Nationalist Challenge to the Israeli Communist Party (1970–1985)," *Studies in Comparative Communism* 22, no. 4 (1989): 337–50, 343.

25. 'Aziz Haidar, "The Nationalist Progressive Movement," in *The Palestinians in Israel: Readings in History, Politics and Society*, edited by Nadim N. Rouhana and Areej Sabbagh-Khoury, 161–74 (Haifa: Mada al-Carmel, 2018), 163.

26. Haidar, "Nationalist Progressive Movement," 163; Don Peretz and Sammy Smooha, "Israel's Eleventh Knesset Election," *Middle East Journal* 39, no. 1 (Spring 1985): 86–103, 91.

27. Peretz and Smooha, "Israel's Eleventh Knesset Election," 101.

28. Haidar, "National Progressive Movement," 109; Mustafa, "Sons of the Village," 154.

29. Nadim Rouhana, "The Intifada and the Palestinians of Israel: Resurrecting the Green Line," *Journal of Palestine Studies* 19, no. 3 (Spring 1990): 58–75, 59.

30. Elia Zureik and 'Aziz Haider, "The Impact of the Intifadah on the Palestinians in Israel," *International Journal of the Sociology of Law* 19, no. 4 (1991): 475–99, 487.

31. Zureik and Haider, "The Impact of the Intifadah," 487.

32. Rashid Khalidi, "The Resolutions of the Nineteenth Palestine National Council," *Journal of Palestine Studies* 19, no. 2 (Winter 1990): 29–42.

33. Palestine National Council, "Communique, Algiers, 15 November 1988," *Journal of Palestine Studies* 18, no. 2 (Winter 1989): 216–23, 220.

34. Rouhana, "Intifada and the Palestinians of Israel," 72.

35. Haidar, *Palestinians in Israel*, 141.

36. Haidar, *Palestinians in Israel*, 143–48.

37. Haidar, *Palestinians in Israel*, 151–54.

38. Hassan Jabareen, "Twenty Years of Oslo: The Green Line's Challenge to the Statehood Project," *Journal of Palestine Studies* 43, no. 1 (Autumn 2013): 41–50, 42.

39. Awad Abdel Fattah, "Before There Was Balad," interview by David Sheen, video, 12:43, January 14, 2013, https://www.youtube.com/watch?v=hMr-dfZuNOQ.

40. 'Azmi Bishara, Sara Scalenghe, Steve Rothman, and Joel Beinin, "On Palestinians in the Israeli Knesset: Interview with 'Azmi Bishara," *Middle East Report* 201 (Oct.–Dec. 1996): 27–28, 27.

41. Nimer Sultany, "The National Democratic Assembly," in *The Palestinians in Israel: Readings in History, Politics and Society*, edited by Nadim N. Rouhana and Areej Sabbagh-Khoury, 216–29 (Haifa: Mada al-Carmel, 2018), 218.

42. Yitzhak Rabin, "Ratification of Interim Agreement," Israel Ministry of Foreign Affairs, October 5, 1995, https://tinyurl.com/y28gqwhc.

43. Nadim Rouhana, "Israel and Its Arab Citizens: Predicaments in the Relationship between Ethnic States and Ethnonational Minorities," *Third World Quarterly* 19, no. 2 (1998): 277–96.

44. ʿAzmi Bishara, "Bridging the Green Line: The PA, Israeli Arabs, and Final Status. An Interview with ʿAzmi Bishara," *Journal of Palestine Studies* 26, no. 3 (Spring 1997): 72–73.

45. ʿAzmi Bishara, "'Asmi Bishara: His Nomination for Prime Minister," interview by ʿAbdallah al-Saʾafin, *Al-Jazeera*, January 9, 1999, https://tinyurl.com/y43m7qro.

46. Majid Al-Haj, "Whither the Green Line? Trends in the Orientation of the Palestinians in Israel and the Territories," *Israel Affairs* 11, no. 1 (Spring 2005): 183–206, 197.

47. Yousef T. Jabareen, "Critical Reflection on Law, Equal Citizenship and Transformation," in *Plurality and Citizenship in Israel: Moving Beyond the Jewish/Palestinian Civil Divide*, edited by Yotam Benziman and Dan Avnon, 94–118 (New York: Routledge, 2010).

48. Cited in Dan Rabinowitz and Khawla Abu-Baker, *Coffins on Our Shoulders: The Experience of the Palestinian Citizens of Israel* (Berkeley: University of California Press, 2005), 159–61.

49. Jabareen, "Twenty Years of Oslo."

50. Rabinowitz and Abu-Baker, *Coffins on Our Shoulders*, 3.

51. Sorek, *Palestinian Commemoration in Israel*.

52. Omar Jabary Salamanca, Meza Qato, Kareem Rabie, and Sobhi Samour, "Past Is Present: Settler Colonialism in Palestine," *Settler Colonial Studies* 2, no. 1 (2012): 1–8.

53. "Haifa Declaration," 2007, available at http://mada-research.org/en/files/2007/09/haifaenglish .pdf, 12. Ghaida Rinawie- Zoabi, ed., "The Future Vision of the Palestinian Arabs in Israel" National Committee for the Heads of the Arab Local Authorities in Israel, 2006, https://www.adalah.org /uploads/oldfiles/newsletter/eng/dec06/tasawor-mostaqbali.pdf, 9.

54. Jabareen, "Twenty Years of Oslo."

55. Ilan Peleg and Dov Waxman, *Israel's Palestinians: The Conflict Within* (Cambridge: Cambridge University Press, 2011).

56. "The Nakba Law: Amendment No. 40 to the Budgets Foundations Law," Adalah, 2011, https:// www.adalah.org/en/law/view/496.

57. Nadim Rouhana and Areej Sabbagh-Khoury, "Memory and the Return of History in a Settler-Colonial Context: The Case of the Palestinians in Israel," *Interventions* 21, no. 4 (2018): 527–50, 528.

58. Mustafa, "Sons of the Village," 158.

59. "Founding Statement, English," Popular Movement for One Democratic State on Historic Palestine, November 26, 2013, https://www.antiimperialista.org/en/ods_founding_statement.

60. Rabi ʾId, "Ayman Odeh to *al-Modon*: 'We Cannot Abandon the Two-State Solution,'" *al-Modon*, April 26, 2015, https://tinyurl.com/yby6hjbq.

61. Shehadeh and Saʾabnah, "The Role of ʾ48 Palestinians," 55.

62. Shehadeh and Saʿabnah, "The Role of ʾ48 Palestinians," 56.

63. Mtanes Shehadeh, "Ayman Odeh and the Delusion of Betting on the Israeli Left," *Kul al-ʿArab*, May 30, 2017, https://www.alarab.com/Article/809978.

64. "Basic Law: Israel—The Nation-State of the Jewish People," unofficial translation, July 25, 2018, available at https://www.adalah.org/uploads/uploads/Basic_Law_Israel_as_the_Nation_State _of_the_Jewish_People_ENG_TRANSLATION_25072018.pdf.

65. Jeff Halper, "The 'One Democratic State Campaign' Program for a Multicultural Democratic State in Palestine/Israel," *Mondoweiss*, May 3, 2018, https://mondoweiss.net/2018/05/democratic-multi cultural-palestine/.

66. PCPSR, "A Joint Poll."

67. Shakir Jarrar, "Have the Arab Parties Turned into Parliamentary Parties? A Conversation on Participating in the Knesset," *Hiwar*, April 19, 2019, https://tinyurl.com/y2vsuh9s; Lana Tatour, "Zionism's Last Hope: The Joint List Cannot Reform Israeli Colonialism," *Middle East Eye*, March 10, 2020,

https://www.middleeasteye.net/opinion/palestinian-voters-israel-should-not-stake-their-struggle
-masters-tools.

68. Institute for National Security Studies, "A Political-Security Framework for the Israeli-Palestinian Arena," Institute for National Security Studies, October 8, 2018, http://www.inss.org.il/research /political-security-framework-israeli-palestinian-arena/.

69. US White House, "Peace to Prosperity: A Vision to Improve the Lives of the Palestinian and Israeli People," January 28, 2020, https://www.whitehouse.gov/wp-content/uploads/2020/01/Peace -to-Prosperity-0120.pdf, no longer available.

BIBLIOGRAPHY

Al-Haj, Majid. "Whither the Green Line? Trends in the Orientation of the Palestinians in Israel and the Territories." *Israel Affairs* 11, no. 1 (Spring 2005): 183–206.

Bishara, 'Azmi. "Bridging the Green Line: The PA, Israeli Arabs, and Final Status. An Interview with 'Azmi Bishara." *Journal of Palestine Studies* 26, no. 3 (Spring 1997): 67–80.

Bishara, 'Azmi, Sara Scalenghe, Steve Rothman, and Joel Beinin. "On Palestinians in the Israeli Knesset: Interview with 'Azmi Bishara." *Middle East Report*, no. 201 (Oct.–Dec. 1996): 27–28.

Dallasheh, Leena. "The Al-Ard Movement." In *The Palestinians in Israel: Readings in History, Politics and Society*, edited by Nadim N. Rouhana and Areej Sabbagh-Khoury, 139–48. Haifa: Mada al-Carmel, 2018.

El-Asmar, Fouzi. "Israel Revisited, 1976." *Journal of Palestine Studies* 6, no. 3 (Spring 1977): 47–65.

Haidar, 'Aziz. "The Nationalist Progressive Movement." In *The Palestinians in Israel: Readings in History, Politics and Society*, edited by Nadim N. Rouhana and Areej Sabbagh-Khoury, 161–74 (Haifa: Mada al-Carmel, 2018).

———. *The National Progressive Movement—Abna' al-Balad*. Beir Zeit: Markaz dirasat wa-tawthiq al-mujtama' al-filastini, 1989. [Arabic].

———. *The Palestinians in Israel in the Shadow of the Oslo Accord*. Beirut: Mu'assasat al-dirasat al-filastiniya, 1997. [Arabic].

Institute for National Security Studies. "A Political-Security Framework for the Israeli-Palestinian Arena." Institute for National Security Studies, October 8, 2018. http://www .inss.org.il/research/political-security-framework-israeli-palestinian-arena/.

Jabareen, Yousef. "Critical Reflection on Law, Equal Citizenship and Transformation." In *Plurality and Citizenship in Israel: Moving beyond the Jewish/Palestinian Civil Divide*, edited by Yotam Benziman and Dan Avnon, 94–118 (New York: Routledge, 2010).

———. "Twenty Years of Oslo: The Green Line's Challenge to the Statehood Project." *Journal of Palestine Studies* 43, mo. 1 (Autumn 2013): 41–50.

Jamal, Amal. "The Political Ethos of Palestinian Citizens of Israel: Critical Reading in the Future Vision Documents." *Israeli Studies Forum* 23, no. 2 (Winter 2008): 3–28.

Jiryis, Sabri. "The Arabs in Israel, 1973–1979." *Journal of Palestine Studies* 8, no. 4 (Summer 1979): 31–56.

Khalid, Mahmud. *The Israeli Left Camp*. Amman: Manshurat Dar al-Karmal, 1986. [Arabic].

Khalidi, Rashid. "The Resolutions of the Nineteenth Palestine National Council." *Journal of Palestine Studies* 19, no. 2 (Winter 1990): 29–42.

Landau, Jacob. *The Arabs in Israel: A Political Study*. London: Oxford University Press, 1969.

Mustafa, Mohaned. "Sons of the Village Movement." In *The Palestinians in Israel: Readings in History, Politics and Society*, edited by Nadim N. Rouhana and Areej Sabbagh-Khoury, 149–59 (Haifa: Mada al-Carmel, 2018).

Nassar, Maha. *Brothers Apart: Palestinian Citizens of Israel and the Arab World*. Stanford, CA: Stanford University Press, 2017.

Palestine National Council, "Communique, Algiers, 15 November 1988." *Journal of Palestine Studies* 18, no. 2 (Winter 1989): 216–23.

Palestinian Center for Policy and Survey Research. "Palestinian-Israeli Pulse: A Joint Poll." Palestinian Center for Policy and Survey Research, December 2017. http://www.pcpsr.org/sites/default/files/Table%20of%20Findings_English%20Joint%20Poll%204%20dec2017.pdf.

Peleg, Ilan, and Dov Waxman. *Israel's Palestinians: The Conflict Within*. Cambridge: Cambridge University Press, 2011.

Peretz, Don. "Arab Palestine: Phoenix or Phantom?" *Foreign Affairs* 48, no. 2 (January 1970): 322–33.

Peretz, Don, and Sammy Smooha. "Israel's Eleventh Knesset Election." *Middle East Journal* 39, no. 1 (Spring 1985): 86–103.

Rabin, Yitzhak. "Ratification of Interim Agreement." Israel Ministry of Foreign Affairs, October 5, 1995. https://tinyurl.com/y28gqwhc.

Rabinowitz, Dan, and Khawla Abu-Baker. *Coffins on Our Shoulders: The Experience of the Palestinian Citizens of Israel*. Berkeley: University of California Press, 2005.

Rekhess, Elie. "The Arab Nationalist Challenge to the Israeli Communist Party (1970–1985)." *Studies in Comparative Communism* 22, no. 4 (1989): 337–50.

Rinawie-Zoabi, Ghaida, ed. *The Future Vision of the Palestinian Arabs in Israel*. Nazareth: National Committee for the Heads of the Arab Local Authorities in Israel, 2006.

Robinson, Shira. *Citizen Strangers: Palestinians and the Birth of Israel's Liberal Settler State*. Stanford, CA: Stanford University Press, 2013.

Rouhana, Nadim. "The Intifada and the Palestinians of Israel: Resurrecting the Green Line." *Journal of Palestine Studies* 19, no. 3 (Spring 1990): 58–75.

———. "Israel and its Arab Citizens: Predicaments in the Relationship between Ethnic States and Ethnonational Minorities." *Third World Quarterly* 19, no. 2 (1998): 277–96.

Rouhana, Nadim, and Areej Sabbagh-Khoury. "Memory and the Return of History in a Settler-Colonial Context: The Case of the Palestinians in Israel." *Interventions* 21, no. 4 (2018): 527–50.

Salamanca, Omar Jabary, Mezna Qato, Kareem Rabie, and Sobhi Samour. "Past Is Present: Settler Colonialism in Palestine." *Settler Colonial Studies* 2, no. 1 (2012): 1–8.

Shehadeh, Mtanes, and 'Amid Sa'abnah. "The Role of '48 Palestinians and Their Place in the Palestinian National Project." *Majallat al-Dirasat al-Filastiniyah*, no. 105 (Winter 2015): 53–60 [Arabic].

Sorek, Tamir. *Palestinian Commemoration in Israel: Calendars, Monuments and Martyrs*. Stanford, CA: Stanford University Press, 2015.

Sultany, Nimer. "The National Democratic Assembly." In *The Palestinians in Israel: Readings in History, Politics and Society*, edited by Nadim N. Rouhana and Areej Sabbagh-Khoury, 216–29. Haifa: Mada al-Carmel, 2018.

Zureik, Elia, and 'Aziz Haider. "The Impact of the Intifadah on the Palestinians in Israel." *International Journal of the Sociology of Law* 19 (1991): 475–99.

11

Indigeneity as Resistance

Ilan Pappe

"We are not red Indians," Yasser Arafat declared when presented for the first time with the notion of Palestinians as an indigenous people.[1] Understandably, the leader of the Palestine Liberation Organization (PLO) dreaded the political implications of comparing the Palestinians to indigenous groups who had lost the struggle for sovereignty and independence, particularly to a group that had been enclaved in reservations and pushed to the social and geographical margins of the American reality. A group, one should hasten to remark, that nonetheless is still struggling and has not, all in all, accepted defeat.

This chapter deals with the delicate relationship between nationalism and indigeneity, and specifically in the north of historic Palestine. It begins by revisiting the common apprehension, articulated above by Arafat, about framing the Palestinian struggle as an indigenous one. By now, this issue has been addressed by the rich scholarship that applies the settler-colonial paradigm to the case study of Palestine. In this literature, the Zionist project, and the state of Israel, are presented as clear examples of a settler-colonial movement, implying that if the Zionists are the settlers, the Palestinians are the indigenous people of the land. What this indigeneity means and how it relates to the Palestinian national struggle is an ongoing discussion among academics and activists, one that will contribute significantly to the meaning of political struggle for liberation in this century.

This chapter claims that the people who have carried out the Palestinian struggle within the state of Israel in recent years articulate, by their actions, aspirations, and visions, their own version of a national indigenous struggle for liberation. At the heart of this struggle is the wish to decolonize historic Palestine as a whole, while being willing to achieve this incrementally and from below. It is an approach quite different from other modes of Palestinian resistance, such as the ones carried out in the past and the ones chosen by Palestinians in the Gaza Strip and the West Bank.

My central contention here is that indigeneity has become a signifier of cultural and political Palestinian struggle within the state of Israel, with possible implications for Palestinians in parts of the West Bank, in Areas B and C, and the greater Jerusalem area. It is important to stress that indigeneity is not treated here as a fixed identity but rather as a dynamic one that activists articulate and grow into.[2] This particular resistance complements current modes of existence and resistance among the Palestinian community in Israel. In view of recent political developments in Israel and the choices confronting the Palestinian community, indigeneity is unfolding as a powerful tool that can enhance the project of the liberation of Palestine as a whole, and of the Palestinians in Israel in particular. This does not mean that it would be possible to liberate Palestine fully without a total dismantlement of the Zionist institutions of the Jewish state and the creation of one democratic state as the endgame of this struggle. The discourse and practice of indigeneity described here help shed light on new ways to reach this goal.

INDIGENEITY AS AN ALTERNATIVE POLITICAL DISCOURSE

Ever since indigeneity became an analytic prism for explaining the Palestinian struggle, it has been a bone of contention within the area of Palestinian studies. The origins of the debate are a bit peculiar. It should have been triggered by the almost unanimous scholarly embrace of the settler-colonial paradigm as the paradigm for understanding the Palestinian condition, given that the embedded logical assumption is to define the Palestinians as either natives or indigenous in view of the fact that the Zionists are settlers. However, the indigeneity debate was instead prompted when scholars started to study one particular group of Palestinians: the Bedouins of the Naqab.[3] Many nationalists feared that using such a framework of analysis would differentiate one Palestinian group from another and thereby contribute to fragmentation of the Palestinian people through what one scholar called "divisive classification."[4] The danger is that such a practice will tally with Israeli policies of dividing the Palestinians into religious and cultural minorities, thereby questioning their cohesive national identity.

However, the debate surrounding the applicability of the discourse of indigeneity to the Palestinians is not simply an academic one. The principal conceptual concern among scholars who object to this designation lies in the limited nature of the UN Declaration on the Rights of Indigenous Peoples (adopted in 2007) when applied to the Palestinian struggle, as this declaration does not include a clear endorsement of a people's right to independent statehood. It is also possible that those scholars have reservations regarding the use of the prism of indigeneity when it comes to describing the Palestinian struggle because of some preconceived dominant stereotypes concerning the "primitivism" and vulnerability of indigenous people.[5]

One of the most detailed challenges to the indigeneity framework was voiced by Nadim Rouhana.[6] He claimed that the Zionist settler-colonial project was different from what he called "triumphant" settler-colonial projects—in which the natives were conquered and subdued, as in North America and Australia. Since Zionism has not as yet "triumphed," the struggle against it is still national, including for the Palestinians inside Israel. He therefore prefers to use the term "homeland nationalism" to designate the efforts of Palestinians in Israel to reclaim Palestine as their national homeland. For Rouhana, this "homeland nationalism" complements the broader Palestinian nationalism of claiming Palestine as the homeland of the Palestinian people.

I believe that the political nature of the Palestinian struggle can be enriched by incorporating the concept of cultural indigenous resistance into it, in particular at a time when there is no space or scope for the notion of armed struggle. As Edward Said had clarified, culture is political, especially when we focus on an expanded, rather than narrow, definition of what culture is. The narrow definition relates to the aesthetic and literary assets of a society: "Culture is a concept that includes a refining and elevating element, each society's reservoir of the best that has been known and thought." The expanded definition of culture, by contrast, sees it as the theatre of life "where various political and ideological causes engage one another."[7] Culture, in the eyes of the settler state, is defined within the narrow definition put forward by Said. For the indigenous population, it is understood within the expanded version.

This chapter contends that the indigenous cultural struggle is not an antithesis, or alternative, to the political national one, but rather the optimal struggle available, in view of the historical junction the Palestinian question finds itself in. An indigenous cultural struggle is, in its essence, part of a political resistance, especially given that other modes of resistance have not been very successful so far. As pointed out by Amara, framing the Palestinian people within the settler-colonial paradigm is a "manifestation of a resistant approach to the Palestinian political project" of state formation.[8] The Palestinian wish for decolonization remains the same, but the nature of the struggle has changed.

There is a growing recognition among other Palestinian scholars that Palestinians share a common fate with quite a few indigenous peoples. According to Rana Barakat, this shared fate with other indigenous people should be the focus of Palestinian research on settler-colonialism moving forward. She argues that it is time to leave aside the already saturated deconstruction of Zionism as a settler-colonial movement and focus instead on the potency of indigeneity as a conceptual and political framework moving forward.[9] Her views are in line with the useful comparisons that Mahmoud Mamdani makes between the Native American and Palestinian predicaments. Mamdani suggests that in both cases the main struggle between the settler states and the natives is about citizenship and land.[10] Both indigenous communities (and here he refers not necessarily to Palestinians in general, but specifically to those in Israel) have employed legal and civil means to change their status within the settler state. The legal struggle for citizenship rights in both contexts reflects the settlers' view of indigeneity: American Indians were "declared" citizens in 1924 with the Indian Citizenship Act, thus they were considered naturalized citizens, as distinct from those who gained citizenship rights through birth. Palestinians in Israel were declared citizens by means of a similar act, the 1952 Nationality Law. This law immediately created two types of citizenship: one for Jews by virtue of a "birthright," and one for Palestinians by a process akin to naturalization. In both cases, the natives were depicted, or framed, by the settlers as aliens who needed to be naturalized. The struggle against this particular injustice can be therefore better understood within the field of native and indigenous studies than within conventional national or nationalist paradigms.[11]

Those who insist on employing indigeneity as a useful lens to interpret the reality of the Palestinians in Israel stress that the application of the indigenous framework does not affect the subjective Palestinian sense of identity. Indigeneity stems from a more complex and dialectic process in which native people respond to their role or place within the settler-colonial narrative and policies. Thus, the comparison to Native Americans does not focus on the success or failure of the settler-colonial project of eliminating the natives but compares their place (or rather their absence) within the ethos of settlers' communities: their construction as the savage Native Americans who will disappear with the completion of the "errand in the wilderness" of the white settlers in North America and the primitive Arabs who will wilt under the Zionist project of "blooming of the desert."[12] This process has profound impacts on Israeli policies and the Palestinian community in Israel, since it reflects not simply an assault on Palestinian national dignity, as Rouhana argues, but also a threat to their indigenous survival.[13]

INDIGENEITY AS A POLITICAL STRATEGY

Israeli politics has undergone a drastic transformation since the collapse of the Camp David negotiations in 2000. The Israeli regime has become more nationalist, religious, and extreme. The orientation is towards a unilateral expansion of the state over the Occupied Territories and a fierce struggle against any manifestation of Palestinian national sentiment or agenda within areas defined as Israel proper. This new attitude has been legalized through the Jewish Nation-State Basic Law in July 2018. Meanwhile, Israeli processes of land expropriation, informal and formal annexation, and the imposition of Israeli law in various parts of the West Bank have inflicted a final deathblow to the Israeli Palestinian "peace process" and to the chances of a two-state solution.

Within Palestinian politics, as well as in the scholarly world, however, a clear distinction continues to be made between the Palestinian struggle for statehood in the West Bank and the Gaza Strip and the Palestinian civic struggle inside Israel. To this day, the Palestinian leadership on both sides of the Green Line, notwithstanding their cooperation and constant dialogue, regard their struggles as distinct and different.[14] The implication of such a position is that Palestinian citizens in Israel are not present in the classical anticolonialist struggle to achieve an independent state, which those in the Occupied Territories still hope to attain. As 'Azmi Bishara commented years ago, the Palestinian strategy in Israel has never been about destroying the Jewish state from within or about gaining sovereignty.[15]

These debates reveal the importance of clearly distinguishing between the terms *indigenous* and *native*, which activists tend to use interchangeably. In this chapter, native is a more neutral, static term, almost an ecological statement, that defines a group's location and attachment. Indigenous, on the other hand, is an evolving position of empowerment and resilience against the oppression that natives face. It is the political framework in which communities express their national, or group, identity. In this regard, the Palestinians in Israel are indigenous, native, and a national minority. They are separated from the other Palestinian groups and yet are reintegrated with the Palestinians in the West Bank by virtue of Israel's policies of expansion and colonization, which continue within the Green Line and outside it.[16]

Affirming national identity undoubtedly can entail affirming the Palestinian right to their own state next to Israel. However, the claim for indigenous rights goes beyond a claim for a sovereign state over 22 percent of one's homeland. It refers to the historical homeland in its totality as much as entails a demand for redistributing land ownership and wealth. When it becomes part of a campaign for a change of regime from the Jordan River to the Mediterranean, it is also an aspiration to dismantle settler-colonial institutions as well as reshape the debate surrounding state immigration policy and its symbolic nature. An incremental political, cultural struggle in line with such a vision can produce partial but meaningful achievements, even without bringing about a change of sovereignty, as can be seen in other parts of the world.[17]

The visions that one has of the future, or of the possible political solutions available, undoubtedly impact, consciously or unconsciously, one's understanding of the present. For Palestinians inside Israel, be they activists, scholars, or both, full independence, that is, complete territorial decolonization, is not a realistic goal. In such a context, indigeneity becomes another form of self-assertion against the settler state of Israel. Willingness to adopt indigeneity as a social and political framework of resistance is more clearly evident, and acceptable, among the Palestinian community inside Israel than among the Palestinians in the Occupied Territories, where quite a few still adhere to a national liberation agenda that seeks the creation of an independent Palestinian state next to Israel.

This willingness to define oneself as indigenous can clash with more explicit national self-definition. Yet, the tension that the Palestinian population inside Israel has felt between these two definitions has been eased in recent years. This is largely due to two developments: on the one hand, the despair that many feel regarding the prospect of substantial political solutions, or a viable Palestinian state, in the foreseeable future, and on another hand, a determination to work more locally and less ambitiously against a settler state that with every passing year becomes less tolerant and more discriminatory. Both processes, political despair and bottom-up activism, have meant that activists are avoiding macro-level political and ideological projects and focusing instead on tangible actions that protect the Palestinian community.

It is important to note, though, that the transition from political to cultural activism that various activists are embarking on is not part of a conscious attempt to substitute, or avoid, the need to redefine the Palestinian liberation project moving forward. It is rather a pragmatic adaptation to an ongoing struggle in light of the failure of one hundred years of resistance to liberate the homeland and given the existential threats that the neo-Zionist state of Israel poses to Palestinians in the twenty-first century.

There is also another impulse encouraging a new civil and scholarly understanding of the Palestinian struggle. It is the wish not to repeat past failures such as the unsuccessful attempt to internationalize the struggle of the Palestinians in Israel. Neither the PLO nor Israel allowed the case of the Palestinians in Israel to be discussed in the peace process. The international community regarded the relationship of the Jewish state with its Palestinian minority as a domestic issue pertaining to those living inside Israel. The PLO in the 1970s explained this exclusion of the Palestinians in Israel from its overall national struggle by stating that each group of Palestinians knew best what kind of a struggle it should conduct according to its specific context. This has never undermined the PLO's standing among Palestinians in Israel as is so accurately and beautifully manifested in the poetic correspondence between Mahmoud Darwish and Samih al-Qassem.[18]

Within the framework of the conventional Palestinian national struggle, the Palestinians in Israel did not constitute a matter of international concern, but were a domestic Israeli problem. Framing this minority as indigenous enables it to be associated with the global struggle of indigenous people, and therefore internationalizes its cause. The international dimension of the comparative study on indigeneity was highlighted by the case of Steven Salaita, a Palestinian scholar in the United States who compared American Indian literature and political history with that of Palestine.[19] In his work, and in the campaign that ensued in the wake of a university decision to withdraw its offer of employment on ideological grounds, the international connection between the victims of both settler-colonial projects showed that academically and politically this is a valid and useful struggle. It recruited many in the complex matrix of American ethnicity and multiculturalism to the Palestinian struggle, though in the past they had been distanced from it. The connection had been recognized before, due to Edward Said's influence on native studies in America and his twin scholarship on Orientalism and Palestine, which reinforced these links and made them a potent factor in the struggle for Palestine in American and international public spaces.

The recognition of this international dimension can be seen in the United States, where efforts to draw parallels and organize joint solidarity activities between indigenous and Palestinian groups have intensified over the past years. For example, the Palestine Youth Movement of San Diego and Collectivo Zapatista came together in Fall 2013 for a five-kilometer run along the US-Mexico border, to show the parallels between the settler-colonial projects in Mexico and Palestine.[20]

This being said, it is important to make a clear the distinction between indigeneity as understood within the liberal Zionist position, which grants cultural autonomy to Palestinians, and the nature of the indigenous cultural struggles described here. Liberal Israeli bodies such the mainstream Israeli Association for Civil Rights see their mobilization on behalf of Palestinian citizens in recent years as a struggle over the soul of Israeli democracy. In this they are similar to the anti-occupation Jewish movement, which wished to end the occupation because of the moral damage it causes to the Jewish state. The indigenous struggle for the Palestinians in Israel, however, centers on Palestinian attachment to the land. The Israeli democracy, or alleged democracy, can hide its settler-colonial nature in many aspects of life, but not on the question of land ownership. As the Palestinians in the north of Israel say, the land speaks Arabic in the Jewish state.

Palestinian engagement with Israeli democracy is not an end in itself, but a means of ensuring first of all the survival of the indigenous population, then its equality, and finally its role in shaping the future solution of Israel/Palestine. As the discussion below shows, the projects initiated by Palestinian citizens of Israel to assert their rights to the land and to equality are part of an indigenous cultural and political resistance now taking precedence over old forms of resistance such as armed struggle or state-building. These young Palestinians navigate carefully between respect for the national struggle and its legacy, on the one hand, and the need to find new forms of struggle, on the other.

INDIGENOUS PALESTINIAN STRUGGLES WITHIN ISRAEL: CULTURE AS POLITICAL RESISTANCE

Cultural resistance has become quite a common scholarly reference in cultural studies, one that is "located in countless non-heroic practices that make up the realm of the everyday and its multiple connections with contemporary global life," as Roland Bleiker put it.[21] Cultural resistance underscores how various cultural practices are employed to contest and combat a dominant power, often constructing a different vision of the world in the process. As Gramsci pointed out, power resides not only in institutions, but also in the ways people make sense of their world; hegemony is a political and cultural process.[22] Armed with culture instead of guns, one fights a different type of battle. Whereas traditional battles were "wars of maneuver," frontal assaults that seized the state, cultural battles are "wars of position," flanking maneuvers, commando raids, and infiltrations, staking out positions from which to attack and then reassemble civil society.

It is precisely in the popular cultural resistance that indigeneity plays an important political role. From the point of view of the Jewish state, "traditional" or "Arab" frames for social mobilization are not associated with challenging Jewish statehood or sovereignty. The main assault on the Palestinian claim of indigeneity comes rather from Israeli scholars who are embedded in the settler-colonial project and do all they can to deindigenize the Palestinians in the academic discourse. The Israeli government, on the other hand, is far more simplistic in its approach, and regards only clear-cut national framings of the struggle as a danger to the Jewish state.[23] Although one should say that this is beginning to change: in part as a result of the effectiveness of cultural resistance and in part due to the Israeli political system moving further to the extreme right, indigenous cultural projects have been more systemically targeted since 2016 as constituting a threat to Israeli national security.

In this respect, it would be useful to note that cultural resistance can be political without being outwardly nationalistic. It has a political message even if it is not about gaining seats in parliament or winning elections, or seats, at the negotiation table. As the case studies below will illuminate, efforts to de-erase the settler-colonial state imprint, which has become the major focus of the cultural resistance inside Israel, are based on a sense of indigeneity. These current practices can be analyzed as a new shift of emphasis, one which also responds to the drastic changes of the past two decades. Protecting the indigeneity of the Palestinian people living inside Israel as a set of rights can be the principal cultural struggle against a regime that has the appearance, and some of the practices, of a liberal democracy, but in essence is not. Liberal democracy in the Israeli case has instead proven to be a tool of a settler-colonial movement that has not as yet completed its overall objective, namely its vision of a Jewish state in Palestine.

It is also worth noting that blurring national and indigenous struggles might be less detrimental to the national project than originally thought while being more beneficial to the community on the ground. As Stephen Duncombe remarks, with the immediacy of global media, the local becomes national and at the same time global: cultural resistance becomes a space for developing tools for political action, a dress rehearsal for the actual political act or a political action in itself, one which operates by redefining the meaning of politics.[24] The potential relevance of this conception in the case of the perpetual Palestinian demand for the right of return is particularly poignant.

De-Judaizing the Judaization

The Israeli double project of indigenizing Jewish society while de-indigenizing the Palestinian minority in Israel began in 1948 and has not ceased. The Galilee is the main space where this double process has been taking place, the site of the Israeli government project of "Judaization of the Galilee." In this Israeli campaign, the Galilee is presented as a cradle of the Jewish nation, articulating one narrative while seeking to obliterate another. The Judaization of the Galilee necessitates not only settling the Galilee with Jews, but also altering the landscape so that Jews will no longer be considered settlers in the Palestinian Galilee. The establishment of national parks around sites that were regarded as important for the Jewish national historical narrative served to foster a Jewish self-perception of indigeneity.

The Judaization of the Galilee is portrayed officially as a successful transformation of the Jews in the region into the indigenous population in the Galilee, and the transmutation of the native Palestinians into settlers. However, if in this narrative the Galilee was perceived as an ancient Jewish land that was to be redeemed by its native sons, there was a functional need to leave intact those parts of the landscape that signify the antiquity of the Galilee, even if these were located in emptied Palestinian villages and quarters. This revision of spatial narrative thus produced a paradoxical reality: the venues in which much of the indigenous cultural resistance in the Galilee takes place are located within Israeli tourist sites. Thus, for instance, the ancient archaeological sites of Safuriyya and Bir'im are the spaces in which young Palestinians chose to declare their right of return as a second generation of internal refugees.

So far, the indigenous resistance movement is not counted for much by the Israelis themselves and this is the reason why it can still prosper and be expanded. The focus of Palestinian counter policy is the commemoration of the catastrophe, the Nakba. It consists of efforts to reconstruct life and landscape as it was before the catastrophe. Israel does not regard 1948 as a catastrophe, but for now it also does not see the connection between the reconstruction of erased life before 1948 and the commemoration of the catastrophe. In recent years though, Israel has enacted a new policy that entails closing access to material in its archives that deals with the Nakba and has put serious hurdles in the way of the attempts of Palestinians in Israel to commemorate the Nakba. That being said, such commemorations are still allowed and are largely carried out by the younger generation of the Palestinians in Israel.

Palestinians' use of indigeneity as a powerful motif can been seen in the kinds of projects activists have been initiating in various domains, such as art, education, and architecture, among others, as part of a cultural resistance that is deeply political. These initiatives, some of which are described below, are indicative of a bottom-up, daily, and nondramatic resistance to a Jewish state determined to wipe out the Palestinian indigeneity.

Graffiti

The theoretical literature on graffiti depicts it as an urban and suburban phenomenon but in Israel and Palestine it is mainly rural. Scholars writing about youth graffiti usually see it as part of youth delinquency. Among the Palestinians in Israel it is precisely the opposite—graffiti is a manifestation of the commitment and struggle of Palestinian youth. It is possible, however, to argue, in line with some of the general literature, that graffiti represents a means to share values, ethics, and codes of behavior via where and how it is produced.

In several villages in the Galilee murals painted on private homes and public buildings draw the pre-1948 village scenery. Once they were drawn in one village, they were emulated elsewhere. They are drawn by local artists, encouraged by cultural NGOs and local municipalities. The murals convey a very clear message: different communities coexisted in peace before the Nakba. In many ways, the murals are a virtual attempt to reruralize a community that was long ago forced to abandon agriculture and commerce as a way of life.[25]

Reconstructing the Palestinian "Home"

In 1948, half of Palestine's villages were destroyed within nine months of the Nakba. The lost Palestinian villages are not the same villages that can been seen today all over Israel/Palestine. The pre-1948 Palestinian village was a place where people of different religions lived together, where agriculture was the main source of subsistence. The village was organically connected to the ecological cycle of life in the country, respecting its flora and fauna, utilizing its water resources and natural herbs well and responsibly, and built according to the topography and climate of each region.

In 2017, the cultural NGO al-Manar (situated in Majdal Krum), together with the firm al-Arkan (located in Kabul), embarked on a unique project that seeks to reconstruct the heritage of Palestine as a legacy for the future. The project is called Hadara ("civilization") and focuses on the reconstruction of archetypal pre-1948 Palestinian villages. In some villages, such as Kefar Yasif, murals were painted and the village piazza and residences were reconstructed. In some houses, people scraped away new mortar covering old walls in order to restore the old style of building, which provided cool houses in the summer and warm ones in the winter. Very few architects or builders today are capable of building in such a way—an artisanship that was lost, together with other cultural knowledge, in the Nakba.

The uniqueness of this project lies in the fact that the reconstructions were accomplished with materials that came directly from the destroyed villages: organic, authentic, natural materials that are part of the Palestinian heritage. The reconstructed villages were built with the support of eyewitnesses from the period, as well as their photographs and narratives. The terraces were built with stones from the destroyed villages; trees and herbs were extracted from the original sources. Even the coloring of the houses was sourced from local natural resources. A group of highly professional artisans from Russia and the Ukraine, with local architects and historians, have also helped to make models of these reconstructions that were distributed in recent years to the public. These models were supplied to more than one hundred Palestinian schools in Israel and the West Bank. In each they are placed at the entrance of the school, surrounded by posters that highlight aspects of pre-1948 rural Palestine.

Meanwhile, a number of Palestinian individuals and NGOs are working on having old Palestinian houses—the few that remain in urban spaces—recognized as UNESCO heritage sites. In downtown Haifa, local organizations are trying to dissuade the local municipality from demolishing these houses, such as the house of Emil Touma, who was one the leading intellectuals and journalists of the late Mandate and early Israeli statehood periods.

These projects of rehabilitation of houses and villages may appear cultural in nature, since they do not focus on sovereignty or liberation. They remain political insofar as they attempt to commemorate and rectify the dislocation of the native population by reconstructing the architectural face of indigeneity.

Indigeneity as Educational Resistance

Education is another important space for indigenous resistance, a struggle for Palestinian autonomy in an educational system that has been under Israeli scrutiny since 1948. The Israeli secret service has long vetted teachers and school heads alike, while punishing whoever challenged the curriculum by teaching the Palestinian narrative.[26] Today, activists need to navigate carefully between the regime's refusal to recognize the Palestinians in Israel as a national minority and the latter's own refusal to accept the imposed Zionist narrative of the Israeli educational system.

The importance of indigeneity for the struggle of Palestinians in Israel—and the role of education in that struggle—is clearly articulated in the "Vision Papers," composed by Palestinian political and intellectual elites inside Israel. These are four documents prepared and publicized by Palestinian NGOs in Israel in 2006 and 2007. In 2006, the first two were published by the NGO Musawa in Haifa and by the Follow-Up Committee (the main representative body of the Palestinian minority in Israel, composed of members of Knesset, all heads of local Arab councils and municipalities, and heads of NGOs). In 2007, Mada al-Karmil, the leading independent research center in Haifa, and Adalah, the leading legal NGO of Palestinians in Israel, published their own vision papers. All of these papers successfully articulate the Palestinian minority's political aspirations to be recognized as "a native national group" (and as a minority according to the relevant definitions in international law), who aspires to live in a democratic state as equal citizens. Several times they mention indigeneity as the main moral and legal basis for demanding equality and international protection.[27]

The authors of these documents demand "cultural educational autonomy," on the grounds that "the Arab Palestinians in Israel—as natives—have the right to run their own educational system."[28] They elaborate these educational demands, arguing for a "territorial cultural statutory autonomy" and demanding the creation of a separate Arab educational authority within the Israeli Ministry of Education.[29]

The structures requested are familiar—they are borrowed from Canada and the Swedish minority in Finland. However, to understand why these efforts represent an affirmation of indigeneity and not just an affirmation of national rights, it is worth pointing out that in a way such a structure already exists; namely, a separate educational office for "Arabs" is part of the Israeli Ministry of Education, but it has a different cultural vision of what the "Arabs" need to learn than the Palestinians in Israel themselves do. Without the defining aspirations of the "Vision Papers" within the settler/indigenous binary, it would be very difficult to see any fundamental difference in the power relations between an Israeli Zionist Ministry of Education and its Arab educational office (as it is now) and an autonomous one (as envisaged in the "Vision Papers").

Meanwhile, the Follow-Up Committee expanded an effort begun in 2008 by an NGO, Ibn Khaldun, to "shadow" every textbook and official program of the Israeli Ministry of Education with a counter textbook and program, which teachers could use as they deemed right. For instance, when the Israeli Education Ministry provided a booklet of "One Hundred Basic Notions about Zionism" as part of the curriculum, Ibn Khaldun produced a counter, "One Hundred Basic Notions about Palestine."[30]

There is not, as yet, comprehensive research on educational efforts by educators and parents in the Palestinian community to circumvent the official curriculum. It appears that widespread informal home-schooling provides an alternative narrative to the official one. There is also a local Palestinian academic effort to deconstruct the "Arab" school curriculum in Israel as a way to de-educate indigenous Palestinians. The danger of producing an overtly national narrative is being replaced by efforts to create a less conspicuous, indigenous one. It should be noted that while the liberal Zionist project tries hypocritically to universalize both the Jewish and Arab narratives (by stressing human and civil rights, but ignoring indigenous rights), Palestinian activists and NGOs focus on indigeneity as a cultural project from below, one that seeks to counter the erasure produced by the settler-colonial project's false universalizing mission.

Indigenizing Segregated Spaces

The "Vision Papers" devote considerable space to discussing land ownership and rights, which remain indeed the most pressing issue for the Palestinian community in Israel. In the early years of the state, the communist party led a national struggle to save Palestinian lands from an Israeli policy of expropriation, especially in the Galilee. The struggle continues today as a civic one, with a strong emphasis on how expropriation, and the severe difficulties of buying land, are violations of the indigenous rights of the minority.

There are, however, two ways of living in a mixed community nowadays in Israel. Palestinians who live in originally mixed towns are discriminated against at all levels of municipal and governmental services. There, the indigenous struggle is about regaining space for expansion according to the population's needs, demolishing segregation walls, safeguarding Arabic names of streets and neighborhoods, and overall improving the physical infrastructure. In Acre and Jaffa, for example, the struggle has been mainly against governmental policies of silent de-Arabization and transfer of Arab neighborhoods to Jewish ownership and identity. Ad hoc organizations help residents to remain steadfast, providing them with legal aid and attracting international attention to their plight and to the danger of their eviction. The town of Ramleh is a case in point. There, Palestinians are resisting a municipality that deems them aliens and *mitrad*— "nuisance" in Hebrew, a term used for physical objects such as garbage. An NGO called al-Bayt ("Home") has succeeded in persuading the UNESCO to recognize some Palestinian buildings as cultural heritage sites. What remains ominous is the fact that the Palestinian neighborhoods in Ramleh are not included in the city's overall municipal strategic planning.[31]

The second way of challenging spatial segregation is seen in Palestinians moving into what were meant to be exclusively Jewish towns. There is no way of knowing how many Palestinians have succeeded in moving into towns and settlements in the Galilee that are designated by the state as exclusively Jewish. Approximately seventy thousand Palestinians are estimated to live in either officially Jewish spaces or traditionally Jewish neighborhoods in mixed towns. Also striking is the increase in the number of Jews living in Palestinian villages. This latter phenomenon is even more subversive, given the settler-colonial and segregating structure of present-day Israel.[32] There is a socioeconomic dimension to both developments: poor Jews move to Arab areas because they are more affordable, while Palestinians who are higher earners move to exclusively Jewish spaces. The latter can afford paying double, and at times triple, the rent that Jewish house owners would demand from Jewish renters. Their wish to live in these particular spaces corresponds to the overall desire to remain within the pre-1967 Israel borders in the eventuality of a two-state solution being implemented.

The government has attempted to stop such developments. There is an explicit discourse in Israel, which is translated into recent legislation, about "saving" Jewish towns and settlements from further Palestinian "invasion." One such legal act was the Acceptance to Communities bill of 2011, which formalized the establishment of admission committees to review potential new residents of communities of up to four hundred family units in the Naqab and Galilee regions, where the Palestinian population in Israel is largely concentrated. The law's central intention is to prevent Palestinians from settling in Jewish communities.

Commemoration as Cultural Resistance

Following the failure of the 1991 Madrid Conference to broach the subject of refugees, the principal body representing the internal refugees in Israel (more than a quarter of a million people) founded a new NGO, the Association for the Defense of the Rights of the Internally Displaced in Israel (ADRID). Since 1998 it has organized an annual March of Return on Israel's Independence Day (which is celebrated according to the lunar Hebrew calendar), marching to the site of a different 1948-destroyed village each year, as a way to remind the Jewish public of Israel of the price the Palestinians paid for Jewish independence.

Starting in the early 1990s, the Palestinian community in Israel also began commemorating Nakba Day on May 15, like all other Palestinian communities in the world. These events are closely coordinated with other Palestinian groups in Palestine and beyond. The ceremonies organized by Palestinians in Israel prioritize the return of internally displaced refugees to their villages before the implementation of the general right of return for all the Palestinians.

Commemoration of the Nakba by Palestinian citizens of Israel is now a widespread annual act, manifested in a March of Return, by thousands of people, to one of the many destroyed 1948 villages. These marches are attended by all the Palestinian politicians and have become a focus of cultural, as well as political, struggle against the 2011 Israeli Nakba law, which prevents public funding to anyone who commemorates the 1948 events as the Nakba. It is also a day of solidarity with oppressed Palestinians elsewhere, in which speakers are invited by video call from Gaza to emphasize the joint struggle to remove the blockade and end the siege. The indigenous dimension of the commemoration is accentuated by the Jewish, in particular liberal Jewish, objection to it. One of the gurus of liberal Zionism, Professor Shlomo Avineri, criticized it as an act of delegitimizing the state, since he saw the commemoration as revealing the hidden national wish of Palestinian citizens to lay the foundation of a Palestinian state all over historical Palestine.[33]

ADRID's vision of the future is to create clear educational and cultural spaces in which to de-erase what was wiped out in the 1948 Nakba. They do this through constant exploration of the legal possibilities for return to demolished villages and for compensation. Their strategies, such as the demand for the collective memory of the Nakba to be part of the identity and ethos of any future political entity that would come out of a process of reconciliation and peace, are similar to those used in other indigenous struggles. The very term *internal refugees* emphasizes indigeneity and is capable of protecting Palestinian rights in the face of efforts to denationalize the Palestinian political struggle. The implications that such a denationalization would have for the struggle of Palestinians in refugee camps in Lebanon and Syria, as well as Palestinians who might find themselves in a new reality if Israel annexes Area C in the West Bank or the West Bank as a whole (as the option that would make the return to "only" the Palestinian state in the Occupied Territories irrelevant), would be major.

CONCLUSIONS

The international legitimacy that the Jewish state enjoys has pushed the Palestinian minority in Israel to use new frameworks in the political struggle for their rights. The political elite of this minority still operates with reference to the two-state solution; it sees the struggle inside Israel as concerned with protecting their collective national rights and encouraging democratization of the Israeli political system. However, the death of this solution and the formation of a de facto single state, a variation on the South African apartheid model, has brought changes in the civil and cultural struggle of the Palestinians inside Israel that might also affect those living in Jerusalem and Area C in the West Bank, areas which are incrementally being annexed to Israel.

The success of these Palestinian struggles inside Israel will continue to depend on the ways in which the Palestinian liberation project will be redefined to fit the new reality and thereby stop relying on nostalgic national notions of the 1960s and 1970s. While the Palestinian national political limbo persists, Palestinians activists inside pre-1967 Israel are stressing Palestinian indigeneity. They thus offer an alternative language to the banned demand for national Palestinian rights in Israel while highlighting both the continuous settler-colonial nature of the regime and possible ways toward decolonization.

Designing and teaching, even if informally, alternative school curricula, or organizing Nakba commemorations and return marches are struggles for indigeneity. They are particularly important in the face of Israel's attempts of indigenization, or Judaization, that not only come at the expense of the native Palestinian population but also are meant to continue their displacement and destitution. Thus space, place, and counter-settlements are the means of the modern-day struggle against the settler-colonial state, and not only against the occupation in the West Bank or the Gaza Strip.[34] Although the Israeli unilateral annexation of large parts of the West Bank since 2000 blurs the boundaries of post- and pre-1967 Israel, it expands the options of struggle within the West Bank, or the part of it that would be annexed to Israel.

The Palestinian struggle is and will continue to be a struggle against the privileges granted to the settlers over the natives. However, as long as the democratic game is played in Israel, an Islamic movement can win (as it did in municipal and national elections) and create a countercultural religious space in the public arena, one that is both religious and national. Once Israel outlawed the Islamic movement, it became clear that countercultural spaces, defined in either national or Islamic terms, would not be tolerated by the state. The Islamic movement has moved since then towards claiming religious spaces as "traditional" and "Islamic cultural" centers as part of their indigenous rights. This move must be read as a strategy of survival against, rather than submission to, Israeli settler-colonial erasure policies. Such cultural resistance, as has been shown, is daily, routine, and everywhere. It is performed in community centers, in youth and football clubs, in the sites of informal education, and in plays and films.[35]

It is too early to tell whether present-day Israel, with it nationalist and extremist ideology, will try to block any activity that is defined as indigenous and label it as either nationalist or terrorist. Demanding normality may seem a modest claim from a radical perspective that continues to insist on national liberation defined in terms of exclusive political sovereignty. The demand for normality, however, is existential given the ongoing setter-colonial reality. Unlike the political elites on both sides who associate demands for equality with grand political solutions, the daily cultural struggles of Palestinians who have lived in Israel for more than seventy years are centered on the demand for equality now in the name of civic and indigenous rights. Theirs is a struggle for equality as much as it is for national liberation. It goes beyond the demand for equal rights; it is an antidote to the dehumanization ingrained in a settler-colonial project—a call for humanizing the Palestinians in Israel.

NOTES

Parts of this chapter are drawn from Ilan Pappe, "Indigeneity as Resistance: Notes on the Palestinian Struggle within Twenty-First-Century Israel," *South Atlantic Quarterly* 117, no. 1 (2018): 157–78.

1. Yasser Arafat, "An Interview with Yasser Arafat," by Scott MacLeod, *New York Review of Books*, June 11, 1987.

2. James Clifford, "Indigenous Articulations," *The Contemporary Pacific* 3, no. 2 (2001): 468–90.

3. See for example, Ahmad Amara, Ismael Abu-Saad, and Oren Yiftachel, eds., *Indigenous (In) Justice: Human Rights Law and Bedouin Arabs in the Naqab/Negev* (Cambridge, MA: Harvard Law School Publications, 2012) and in particular the chapter there by Rodolfo Stavenhagen and Ahmad Amara, "International Law of Indigenous Peoples and the Naqab Bedouin Arabs," 158–93.

4. A point discussed at length by Oren Yiftachel, "Epilogue: Studying Naqab/Negev Bedouins –Towards a Colonial Paradigm?" *HAGAR: Studies in Culture, Polity and Identities* 8, no. 2 (2008): 83–108.

5. Mansour Nasara, "The Ongoing Judaisation of the Naqab and the Struggle for Recognizing the Indigenous Rights of the Arab Bedouin People," *Settler Colonial Studies* 2, no. 1 (2012): 81–107.

6. Nadim N. Rouhana, "Homeland Nationalism and Guarding Dignity in a Settler-Colonial Context: The Palestinian Citizens of Israel Reclaim their Homeland," *Borderland e-Journal* 14, no. 1 (2015).

7. Edward Said, *Culture and Imperialism* (New York: Vintage Books, 1993), xiv.

8. Ahmad Amara, "Indigeneity in Palestinian Studies: Between Political and Legal Indigeneity," paper presented at the 2016 Palestinian Studies Workshop, Brown University, https://palestinianstudies .files.wordpress.com/2015/12/amara-ahmad.docx, 3.

9. Rena Barakat, "Writing/Righting Palestine Studies: Settler Colonialism, Indigenous Sovereignty and Resisting the Ghost(s) of History," *Settler Colonial Studies* 8, no. 3 (2018): 349–63.

10. Mahmoud Mamdani, "Settler Colonialism: Then and Now," *Critical Inquiry* 4, no. 3 (2015): 596–614.

11. Elizabeth Povinelli, *The Cunning of Recognition: Indigenous Alterities and the Making of Australian Multiculturalism* (Durham, NC: Duke University Press, 2002); Audra Simpson, *Theorizing Native Studies* (Durham, NC: Duke University Press, 2014).

12. Eric Cheyfitz, "Response to Steven Saliata's Inter/Nationalism from the Holy Land to the New World: Encountering Palestine in American Indian Studies," *Native American and Indigenous Studies* 1, no. 2 (2014): 145–47.

13. Rouhana, "Homeland Nationalism." See also Clifford, "Indigenous Articulations."

14. 'Azmi Bishara, "On the Question of the Palestinian Minority in Israel," *Theory and Criticism* 3 (1993): 7–21 [Hebrew]. See Maha Nassar, *Brothers Apart: Palestinian Citizens of Israel and the Arab World* (Stanford: Stanford University Press, 2017).

15. Bishara, "On the Question of the Palestinian Minority in Israel."

16. There is not yet a census of how many Palestinians from Israel work, study, and live in the West Bank, but their growth is exponential

17. In the Philippines, for instance, indigenous struggles resulted in a legal reform in the country's laws of land ownership, while in Ecuador they contributed to change in the civil rights agenda and land reform. For more details see Jose Mencio Molinatas, "The Philippine Indigenous Peoples' Struggle for Land and Life: Challenging Legal Texts, Arizona," *International and Comparative Law* 21, no. 1 (2004): 269–303; and Karla Peña, "The Struggle for Land Reforms ad Food Sovereignty in Ecuador," *Telesur*, August 20, 2015, https://www.telesurenglish.net/opinion/The-Struggle-for-Land -Reforms-and-Food-Sovereignty-in-Ecuador-20150820-0014.html.

18. Samih al-Qassem and Mahmoud Darwish, *A Correspondence between the Two Halves of the Orange* (Haifa: Kul al-Arab, 1990).

19. Steven Salaita, *Uncivil Rites* (Chicago: Haymarket Books, 2015).

20. See US Campaign for Palestinian Rights, "From Palestine to Mexico, All the Walls Have Got to Go," https://uscpr.org/nowalls, accessed May 2021.

21. Roland Bleiker, *Popular Dissent, Human Agency and Global Politics* (Cambridge: Cambridge University Press, 2000), 278.

22. Antonio Gramsci, *Prison Notebooks*, eds. Quentin Hoare and Geoffrey Nowell Smith (New York: International, 1971), 229–39.

23. In this respect should be noted the importance of the volume edited by Rebecca L. Stein and Ted Swedenburg, *Palestine, Israel and the Politics of Political Culture* (Durham, NC: Duke University Press, 2005), which opened the way for seeking the role of cultural studies in general, and popular culture in particular, by examining the Palestinian case study. In a similar vein, the role cultural resistance plays beyond national or political boundaries was recognized earlier by Helga Tawil-Souri, "Towards a Palestinian Cultural Studies," *Middle East Journal of Communication and Culture* 2, no. 2 (2009): 181–85.

24. Stephen Duncombe, "Introduction," in *Cultural Resistance Reader*, edited by Stephen Duncombe, 1–16 (London: Verso, 2002).

25. Majid al-Haj, *Education, Empowerment and Control: The Case of Arabs in Israel* (Albany: State University of New York Press, 1995), 16–17.

26. Such as banishment for long periods from their villages or towns and imprisonment.

27. Follow-up Committee of the Arabs in Israel, "The Future Vision of the Palestinian Arabs in Israel," 10 [in Hebrew], available at http://www.reut-institute.org/he/Publication.aspx?PublicationId=1428.

28. As'ad Ghanem and Mohanad Mustafa, "The Future Vision as a Collective Political and Theoretical Platform of the Palestinians in Israel," in *Between Vision and Reality: The Vision Papers of the Arabs in Israel 1006–2007*, edited by Sarah Ozacky-Lazar and Mustafa Kabha, 156–87 (Jerusalem: Citizens' Accord Forum, 2009) [in Hebrew].

29. Follow-up Committee of the Arabs in Israel, "The Future Vision of the Palestinian Arabs in Israel," 25.

30. Asad Ghanem, "'Identity and Belonging': A Pioneering Project, Which Must be the Starting Point for an Alternative, Comprehensive Educational Plan," *Adalah Newsletter* 27 (July–August 2006), www.adalah.org/uploads/oldfiles/newsletter/eng/jul-aug06/ar2.pdf.

31. Ghazi Falah, Michael Hoy, and Rachel Sarker, "Co-existence in Selected Mixed Arab-Jewish Cities in Israel: By Choice or by Default," *Urban Studies* 37, no. 4 (2000): 775–96.

32. *Yediot Achronot*, April 27, 2013.

33. Shlomo Avineri, "A Jewish State of all its Citizens," *Haaretz*, October 6, 2012.

34. Rouhana, "Homeland Nationalism."

35. When the only Palestinian theater in Israel attempted to adopt a more national repertoire, it was faced with the wrath of the Minister of Culture, Miri Regev, as was the Arab-Hebrew Theatre in Jaffa for similar "offences."

BIBLIOGRAPHY

al-Haj, Majid. *Education, Empowerment and Control: The Case of Arabs in Israel*. Albany: State University of New York Press, 1995.

al-Qassem, Samih, and Mahmoud Darwish. *A Correspondence between the Two Halves of the Orange*. Haifa: Kul al-Arab, 1990. [Arabic.]

Amara, Ahmad. "Indigeneity in Palestinian Studies: Between Political and Legal Indigeneity." Paper presented at the 2016 Palestinian Studies Workshop, Brown University. https://palestinianstudies.files.wordpress.com/2015/12/amara-ahmad.docx 2016.

Amara, Ahmad, Ismael Abu-Saad, and Oren Yiftachel, eds. *Indigenous (In)Justice: Human Rights Law and Bedouin Arabs in the Naqab/Negev*. Cambridge, MA: Harvard Law School Publications, 2012.

Barakat, Rena. "Writing/Righting Palestine Studies: Settler Colonialism, Indigenous Sovereignty and Resisting the Ghost(s) of History." *Settler Colonial Studies* 8, no. 3 (2018): 349–63.

Bleiker, Roland. *Popular Dissent, Human Agency and Global Politics*. Cambridge: Cambridge University Press, 2000.

Bishara, 'Azmi. "On the Question of the Palestinian Minority in Israel." *Theory and Criticism* (1993) 3: 7–21. [Hebrew.]

Cheyfitz, Eric. "Response to Steven Saliata's Inter/Nationalism from the Holy Land to the New World: Encountering Palestine in American Indian Studies." *Native American and Indigenous Studies* 1, no. 2 (2014): 145–47.

Clifford, James. "Indigenous Articulations." *The Contemporary Pacific* 3, no. 2 (2001): 468–90.

Duncombe, Stephen. "Introduction." In *Cultural Resistance Reader*, edited by Stephen Duncombe, 1–16. London: Verso, 2002.

Falah, Gahzi, Michael Hoy, and Rachel Sarker. "Co-existence in Selected Mixed Arab-Jewish Cities in Israel: By Choice or by Default." *Urban Studies* 37, no. 4 (2000): 775–96.

Follow-up Committee of the Arabs in Israel. "The Future Vision of the Palestinian Arabs in Israel" [in Hebrew]. Available at http://www.reut-institute.org/he/Publication.aspx?PublicationId=1428.

Ghanem, As'ad, and Mohanad Mustafa. "The Future Vision as a Collective Political and Theoretical Platform of the Palestinians in Israel." In *Between Vision and Reality: The Vision Papers of the Arabs in Israel 1006–2007*, edited by Sarah Oszacky-Lazar and Mustafa Kabha, 156–87. Jerusalem: Citizens' Accord Forum, 2009.

Gramsci, Antonio. *Prison Notebooks*. Edited by Quentin Hoare and Geoffrey Nowell Smith. New York: International, 1971.

Jamal, Amal. *Arab Minority in Israel: The Politics of Indigeneity*. Abingdon: Routledge, 2011.

Mamdani, Mahmoud. "Settler Colonialism: Then and Now." *Critical Inquiry* 4, no. 3 (2015): 596–614.

Molinatas, Jose Mencio. "The Philippine Indigenous Peoples' Struggle for Land and Life: Challenging Legal Texts, Arizona." *International and Comparative Law* 21, no. 1 (2004): 269–303.

Nasasra, Mansour. "The Ongoing Judaisation of the Naqab and the Struggle for Recognising the Indigenous Rights of the Arab Bedouin People." *Settler Colonial Studies* 2, no. 1 (2012): 81–107.

Nassar, Maha. *Brothers Apart: Palestinian Citizens of Israel and the Arab World*. Stanford, CA: Stanford University Press, 2017.

Povinelli, Elizabeth. *The Cunning of Recognition: Indigenous Alterities and the Making of Australian Multiculturalism*. Durham, NC: Duke University Press, 2002.

Rouhana, Nadim, "Homeland Nationalism and Guarding Dignity in a Settler-Colonial Context: The Palestinian Citizens of Israel Reclaim Their Homeland." *Borderland e-Journal* 14, no. 1 (2015).

Said, Edward. *Culture and Imperialism*. New York: Vintage Books, 1993.

Salaita, Steven. *Uncivil Rites*. Chicago: Haymarket Books, 2015.

Simpson, Audra. *Theorizing Native Studies*. Durham, NC: Duke University Press, 2014.

Stavenhagen, Rodolfo, and Ahmad Amara. "International Law of Indigenous Peoples and the Naqab Bedouin Arabs." In *Indigenous (In)Justice: Human Rights Law and Bedouin Arabs in the Naqab/Negev*, edited by Ahmad Amara, Ismael Abu-Saad, and Oren Yiftachel, 158–93. Cambridge, MA: Harvard Law School Publications, 2012.

Stein, Rebecca L., and Ted Swedenburg. *Palestine, Israel and the Politics of Political Culture*. Durham, NC: Duke University Press, 2005.

Tawil-Souri, Helga. "Towards a Palestinian Cultural Studies." *Middle East Journal of Communication and Culture* 2, no. 2 (2009): 181–85.

Veracini, Lorenzo. *Israel and Settler Society*. London: Pluto Press, 2006.

———. "The Other Shift: Settler Colonialism, Israel and the Occupation." *Palestine Studies* 42, no. 2 (2013): 26–42.

Yiftachel, Oren. "Epilogue: Studying Naqab/Negev Bedouins: Towards a Colonial Paradigm?" *HAGAR: Studies in Culture, Polity and Identities* 8, no. 2 (2008): 83–108.

Conclusion

Leila Farsakh

The Palestinian quest for an independent state has been unsuccessful but it was not in vain. It undoubtedly affirmed Palestinians' right to self-determination and thereby their political presence, which UN Resolution 242 denied. The struggle for independent statehood, however, was not able to bring about liberation, let alone justice, because it was confined within an international consensus based on territorial partition as a solution to the Israeli-Palestinian conflict. The partition paradigm, or the two-state solution, does not question the settler-colonial structure of Zionism nor address the injustices that Israel has inflicted on the Palestinians since 1948. Partition was bound not only to compromise Palestinian political aspirations but also to deepen Israel's settler-colonialism, as best manifested by Israel's 2018 nationality law. That law, which upholds the right to self-determination only for Jewish people in the land that Israel controls, has effectively wrapped the dispossession of the Palestinian people with another veneer that voids the Palestinian state project of any emancipatory promise. It demonstrates the dangers, and embedded racial-exclusionary connotations, of linking self-determination to territorial statehood and ethnic nationhood.

As this volume has stressed, the right to self-determination cannot be protected within the confines of a strict territorial understanding of sovereignty nor within the boundaries of an ethno-nation-state. A central question that will continue to dominate Palestinian politics and Palestine studies moving forward is whether it is possible to transcend the state in the attempt to exercise the right of self-determination. As Adam Hanieh discusses in this volume, the state is not a neutral or technical entity, but rather a social relation situated within a dynamic global capitalist reality. Analyzing the evolving nature of this political economy, including the impact of Covid-19 on regional economies, the direction of capital flows, and the process of class formation, is critical to understanding the kind of state and system of government being built and their ability to enhance, or further compromise, the Palestinian struggle for justice and equality. De-exceptionalizing Palestine and situating it in its regional context is also key, given the genealogy of capital accumulation and investment in Palestine and the Middle East more generally. This contextualization is all the more important given that the Palestinian history of displacement, inequality, and oppression is no longer distinctive, as the experiences of Syrian, Iraqi, and Lebanese refugees attest. The demand for the right to self-determination and equality has never been unique to the Palestinians; it is a demand shared by Arab citizens in the entire region, as the Arab uprising of 2011 clearly demonstrated.

One of the conclusions drawn from the various chapters in this volume is that the state cannot be transcended but needs to be rethought. Because the state is not simply about security and order, its power needs to be tamed. The state remains, in its essence, a constitutive political community that must be accountable to, and representative of, its citizens, who are the source of sovereignty and are entitled to full equality. Articulating how the state is to be held accountable in a regional and international context that is increasingly integrated economically and is deeply unequal is not evident, however, and warrants further research. The signing of the Abraham Accords by Israel, the United Arab Emirates, and Bahrain at the White House on September 14, 2020 shows that the economic interests of Arab regimes effectively converge with those of colonial states. These accords formalized long-standing informal economic and security relations between these states and signaled the official end of the 2002 Arab Peace Initiative, which conditioned Israel's regional normalization on it ending the occupation of the West Bank and Gaza and establishing a Palestinian state with East Jerusalem as its capitol. Together with the Trump Administration's 2020 peace plan, these accords entrench an authoritarian understanding of statehood as well as mark the end of an era in Arab politics in which the resolution of the Israeli-Palestinian conflict was considered central—if only rhetorically—to attaining peace in the region.

Some would argue that these recent developments confirm the demise of the liberatory promise of statehood, and of the Palestine question. A more careful analysis, however, would suggest that the changes precipitated by the 2011 Arab uprisings and their aftermath are indicative of the symbiotic relationship that exists between Palestine and the larger Arab region. Moreover, the "Ferguson to Palestine" rallies, the Black Life Matters demonstrations, and the international outcry against Israel's latest war on the Palestinians in 2021 show again both the resonance that the Palestinian cause has worldwide and the intersectionality of people's struggle for freedom. The deep connections between race, class, and decolonization in the struggle against authoritarian oppression are increasingly evident and warrant further research, especially since they are redefining the meanings of political liberation and citizenship in the twenty-first century.

As Masen Masri reminds us in this volume, statehood is inherently intertwined with the law. The law delineates the power of the state, its relationship to its citizens, and the rights of citizens. In any democratic society, the law is produced by the people and for the people, for they are the only sovereign. Putting the law, especially international law, at the service of the Palestinian cause has remained a central feature of Palestinian resistance and research. The law continues to affirm Palestinians' individual right of return, their collective right to fight colonialism, and the legal validity of the notion of a Palestinian nationality, as Susan Akram demonstrates in this volume. How to translate these legal tools into a political program of decolonization needs further study since, as Noura Erekat has shown, the law, whether domestic or international, can be a weapon of oppression just as much as an instrument for liberation.

The trajectory of the Palestinian struggle so far has shown that political liberation cannot be achieved by accepting Israel's colonial structure in the hope of containing it. The meaning of decolonization in the twenty-first century and how to achieve it, however, remains unclear, both from an academic and from a political point of view, given that Palestinians do not all face the same material realities or embrace the same forms of resistance, even if they share a common history, an ongoing Nakba, and a recognized set of rights. While for the Palestinian diaspora, decolonization is associated with return, for the Palestinians in the West Bank and Gaza, it continues to be tied to independent statehood. For Palestinian citizens of Israel, decolonization demands transforming Israel into a state that ensures equality for all of its citizens. Attempting to harmonize these different visions into a single political project is daunting, especially in view of the absence of institutional platforms that would enable different constituencies to dialogue and articulate a clear political project moving forward.

Moreover, it is far from clear which Palestinian constituency can best articulate the political shape of liberation in the twenty-first century. Some argue that Palestinian citizens of Israel are best poised to articulate the elements of decolonization, given the historical juncture at which the Palestinian question finds itself today. Others see the primary agents of decolonization as the refugees and people in the diaspora, given the centrality of their right of return to the question of Palestine. Whether Palestinian citizens of Israel should, or would, become the center of gravity of the Palestinian nationalism, as refugees did in the 1970s and 1980s, and Palestinians in the West Bank and Gaza have over the past three decades, remains an open question. Only further research can shed light on this question and help untangle what at times appears as the dialectical relationship between Palestine and the Palestinians.

As has been argued, settler-colonialism is not an event but an ongoing process. Its dismantlement entails not only decolonizing the land but, above all, decolonizing Israeli-Palestinian relations. It requires that Israelis give up their colonial privileges and address questions of historical injustices and reconciliation with the Palestinians. Palestinians, in turn, will need to address the issue of Israelis' collective and individual rights once their colonial privileges are revoked. The question of Israeli rights, however, remains among the thorniest issues for Palestinian activists and researchers. The success of any constitutional design for a democratic decolonized polity, be it binational, federal or confederal, will hinge on the willingness of those involved to work and live together as equals. As Nadim Khoury explains in this volume, decolonization entails a process of reconciliation. It requires engaging with the enemy and confronting the issue of historical responsibility by developing mechanisms for reconciliation, both between Israel and the Palestinians and also within Israeli and Palestinian societies. Further research can help identify the inherent challenges and the means by which such mechanisms of reconciling with the "other" can be developed and implemented, not only in Palestine but also in the whole Arab world, where the scars of the past ten years of war would need to healed to ensure stability moving forward.

On both the epistemological and political levels, the issue that will continue to face Palestinian and Arab liberation struggles is how to move beyond the grand narrative of national liberation without falling into the neoliberal discourse of rights, which privileges individuality and inequality. Some academics, such as Ilan Pappe among others, argue that the discourse of indigeneity offers a more productive approach for decolonizing the land. It still remains to be seen, however, how far indigeneity can become an effective tool to understand the political shape of self-determination moving forward. Further research can shed light on how far the Palestinians can relinquish the dream of unifying their fragmented nation within the boundary of a state, as opposed to accepting the diversity of Palestinians' political experiences and modes of resistance. The political manifestation of this dilemma can be heard in the contrast between those who call for reviving the PLO, on the one hand, and those who accept its demise and advocate for a new reliance on grassroots forms of resistance. These forms of popular resistance can be seen in the yearly commemoration the Nakba by Palestinian citizens of Israel inside the Green Line, in the 2017–18 Great March of Return in Gaza, and in the Palestinians' uprising in Spring 2021 against Israel's war on Gaza, house evictions of Palestinians in East Jerusalem, and Jewish mob attacks against Palestinian citizens in Israel. They express new ways of unifying the Palestinian body politic without ossifying it in rigid institutions.

At the heart of the question of Palestine is the desire for freedom and justice. This desire is also at the center of the struggles of Arab citizens against their oppressive regimes and the struggles of all those fighting injustice globally, be they indigenous peoples in the Americas and Australia, people of color in the United States, refugees waiting at the doors of Europe, or Iranians waging the Green Revolution, among so many others. If this book has shown that Palestinians are rethinking statehood beyond partition and continue to resist their ongoing colonial reality, further research can illuminate what kind of political and legal actions are needed to create a decolonized polity that ensures liberation and equality for all.

SUSAN M. AKRAM is clinical professor and director of Boston University's International Human Rights Clinic. Her most recent books include *Still Waiting for Tomorrow: The Law and Politics of Unresolved Refugee Crises*, edited with Tom Syring (New York: Routledge, 2014); and *International Law and the Israeli-Palestinian Conflict: A Rights-Based Approach to Middle East Peace*, edited with Mick Dumper, Michael Lynk, and Ian Scobbie (New York: Routledge, 2011). Her articles and book chapters include "Palestinian Exceptionalism, Whether It Matters, and the Role International Agencies Play," in *The Oxford Handbook of Refugee and Forced Migration Studies* (Oxford: Oxford University Press, 2014); with Michael Lynk, "The Arab Israel Conflict," in the *Max Planck Encyclopedia of International Law* (2013); and "Temporary Protection as an Instrument for Implementing the Right of Return for Palestinian Refugees," in *Boston University International Law Journal* 22, no. 1 (2004).

HANIA WALID ASSALI is a Palestinian born and raised in Jerusalem. She holds a law degree from the University of Montpellier, France. She worked as in-house general counsel to the Jordanian affiliate of a major international company for several years. She is now working as a freelancer consultant and researcher.

TAREQ BACONI is the Crisis Group's senior analyst for Israel/Palestine and Economics of Conflict and author of *Hamas Contained: The Rise and Pacification of Palestinian Resistance* (Stanford, CA: Stanford University Press, 2018). His writing has appeared in Arabic in *Al-Ghad* and *Al-Quds al-Arabi*, and in English in *The New York Review of Books Daily*, *The Washington Post*, *Foreign Affairs*, *The Guardian*, *The Nation*, *The Daily Star* (Lebanon), and *al-Jazeera*. Dr. Baconi holds a Ph.D in international relations from King's College London and an MPhil degree from the University of Cambridge.

LEILA FARSAKH is an associate professor and chair of the Political Science Department at the University of Massachusetts, Boston. Her books include *Palestinian Labour Migration to Israel: Labour, Land and Occupation* (London: Routledge, 2005; 2nd ed. 2012); and *The Arab and Jewish Questions: Geographies of Engagements in Palestine and Beyond*, edited with Bashir Bashir (New York: Columbia University Press, 2020).

ADAM HANIEH is a professor of development studies at the Institute of Arab and Islamic Studies, University of Exeter. He is author of *Capitalism and Class in the Gulf Arab States* (New York: Palgrave Macmillan, 2011) and *Lineages of Revolt: Issues of Contemporary Capitalism in the Middle East* (Chicago: Haymarket Books, 2013). His most recent book is *Money, Markets, and Monarchies: The Gulf Cooperation Council and the Political Economy of the Contemporary Middle East* (Cambridge: Cambridge University Press, 2018).

NADIM KHOURY is an associate professor in international studies at Lillehammer University College. Prior to moving to Norway, Professor Khoury taught and ran the political studies program at Al-Quds Bard College in Palestine (2012–2014). His research interests include contemporary political theory, nationalism, collective memory, and the Israeli-Palestinian conflict. He has published on these issues in *Constellations, Philosophy and Social Criticism, European Journal of International Relations, Nations and Nationalism*, and in edited volumes. Currently, he is completing a book manuscript entitled *Partitioning Memory* that critically examines the politics of memory of the Oslo peace process

MAZEN MASRI is a senior lecturer in law at the City Law School, City University of London. His areas of teaching and research are constitutional law and public international law with special interest in comparative constitutionalism. His work has appeared in legal and interdisciplinary journals such as *Social and Legal Studies, Asian Journal of International Law*, and *International Journal of Law in Context* as well as scholarly e-zines and blogs. His book *The Dynamics of Exclusionary Constitutionalism: Israel as a Jewish and Democratic State* was published as part of the Hart Studies in Comparative Public Law Series (Oxford: Hart Publishing, 2017).

YOUSEF MUNAYYER is a nonresident senior fellow at the Arab Center Washington, DC. He holds a Ph.D from the University of Maryland in government and politics. Previously he served as executive director of the US Campaign for Palestinian Rights as well as of the Jerusalem Fund. He has written widely on US policy toward Israel/Palestine and his research interests include the politics of human rights and political repression.

MAHA NASSAR is an associate professor in the School of Middle Eastern and North African Studies at the University of Arizona, where she specializes in the cultural and intellectual history of the modern Arab world. Her book *Brothers Apart: Palestinian Citizens of Israel and the Arab World* (Stanford, CA: Stanford University Press, 2017) examines how Palestinian intellectuals in Israel have connected to global decolonization movements through literary and journalistic writings.

ILAN PAPPE is the director of the European Center for Palestine Studies and a fellow of the Institute of Arab and Islamic Studies at the University of Exeter. Pappe is the author of twenty books, among them *The Ethnic Cleansing of Palestine* (Oxford: OneWorld, 2007), *A History of Modern Palestine* (Cambridge: Cambridge University Press, 2006), and *On Palestine*, with Noam Chomsky (Chicago: Haymarket, 2015. His two latest books are *Ten Myths about Israel* (London: Verso, 2017) and *The Biggest Prison on Earth: A History of the Israeli Occupation* (Oxford: OneWorld, 2017).

HANAN TOUKAN is assistant professor at Bard College Berlin. She was also a visiting assistant professor in Middle East studies at Brown University (2016–2018) and visiting professor of the cultural studies of the Middle East at the University of Bamberg (2018–2019). Her research focuses on media, film studies, and the visual politics of museums. She is author of *The Politics of Art: Dissent and Diplomacy in Lebanon, Palestine and Jordan* (Stanford: Stanford University Press, 2021). Professor Toukan's work has also been published in *International Journal of Cultural Studies, Cultural Politics, Arab Studies Journal, Radical Philosophy, Journal for Palestine Studies, Review of Middle East Studies, Jerusalem Quarterly, SCTIW Review*, and *Jadaliyya*, among others.

INDEX

Founded in 1893,
UNIVERSITY OF CALIFORNIA PRESS
publishes bold, progressive books and journals
on topics in the arts, humanities, social sciences,
and natural sciences—with a focus on social
justice issues—that inspire thought and action
among readers worldwide.

The UC PRESS FOUNDATION
raises funds to uphold the press's vital role
as an independent, nonprofit publisher, and
receives philanthropic support from a wide
range of individuals and institutions—and from
committed readers like you. To learn more, visit
ucpress.edu/supportus.